Keynote

Upper Intermediate
Teacher's Book

Claire Hart
Communicative Activities by Karen Richardson

NATIONAL GEOGRAPHIC LEARNING | **CENGAGE Learning**

Keynote Upper Intermediate
Teacher's Book
Claire Hart
Karen Richardson

Publisher: Gavin McLean

Publishing Consultant: Karen Spiller

Project Manager: Karen White

Development Editor: Liz Driscoll

Editorial Manager: Alison Burt

Head of Strategic Marketing ELT: Charlotte Ellis

Senior Content Project Manager: Nick Ventullo

Production Intern: James Richardson

Manufacturing Manager: Eyvett Davis

Cover design: Brenda Carmichael

Text design: MPS North America LLC

Compositor: MPS North America LLC

National Geographic Liaison: Leila Hishmeh

Audio: Tom Dick and Debbie Productions Ltd

DVD: Tom Dick and Debbie Productions Ltd

Cover Photo Caption: View of speaker Nilofer Merchant from the very top of the house at TED2013 – The Young The Wise The Undiscovered, Long Beach, California. February 25 – March 1, 2013. Photo: © Michael Brands/ TED.

ISBN: 978-1-305-57959-0

National Geographic Learning
Cheriton House, North Way, Andover, Hampshire, SP10 5BE
United Kingdom

Cengage Learning is a leading provider of customized learning solutions with employees residing in nearly 40 different countries and sales in more than 125 countries around the world. Find your local representative at **www.cengage.com**.

Cengage Learning products are represented in Canada by Nelson Education Ltd.

Visit National Geographic Learning online at **ngl.cengage.com**

Visit our corporate website at **www.cengage.com**

CREDITS

The publishers would like to thank TED Staff for their insightful feedback and expert guidance, allowing us to achieve our dual aims of maintaining the integrity of these inspirational TED Talks, while maximising their potential for teaching English.

The publishers would like to thank the following for permission to use copyright material:

Illustrations by MPS North America LLC.

Cover: © Michael Brands/TED.

Printed in Greece by Bakis SA
Print Number: 01   Print Year: 2015

Contents

Introduction

1 What is *Keynote*?

Keynote is a six-level, multi-syllabus English course that takes learners from Elementary level (A1) to Proficient (C2). It is suitable for all adults or young adults in higher education or in work who need English in their professional or personal lives. It is suitable for all teachers, however experienced – extensive teaching notes will help the inexperienced teacher plan lessons, while valuable background information, teaching tips and extension activities will be of great use to even the most experienced teacher.

The units in *Keynote* each take a TED Talk as their point of departure. These talks are given by speakers from all walks of life, countries and fields of work and provide a rich and varied basis for the teaching and learning of authentic English. See section 2 for more about TED.

Each level contains enough material for between 90 and 120 hours' classroom work. Teachers can reduce this time by giving some preparation tasks to students to do at home (such as watching the TED Talks) or extend it with the extra activities in the teaching notes and the photocopiable communicative activities at the back of this book.

What are the components of *Keynote*?

Student's Book

- twelve units of five double-page lessons each (See section 3 below for details.)
- six double-page Review lessons, one after every two units
- a grammar summary and extra exercises to accompany each unit
- audioscripts and TED Talk transcripts
- DVD-Rom with all TED Talks, Vocabulary in context exercises, Presentation skills montages, and recordings for listening and pronunciation exercises

Workbook

- consolidation and extension of all the learning objectives in the Student's Book
- additional TED input via biographical information about the speakers featured in the Student's Book, playlists related to the featured talks and audio of podcasts given by members of the *Keynote* team
- six two-page Writing lessons that provide detailed practice of the kinds of texts that come up in the Cambridge exams. These process-based lessons help students generate ideas, provide them with a model, give them useful language, and help them plan, draft, revise and analyse.

- six two-page Presentation lessons that allow students to practise the presentation skills from the Student's Book and build up a bank of personalized presentation language

Teacher's Book

- full teaching notes for all the units and Review lessons, containing answers, TED Talk and audio transcripts, teaching tips, optional and alternative ways of dealing with the Student's Book exercises, extension activities and background information
- six photocopiable progress tests, with sections looking at the vocabulary, grammar, reading, listening, speaking and writing from the previous two units, with answer key
- twenty-four photocopiable communicative activities, two for each unit, with full teaching notes, containing a variety of activities such as information gap, card games and surveys. While most of the worksheets are copied and given to the students, some are to be cut into cards and given to the students. In these cases, it may be best to copy the page onto card (and possibly laminate it), so that the cards are sturdier and can be used several times if necessary.

Website

- video streaming of the TED Talks from the Student's Book, Vocabulary in context and Presentation skill montages
- worksheets organized by industry (e.g. manufacturing, tourism, education) and business function (e.g. human resources, marketing, research and development) that provide highly targeted practice of the language specific to the learners' field of work. They can be used in class or for self study.
- mid- and end-of-year tests
- Word versions of all the audio/video scripts and reading texts that can be 'repackaged' by teachers to create additional practice material or tests

2 What is TED?

TED is a non-profit organization based on the idea that many people from all areas of life have 'ideas worth spreading', and should be given a platform to spread those ideas. There are currently more than two thousand TED Talks on the TED website, and new talks by leading thinkers and doers across a wide range of fields are constantly being added. TED originated at a conference in 1984 centred on Technology, Entertainment and Design, but the talks now cover far more than those three areas. The talks are given by speakers from across the world, ranging from highly-respected business leaders to school students, all of whom have an idea worth spreading. The talks can last as long as eighteen minutes but are generally much shorter. By providing this platform, TED aims to 'make great ideas accessible and spark conversation'. For more on TED, see www.TED.com.

Why are TED Talks great for learning English?

TED Talks feature remarkable people communicating passionately and persuasively, and are a unique source of engaging and often amusing real language. The talks are intrinsically interesting, and are watched by millions of people around the world. In the ELT classroom they provide:

- motivating content that learners choose to watch in their leisure time for entertainment and edification
- educational content, i.e. students learn about the world as well as learning English
- authentic listening input
- exposure to different language varieties: *Keynote* has a mix of talks given by British English, American English, Australian speakers and includes a glossary in each TED Talk lesson to compare and contrast language (See Teaching tip 1 below.)
- exposure to different accents (native, such as British and US, as well as non-native)
- up-to-date language
- ideal material for developing critical thinking skills
- probably the best models in existence for presentation skills

3 How do I teach with *Keynote*?

Unit structure

Each unit in the Student's Book contains five lessons around an overarching theme:

- the first provides an introduction to the TED Talk for the unit, including preparation by pre-teaching key vocabulary and practising skills that will help students when listening to authentic English
- the second is the TED Talk lesson where students watch and listen to the talk, both in its entirety and in short sections, and do further vocabulary work (mining the talk for interesting vocabulary and collocations) as well as work on critical thinking and presentation skills (See Teaching tip 2 below.)
- the third is the grammar lesson, with real input in the form of an infographic that provides a context for the presentation of the grammar and its practice, and ends in a spoken output using the new language

- the fourth lesson is based on a reading text, drawn from the theme of the unit and addressing real-life topics, with a variety of comprehension, reading skills and vocabulary exercises
- the last lesson in each unit focuses on functional language, and comprises listening and speaking with accompanying vocabulary work, as well as a section on writing, focusing on text type and writing skills

The grammar, reading and functional lessons in each unit have 21st century outcomes, i.e. the lessons provide and practise the skills and knowledge needed by students to succeed in their professional and personal lives in the 21st century.

The grammar, vocabulary and skills presented in each unit are practised further in the Review lesson after every two units. (See Teaching tip 3 below.)

Grammar

Grammar is presented in a natural and clear context using an infographic, which means that there is not a huge amount of reading for the students to do in order to find examples of the grammar. Students are led to understanding of the grammatical points through guided discovery, focusing on language from the infographic picked out in one or two grammar boxes, and studied through the use of concept check questions. Students are then directed to the Grammar summary at the back of the book to read about the grammar in more detail. The exercises accompanying the Grammar summaries focus mainly on form and can be done at this point before students tackle the exercises in the unit, which focus more on meaning and use, or they can be done for homework.

The Workbook consolidates the grammar presented in the Student's Book and extends it (often looking at more idiomatic grammar) in the 'Grammar Extra' exercises.

Vocabulary

There are three different categories of vocabulary presentation and practice in *Keynote*:

Key words

The Key words section always appears in the first lesson. In this section some of the words and phrases that are central to the TED Talk are matched with definitions in order to enable students to understand the talk more easily. Note that these words are sometimes above the relevant CEFR level and are not intended for productive use. (See Teaching tip 4 below.)

Vocabulary in context

The Vocabulary in context section always appears in the second lesson, after students have watched the TED Talk. Here, short excerpts which contain useful words, phrases or collocations are repeated and the lexical items are matched with synonyms and then practised in a personalization activity.

Vocabulary development

Further vocabulary work focuses on vocabulary relevant to the theme taken from the reading and listening texts, building on it in the form of work on lexical sets, phrases and collocation.

There is further work on vocabulary in context and the lexical sets of the units in the Workbook. Additionally the Workbook provides more practice of wordbuilding and common collocations of a topic word.

Skills

Reading

Each unit has a reading lesson based on a contemporary and real-world text. The accompanying exercises cover reading comprehension, reading skills and vocabulary work, but also elicit a personal response to the content of the text.

Writing

There is a focus on writing in each final lesson, covering a text type and writing skill, such as using linking words. There are on-page models for students to analyse and follow in their own writing. Writing is further practised in the Workbook where there are six process-based, double-page lessons that provide detailed practice of the kinds of texts that come up in the Cambridge exams (matched to the level of the book).

Listening

Listening is a key component of the course and is dealt with in various ways. To help students deal with the authentic, native speaker-level language of the TED Talks, *Keynote* has a comprehensive authentic listening skills syllabus that – together with a focus on key words from the Talk and background information – allows students to understand listening material which is usually well above their productive level. (See Teaching tip 5 below.) There is often listening in the grammar lessons, consolidating the new language, and there is also graded listening material in the final lesson of each unit, using a wide variety of listening comprehension task types.

Speaking

Each unit has a lesson that focuses specifically on functional and situational language that is relevant to working adults. This is supported by a Useful language box containing a number of expressions relevant to the function or situation. There are also speaking activities throughout the units.

Pronunciation

There is a pronunciation syllabus, integrated with the grammar and speaking lessons where there is a relevant pronunciation area.

4 Teaching tips

The following teaching tips apply throughout the course. There are lesson-specific teaching tips through the units.

Teaching tip 1 Which variety of English?

This deals with the notes comparing North American and British English in the TED Talk lesson. Find out whether your students are interested in learning about the different pronunciation and vocabulary of these two varieties. Ask them what varieties of English they prefer to listen to (native and non-native) and why. Explore any prejudices the class may have around variety. Discuss students' long-term pronunciation goals and whether they hope to sound like native speakers or whether it is better to aim for a clear accent that reflects their identities more accurately. The conclusions to this discussion will determine what you do with the footnotes. If your students are very interested in the two varieties, you may decide to get them practising saying the words in the different accents. Similarly, where the spelling or vocabulary is different, you could encourage students to use the variety they feel most comfortable with in their learning, but ensure that they use one variety consistently.

Where students are interested, you could spend some time investigating the differences further. For example, with spelling differences, you could ask the students to look for patterns (in the glossaries in the book or using online dictionaries). They should be able to identify patterns such as the -or/-our ending in North American *color/favor* and British *colour/favour.* With differences in vocabulary, you could encourage students to speculate on how the differences have come about. For example: *Is* sidewalk *a more literal word than* pavement?

Teaching tip 2 Developing presentation skills

After students have watched a TED Talk in each unit, they focus on a particular aspect of presentation skills such as 'using props' or 'pace and emphasis'. Before embarking on the Presentation skills sections, it's probably worth finding out from your students the kinds of situations when they might have to present (in their first language or in English). Many of your students will need to present information at work and students in academic situations will have to present their research. Even students who don't often give presentations will benefit from presenting in your class because it's an opportunity to build confidence in speaking in English and to develop a key communication skill.

At first, some of your students might not feel comfortable with giving presentations in English. That's why many of the presentations tasks in *Keynote* can be done in pairs, with students taking turns to present to each other. As the course progresses, you could ask students to present to larger groups and once they are more confident, to the whole class.

Remember to allow plenty of preparation time for the presentations. Often it's a good idea to set a presentation task and ask students to work on it for homework before they give their presentation in the next lesson. It's also useful to provide students with preparation strategies such as making notes on pieces of card to refer to, rehearsing in front of a mirror, or presenting to family and friends at home. You will find more tips on setting up and delivering classroom presentations in the relevant part of each unit of this Teacher's Book.

Teaching tip 3 Using the Review lessons

The Review lesson is an opportunity for reflection and consolidation. Encourage students to see the benefits of reviewing recently encountered language as a means to strengthening their learning and for diagnosing which areas they need to study again.

The Review lessons could be set as homework, but by doing them in class you will be available to clarify areas of difficulty, answer questions and see for yourself where students are doing well and where not so well. Ask students how hard they found the exercises as a means of diagnosing what needs reviewing more thoroughly. Also, consider putting students into small groups to work through the grammar, vocabulary, speaking and writing activities on their own while you conduct one-to-one sessions with individuals. Speak to students to find out how they are progressing, what they need to work on, whether they are experiencing any difficulties in the class or any other matters.

Teaching tip 4 Key words

One way of dealing with the Key words activity in the first lesson of each unit is to write the key words on the board. Read out the first definition and nominate a student to say the correct word. If they guess correctly, read out the second definition and nominate another student to guess that word. Continue until they have matched all the words and their definitions in this way. However, whenever a student guesses incorrectly, start from the very beginning again and read out the first definition, nominating a different student each time. The activity ends once the class has correctly matched all the words and definitions in a row without any mistakes.

Teaching tip 5 Dealing with difficult listening activities

The TED Talks are authentic English and may be challenging for some students, which can be a cause of frustration. Here are some ideas to increase your students' ability to deal with authentic language:

• Don't miss out any of the pre-listening exercises in the first lesson, such as Key words or Authentic listening skills. These are designed to make listening easier.

• Students need time before and after listening to prepare and compare: before, to read the task, to ask questions and to predict possible answers, and after, to write their answers and to compare them with a partner.

• Time for writing answers is particularly important when watching clips rather than listening because it is hard to watch the video and write at the same time. This is one reason the TED Talks are broken into small segments.

• Let students read the transcript while they listen or watch.

• Isolate the few seconds of the audio or video where the answer to a question lies and let students listen to it a number of times.

• It's hard in long clips to keep concentrating all the time, so pause just before an answer comes up in order to warn students that they should refocus.

• There are ways of changing the speed that video is played back. You may want to investigate how to slow down talks slightly for your students using certain media players.

• If a task is difficult, make it easier. For example, if students have to listen for words to fill gaps, you could supply the missing words on the board, mixed up, for them to choose.

• Celebrate the successes, however small. If a student hears only one thing, praise them for that. Don't supply extra information which you heard but they did not, unless you have a good reason.

• Remind students now and again of the advice they read about listening to authentic speech in the first lesson of each unit, especially the advice not to try to understand every word, to stay relaxed and to keep listening. Reassure them that listening improves with repeated practice and that the best thing they can do for their listening skills is to persevere.

1 Identity

THEME: Identity and brands – both company and individual

TED TALK: *404, the story of a page not found.* In this TED Talk, Renny Gleeson talks about how companies can use messages saying that webpages can't be found on the server to communicate with their online audience and, therefore, repair the feeling of a broken relationship that people experience when they come across this message.

AUTHENTIC LISTENING SKILLS: Recognizing key terms

CRITICAL THINKING: Relevant examples

PRESENTATION SKILLS: Giving examples

GRAMMAR: Present tenses: active and passive

VOCABULARY: Tasks and interests

PRONUNCIATION: Word stress, Using intonation to ask a question

READING: A personal view on personal branding

LISTENING: Networking

SPEAKING: The Internet and me, Personal branding, Making an impression (Meeting people)

WRITING: An online profile

WRITING SKILL: Symbols and notes

LEAD IN

• Books open. Draw students' attention to the unit title, and to the photo on page 8 and its caption. Ask: *What elements does your identity consist of?* Possible answers could be: *the place where you grew up, your race, your nationality, the language(s) you speak, the clothes you wear, the job you do, your hobbies and interests.*

• To gauge students' prior knowledge of the unit vocabulary, ask: *What can we a) read, b) watch, c) interact with online?* Possible answers could be: *a) information on websites, articles, blog posts, Facebook statuses, tweets, advertisements; b) short videos, TV programmes, film trailers; c) social media sites, blogs and articles (by leaving a comment).*

• Bring in students' own experiences. Ask: *What aspects of your identity do you share online, and how? What factors influence your decisions about what you share?*

• Explain to the class that every unit in *Keynote* begins with a TED Talk. Ask students if they are familiar with TED Talks and if they have ever watched one.

TEDTALKS
BACKGROUND

1

• Ask students to read the text about Renny Gleeson and his talk. If necessary, clarify the meaning of:

new media – channels for mass communication using digital technologies, such as the Internet (line 2)

build relationships – create and strengthen relationships with other people (lines 6–7)

• Put students into pairs to discuss the questions. Alternatively, they could work in groups of three.

• **Question 1.** You could ask students: *What is your usual reaction to seeing this page?* Possible answers could be: *frustration, irritation.*

• **Question 2.** If students haven't seen any funny 404 pages before, tell them that a lot of these pages can be found online. Many of these pages are very creative, and they usually include text and images based on the theme of making an error / getting something wrong / something bad happening. They sometimes include figures from popular culture, such as Batman or Justin Bieber. If you have internet access, you can look up some examples of funny *404, page not found* pages to show the class. Alternatively, or in addition, if students are allowed to use their mobile devices in class, they could look for funny 404 pages themselves.

• **Question 3.** When students are talking about examples of new media, encourage them to be specific and to focus on examples they're already familiar with. Elicit how they use them and how they use different types of new media to do or to share different things.

Suggested answers

1 This is a message you see when a webpage you want to look at cannot be found.

2 Students' own answers

3 Facebook, YouTube, Pinterest

KEY WORDS

2

• Explain that the aim of this section in every unit is to pre-teach some of the key words students will need to know in order to understand the TED Talk. It will also help them to prepare to think about the main themes of the talk.

• Ask students to read the sentences and to try to guess the meaning of the words in bold.

• When students have finished matching the words with their definitions, you could put them into pairs to compare their answers before you check with the whole class.

AUTHENTIC LISTENING SKILLS
Recognizing key terms

3a

• Explain that the Authentic listening skills box on the opening spread of every unit is to help students to develop their listening skills.

• Ask students to read the information about recognizing key terms in the Authentic listening skills box. If necessary, clarify the meaning of:

abbreviation – a shortened form of a word or phrase (line 2)

jargon – special words or expressions that are used by a specific group, e.g. a group of professionals working in the same field (line 2)

• You could put students into pairs to practise saying the terms. Don't correct their pronunciation at this stage.

3b

• Students read the sentences from the TED Talk. Elicit or explain that the words in brackets have been included in sentences 2 and 4 to make clear the meaning of *these things* and *these*. You could put students into pairs to predict the missing term(s) in each sentence.

• 🔊1 Play the recording so that students can complete the sentences with the terms from Exercise 3a. If necessary, play the recording twice. Students can then compare their answers in pairs, but don't confirm answers at this stage.

Transcript and answers

1   At <u>4.04</u> the next day, we gave out <u>$404</u> in cash.

2   But these things [404 pages] are everywhere. They're on <u>sites</u> big, they're on <u>sites</u> small.

3   The 404 page is that. It's that broken experience on the Web. It's effectively the <u>default</u> page when you ask a website for something and it can't find it.

4   You can type in an <u>url</u> and put in 404 and these [webpages] will pop.

Background information

Pronunciation of *url*

In this TED Talk, Renny Glesson says 'an url'. However, this isn't standard English usage. Because 'url' starts with a /juː/ sound instead of a /ʌ/, we would normally say 'a u-r-l' instead and spell out the letters.

3c

• 🔊1 Play the recording again so that students can check their answers.

• Conduct whole-class feedback and ask students if they pronounced the words correctly.

• Put students into pairs to read out the sentences and then to practise saying the terms. Students can help each other with pronunciation.

• **Optional step.** Draw students' attention to the different ways we can say times, e.g. *4.00* could be *four hundred hours, sixteen hundred hours (*if you're using the 24-hour clock), *4 pm, 4 am* or *four o'clock (in the morning / in the afternoon).* Remind students that native English speakers use the 12-hour clock more frequently than the 24-hour clock when talking about time: the 24-hour clock is more often used in schedules (train departures/arrivals, TV programme listings, etc.) You could also elicit or explain that British-English speakers usually add *and* between *hundred* and the rest of the number, e.g. *four hundred and four,* whereas American-English speakers typically say *four hundred four.* Then get students to try saying other times and numbers in different ways.

Extra activity

Numbers, abbreviations and jargon

Ask students to write down examples of numbers, abbreviations and jargon that are used in their area of work or study. Then put students into pairs to say and to explain the meaning of these examples. Conduct whole-class feedback and focus on any differences in the pronunciation of these examples in British and North American English, e.g. the letter *z* is pronounced differently by British English speakers (zed) and North American English speakers (ziː).

1.1 404, the story of a page not found

TEDTALKS

1

• Books open. Explain that students are now going to watch an edited version of the TED Talk.

• Ask students to read the list of three things that Renny Gleeson does in the TED Talk. Tell them to focus on which of the three things he does in each part of the talk while they're watching and not to worry about understanding every word he says.

• ▶1.1 Play the whole talk once so that students can put the three things in order. You could put students into pairs to compare their answers before you check with the whole class.

Transcript

0.11 *So what I want to try to do is tell a quick story about a 404 page and a lesson that was learned as a result of it. But to start it probably helps to have an understanding of what a 404 page actually is.*

0.24 *The 404 page is that. It's that broken experience on the Web. It's effectively the default page when you ask a website for something and it can't find it. And it serves you the 404 page. It's inherently a feeling of being broken when you go through it. And I just want you to think a little bit about, remember for yourself, it's annoying when you hit this thing. Because it's the feeling of a broken relationship.*

1.14 *But these things are everywhere. They're on sites big, they're on sites small. This is a global experience.*

1.22 *What a 404 page tells you is that you fell through the cracks. And that's not a good experience when you're used to experiences like this. You can get on your Kinect and you can have unicorns dancing and rainbows spraying out of your mobile phone. A 404 page is not what you're looking for. You get that, and it's like a slap in the face.*

1.28 *So where this comes into play and why this is important is I head up a technology incubator, and we had eight startups sitting around there. And those startups are focused on what they are, not what they're not, until one day Athletepath, which is a website that focuses on services for extreme athletes, found this video.*

1.46 *(Video) Guy: Joey!*

1.51 *Crowd: Whoa!*

1.55 *Renny Gleeson: They took that video and they embedded it in their 404 page and it was like a light bulb went off for everybody in the place. Because finally there was a page that actually felt like what it felt like to hit a 404.*

2.11 *So this turned into a contest. Dailypath that offers inspiration put inspiration on their 404 page. Stayhound, which helps you find pet sitters through your social network, commiserated with your pet. Each one of them found this. It turned into a 24-hour contest. At 4.04 the next day, we gave out $404 in cash. And what they learned was that those little things, done right, actually matter, and that well-designed moments can build brands. So you take a look out in the real world, and the fun thing is you can actually hack these yourself. You can type in an URL and put in 404 and these will pop. This is one that commiserates with you. This is one that blames you. This is one that I loved. This is an error page, but what if this error page was also an opportunity?*

2.54 *So it was a moment in time where all of these startups had to sit and think and got really excited about what they could be. Because back to the whole relationship issue, what they figured out through this exercise was that a simple mistake can tell me what you're not, or it can remind me of why I should love you.*

3.12 *Thank you.*

3.14 *(Applause)*

Answers

1 b   2 c   3 a

- Note the differences in North American English and British English shown at the foot of the spread. Renny Gleeson uses North American English in this TED Talk, so North American versions are listed first. In this unit, these focus on spelling, pronunciation and vocabulary differences. Note that Renny Gleeson uses *mobile phone* in his talk, whereas most North Americans would say *cellphone*. See page 6 of the Introduction for ideas on how to present and practise these differences.

2

- Give students time to read the sentences. You could ask them to predict whether the sentences are true or false based on what they can remember from the first time they watched this part of the talk. This should make students more focused when they watch the first part of the talk again and listen for detail.

- ▶ **1.1** Play the first part (0.00–1.28) of the talk so that students can check whether the sentences are true or false.

- You could put students into pairs to check their answers before you check with the whole class. You could also ask students to correct the false sentence(s).

Answers

1 F (There are lots of examples in the TED Talk which show that 404 pages are different and non-standardized.)

2 T

3 T

- **Optional step.** Put students into pairs or small groups to discuss whether they agree or disagree with the sentences, and why / why not.

3

- Give students time to read the sentences. You could ask them to predict the correct option based on what they can remember from the first time they watched this part of the talk.

- ▶ **1.1** Play the second part (1.28 to the end) of the talk so that students can check their answers.

Answers

1 startups   2 found   3 24 hours   4 identity

4

- Put students into pairs to discuss the questions.

Suggested answers

1 They put things related to their business on their 404 page.

2 Successful brands are important to companies because they give them their identity, and promote and sell their business.

3 Students' own answers

- **Optional step.** Students look at the brands they can see on their things, such as their clothes, car keys, food and drinks. Ask students if they identify with any of these brands and, if so, why? Put students into small groups to discuss these questions: *How do you know that a brand is successful? What are the elements of a successful brand? How are brands positioned to appeal to different target groups?* Conduct whole-class feedback.

Reflecting on what you've learned

Reflecting on what they've learned may be something that students aren't used to doing. You can guide students through this process by first giving time and space for them to just think about what they've learned. Then give students a range of options for reflection. Some people prefer not to discuss their reflections with others, some need to discuss them in pairs or in small groups. Some prefer to talk, others prefer to write. Suggest that students who are comfortable with writing their reflections down keep a journal which they can add to throughout the course. They could build up a series of sentences that start: *(Today) I've learned …* or *(Today) I've learned … about …*

VOCABULARY IN CONTEXT

5

- Explain that students are going to watch some clips from the TED Talk which contain some new words and phrases. They need to choose the correct meaning of the words.

- ▶1.2 Play the clips from the talk. When each multiple-choice question appears, pause the clip so that students can choose the correct definition. Discourage the more confident students from always giving the answer by asking students to raise their hand if they think they know.

Transcript and subtitles

1   *It's annoying when you **hit** this thing.*
    a meet
    b make
    c strike

2   *What a 404 page tells you is that you **fell through the cracks**.*
    a didn't do anything
    b made a mistake
    c were lost or forgotten

3   *You get that, and it's like a **slap in the face**.*
    a funny thing
    b insult
    c discovery

4   *So where this **comes into play** and why this is important …*
    a game begins
    b information is new
    c starts to have an effect

5   *It was like **a light bulb went off** for everybody in the place.*
    a someone turned off the lights
    b there was a power cut
    c a moment of understanding something

6   *… what they **figured out** through this exercise …*
    a understood
    b added up
    c thought

Answers

1 a   2 c   3 b   4 c   5 c   6 a

6

- The aim of this exercise is to make sure that students can use some of the new vocabulary in a personal context.

- Ask students to underline the words from Exercise 5: *fell through the cracks, slap in the face* and *figured (it) out*. Elicit the meaning of the three expressions.

- Make sure that students understand that the sentences should be true for them. Give examples from your own life to make this clear. For example: *When my friend told me I should have visited her more often when she was in hospital, it felt like a slap in the face.*

- Monitor students while they're writing, offering help where necessary. Make sure that they are using the correct meaning of the words and phrases, e.g. the figurative meaning of *slap in the face* used in the video rather than its literal meaning.

- Put students into pairs or small groups to compare their sentences. You could then invite individual students to read out a sentence each to the rest of the class.

CRITICAL THINKING Relevant examples

7

- Explain or elicit that 'critical thinking' refers to the skill of thinking more deeply about a topic and considering the main arguments and evidence. It involves being able to analyse situations and to use this analysis to draw conclusions based on existing knowledge or theory, problem-solving skills, being able to give reasons and relevant examples to support your opinions, being aware of different nuances of meaning, being open-minded and able to approach an issue or problem from different angles. Critical thinking is especially useful at higher levels because it will help students to use language more creatively. Point out that after every TED Talk in this book, students will focus on a different aspect of critical thinking.

- Put students into pairs to discuss the questions. Then conduct whole-class feedback.

8

- Tell students that these comments have been created for the book, but they're based on comments that people leave on the TED website. Here we have an example of someone posting a comment and then two other people replying to that original comment: something we also see online.

- Bring in students' own experiences. Ask: *Do you ever read the comments at the bottom of web articles? Why do you think people usually write these comments? Have you ever written comments yourself and, if so, can you remember what you wrote?*

- Ask students to decide which viewer(s) give(s) a good example of what Renny Gleeson explained. Elicit or explain that *viewer(s) give(s)* suggests that either one or more viewers – but we are not told how many – give a good example.

- Put students into pairs to compare their answers. Encourage them to give reasons for their choices.

- Ask students to write a reply to one of the comments. Students could write their reply on a small piece of paper and the replies could be stuck on the classroom noticeboard or made available for everyone to read.

- **Optional step.** Discuss examples of Google doodles with the class. Ask: *Do you think Google doodles help to strengthen the Google brand? Why? / Why not?*

PRESENTATION SKILLS Giving examples

9

- Ask students if they ever have to give presentations as part of their work or studies. Explain that in every unit there is a focus on Presentation skills.

- Ask students to read about giving examples in the Presentation tips box. If necessary, clarify the meaning of:

  relate to something – understand it because you've experienced the same thing or something similar (fourth bullet)

- Ask students if they feel that Renny Gleeson used more stories or more visuals in his talk. They will probably agree that he used more visuals, though he also told the story of the startup competition and illustrated this with visuals.

- **Optional step.** Ask students to talk about their experiences of making, using and looking at visuals during presentations, either in pairs or as a whole class. Ask: *What role do slides play in a presentation and how important are they? Can you think of any examples of good or bad use of slides in either presentations that you've given or that you've watched?*

- ▶ 1.3 Play the clip so that students can identify examples of the three types of experiences. Put students into pairs to discuss the examples and whether or not they follow the techniques in the box. Encourage them to give reasons for their answers.

Transcript

But these things are everywhere. They're on sites big, they're on sites small. This is a global experience.

What a 404 page tells you is that you fell through the cracks. And that's not a good experience when you're used to experiences like this. You can get on your Kinect and you can have unicorns dancing and rainbows spraying out of your mobile phone. A 404 page is not what you're looking for. You get that, and it's like a slap in the face.

- Conduct whole-class feedback. You might like to ask students if they know of any other 404 pages which illustrate good and bad experiences.

10

- Look at the instructions with the class. If necessary, clarify the meaning of:

  a viral video – a video that becomes popular because people watch it and share it with others who, in turn, share it with even more people, creating a *viral* effect (second bullet)

- Put students into pairs to discuss whether they would use a story or a visual in a presentation to give an example of each of the three items. Encourage them to give reasons for their preference.

- Students choose one of the items and prepare a presentation, using either a story or a visual. Tell students that their presentation should be around 30 seconds long and not more than one minute.

- If students have chosen to use a visual, they can create their own visual with paper and pen or use an image they have on their smartphones, tablets or laptops.

- Students practise presenting their example to their partner. Remind them to use the techniques in the Presentation tips box.

11

- Put students into new pairs. They take turns to give their presentation and to give each other feedback on how well their example works.

- Monitor students while they're presenting, noting any examples of good use of the techniques in the Presentation tips box.

- Conduct whole-class feedback. Gauge how well students think their examples work. Invite individual students to demonstrate examples of good use of the techniques that you have noted.

▶ Set Workbook pages 4–5 for homework.

1.2 Building identity

GRAMMAR Present tenses: active and passive

1

- This section is intended to provide revision of present tenses in the active and passive form. It's assumed that students will have already encountered these during their previous learning experience.

- Books open. Put students into pairs to discuss the questions. If students are allowed to use their mobile devices in class, they could show each other videos they like.

- Conduct whole-class feedback. Find out which videos have been particularly popular.

2

- This may be the first time students have seen an infographic. If necessary, briefly explain that infographics are diagrams that represent information in visual form.

- Tell students to look at the infographic. Elicit that the icons represent: mobile phones (purple), email (brown), social media (green), Twitter (blue). Then ask: *What does the infographic tell us about how a viral video spreads?*

- You could put students into pairs to discuss how a viral video spreads. Partners could take turns to describe a step in the process.

- Conduct whole-class feedback on how a viral video spreads.

Answer

A video goes viral when it is shared online. Someone watches the video and shares it online – for example, on social media. More people then watch it, some of those people also share it and the number of people who've seen the video multiplies through this 'viral' process.

3

- Explain that students are going to listen to part of a radio programme about viral videos. Give them time to read the questions. You could put students into pairs to discuss the questions.

- 🔊 2 Play the recording so that students can answer the questions.

Transcript

Every day, millions of videos are uploaded to the Internet, but very few of them go viral. If you think that it's impossible to predict what kind of videos go viral, you might be right. But the phenomenon of viral videos is fast-growing. And more people than ever are posting videos online. The whole phenomenon is being studied closely, because there's a lot of money to be made if you can reach an audience of millions with your video. But the key to a viral video isn't how it's spread – it's the content. The mechanism for the spread of viral videos is clear and it's quite different to traditional mass media. Millions of people watch mass media every day and they all see a broadcast at the same time, whereas online videos are seen by a much smaller number at first, and then they are shared with the viewers' contacts. They can be seen multiple times and at any time the user chooses. A viral video is ultimately viewed by a huge, global audience. A lot of people who started out posting videos as a hobby now host adverts on their sites and so they've turned their hobby into a source of income. Later on in the programme, we'll be talking to three people who have done exactly that. But first, the business news headlines.

- Students could check their answers in pairs before you check with the whole class. You could play the recording again either before or after checking answers.

> ### Answers
>
> 1 Because you can make lot of money if your video reaches an audience of millions.
>
> 2 Millions of people watch mass media every day and they all see a broadcast at the same time, whereas online videos are seen by a much smaller number at first, and then they are shared with the viewers' contacts.
>
> 3 Yes. A lot of people who started out posting videos as a hobby now host adverts on their sites and earn money from this.

- **Optional step**. Put students into pairs or small groups to reflect on and discuss their own experiences. Ask: *Are there any differences between how you view online and more traditional video content? Which do you prefer viewing, and why? Do you know of anyone who has made money from viral videos and, if so, how did they do this?*

4

- Look at the Grammar box with the class. Elicit or remind students that the *present tenses* are the present simple and the present continuous. Present tenses can have active and passive forms.

- Ask students to read the sentences – which are from the recording. If necessary, clarify the meaning of:

  temporary – referring to something that only exists or happens for a short period of time (question 2)

  in progress – referring to an activity that has started but hasn't finished (question 2)

- Students can check their answers and overall understanding of present tenses: active and passive by turning to the Grammar summary on page 140.

> ### Answers
>
> 1 present simple   2 present continuous

- If you feel that students need more controlled practice before continuing, they could do some or all of the exercises in the Grammar summary. Otherwise, you could continue on to Exercise 5 in the unit and set the Grammar summary exercises for homework.

> ### Answers to Grammar summary exercises
>
> **1**
>
> 1 Are (you) watching   2 don't finish   3 records
> 4 don't want   5 'm/am reading   6 stays   7 is getting
> 8 make
>
> **2**
>
> 1 are reported   2 are hacked   3 are stolen   4 is posted
> 5 are being exposed   6 are being investigated
> 7 are being carried out   8 is done
>
> **3**
>
> 1 Hundreds of films are made every year.
>
> 2 Do they update their website weekly?
>
> 3 In the cinema, they don't interrupt films to show adverts.
>
> 4 A lot of films are being downloaded illegally.
>
> 5 The new 'superhero' film isn't being released until next week.
>
> 6 They are / Someone is rewriting a popular 'superhero' comic for the cinema.
>
> **4**
>
> 1 don't enjoy   2 change   3 are appearing   4 Is the video channel checked   5 aren't accepted   6 are kept
> 7 are needed   8 is using
>
> **5**
>
> 1 are started   2 don't have   3 come up with
> 4 aren't required   5 are attracted   6 need
> 7 don't make   8 are trying
>
> **6**
>
> 1 Hi, my name's Monica and I'm living **I live** in London. I was born there.
>
> 2 How much do **are** you paid in your job?
>
> 3 What's the matter? What happens? **What's happening?**
>
> 4 I'm a teacher and I'm **I** work in a primary school.
>
> 5 In my family, we don't watch usually **usually watch** much TV.
>
> 6 On my English course, we assess **are assessed** once a term.

5

- Ask students to look quickly at the sentences. Elicit that in each sentence one option is active and the other is passive. You could ask students to identify the tense of each verb.

- Students choose the correct option to complete the sentences. They could then check their answers in pairs before you check with the whole class.

- **Optional step.** Get students, especially fast finishers, to write sentences using the unused options. For example: *1 Three people are teaching the new course.*

6

- Look at the example with the class. If necessary, review how to form questions in the present simple and present continuous.

- Ask students to complete the questions and answers on their own. They could then check their answers in pairs before you check with the whole class.

7

- Explain that the *Videos Go Viral Award* is a made-up award, but awards for viral videos such as the Viral Video Award are given.

- Ask students to look quickly at the text. If necessary, clarify the meaning of:

   hold a completion – organize a competition (line 1)

   amateur – the opposite of professional, something which is done as a free-time activity, usually without payment (line 8)

- Ask students to complete the text with active and passive forms. They could then check their answers in pairs before you check with the whole class.

8

- Explain that students should write a sentence for each noun in the word list and that they should use either an active or passive form of each verb, but that the nouns and verbs in the word list don't have to be combined.

- Look at the example with the class. Ask students to suggest other sentences using the word *information*. For example: *Some online videos are funny and others give lots of information.*

- Remind students to draw on their own personal experience of using the Internet when writing their sentences.

- Give students 10–15 minutes to write their sentences. Monitor students while they're writing, offering help where necessary. Note examples of good sentences.

- Conduct whole-class feedback. Invite students to read out example sentences that you have noted.

Pronunciation Word stress

9a

- Look at the instructions and the example (1a) with the class. If necessary, clarify what a *part* of a word is by writing a multi-syllable word on the board and asking students to identify its parts, e.g. ad-jec-tive. You don't need to introduce the word *syllable* unless students explicitly ask you for the name for that *part* of a word. Elicit or explain that the first part of *download* is stressed in the example.

- **Optional step.** If the concept of word stress is unfamiliar to students, give an example. Say *record* and then *record*. Elicit that the difference between the way you said the two words was that a different part of the word was stressed each time. Write *record* on the board twice with the first syllable and then the second syllable underlined to visualize this. Then ask students to use the word in a sentence, for example: *I've got a re<u>cord</u> of everything we did, When did they re<u>cord</u> their last CD?* Elicit that *record* is a noun and *re<u>cord</u>* is a verb. You could then elicit or explain that *down<u>load</u>* in the example (1a) is a noun.

- ▲ 3 Play the recording so that students can underline the stressed syllables.

Transcript

1a	*You can get that music as a download quite cheaply.*
1b	*Do you know how to download music files?*
2a	*How often do you use online shopping sites?*
2b	*When I go online, I usually check my emails first.*
3a	*I never update my Facebook status. Do you?*
3b	*I don't know how to install this software update.*
4a	*With this app, you can upload photos really quickly.*
4b	*What's the difference between an upload and an attachment?*

- Students could check their answers in pairs before you check with the whole class. You could play the recording again either before or after checking answers.

• You could elicit or explain these rules: 1 in two-syllable nouns and adjectives, the word stress is always on the first syllable; 2 in two-syllable verbs and adverbs, the word stress is always on the second syllable. Explain that this difference in word stress helps us to differentiate between noun and verb forms, and between adjective and adverb forms.

9b

• Ask students to prepare sentences using the words from Exercise 9a. Give weaker students time to prepare sentences of their own. These don't need to be long and complex – relatively short sentences like the ones they've just listened to would be ideal.

• Put students into pairs to say their sentences. Monitor students while they're saying their sentences, but ask students to give each other peer feedback, rather than deferring to you for confirmation of whether they're saying a word correctly first. Only intervene and correct if you become aware of the fact that neither of the students in a pair know the correct syllable stress.

SPEAKING The Internet and me

10 *21st* CENTURY OUTCOMES

• Before starting this exercise, refer students to the 21st CENTURY OUTCOMES at the foot of the page, which is *ICT LITERACY Use technology as a tool to evaluate and communicate information.* If necessary, clarify the meaning of:

   ICT — an abbreviation of Information, Communications and Technology

   literacy — the ability to read or write or, as it's used here, the ability to use something, e.g. technology, as a tool

• Explain or elicit that this exercise encourages students to think about how they use technology to communicate information in order to fulfil this 21st CENTURY OUTCOME.

• Tell students to turn to page 164 and to read the profiles quickly. Ask: *Have you seen this kind of categorization before? Do you know of any other ways of categorizing people according to their interactions with the Internet?*

• Bring in students' personal experiences of taking part in this kind of personality or lifestyle quiz. Ask: *Have you ever done a quiz like this before? If you have, what did you learn about yourself from doing it?*

• Tell students to turn back to page 13. Put them into pairs to complete the questions for each topic and then to write two more questions of their own.

• Monitor students while they're writing questions, offering help where necessary. Word order may be a problem area, so look out for correct word order.

11

• Put students into new pairs to ask and answer their questions. Remind them to actually ask the questions, rather than just give them to their partner to read.

• Tell students to turn to page 164 again and to decide which profile fits their partner. Ask students to use their partner's answers from the quiz to explain why they've chosen that category. Partners should say whether they agree or disagree with the categorization.

• Students can work with more than one different partner and repeat the activity more than once.

▶ Photocopiable communicative activity 1.1: Go to page 213 for practice of present tenses: active and passive, and computer- and website-related vocabulary. The teaching notes are on page 237.

▶ Set Workbook pages 6–7 for homework.

1.3 Who am I?

READING A personal view on personal branding

1

• Books open. Draw students' attention to the spread title: *A personal view on personal branding.* Although students will already be familiar with what a *brand* is, they may not know what *personal branding* is. Write *personal branding* on the board, draw a circle around it and add three lines going out from the circle, each of which leads to one of the following: *my image / what I want people to think about me / what I want people to associate me with.* Explain that these are three important ingredients of personal branding. Invite students to suggest other words or phrases which could be added to the spider diagram, and add these.

- Bring in students' own experiences. Ask: *What have you done to brand yourself as a person or as a professional? Do you know other people who have branded themselves in a particular way?* Encourage students to talk about people they know or people in the public eye.

- Look at the questions with the class. Elicit or explain that a blog can be part of someone's personal brand.

- Put students into pairs to discuss the questions.

- Conduct whole-class feedback. Write the things blogs can be about and the reasons why people read them on the board as students mention them. If students don't mention this during whole-class feedback, remind them that one reason for writing a blog is to have a platform for your personal brand and to promote it.

2

- Look at the instructions with the class. The words *acupuncture* and *therapist* are cognates in many European languages. However, speakers of other languages may need clarification of the meaning:

- *acupuncture* – a treatment for pain or illness in which thin needles are positioned just under the surface of the skin at special points around the body

- *therapist* – someone whose job is to treat an illness

- Model and drill the pronunciation of *acupuncture* /ˈækjʊˌpʌŋ(k)tʃə/ and *therapist* /ˈθɛrəpɪst/.

- Bring in students' own experiences. Ask: *Have you ever had acupuncture? If yes, did it help you?*

- Explain that students are going to read the blog post and decide the writer's purpose. They should also look for evidence in the blog post in order to support their decision. Explain that students will be reading for general information or gist, so they should read the text quite quickly and focus on identifying the writer's purpose. Remind them that understanding every word in the text will not be necessary in order to complete the task.

- Ask students to read the blog post and think about their answer.

- You could put students into pairs to discuss their answer.

Answers

b

The writer doesn't talk about selling products connected to personal branding and she doesn't explain why personal branding is important.

In paragraph B, she says 'So I decided to look more closely at how well I'm developing my own personal brand. And this is what I found out.' In paragraphs C–E, she then outlines how well she feels she is doing at developing her own brand.

3

- Explain that students are now going to focus on the paragraphs in the blog post in greater detail. Their aim is to identify the main focus in each paragraph, which is a useful reading skill.

- Ask students to match the headings with the paragraphs.

Answers

1 A 2 D 3 C 4 E 5 B

- Elicit or explain that the T-shirt with the blog post isn't the acupuncturist's T-shirt.

4

- Explain that students are now going to focus on reading the blog post for specific information.

- Ask students to read the blog post again and to find the best option to complete the sentences.

- Students could check their answers in pairs before you check with the whole class. Encourage them to give reasons or evidence to support their answers.

Answers

1 b 2 c 3 c

Sentence 1: your vision of yourself (lines 1–2) doesn't mean 'picture, photograph, etc.'. The word vision in this context means 'an idea or image in your mind'.

Sentence 2: the writer talks about communicating with the world (line 12) – but she doesn't mean 'the whole world'; she means 'other people'.

5

- Look at item 1 as an example with the class. If necessary, clarify the meaning of *presence* in this context:

  presence – being seen or noticed in a place, in this case the place is the Internet

- Elicit that the writer is positive about her presence on social media.

- Put students into pairs to find the words and to decide whether the writer is positive or negative about these aspects of her 'personal brand'. Then check answers with the class.

Answers

1 positive   2 positive   3 negative   4 negative
5 negative   6 positive   7 positive   8 positive
9 positive   10 positive   11 positive   12 positive

6

- Put students into pairs to discuss the questions. These questions, especially question 1, will generate a lot of discussion, so remind students to speak English as much as possible throughout.

- Encourage students to use examples to support their opinions. If possible, these should be examples from their own experiences or those of people they've come into contact with. For example, you could ask: *Have you benefitted from personal branding yourself? Do you know anyone who's benefitted from personal branding? If so, what positive effects has it had on you/them?*

• **Optional step.** Students who finish early or need an extra challenge, could discuss in pairs this question: *Is personal branding more or less important in the 21st century than it was in the 20th century? Give reasons to support your answer.*

VOCABULARY Tasks and interests

7

• Elicit that *tasks* are specific things you have to do, usually while you're at work, and *interests* are things you find interesting and want to learn more about.

• Ask students to match the words in bold in the sentences with the words with a similar meaning in the box.

• **Optional step.** Draw students' attention to the verb + preposition combinations in some of the sentences, e.g. *head up* (sentence 1), *focus on* (sentence 3), *deal with* (sentence 9). Elicit or explain that these verbs are always followed by these prepositions.

TEACHING TIP

Synonym building

Creating lists of synonyms (words with the same or similar meaning) can be a helpful way to build vocabulary. Encourage students to think of and write down synonyms for new words that they learn. At this stage, students should also be able to identify and use more interesting synonyms for commonly used words, e.g. more interesting synonyms for *big* include *massive, huge, extensive, immense*.

8

• Give students 10–15 minutes to write ten sentences on their own.

• Make sure students understand that the sentences should be true for them. Give examples from your own life to make this clear, e.g. *Our school offers a range of English courses to meet the needs of different students, I'm also involved in test writing, The school secretary deals with course administration.*

• Monitor students while they're writing, offering help where necessary.

• Look at the example with the class. Elicit that *Oh?* is used as a response to the statement in order to show interest in what speaker A has said.

• **Optional step.** Elicit or give students examples of other expressions for showing interest in what someone has just told us, e.g. *Really?, That's interesting, I didn't know that, Fantastic.* Then encourage students to use different expressions in response to the different sentences their partner says.

• Put students into pairs to compare their sentences and to ask follow-up questions. Encourage students to form their follow-up questions as spontaneously as possible.

• Conduct whole-class feedback. Invite pairs of students to read out their sentences and ask follow-up questions in front of the rest of the class.

SPEAKING Personal branding

9   **21st** **CENTURY OUTCOMES**

• Before starting this exercise, refer students to the 21st CENTURY OUTCOMES at the foot of the page, which is *CRITICAL THINKING Effectively analyse and evaluate evidence, claims and beliefs.* Ask students to say what they think it means to be able to analyse evidence, claims and beliefs. When do they have to be able to do this either at work or in their studies?

• Ask students to think of three people they know who they could answer the questions about. Encourage them to include at least one person they know personally because this should help to make the topic feel more relevant for them.

• Put students into pairs to discuss the questions.

• Conduct whole-class feedback. Ask as many students as possible to talk about one of the people they thought of.

▶ Set Workbook pages 8–9 for homework.

1.4 I don't think we've met

LISTENING Networking

1

• Books open. Draw students' attention to the spread title: *I don't think we've met.* Ask: *In which type of social situation would someone say this? What could come after this statement in a conversation?*

• Draw students' attention to the section heading: *Networking.* Elicit or explain that *networking* involves meeting and building relationships with people who can help you in your career or help your company.

- Elicit or give examples of how networking can happen, e.g. at an evening reception or conference dinner where people working in the same area can meet, talk and exchange business cards. There's also online networking where people post details of their professional experience on websites and form a network of contacts.
- Ask students to read the list of situations and to think about possible conversation topics for each one. They can do this in pairs.

- **Optional step.** Elicit that conversation topics that would be appropriate in some cultures aren't in others. Ask students to formulate advice about what people unfamiliar with their culture should and shouldn't talk about when attending a networking event in their country.

2

- Put students into pairs to discuss the questions.
- **Question 2.** Encourage students to think about how different forms of follow-up communication would be more or less appropriate in the different situations.
- Monitor students while they're speaking, offering help where necessary. Then conduct whole-class feedback.

3

- Look at the instructions and the table with the class. If necessary, clarify the meaning of:

  mutual acquaintance – a person who's known to two or more different people (last line of table)

- 🔊 4 Play the recording so that students can decide which statements in the table are true for the speakers.

Transcript

1

P = Paul, R = Rowan

P: *Do you mind if I join you?*

R: *No, not at all.*

P: *I'm Paul, TGB systems. How are you finding the conference?*

R: *It's pretty good so far. I'm Rowan, by the way. I'm with Alliance Graphics.*

P: *Pleased to meet you. Alliance Graphics … you're based in Edinburgh?*

R: *Yes, that's right, but we're opening up a couple of new offices in other cities too.*

P: *So things are going well, then?*

R: *Actually, yes. And that's why I'm here really, at this conference. It's got a lot to offer us right now.*

2

J = Joan, N = Nikolai

J: *Hello. I'm Joan, I live on Rowan Street.*

N: *Hi, nice to meet you.*

J: *I believe you live near Marco? Is that right?*

N: *Yes, we're next-door neighbours. We moved in last year, number 25. I'm Nikolai.*

J: *Ah yes, Nikolai. Marco and I used to work together on the neighbourhood committee.*

N: *Really? I didn't know he'd been on the committee. What was that like?*

J: *Oh, you know – interesting but time-consuming. So how do you like living here?*

N: *Oh it's great. We're really happy here.*

3

R = Roger, E = Elise

R: *Hi.*

E: *Hello. I don't think we've met. I'm one of BKG's regional co-ordinators, Elise Binoche.*

R: *My pleasure. I'm Roger Kennedy, Global Digital Strategies Director at Lynne Robson Jones.*

E: *Digital Strategies? What kind of things does that involve?*

R: *Well, I work primarily in web technologies. I handle viral marketing and social media for our international clients.*

E: *That sounds interesting. Viral marketing is a really exciting thing to be involved in, I guess.*

R: *It is. It's fun too.*

- Students could check their answers in pairs before you check with the whole class. You could play the recording again either before or after checking answers. Ask students to give reasons for the choices they've made about the relationships between the speakers.

Answers

	1	2	3
they haven't met before	✓	✓	✓
they don't work in the same field	✓		✓
they work for different companies	✓		✓
they live in the same area		✓	
they are connected by a mutual acquaintance		✓	

- **Optional step.** After listening to the recording, students may be confused by the fact that we use 'no' in positive answers to the questions: *Do you mind … ?* (conversation 1, line 1) or *Would you mind …-ing?* Explain that when we use these questions, we're asking if something would be a problem for the other person. 'No' therefore indicates that this is not a problem. 'Yes' would be a negative answer because it would indicate that it *is* a problem. Questions with *mind* are commonly used by native English speakers in conversation.

4

- Look at the Useful language box with the class. Ask: *How important do you think it is to make a good impression when you meet someone for the first time at a networking event? There's a saying in English: 'You never get a second chance to make a first impression.' Would you agree?*

- Ask students to match the three groups of expressions in the Useful language box with the techniques for making a good impression. They can do this in pairs. Students can then think of other techniques you can use when networking.

- Conduct whole-class feedback. Elicit and write a list of other techniques on the board.

- **Optional step.** Draw students' attention to the fact that asking open questions can make it easier to keep the conversation going than asking closed questions. Elicit the difference between a closed question (a question to which the answer can only be *yes* or *no*) and an open question (a question to which you can give any answer). Then give students some closed questions to change into open questions. For example, instead of asking the closed question: *Do you live nearby?* you can ask: *Where do you live?* Instead of asking: *Do you travel a lot?* you can ask: *How often do you travel?*

Answers

1 b   2 c   3 a

Other techniques could be: showing interest in the person you're talking to or their comment, finding points of common interest, giving and responding to compliments, showing how experienced you are, showing how well-connected you are (name-dropping), showing modesty, involving everyone in the conversation (if you're talking in a group), not dominating the conversation, not interrupting when the other person is talking, asking follow-up questions.

5

- Explain that students are going to listen to the recording again and identify which one of the two people in each conversation uses the expressions in the Useful language box.

- ▲ 4 Play the recording so that students can choose the correct option.

- Students could check their answers in pairs before you check with the whole class. You could play the recording again either before or after checking answers. You could also direct students to the transcript on page165 if they would like to look at the expressions the speakers used.

Answers

1 Paul   2 Joan   3 Elise

Pronunciation Using intonation to ask a question

6a

- Look at the Pronunciation section heading with the class. If necessary, clarify the meaning of:

> *intonation* – the rhythm we give to our words as we say them

- Elicit or explain that *grammatical question forms* can be identified as questions because they contain auxiliary verbs, e.g. *do, does, did, have, has.* For example, *How do you like living here?* (from this recording) contains the grammatical question form *do you* + verb. In contrast, *You're based in Edinburgh?* (also from this recording) doesn't contain a grammatical question form, but could be made into a question through the intonation the speaker uses.

- ▲ 5 Play the recording so that students can identify which question has a grammatical question form.

Transcript

1   *You're based in Edinburgh?*

2   *So things are going well, then?*

3   *I believe you live near Marco?*

4   *How do you like living here?*

5   *Digital Strategies?*

- Students could check their answers in pairs before you check with the whole class. You could play the recording again either before or after checking answers. You could also direct students to the transcript on page165 if they would like to look at the questions as they listen.

> **Answer**
>
> Question 4 has a grammatical question form.

6b

- 🔊 **6** Play the recording, pausing after each question to give students time to repeat.

Transcript

1   You're based in Edinburgh?

2   So things are going well, then?

3   I believe you live near Marco?

4   Digital Strategies?

- **Optional step.** Get students to use intonation to ask their own questions, e.g. *You're working on page 16?*

SPEAKING Meeting people

7

- Bring in students' own experiences. Ask: *Have you ever attended a social event with other students and teachers? If yes, did you talk to new people at the event? What impression did they make on you?*

- Put students into groups (5–6 students) to introduce themselves. Try and organize groups so that students work with people they haven't worked with before. Tell students to decide whether they're going to be a student or a teacher and to introduce themselves to at least three other people in the group. Alternatively, students can move around the classroom and speak to people they don't particularly know.

- Remind students to use the expressions from the Useful language box. They could write down some expressions they would like to use on a card or small piece of paper. They can refer to these during their conversations.

- **Optional step.** Ask students to reflect on how successful their conversations were and how good an impression they made on the people they talked to. They can do this in pairs.

8

- Put students into pairs to talk about who they spoke to and what impression these people made. They then tell each other which person or people they would contact again, and why.

- Conduct whole-class feedback. Ask students to tell the rest of the class about people that made a positive impression.

WRITING An online profile

9

- Books open. Bring in students' own experiences. Ask: *Have you read any profiles from networking websites before? What features of online profiles do you like and dislike? Have you ever created your own online profile?*

- Ask students to read the profile. Then put them into pairs to discuss how this profile compares with other online profiles they've seen.

- If students haven't seen any online profiles before, you could show some examples from websites such as LinkedIn.

10

- Students match the symbols with the words. They should be able to do this relatively quickly.

- Check answers with the class. Invite individual students to draw one symbol each on the board.

> **Answers**
>
> 1 @   2 .   3 /   4 #   5 _

- **Optional step.** Ask students where you would see or use these symbols, e.g. *at* symbols are used in email addresses and Twitter handles, dots are used in website and email addresses, hashtags are used on Twitter, Facebook and Instagram.

Writing skill Symbols and notes

11a

- Look at item 1 as an example with the class. Get students to find the words in the online profile. Elicit or explain that this is a concise form and that you would add *I* before *moved* in a conversation.

- Ask students to decide how they would give the other pieces of information in a conversation. They can write out the full sentences they would use. They can do this in pairs.

- Conduct whole-class feedback by inviting individual students to write the full sentences on the board. Accept slight variations on the sentences given in the answers if the sentence is still accurate and communicates the original information.

> **Answers**
>
> 1 but I moved into digital advertising
>
> 2 and I created online platforms
>
> 3 where I handle international clients
>
> 4 My Skype name is R O Kennedy.
>
> 5 My Twitter username is R O K E N.
>
> 6 I speak English and Italian.
>
> 7 I work in web technologies.
>
> 8 I studied at Yale University and the University of Pennsylvania.

11b

• Give students about ten minutes to write the profile information as full sentences.

• Students could check their answers in pairs before you check with the whole class. You could invite individual students to write their sentences on the board again, as in Exercise 11a. As above, accept slight variations on the sentences given in the answers if the sentence is still accurate and communicates the original information.

Answers

1 I studied at the London School of Economics from 1999 to 2002.

2 I have worked on software development for five years.

3 My email address is Amelia at Cruz dot com.

4 I work in customer care and online client support.

5 I joined Gaming Inc in 2009 and created a new online format.

6 I'm currently an assistant manager at B&T Ltd.

7 My interests are marathon running and attending a theatre group.

8 My previous posts were as a personal assistant at Greenly Foods and an office manager at Dairy International.

11c

• Tell students to identify the main focus of each sentence and then to summarize the sentence in note form. They should use the concise forms from Exercise 11a as a model.

• Monitor students while they're writing, offering help where necessary. Then check answers with the class.

Answers

1 email: c_trott@revlon.com

2 Skype: claratrott

3 Languages: German, Spanish

4 area of expertise: accounts management

5 Experience: financial planning, ten years

6 Interests: (various) children's charities

7 left post and set up own company

8 currently head up research department and direct new projects

12 `21st` **CENTURY OUTCOMES**

• Before starting this exercise, refer students to the 21st CENTURY OUTCOMES at the foot of the page which is *PRODUCTIVITY AND ACCOUNTABILITY Present yourself professionally and in the accepted way.* If necessary, clarify the meaning of:

accountability – taking responsibility for what you do

• Ask students why presenting yourself professionally and in the accepted way is important. Elicit or explain that this is not only polite when meeting someone, but it's also a way to make a good impression either in person or in writing.

• Encourage students to reflect on what they could do to give a positive impression of themselves before they start writing.

• Give students 10–15 minutes to complete their profile.

• Monitor students while they're writing, offering help where necessary.

> **TEACHING TIP**
>
> **Students writing/talking about themselves**
>
> What or how much information students are able to complete about themselves will depend on the stage in their working lives that they've reached. Some students may already have a lot of work experience and others may still be in full-time education. However, even if your students haven't yet entered full-time employment, they will still have interests and areas of expertise, for example in academic subjects. They may also have done some form of community service or voluntary work during their studies which they could add to their profile.

13

• Put students into pairs to exchange profiles. Encourage them to ask and to respond to follow-up questions based on what they've read in their partner's profile. Remind them that they can ask about both professional and non-professional interests.

• Ask students to imagine they're at a networking event where they're asking each other follow-up questions. Their goal is to find out more information about the other person so that they know whether they would like to build a relationship.

• **Optional step.** Students work in groups of three. They each create a message that they could send to someone they met at a networking event to follow up the conversation they had there. Each person in the group should create their message for a different media: 1 a voicemail message, 2 an email, 3 a message you'd send through a social media site. They could use a voice recording app on their smartphones to make a recording of the voicemail message. Students can then compare and contrast the different versions, identifying reasons for any differences.

▶ Photocopiable communicative activity 1.2: Go to page 214 for further practice of small talk / networking language: making an impression, vocabulary for talking about yourself, and open-ended questions and reflecting comments. The teaching notes are on page 237.

▶ Set Workbook pages 10–11 for homework.

▶ Set Workbook Presentation 1 on pages 12–13 for homework.

2 Careers

LEAD IN

• Books open. Draw students' attention to the unit title, and to the photo on page 18 and its caption. Ask: *What's the difference between a job and a career?* Possible answers could be: *A job is something that you get, but a career is something that you build for yourself*; *A career is a series of jobs or positions done by someone who wants to advance and build on their skills and experience to achieve a specific work-related goal.* Then ask: *Do you think the men in the photo have a job or a career? Would you like to do this work?*

• To gauge students' prior knowledge of the unit vocabulary, ask: *How would you know that someone has a successful career?* Possible answers could be: *they earn a lot of money, they have a lot of power or responsibility, they're well-respected, they've developed a lot of knowledge of and skills in their area.* Then ask: *What do you need in order to have a successful career?* Possible answers could be: *academic qualifications, interpersonal skills, commitment, ambition.*

• Bring in students' own experiences. Ask: *What goals would you like to achieve during your working life?*

TEDTALKS
BACKGROUND

1

• Ask students to read the text about Derek Sivers and his talk. If necessary, clarify the meaning of the following:

founder – someone who starts, or founds, a company (line 2)

proceeds – money that you get from events or activities (line 4)

charitable trust – a non-profit organization that provides help or support where it is needed (lines 4–5)

• If culturally relevant, elicit times of year when people usually set themselves objectives, e.g. New Year when people make New Year's resolutions, and what kind of goals they set at those times, e.g. get fit, give up smoking. Ask: *Have you ever set yourselves objectives at these times of year? If so, would you like to share them?*

• **Optional step.** Based on what students have read about Derek Sivers and the title of the TED Talk, elicit some possible sentences they would expect him to say in this talk. Students write these sentences down so that they can compare them with what Derek Sivers actually says later.

KEY WORDS

2

• Ask students to read the sentences and to try to guess the meaning of the words in bold.

• When students have finished matching the words with their definitions, you could put them into pairs to compare their answers before you check with the whole class.

• Check that students can say the words in bold correctly. The words *acknowledge*, *conventional* and *gratification* may prove difficult for students to pronounce, depending on their first language background. If necessary, model and drill the pronunciation.

> **Answers**
>
> 1 c   2 f   3 b   4 d   5 e   6 a

AUTHENTIC LISTENING SKILLS Listening for signposts

3a

- Ask students to read the information about signposts in the Authentic listening skills box.

- Give students time to read the first four sentences of the TED Talk. Explain that one of these sentences is a signpost. Ask students to put the sentences in order. They can then compare their answers in pairs, but don't confirm answers at this stage.

- ⚡ 7 Play the recording so that students can check their answers.

> **Transcript and answers**
>
> 1 *Everyone, please think of your biggest personal goal.*
>
> 2 *For real – you can take a second.*
>
> 3 *You've got to feel this to learn it.*
>
> 4 *Take a few seconds and think of your personal biggest goal, OK?*

3b

- Ask students to read and match the signpost sentences (1–4) with what Derek Sivers says next (a–d). They can then compare their answers in pairs, but don't confirm answers at this stage.

3c

- ⚡ 8 Play the recording so that students can check their answers.

Transcript

1 *Well, bad news: you should have kept your mouth shut, because that good feeling now will make you less likely to do it.*

2 *So, let's look at the proof. 1926, Kurt Lewin, founder of social psychology, called this 'substitution'.*

3 *It goes like this: 163 people across four separate tests – everyone wrote down their personal goal*

4 *So, if this is true, what can we do? Well, you could resist the temptation to announce your goal.*

> **Answers**
>
> 1 d 2 b 3 a 4 c

- **Optional step.** Play the recording again and ask students to focus their attention on the words that Derek Sivers stresses as he says the signpost expressions. Model and drill this. Students can then practise saying the expressions in pairs.

1 <u>Well</u>, bad news:

2 <u>So</u>, let's look at the proof.

3 It goes like <u>this</u>:

4 <u>So</u>, if this is <u>true</u>, what can <u>we</u> do?

2.1 Keep your goals to yourself

TEDTALKS

1

- Books open. Look at the instructions, the words and the summary with the class. If necessary, clarify the difference between *prove* and *test*. Elicit or explain that *prove* is a verb only (meaning 'to show that something is true'), whereas *test* can be a verb or a noun (meaning '[to give someone] a set of questions to measure their ability'). These may be false friends in students' first language.

- Students complete the summary.

- ▶ 2.1 Play the whole talk once so that students can check their answers.

Transcript

0.14 *Everyone, please think of your biggest personal goal. For real – you can take a second. You've got to feel this to learn it. Take a few seconds and think of your personal biggest goal, OK? Imagine deciding right now that you're going to do it. Imagine telling someone that you meet today what you're going to do. Imagine their congratulations and their high image of you. Doesn't it feel good to say it out loud? Don't you feel one step closer already, like it's already becoming part of your identity?*

0.43 *Well, bad news: you should have kept your mouth shut, because that good feeling now will make you less likely to do it. Repeated psychology tests have proven that telling someone your goal makes it less likely to happen. Any time you have a goal, there are some steps that need to be done, some work that needs to be done in order to achieve it. Ideally, you would not be satisfied until you had actually done the work. But when you tell someone your goal and they acknowledge it, psychologists have found that it's called a 'social reality'. The mind is kind of tricked into feeling that it's already done. And then, because you felt that satisfaction, you're less motivated to do the actual hard work necessary. (Laughter) So this goes against the conventional wisdom that we should tell our friends our goals, right – so they hold us to it.*

1.28 *So, let's look at the proof. 1926, Kurt Lewin, founder of social psychology, called this 'substitution'. 1933, Vera Mahler found, when it was acknowledged by others, it felt real in the mind. 1982, Peter Gollwitzer wrote a whole book about this and in 2009, he did some new tests that were published.*

1.47 *It goes like this: 163 people across four separate tests – everyone wrote down their personal goal. Then half of them announced their commitment to this goal to the room, and half didn't. Then everyone was given 45 minutes of work that would directly lead them towards their goal, but they were told that they could stop at any time. Now, those who kept their mouths shut worked the entire 45 minutes, on average, and when asked afterwards, said that they felt that they had a long way to go still to achieve their goal. But those who had announced it quit after only 33 minutes, on average, and when asked afterwards, said that they felt much closer to achieving their goal.*

2.26 *So, if this is true, what can we do? Well, you could resist the temptation to announce your goal. You can delay the gratification that the social acknowledgement brings, and you can understand that your mind mistakes the talking for the doing. But if you do need to talk about something, you can state it in a way that gives you no satisfaction, such as, 'I really want to run this marathon, so I need to train five times a week and kick my ass if I don't, OK?'*

2.55 *So audience, next time you're tempted to tell someone your goal, what will you say? (Silence) Exactly, well done.*

3.03 *(Applause)*

> **Answer**
> _____
> 1 secret   2 plans   3 proves   4 tests   5 suggestions

- Draw students' attention to the following verb + noun collocations: *keep something secret, tell somebody something, prove a claim, do a test, make a suggestion*.

Extra activity

Verb + noun collocations

Give students further practice of verb + noun collocations. Give each student or pair of students a different noun. Keep the nouns quite simple, e.g. *decision, test, suggestion, arrangement*. Ask students to write their noun on the right side of a page in their Vocabulary notebooks. Tell students to think of as many verbs as they can which could go in front of their noun and to write these as a list on the left side of the page. They should write as many verbs as they can think of. You could make this into a competition to see who can find the most. When students have finished making their lists, they could present their collocations to the whole class or to small groups.

- Note the differences in North American English and British English shown at the foot of the spread. Derek Sivers uses North American English in this TED Talk, so North American versions are listed first. In this unit, these focus on vocabulary, spelling and pronunciation differences. See page 6 of the Introduction for ideas on how to present and practise these differences.

2

- Give students time to read the sentences. You could ask them to predict the correct options based on what they can remember from the first time they watched this part of the talk.

- ▶ 2.1 Play the first part (0.00–1.28) of the talk so that students can choose the correct options.

- Students could check their answers in pairs before you check with the whole class. Elicit or explain that Derek Sivers' advice (*Don't tell anyone your goal*) is counter-intuitive, i.e. not what you would expect.

> **Answers**
> _____
> 1 less   2 less   3 should

3

- Ask students to read the sentences about the 2009 psychology test that Derek Sivers refers to.

- ▶ 2.1 Play the second part (1.28–2.26) of the talk so that students can identify the sentence which isn't true.

> **Answer**
> _____
> e is not true

- **Optional step.** Put students into pairs or small groups to discuss how convincing they think this research is. Ask students to give reasons to support their opinions.

4

- Give students time to read the suggestions. You could ask them to predict the suggestions Derek Sivers makes based on what they can remember from the first time they watched this part of the talk.

- ▶ 2.1 Play the third part (2.26 to the end) of the talk so that students can check their answers.

> **Answers**
> _____
> Derek Sivers makes these suggestions:
> b, c, d

5

- Put students into pairs to discuss the questions.

- Monitor students while they're speaking, noting any examples of good points.

- Conduct whole-class feedback. Encourage individual students to tell the class of any examples of things Derek Sivers suggests that they've done.

> **Suggested answers**
> _____
> 1 Telling somebody your goal will make you less likely to do it.
> 2 Students' own answers
> 3 Students' own answers

VOCABULARY IN CONTEXT

6

• ▶2.2 Play the clips from the TED Talk. When each multiple-choice question appears, pause the clip so that students can choose the correct definition. Discourage the more confident students from always giving the answer by asking students to raise their hand if they think they know.

Transcript and subtitles

1   *Everyone, please think of your biggest personal goal.* **For real** *– you can take a second.*
    a *honestly*
    b *I don't believe you*
    c *really big*

2   **Well, bad news**: *you should have kept your mouth shut*
    a *guess what happened*
    b *I'm sorry to say this*
    c *that's sad*

3   *The mind is* **kind of** *tricked into feeling that it's already done.*
    a *completely*
    b *often*
    c *in some way*

4   *So this goes against the conventional wisdom that we should tell our friends our goals,* **right**?
    a *do you do this?*
    b *don't you agree?*
    c *is that OK?*

5   *in 2009, he did some new tests that were published.* **It goes like this**: *163 people across four separate tests*
    a *this is the explanation*
    b *this is where it goes*
    c *this is why they did it*

Answers

1 a 2 b 3 c 4 b 5 a

7

• Elicit the meaning of the three expressions. Also elicit that Derek Sivers used *right* to turn a statement into a question and that he used an upward intonation with his question. Model and drill this upward intonation using the example sentence from the TED Talk.

• Put students into pairs to tell each other their stories about something unusual they've heard recently. Point out that this doesn't have to be anything extraordinary, just something that surprised or interested them.

Using target expressions in discussions

Sometimes, just asking students to use target expressions in a discussion isn't enough. They often concentrate on getting their words out and forget about the target language completely. In order to increase the chances of students using target expressions, you could do one of the following:

1 Ask students to prepare sentences incorporating the target expressions before they start speaking. They can also think in advance about how and when they'll use the sentences.

2 Put the target expressions onto cards or strips of paper that students hold in their hands. They then put the cards down on the table as they say each expression.

3 Students focus on using the target expressions to ask their partner(s) questions, for example: *So you … , right? Was it kind of … ?*

CRITICAL THINKING Using appropriate evidence

8

• Look at the section heading with the class. If necessary, clarify the meaning of:

  using appropriate evidence – choosing information or statistics which support your argument

• Ask students to read the comments and to decide whether the writers think Derek Sivers used appropriate evidence.

Answers

Jian – no, Lianne – yes, Kevin – yes

• **Optional step.** Students write their own short comment, giving their opinion of or reaction to Derek Sivers' talk. Encourage students to keep their comment general rather than focusing on whether he uses appropriate evidence. Monitor students while they're writing, offering help where necessary. When they've finished writing, put students into pairs or small groups to read and give feedback on each other's comment.

9

• Give students time to think about whether Derek Sivers' evidence was convincing and/or appropriate. If necessary, they can refer to the transcript on page 174 during the activity: this is not a memory test.

• Put students into pairs to discuss their opinions and to give reasons for them.

• Monitor students while they're speaking, noting which students think Derek Sivers used convincing and/or appropriate evidence, and which don't.

• Allow 5–10 minutes for discussion.

• Conduct whole-class feedback. Ask individual students with differing views to discuss their opinions.

10

• Ask students to choose one of the comments to reply to. Encourage them to choose a comment that they either strongly agree or disagree with.

• Elicit the two expressions used in the comments to give the writer's opinion (*personally*, *to my mind*).

• Elicit other expressions you can use to give your opinion, e.g. *for me*, *in my opinion*, *the way I see it*. Encourage students to use one or more of these expressions in their reply.

• Tell students to keep their reply short, i.e. about the same length as the original comment. Give them 2–3 minutes to write their reply.

• When they've finished writing, put students into pairs or small groups to read and give feedback on each other's comment.

PRESENTATION SKILLS Thinking about your audience

11

• Ask students to read about thinking about your audience in the Presentation tips box. If necessary, clarify the meaning of:

> *technical words* – specialist vocabulary used by people working in the same field or area and often unknown to people outside (first bullet)

• Bring in students' own experiences. Ask: *Have you ever watched a talk that you really felt connected to? If so, what did the speaker do or say that helped you feel that connection?*

• ▶ 2.3 Play the clip so that students identify which technique Derek Sivers uses to connect with the audience.

Transcript

Everyone, please think of your biggest personal goal. For real – you can take a second. You've got to feel this to learn it. Take a few seconds and think of your personal biggest goal, OK? Imagine deciding right now that you're going to do it. Imagine telling someone that you meet today what you're going to do. Imagine their congratulations and their high image of you. Doesn't it feel good to say it out loud? Don't you feel one step closer already, like it's already becoming part of your identity?

• Put students into pairs to compare their answers and to discuss the reason(s) why this is a good technique for this talk.

• Conduct whole-class feedback and confirm which technique Derek Sivers uses and why this is useful.

Answers

He directs his audience to think about their own experiences. This means that the audience can then relate their own feelings to what they then hear, which in this case is relevant as the content of the talk is about setting personal goals.

• **Optional step.** Put students into pairs or small groups to discuss these questions or conduct whole-class discussion. Ask: *How connected would you feel to Derek Sivers' talk if you were in the audience? Is it easier to feel connected to a speaker if you're watching a talk live than when you're watching it on a screen? Why? / Why not?*

12

• Look at the example with the class. Ask students to suggest ways of continuing this introduction. For example: *How do you feel? Do you feel nervous? Do you feel excited?*

• Put students into pairs. Explain that they are going to work in pairs to write an introduction to a presentation on some of the topics. They could write an introduction for every topic, and they could either focus on using one technique in each introduction or they could combine techniques.

• Remind students that Derek Sivers' introduction was only 45 seconds long and that their introduction should not be longer than a minute.

• Get students to practise giving their introductions. Monitor students while they're giving their introductions, noting any good examples.

• **Optional step.** You could give each pair a specific audience, e.g. bored teenagers, top corporate executives, retired people, and ask them to think about how they would adapt their introduction to get that audience to connect with the talk. They could then give their introduction to another pair, who would have to guess which group the introduction was for.

13

• Put students into groups of four so that one pair works with another. They take turns to give an introduction and to give each other feedback on how well their introduction works.

• Encourage students to use their voices to convey warmth, enthusiasm and interest in the audience in order to connect with them.

• Monitor students while they're giving their introductions, noting any good examples.

• Conduct whole-class feedback. Gauge how well students think their introductions work. Invite individual students to give examples of good introductions that you have noted.

▶ Set Workbook pages 14–15 for homework.

2.2 Are you looking forward to it?

GRAMMAR Future forms and uses

1

• Books open. Draw students' attention to the spread title: *Are you looking forward to it?* Elicit that this is something we might ask when someone has told us about something they're going to do in the future.

- **Optional step.** Ask students to write a sentence that could have come before this question in a conversation, e.g. *I'm going to a birthday party at the weekend* or *I will start working on a new project next week*. Then invite students to read out their sentences to the rest of the class and write on the board example sentences containing different future forms – they're likely to be *will* + infinitive or *going to* + infinitive. You could provide any necessary help with these sentences at this stage. Alternatively, you could leave this until after students have focused on future forms in the Grammar box, and ask them to look at their sentences again and correct them.

- Put students into small groups to discuss the questions and to give evidence or examples to support their opinions.

- Monitor students while they're speaking. Encourage quieter students to contribute, e.g. by asking them whether they agree with something another student said.

- Conduct whole-class feedback. Ask students to give their opinions and some of the evidence or examples from their discussions.

2

- Ask students to look at the title of the infographic. Encourage them to say what they think the article is about, but don't confirm the answer at this stage.

- Ask students to read the infographic quickly and to check their ideas.

- Students could check their answers in pairs before you check with the whole class. Elicit that only in West Africa are women more optimistic than men.

Answers

There is a gender gap when it comes to how optimistic people are about their children's futures – men are more optimistic than women.

3

- Look at the statements with the class. Explain that students should think about the next generation rather than about children if they don't have children. Ask students to decide whether they would agree or disagree with the statements. Ask: *Would you make the same statement, or would you change it in some way?*

- Put students into small groups to say whether they would agree or disagree with the statements, or to make their own statements.

- If appropriate, conduct quick whole-class feedback to see if any gender differences are apparent in your class.

4

- Look at the instructions with the class. If necessary, clarify the meaning of:

  significant – big enough to show that a difference exists (line 2)

- Ask students to look at the graph and to decide whether the differences between men and women are significant. They could discuss this in pairs.

- Conduct whole-class feedback.

Answers

Except in West Africa, the differences are significant. Men feel much more optimistic than women about their children's future. In West Africa, women are one per cent more optimistic than men.

5

- Ask students to read the sentences in the Grammar box and to choose the correct option to complete the rules. They can do this in pairs.

- Students can check their answers and overall understanding of future forms and their uses by turning to the Grammar summary on page 142.

Answers

1 plans   2 can   3 future perfect   4 future continuous

- If you feel that students need more controlled practice before continuing, they could do some or all of the exercises in the Grammar summary. Otherwise, you could continue on to Exercise 6 in the unit and set the Grammar summary exercises for homework.

Answers to Grammar summary exercises

1

1 'll be opening   2 Will (people) be waiting
3 'll be standing   4 will (they) be getting
5 won't be doing   6 will be talking

2

1 'll have sold   2 will have heard   3 Will (the new business) have made   4 won't have done   5 will (we) have interviewed   6 won't have finished

3

1 will happen   2 will have invented   3 Will the exam have   4 they'll be discussing   5 will be coming
6 she'll be staying   7 will you be doing
8 I'll have found

4

1 d   2 f   3 a   4 e   5 g   6 h   7 c   8 b

5

1 are going to change   2 will fall   3 will have replaced
4 will affect   5 will be working   6 will combine
7 won't think   8 is going to cause

6

1 I don't think the plan is a good idea. ~~I explain~~ **I'll explain**.

2 When ~~I'll~~ **I finish** the course, I'm going to celebrate.

3 Will they have ~~finish~~ **finished** by lunchtime?

4 I expect that tomorrow's exam ~~is~~ **will be** difficult.

5 This time on Monday she'll be ~~start~~ **starting** her new job.

6 I'll ~~apply~~ **be applying** for this job because it looks really interesting.

6

- Ask students to complete the sentences with a future form with *will*. Elicit or explain that they can use *will* + infinitive, *will be* + *-ing* and *will have* + past participle. Students could check their answers in pairs before you check with the whole class.

Answers

1 'll/will be   2 will have spent   3 will be using   4 will change   5 will be supporting   6 will have appeared

- **Optional step.** Encourage students to use the future forms to make sentences about themselves. For example: *I'll have learned more English by the end of the month, I'll help you with your homework this evening, Claudio.*

LISTENING Little people, big plans

7

- Look at the instructions and the options (a–c) with the class. If necessary, clarify the meaning of:

  contestant – someone who takes part in a TV show, normally to win prizes (line 2)

  make your name – become well-known and respected (option 1)

- Bring in students' own experiences. Ask: *Do you ever watch TV shows where contestants are in competition to win a prize or a title? Can you give some examples? Do you like watching these programmes? Why? / Why not?*

- ⏹ **9** Play the recording so that students can match the contestants' names with their ambitions.

Transcript:

1

P = Presenter, G = Giselle

P: *Giselle, you're our youngest contestant. How old are you?*

G: *I'm nine.*

P: *That's very young to be a chef.*

G: *I know, but my family own a restaurant and I've been there since I was like two years old … and I'm crazy about cooking. I'm going to run my own restaurant, with my mom.*

P: *OK! Now Giselle, are you going to make it to the final of Junior Chef?*

G: *Totally!*

P: *Good job! And what will you have learned by then, do you think?*

G: *Some new skills, I guess. Some tricks of the trade … and hopefully I'll learn enough to be a judge on Junior Chef one day.*

2

P = Presenter, J = Jared

P: *So Jared, are you looking forward to today's challenge? What will you be making for us today?*

J: *It's a kind of ravioli with seafood, it's my own recipe.*

P: *Sound delicious. So Jared, you are twelve years old, right? Where do you think you'll be in ten years' time? Do you see yourself in college, maybe?*

J: *College, I don't know … I want to be famous, a really famous chef. I think I'll have made my name by 22.*

P: *With your seafood ravioli as your signature dish?*

J: *Absolutely!*

3

P = Presenter, M = Maisie

P: *Maisie, that looks awesome! Now, what's your food dream?*

M: *I want to have a chain of restaurants.*

P: *A chain?*

M: *Yeah, I hope I'll have opened at least four or five places before I'm 21.*

P: *Right! So how are you feeling about today's challenge?*

M: *I'm cool. It's basically pasta and I do a lot of pasta dishes at home.*

P: *So you're pretty confident?*

M: *I am. Somebody will be going home at the end of today's show, but it's not going to be me.*

Answers

1 c   2 a   3 b

8

- Explain that students are going to listen to the recording again. Again, they're listening for detail.

- Give students time to read the sentences. You could ask them to predict the missing words based on what they can remember from the first time they listened to the recording.

- ⏹ **9** Play the recording so that students can complete the sentences. They could check their answers in pairs before you check with the whole class. You could play the recording again either before or after checking answers. Draw students' attention to the inversion of subject and *will* in direct questions 2 and 4.

Answers

1 are you going to make   2 will you have learned
3 'll learn   4 will you be making   5 you'll be
6 will be going … not going to be

Pronunciation Elision

9a

- Tell students that Exercise 9 focuses on pronunciation and specifically on how some words are pronounced in the recording they have just listened to. Elicit that the speakers in the recording are American.

- 🔊 10 Play the recording and pause after each sentence. Elicit how the speaker says the words in bold and that either a *t* or an *f* sound isn't pronounced in one of the words in bold in each sentence. You could play the recording again so that students can confirm this.

Transcript

1 Are you **going to** make it to the final?

2 It's a **kind of** ravioli with seafood.

3 I **want to** be famous.

4 I do a **lot of** pasta dishes at home.

Answers

1 gonna ('t' is not pronounced in 'to')   2 kinda ('f' is not pronounced in 'of')   3 wanna ('t' is not pronounced in 'want' or 'to')   4 lotta ('f' is not pronounced in 'of')

- If students aren't able to successfully reproduce the elided /t/ and /f/ in the words after listening to the recording, model and drill the pronunciation.

Background information

Elision

Elision (also called deletion) is the omission of one or more sounds from a word by a speaker. The omitted sounds could be consonants, vowels or whole syllables. In English, elision comes naturally to native speakers – perhaps more so to American speakers. You don't have to use elision in English, however – it's equally acceptable to say *going to* or *gonna*. However, in some cases, e.g. in words such as *comfortable* /ˈkʌmfətəbl/, *vegetable* /ˈvedʒɪtəbl/, *temperature* /ˈtemprɪtʃə/, it's essential.

9b

- Explain that *elision* is the term for what happens when one or more sounds in a word or words aren't pronounced. Point out that *elision* is used in linguistics and is not a word students particularly need to know or remember.

- 🔊 10 Play the recording and pause after each sentence so that students can listen and repeat. Remind them to focus on the pronunciation of: *gonna*, *kinda*, *wanna*, *lotta*.

10

- Ask students to look at the direct questions in Exercise 8 (items 1, 2 and 4) and to notice the word order.

- Look at item 1 as an example with the class. Elicit the question *In five years' time, where will you be living?* Elicit or explain that there are currently no future forms among the words, so students will need to choose and add the correct one.

- Students could compare their questions in pairs before you check with the whole class.

Answers

1 In five year's time, where will you be living?

2 At the end of this course, what will you have achieved?

3 By this time next year, will you be working?

4 What will you be doing this weekend?

5 Are you going to use English in the future?

6 Will you have learned a new skill by next year?

11

- Put students into pairs to ask and answer their questions. Tell them to give answers that are true for them.

- Monitor students while they're speaking, offering help where necessary.

SPEAKING Future goals

12 `21st` **CENTURY OUTCOMES**

- Before starting this exercise, refer students to the 21st CENTURY OUTCOMES at the foot of the page which is *INITIATIVE AND SELF-DIRECTION Set personal goals with measurable criteria for success.* If necessary clarify the meaning of:

   initiative – the ability to make decisions and to do things without needing to be told what to do

- Elicit that setting personal goals is one way in which we can demonstrate initiative and self-direction.

- Put students into pairs to discuss the questions. Explain that there are no right or wrong answers to these questions. Students can give their own opinions and agree or disagree with their partners. Remind them to give examples and evidence to support their opinions.

- Conduct whole-class feedback. Elicit examples of personal goals with measurable criteria for success, e.g. earning a certain amount of money.

- **Optional step.** If appropriate, ask students to tell the rest of the class whether they think they're more of a spontaneous person or someone who likes to plan ahead. Gauge which group are in the majority in your class. This may also give you some insights into your students' approach to English learning.

▶ Photocopiable communicative activity 2.1: Go to page 215 for practice of future forms, and vocabulary for plans and goals. The teaching notes are on page 238.

▶ Set Workbook pages 16–17 for homework.

2.3 A job for life?

READING Jobs for the future

1

• Books open. Draw students' attention to the spread title: *A job for life?* Put students into pairs or small groups to discuss the meaning of this expression and the significance of the question mark.

• Elicit or explain that a *job for life* is a job you can stay in all your working life and that the question mark suggests that the idea of 'a job for life' may be something that no longer exists. Ask students whether they would agree with that. They will probably agree that 'a job for life' used to be more common in former times.

• Put students into pairs to discuss the questions. Monitor students while they're speaking, noting any examples of jobs they mention.

• Conduct whole-class feedback. Elicit and write up on the board: a) jobs we do now that we'll still be doing in ten or twenty years' time, b) jobs people will no longer be doing in ten or twenty years' time, c) new jobs that people will be doing.

2

• Draw students' attention to the section heading and title of the article: *Jobs for the future*. Ask students to choose the three jobs people will be doing in ten or twenty years' time that they think they're most likely to read about in the article.

• Students read the article, focusing on the types of jobs that the article says will grow in the next ten years in the USA. If necessary, clarify the meaning of:

  retail sales – the selling of products to customers either face-to-face or online (second heading)

  personal care aide – someone who takes care of someone who needs help with everyday tasks, e.g. washing and eating (third heading)

  post-secondary teacher – someone who teaches students who have completed their secondary school education (eighth heading)

• **Optional step.** Students compare the types of jobs that will grow in the USA with the types of jobs they think will grow in their own country in whole-class or pair discussion. Ask: *Are there any differences or similarities? If so, what could possible reasons for these be?*

3

• Look at the questions with the class. If necessary, clarify the meaning of:

degree – a qualification you get when you complete a course of study at a university, e.g. a Bachelor's or Master's degree (question 3)

• Ask students to read the article again to answer the questions. They could check their answers in pairs before you check with the whole class.

Answers

1 the US Bureau of Labor Statistics

2 personal care aides

3 nursing

4 retail sales, personal care aides, home health aides, (probably, but not stated) food preparation and serving

5 post-secondary teachers

6 retail sales: shopping will never go out of fashion
personal care aides: the population is ageing, so more elderly people need carers
customer service: businesses are increasing their customer service representatives following negative reactions to increased automation in things like phone systems
post-secondary teachers: more students than ever will be continuing their education after high school

---

4

• Elicit reasons why finding synonyms for words can be useful. For example: *finding synonyms can expand and broaden your range of vocabulary, it's useful to know more interesting alternatives to commonly-used words, and knowing synonyms can help you to check you've understood words correctly.*

• Ask students to find the words in the article and to check that they understand them. Then ask them to look at the article again and to find other words with similar meanings.

• Remind students that the words they're looking for will have similar meanings, but the meanings won't be exactly the same.

Answers

1 position   2 think of   3 work   4 job sectors,
5 predict, project, estimate   6 ask for   7 rise
8 chance, opening

5

• Put students into pairs to discuss the questions.

• Monitor students while they're speaking and, if necessary, remind them to give reasons or evidence to support their views.

• Conduct whole-class feedback. If you have a monolingual class, make sure students reach a consensus. If you have a multinational class, invite individual students to tell the rest of the class about the situation in their country.

• **Optional step.** If you have a monolingual class, put students into groups of three. Ask each group to choose three future growth sectors in the economy of their country. Tell each student in the group to write a paragraph about one of these sectors, using the article they read as a model. Students then put their paragraphs together to make a complete article with an introduction that they write together. Monitor students while they're writing, offering help where necessary. If appropriate, put the pieces of writing up on the classroom walls and ask students to walk around, read other students' texts, and give written or oral feedback.

VOCABULARY Career collocations

6

• Draw students' attention to the section heading: *Career collocations.* If necessary, clarify the meaning of:

   collocation – a combination of words, e.g. verb + noun combination or adjective + noun combination, that take on new or added meaning when they're used together

• Explain that students are going to combine A and B words to make collocations connected with careers. Look at the first word *academic* as an example with the class. Elicit that *academic* can be used with *qualifications* and *skills.*

• Students match the words. They could check their answers in pairs before you check with the whole class.

Answers	
academic qualifications	job security
academic skills	professional experience
driving licence	professional qualifications
earn a salary	starting position
employment opportunities	workplace experience
high school diploma	

• Draw students' attention to the fact that *high school diploma* is only used in North American English. Other terms are used for secondary school qualifications in British English.

Background information
School qualifications

Different terminology is used to describe qualifications in different English-speaking countries. In the USA and Canada, for example, students receive a high school diploma when they graduate from high school. In England, Wales and Northern Ireland, however, students sit exams in secondary school and receive qualifications based on their performance. These are the General Certificate of Secondary Education (or GCSE), taken at the age of 16, and the Advanced Level of Secondary Education (or A Level), taken at the age of 18. GCSEs and A Levels are also taken by pupils at international schools all around the world. In Scotland, another set of terminology again is used. Students take National 5s at 16, Highers at 17 and Advanced Highers at 18.

• If students want to translate the secondary school qualifications they have into English, e.g. for a curriculum vitae or job interview, encourage them to use the original name of the qualification in their language, followed by a note that this is the equivalent of a standard or advanced level qualification of secondary education.

7

• Look at sentence 1 as an example with the class. Elicit that the missing expression is *earn a salary.*

• Ask students to complete the sentences with some of the other expressions from Exercise 6. Students could check their answers in pairs before you check with the whole class.

Answers
1 earn a salary   2 driving licence   3 starting position
4 workplace experience   5 job security
6 professional experience   7 academic qualifications
8 employment opportunities

Extra activity

Who wrote what?

Ask students to write sentences about their own lives, opinions and future goals that include the expressions from Exercise 6. They could write each sentence on a different card or strip of paper. Students then work in small groups and mix up all their cards. Each member of the group takes one sentence at a time, reads it out and then either says who they think wrote it and why, or asks questions to find out who wrote it.

SPEAKING Learning skills for the future

8 *21st* CENTURY OUTCOMES

• Before starting this exercise, refer students to the 21st CENTURY OUTCOMES at the foot of the page which is *INITIATIVE AND SELF-DIRECTION Show commitment to learning as a life-long process.* Elicit the meaning of *commitment* – students met this in Key words on page 19.

- Elicit that studying English is one way in which students can show commitment to life-long learning.

- Put students into small groups to discuss the questions. Encourage students to work with students they don't usually work with so that they are able to talk to a range of different people.

- Monitor students while they're speaking. If appropriate, encourage students to elaborate on the points they make and to give examples or supporting evidence.

- Allow 5–10 minutes for discussion. Then conduct whole-class feedback. Get an overview of students' reasons for learning English, the languages they think will be important in the future and the skills they think will become more useful in the future. Ask: *What skills are more important in the 21st century than they were in the past? And why?*

TEACHING TIP

Reasons for learning English

Bear in mind that the question of why students are learning English might be a sensitive one for them. Some may be taking part in the course because they have to, rather than because they have any intrinsic motivation to learn English. Others may be taking part in the course to remedy a lack of English knowledge that they feel uncomfortable about. There's no reason why this should be a taboo issue, but it might need to be handled with tact and sensitivity.

▶ Photocopiable communicative activity 2.2: Go to page 216 for practice of career collocations, and revision of future forms. The teaching notes are on page 238.

▶ Set Workbook pages 18–19 for homework.

2.4 A five-year plan

LISTENING Applying for a job

1

- Books open. Draw students' attention to the photo at the top of the page. Elicit that this person is looking at job advertisements. Ask: *Have you ever looked at advertisements like this when you were looking for a job?*

- If appropriate, ask students to think about the last time they applied for a job. Students who have never applied for a job can think about which things on the list they think they would do when applying for a job and which things are important.

- Look at the list of things to do with the class. Elicit or explain that *CV* is an abbreviation for *curriculum vitae* – a Latin expression meaning 'a short written description of your education, qualifications, previous jobs, and sometimes also your personal interests, that you send to an employer when you are trying to get a job'.

- Put students into groups to discuss the questions.

- Conduct whole-class feedback on things it's important to do when applying for a job, and why. You could create a job-application checklist as a class on the board.

2

- Explain that students are going to listen to a conversation between two friends, Jill and Andy.

- Give students time to read the questions. Elicit possible reasons why two friends would decide to meet and why they would bring something to the meeting. Ask: *What could that something be?*

- 🎧 **11** Play the recording so that students can answer the questions. They could check their answers in pairs before you check with the whole class.

Transcript

J = Jill, A = Andy

J: *Hi, Andy, it's Jill. Do you have a moment? I was just wondering if you could check my application for that job I told you about? The closing date for applications is next week. So it's a bit urgent.*

A: *Yeah, of course. Do you want to email it to me and I'll have a look through it?*

J: *That would be great. I'm sending it through to you now.*

A: *And then do you want to meet up and talk about it? And we could prepare you for the interview too.*

J: *OK, then. I'd really appreciate that! When are you free? I'm not doing anything all week, so any time is good for me.*

A: *Let me look at my schedule … I'm working late on Tuesday and Wednesday, but I should be able to get away early on Thursday.*

J: *Let's say Thursday at six, then. I'll come round to your place, if that's OK with you.*

A: *Yeah, that's fine with me. When are the interviews, by the way?*

J: *Just a moment, let me check … they're on two days – the 12th and 15th of next month.*

A: *Right, so you'll need to do a bit of research and bring some information about the company with you on Thursday.*

J: *Yeah, I can do that. And will you send the checked form back to me?*

A: *Yes, either that or I'll print it out and bring it with me.*

J: *Right, see you on Thursday, then. Thanks again.*

Answers

1 Jill wants Andy to check her application for a job she told him about.

2 They are going to meet on Thursday at 6 pm at Andy's place.

3 Jill will bring some information about the company. Andy will bring the application form (that he has checked).

3

• Explain that students are going to listen to the recording again. This time they're going to focus on specific expressions that the speakers used.

• Give students time to read the expressions. You could ask them to predict the missing words based on what they can remember from the first time they listened to the recording.

• 🎧 11 Play the recording again so that students can complete the expressions.

> **Answers**
> 1 moment 2 great 3 appreciate 4 fine
> 5 interviews 6 again

Pronunciation Elided /d/

4a

• If necessary, elicit or remind students that elision is the omission of one or more sounds from a word or words.

• Tell students that they're going to focus on the elided /d/ sound. Elicit that an elided /d/ is a /d/ which isn't pronounced.

• Ask students to listen and notice how the /d/ sounds in bold aren't pronounced.

• 🎧 12 Play the recording. Check with students that they noticed the elided /d/ sound in *could*, *good* and *round*. Play the recording again if they didn't.

• Remind students that the /d/ is elided here because the first letter of the next word is a consonant. Elicit or explain that the /d/ wouldn't be elided if the first letter of the next word was a vowel.

Transcript
1   I was just wondering if you could check my application …
2   And we could prepare you for the interview too.
3   Any time is good for me.
4   I'll come round to your place, if that's OK with you.

• **Optional step.** Ask students to think of three short phrases or sentences where *could* is followed by a word that starts with a vowel, e.g. *We could explain how to complete the application form*, *I was just wondering if you could access your account*. Then tell them to work in pairs and to practise saying the sentences. They can listen to and feel the difference in the sound made when the /d/ in *could* is pronounced.

4b

• Explain that students are going to listen to four other sentences with an elided /d/ and then repeat them.

• 🎧 13 Play the recording and pause after each sentence so that students can listen and repeat. Draw students' attention to the fact that the letter 'd' in *would* in sentence 1 is much more elided than the letter 'd' in *should* in sentence 2. Explain that this is a matter of speaker preference.

Transcript
1   That would be great.
2   I should be able to get away early on Thursday.
3   You'll need to do a bit of research.
4   Will you send the checked form back to me?

SPEAKING Arranging to help someone

5 **21st CENTURY OUTCOMES**

• Before starting this exercise, refer students to the 21st CENTURY OUTCOMES at the foot of the page which is *COLLABORATION WITH OTHERS Be flexible and willing to be helpful to reach a common goal.* Elicit that the conversation in Exercise 2 showed an example of this.

• Put students into pairs and ask them to choose a situation. Remind students to read the expressions in the Useful language box before they start their conversation. Encourage them to try to use all the expressions.

• Monitor students while they're speaking, noting any examples of useful sentences for arranging to help someone.

• Allow five minutes for the conversations. Invite individual students to tell the rest of the class the useful sentences that you have noted.

▶ Teaching tip: Using target expressions in discussions, Unit 2.1, page 26

WRITING A career goals statement

6

• Explain that students are going to read extracts from four job applications and that the four extracts are career goals statements. Point out that their focus should be on getting an overview of the content of the career goals statements and how clearly the goals are presented.

• Students read the extracts and answer the questions. They could compare their answers in pairs before you check with the whole class.

> **Answers**
> 1 A short text where candidates say what they intend to be doing or will have achieved in their careers in the next five years
> 2 Applicants A, B and D clearly state their career goal.
> 3 Applicant A: enhance his/her leadership skills in more responsible roles
> Applicant B: obtain a managerial position in tele-sales with a leading provider
> Applicant D: secure a position where his/her leadership will improve sales results

Writing skill Formal language

7a

- Look at item 1 as an example with the class. Ask students to match one of the words in bold in the career goal statements with its synonym *get*. Elicit that *get* is a synonym for *obtain*.

- Students could check their answers in pairs before you check with the whole class. Then ask: *Which of the two sets of words has a more positive impact on the reader?*

- Do whole-class feedback. Remind students that context is important. More formal language makes a more positive impact in more formal situations and more informal language makes a more positive impact in more informal situations.

> **Answers**
>
> 1 obtain 2 strong 3 secured a position 4 gained
> 5 achieving 6 intend
>
> The formal words in the career goal statements have a more positive impact on the reader because we use formal words in formal contexts.

7b

- Explain that students are going to replace informal words and expressions in the sentences with more formal synonyms.

- Look at sentence 1 an example with the class. Elicit that the more formal synonym for *I'd like* in this context is *I intend*.

- Check that students are aware of the fact that the underlined expressions aren't wrong – they're just not formal enough for a career goals statement.

- Ask students to replace the underlined words. They could then check their answers in pairs before you check with the whole class.

> **Answers**
>
> 1 intend 2 completed 3 seeking 4 am confident
> ... significant 5 gained 6 effectively 7 possess
> 8 become ... leading

8

- Ask students to think of an imaginary person who's applying for a job that's similar to their own.

- Tell students to write a career goals statements with two goals for that person.

- Monitor students while they're writing their statements, offering help where necessary.

9

- Put students into small groups to compare their statements. Explain that, after reading the statements, they are going to give feedback on the use of formal language.

- Elicit or explain that *praise* is telling someone what a good job they've done, but *feedback* is suggesting ways that someone can do better next time. Encourage students to start their feedback on a positive note, but then go on to areas for improvement.

- Monitor students while they're giving each other feedback. Then conduct whole-class feedback to gauge whether any common problems with the use of formal language have arisen.

- **Optional step.** The 21st CENTURY OUTCOME is also linked to this writing activity. Ask students to reflect on whether their experience of working to create a career goals statement for someone else has helped them to see the importance of being flexible and willing to be helpful to reach a common goal.

- Monitor students while they're making suggestions about how each other's writing could be improved.

▶ Set Workbook pages 20–21 for homework.
▶ Set Workbook Writing 1 on pages 22–23 for homework.

REVIEW 1 | UNITS 1 AND 2

READING About Balance

1

• Explain that students that are going to read an article about a community-interest company (CIC). Ask: *Do you know what a community-interest company is? If you don't, what do you think it could be?* Conduct whole-class feedback on students' answers/ideas, but don't confirm them at this stage.

• Ask students to read the article about Balance and to focus on how it helps people. Tell them to choose the correct option. They could check their answer in pairs before you check with the whole class.

Answer
c

2

• Look at the sentences with the class. If necessary, clarify the meaning of:

  shareholder – shares are parts of or stakes in a public limited company and a shareholder is someone who owns shares (sentence 1)

• Ask students to read the article again. This time they're focusing on the detail and deciding whether the statements are true or false. They can check their answers in pairs before you check with the whole class. You could also ask students to correct the false sentences.

Answers
1 F (Profits are reinvested in the company instead of being paid to shareholders.)
2 F (Balance helps people with autism or Asperger Syndrome, or people who are dealing with stress and anxiety.)
3 T
4 F (Balance can get involved in talking to employers to find solutions to problems.)
5 T
6 F (Lucy is employed in retail sales.)

GRAMMAR

3

• Look at item 1 as an example with the class. Elicit that *provides* goes in the first gap. You could also elicit or explain that we need to use the present simple tense because we're talking about the company's permanent activities; that we add -*s* to the verb because it follows the name of a singular thing or entity; and that we use the active form because the agent (*the company Balance*) is more important than the action (providing something) in this case.

• Ask students to complete the rest of the text with the correct forms of the verbs in brackets. Monitor students while they're doing this, offering help where necessary.

Answers
1 provides   2 need   3 is given   4 are now employed
5 is growing   6 suggest   7 suffers   8 doesn't have

4

• Explain that students are going to focus on future forms.

• Look at item 1 as an example with the class. Elicit that the correct option is *I'm going to stay*. You could also elicit or explain that we use *going to* here because this is a plan that someone has now that *things are different*.

• Ask students to read the rest of the comments and to choose the correct options. Monitor students while they're doing this, offering help where necessary.

Answers
1 I'm going to stay   2 I'll deal   3 I'll do   4 I'll have found   5 we'll be hiring   6 we won't be returning

VOCABULARY

5

• You could put students into pairs to help each other to complete the comments using the correct verb + preposition combinations. Encourage students to use the words that come before and after the gaps and the information in the rest of the sentence to help them to identify the missing combinations.

Answers
1 committed to   2 concentrate on   3 deal with
4 involved in   5 help   6 responsible for

• **Optional step.** If appropriate, students could use these verb + preposition combinations to write true sentences about their own and/or their company's activities.

6

• If necessary, clarify the meaning of *collocations* (see Unit 2.3). Explain that the collocations in this paragraph are all career collocations that students met in Unit 2.3.

• **Optional step.** Books closed. Elicit examples of career collocations and write these on the board as students mention them.

• Ask students to choose the correct options to complete the collocations. Students could check their answers in pairs before you check with the whole class.

Answers
1 qualifications   2 skills   3 opportunities   4 position
5 salary   6 security   7 experience

DISCUSSION

7

• Put students into pairs to discuss the questions. Encourage students to give examples or evidence to support their answers.

• Monitor students while they're speaking, offering help where necessary and collecting interesting examples of language use.

• Conduct whole-class feedback and share the examples of interesting language that you collected. Where appropriate, and especially if there are students from different countries in your class, compare and contrast different students' points of view and experiences.

Suggested answers

1 The main barrier is prejudice, of both employers and the public.

2 Students' own answers, though they may say that lack of job opportunities is the main difficulty. If there are jobs available, then young people won't have any experience or maybe they don't have the necessary qualifications.

3 Students' own answers, though they may suggest work-experience opportunities for people when they're still at school or college courses.

SPEAKING

8

• Ask students to read the whole conversation first to get a feel for what Dina and Martin are saying to each other.

• Ask students to use the word prompts to write complete sentences and questions. They can do this in pairs. They could check their sentences and questions in the Useful language boxes in Unit 1.4 and Unit 2.4.

• You could check answers by asking a stronger pair to read out the conversation to the rest of the class.

Answers

1 How are you finding the course?

2 I was wondering if you could check my presentation?

3 Any time is good for me.

4 Let's say tonight at six.

5 I'll meet you at the main entrance, if that's OK with you.

WRITING

9

• Look at Julianne Brown's profile with the class and elicit that it isn't usual to write information about yourself in the form of complete sentences in a profile like this. Instead, we need to use note forms, which means omitting the personal pronouns and starting with an *-ing* form or a past simple verb form.

• Ask students to use the words in the box and note forms to improve the profile. They can do this in pairs.

• Conduct whole-class feedback and accept variations on the suggested answers below if students have successfully used the verbs in the box, used note forms and succeeded in improving the profile.

Suggested answers

Name: Julianne Brown

Contact: email: julianne@jpbrown.co.uk, Skype: juliannepat

Languages: French, Spanish

Expertise: Completed / Gained Masters in Organizational Psychology, Manchester University; five years in Human Resources

Career goal: Seeking / I intend to gain a job in a social enterprise. I believe I can make an effective contribution to this area.

10

• Put students into pairs to compare the improved versions of the profile they wrote.

• Where appropriate, students can explain why they think their version is better than the original and give reasons for the choices they made. For example: *I decided to use* gained *instead of* completed *because I think that it sounds more positive and more effectively communicates that the person has achieved something.*

3 Growth and development

LEAD IN

• Books open. Draw students' attention to the unit title, and to the photo on pages 30–31 and its caption. Bring in students' own experiences. If appropriate, ask: *What global trends have you seen during the course of your lifetime? What has changed in the world?* Possible answers could be: *An increase in population, Some countries becoming richer while others become poorer, A rise in the use of mobile phones, More and more people using the Internet.* Then ask: *What global trends do you think we will see in the next fifty years?* Possible answers could be: *An increase in population, People living longer than they've ever done before, China becoming the dominant global economic power.* Students could discuss the questions in pairs or small groups.

TEDTALKS
BACKGROUND

1

• Ask students to read the text about Hans Rosling and his talk.

Suggested answers

1 His data will include big numbers: statistics of people with certain illnesses; figures connected with their income and their country's GDP (gross domestic product).

2 In 1965 (50 years before this book was written), the world population was 3.3 billion; in 2010 it was 6.9 billion; in 2015 (when this book was written) it was 7.7 billion; in 2050 it is predicted to be 9.5 billion.

3 stress on the environment; not enough housing, schools, clinics, infrastructure; low ratio of workers to dependents; maternal mortality; unemployment

• **Optional step.** If appropriate and possible, ask students to go online and to find out the actual population figures. Invite individual students to tell the rest of the class. Correct students if they don't say these big numbers correctly.

• Tell the class that this TED Talk was given in 2010 and ask: *What, if any, changes in global population and poverty levels do you think there have been between then and now?* Possible answers could be: *Global population has increased/decreased, Poverty levels have risen/fallen.*

• **Optional step.** Review language for describing trends (see below). Then draw or give students a copy of a graph and ask them to write a description and explanation of the trend it shows or discuss this in pairs.

TEACHING TIP

Language for describing trends

As students will frequently need to use language for describing trends in this unit, you may want to review this language at this stage. Students should already have some awareness of the language for describing trends. Elicit that *increase, rise, grow, improve, climb, jump,* etc. are used to describe upward movement and *decrease, fall, drop, sink, decline, plummet,* etc. are used to describe downward movement. Then elicit the adjectives and adverbs that can be used to describe the speed of movement, e.g. *rapid(-ly), slow(-ly), steady/steadily,* and those which can be used to describe the amount of movement, e.g. *considerable/considerably, significant/significantly, dramatic/dramatically, sharp/sharply.* Elicit that the adjectives are used before nouns and the adverbs after verbs. Another useful verb is *peak,* e.g. *reach a peak, population levels peaked at … .*

KEY WORDS

2

• Ask students to try to guess the meaning of the words in bold and then to match them with their definitions.

• Check that students can say the words in bold correctly. The words *aspiration*, *emerging* and *survival* may prove difficult for students to pronounce, depending on their first language background. If necessary, model and drill the pronunciation.

Background information

The developing world

Hans Rosling uses the term 'the developing world' (sentence 1). However, this term is now considered outdated. Some countries in what was formerly 'the developing world' are now increasingly economically dominant, particularly China, India, Russia and Brazil. An acceptable alternative could be 'less developed country/countries' as this refers to individual countries rather than applying a blanket expression to a diverse group of countries.

Answers

1 c   2 f   3 e   4 d   5 b   6 a

AUTHENTIC LISTENING SKILLS Focused listening

3a

• Ask students to read the information about focused listening in the Authentic listening skills box. Ask: *Have you ever used advance information about what a speaker is going to talk about to focus on the content of the talk? If so, how exactly did you do this? And how helpful did you find it?*

• Ask students to think about what aspect of world population Hans Rosling is going to talk about and write down some possible ideas. They could do this in pairs.

• Point out that Hans Rosling is unlikely to cover all the ideas he wants to talk about in the first minute of his talk. However, based on Exercises 1 and 2, students will probably expect him to talk about population growth.

• ▣ 14 Play the recording so that students can focus on whether Hans Rosling talked about the aspect of world population they had expected him to talk about.

3b

• Explain that students are now going to focus on listening for specific information.

• Give students time to read the extracts. You could ask them to predict the missing words based on what they can remember from the first time they listened to the extracts.

• ▣ 14 Play the recording again so that students can complete the extracts. Draw students' attention to the fact that they will hear two other sentences before the sentence to be completed in extract 3.

• Ask students to reflect on whether reading the sentences in advance and predicting the missing words did make it easier for them to focus on the content while listening.

Transcript and answers

1   *I still remember the day in school when our teacher told us that the world population had become <u>three</u> billion people, and that was in 1960.*

2   *And I'm going to talk now about how world population has <u>changed</u> from that year and into the future.*

3   *And that's what I'm going to show you, because since 1960 what has happened in the world up to 2010 is that a staggering four billion people have been added to the world population. Just look how many. The world population has <u>doubled</u> since I went to school.*

3.1 Global population growth, box by box

TEDTALKS

1

• Books open. Give students time to read the sentences. Explain that the term 'old West' in sentence 6 refers to countries in the western hemisphere – Europe and the USA – which were traditionally seen as being the only or main source of economic power in the world.

• ▶ 3.1 Play the whole talk once so that students can decide whether the sentences are true or false. This is a long talk, so you could pause the recording at 2.13 and check answers for the first three items.

Transcript

0.14   *I still remember the day in school when our teacher told us that the world population had become three billion people, and that was in 1960. And I'm going to talk now about how world population has changed from that year and into the future, but I will not use digital technology, as I've done during my first five TED Talks. Instead, I have progressed, and I am, today, launching a brand new analogue teaching technology that I picked up from IKEA: this box.*

0.50   *This box contains one billion people. And our teacher told us that the industrialized world, 1960, had one billion people. In the developing world, she said, they had two billion people. And they lived away then. There was a big gap between the one billion in the industrialized world and the two billion in the developing world. In the industrialized world, people were healthy, educated, rich, and they had small families. And their aspiration was to buy a car. And in 1960, all Swedes were saving to try to* buy a Volvo like this. This was the economic level at which Sweden was. But in contrast to this, in the developing world, far away, the aspiration of the average family there was to have food for the day. They were saving to be able to buy a pair of shoes. There was an enormous gap in the world when I grew up. And this gap between the West and the rest has created a mindset of the world, which we still use linguistically when we talk about 'the West' and 'the Developing World'. But the world has changed, and it's overdue to upgrade that mindset and that taxonomy of the world, and to understand it.

2.13 And that's what I'm going to show you, because since 1960 what has happened in the world up to 2010 is that a staggering four billion people have been added to the world population. Just look how many. The world population has doubled since I went to school. And of course, there's been economic growth in the West. A lot of companies have happened to grow the economy, so the Western population moved over to here. And now their aspiration is not only to have a car. Now they want to have a holiday on a very remote destination and they want to fly. So this is where they are today. And the most successful of the developing countries, they have moved on, you know, and they have become emerging economies, we call them. They are now buying cars. And what happened a month ago was that the Chinese company, Geely, they acquired the Volvo company, and then finally the Swedes understood that something big had happened in the world. (Laughter)

3.18 So there they are. And the tragedy is that the two billion over here that is struggling for food and shoes, they are still almost as poor as they were 50 years ago. The new thing is that we have the biggest pile of billions, the three billions here, which are also becoming emerging economies, because they are quite healthy, relatively well-educated, and they already also have two to three children per woman, as those have. And their aspiration now is, of course, to buy a bicycle, and then later on they would like to have a motorbike also. But this is the world we have today, no longer any gap. But the distance from the poorest here, the very poorest, to the very richest over here is wider than ever. But there is a continuous world from walking, biking, driving, flying – there are people on all levels, and most people tend to be somewhere in the middle. This is the new world we have today in 2010.

4.25 Here I have on the screen my country bubbles. Every bubble is a country. The size is population. The colours show the continent. The yellow on there is the Americas; dark blue is Africa; brown is Europe; green is the Middle East and this light blue is South Asia. That's India and this is China. Size is population. Here I have children per woman: two children, four children, six children, eight children – big families, small families. The year is 1960. And down here, child survival, the percentage of children surviving childhood up to starting school: 60 per cent, 70 per cent, 80 per cent,

90, and almost 100 per cent, as we have today in the wealthiest and healthiest countries. But look, this is the world my teacher talked about in 1960: one billion Western world here – high child-survival, small families – and all the rest, the rainbow of developing countries, with very large families and poor child survival.

5.25 What has happened? I start the world. Here we go. Can you see, as the years pass by, child survival is increasing? They get soap, hygiene, education, vaccination, penicillin and then family planning. Family size is decreasing. They get up to 90-per-cent child survival, then families decrease, and most of the Arab countries in the Middle East is falling down there. Look, Bangladesh catching up with India. The whole emerging world joins the Western world with good child survival and small family size, but we still have the poorest billion. Can you see the poorest billion, those boxes I had over here? They are still up here. And they still have a child survival of 70 to 80 per cent, meaning that if you have six children born, there will be at least four who survive to the next generation. And the population will double in one generation.

6.18 So the only way of really getting world population to stop is to continue to improve child survival to 90 per cent. That's why investments by Gates Foundation, UNICEF and aid organizations, together with national government in the poorest countries, are so good: because they are actually helping us to reach a sustainable population size of the world. We can stop at nine billion if we do the right things. Child survival is the new green. It's only by child survival that we will stop population growth. And will it happen? Well, I'm not an optimist, neither am I a pessimist. I'm a very serious 'possibilist'. It's a new category where we take emotion apart, and we just work analytically with the world. It can be done. We can have a much more just world. With green technology and with investments to alleviate poverty, and global governance, the world can become like this.

7.20 And look at the position of the old West. Remember when this blue box was all alone, leading the world, living its own life. This will not happen. The role of the old West in the new world is to become the foundation of the modern world – nothing more, nothing less. But it's a very important role. Do it well and get used to it.

7.44 Thank you very much.

7.46 (Applause)

Answers

1 T

2 F (In 1960, there were one billion people in the industrialized world.)

3 T 4 T 5 T

6 F (Hans Rosling believes that the role of the 'old West' in the new world is to become the foundation of the modern world – and it's a very important role.)

- Elicit or explain that Hans Rosling is Swedish and, therefore, a non-native English speaker. Ask students if they noticed any difference between Hans Rosling's pronunciation, speaking style or vocabulary use and that of the speakers from Units 1 and 2. Then ask: *Did you find Hans Rosling easier or more difficult to understand than the native speakers? Or did you not notice any differences? What made Hans Rosling easier or more difficult to understand?*

- Note the differences in North American English and British English shown at the foot of the spread. Hans Rosling uses British English in this TED Talk, so British versions are listed first. In this unit, these focus on spelling differences. See page 6 of the Introduction for ideas on how to present and practise these differences.

2

- ▶ 3.1 Play the first part (0.00–4.25) of the talk so that students can choose the correct options.

Answers
1 aspirations   2 no longer   3 successful   4 just as poor

- **Optional step.** Put students into pairs to discuss whether they agree with Hans Rosling's opinion that the terms 'the West' and 'the developing world' are no longer relevant. Tell students to give reasons and/or examples to support their points of view.

3

- Give students time to read the sentences. If necessary, clarify the meaning of:

   represent – show something in graphic form (sentence 1)

- ▶ 3.1 Play the second part (4.25–6.18) of the talk so that students can complete the sentences. If necessary, play the recording again.

Answers
1 country   2 child   3 children   4 double

4

- Look at the instructions with the class. Elicit or explain that the 'message' someone gives in a talk is the key information that he/she wants to communicate.

- Ask students to complete the summary with the sentence endings. Students can then compare their answers in pairs, but don't confirm answers at this stage.

- ▶ 3.1 Play the third part (6.18 to the end) of the talk so that students can check their answers.

Answers
1 b   2 c   3 a

5

- Put students into pairs to discuss the question.

- Remind students to use language for talking about trends, where appropriate, when describing changes in family size and standard of living. For example: *Family size has decreased significantly.* Encourage them to give examples to support their statements about the trends. If appropriate, these examples could be about their own families and experiences.

- Conduct whole-class feedback. If you have a multinational class, invite individual students to tell the rest of the class about the situation in their country.

Extra activity

Trends in family size and standard of living

If possible, ask students to go online and research trends in family size and standard of living in their own country over the last 50 years. Students could use the statistical data they find to create their own graphs. Then could then use these graphs as visual aids to present the trends to a partner. Alternatively, you could choose a range of countries, preferably a mixture of 'old West' countries and emerging economies, e.g. USA, China, Brazil, UK, Russia, India, etc. and assign a different country to each student. Students then research the trends in that country before presenting them to the rest of the group. This could be followed by a whole-class discussion on differences and similarities in the trends between countries and possible reasons for them.

VOCABULARY IN CONTEXT

6

- ▶ 3.2 Play the clips from the TED Talk. When each multiple-choice question appears, pause the clip so that students can choose the correct definition.

Transcript and subtitles

1   a **staggering** four billion people have been added to the world population
    a huge
    b terrible
    c shocking

2   A lot of companies have happened **to grow** the economy
    a to depend on
    b to develop
    c to become

3   Now they want to have a holiday on a very **remote** destination
    a exotic
    b expensive
    c far away

4   the Chinese company, Geely, they **acquired** the Volvo company
    a bought
    b sold
    c gave up

5 *And will it happen? Well, I'm not an* **optimist**
   a *someone who always thinks good things will happen*
   b *someone who likes to predict the future*
   c *someone who wants happiness*

6 *Well, I'm not an optimist, neither am I a* **pessimist**.
   a *someone who has no opinions*
   b *someone who enjoys unexpected things*
   c *someone who expects bad things to happen*

Answers

1 a 2 b 3 c 4 a 5 a 6 c

7

• **Questions 1 and 2.** Put students into pairs to brainstorm and to discuss the characteristics of an optimist and a pessimist. Tell them to choose examples from people they know who are either optimists or pessimists.

• **Optional step.** Students could organize the characteristics of optimists and pessimists into two mind maps. Alternatively, they could write sentences in which they use linkers to contrast their characteristics. For example: *An optimist will encourage other people to try new things,* <u>*whereas*</u> *a pessimist will point out what could go wrong.*

• Conduct whole-class feedback to find out what students think are the characteristics of optimists and pessimists.

• **Question 3.** Ask students to tell each other about the most remote place they've been to. If appropriate and possible, students could use their mobile phones to show each other a photo of this place as they talk about it. This could be either a photo students have taken or one they've found online.

CRITICAL THINKING Supporting the main argument

8

• If necessary, show students the part of the talk from 5.25–6.18 to remind them of exactly what the graph shows.

• You could put students into small groups to choose which item in the list the graph showed.

• Ask students to discuss how successfully they think the graph was in supporting Hans Rosling's argument, giving reasons to support their answers. If students think the graph wasn't successful, they can make suggestions for a visual aid that they think would do so more successfully.

• Conduct whole-class feedback and ask students to give their views on how successfully the graph supports Hans Rosling's arguments and, if they thought of any, their suggestions for improvements.

Answer

statistical data

9

• Look at the instructions and the comments with the class. If necessary, clarify the meaning of:

   harsh – unkind or too severe (second comment)

   critical – particularly important (third comment)

• Look at Austin's comment as an example with the class. Elicit that *I think that saving children's lives just means more mouths to feed, more poverty, more children in the next generation* is Austin's argument and *I've travelled a lot and seen the situation for myself* is the evidence he uses to support it.

• Explain or elicit that our argument is a statement we believe to be true and evidence to support any argument is information we use to show that our argument is valid. This evidence may be either personal experience, statistical data or something else.

• **Optional step.** Ask students to write their own short comment in response to the TED Talk. They should present their argument, in the form of their opinion of or reaction to what Hans Rosling said, and evidence to support it. When they've finished writing, put students into pairs or small groups to read and to give feedback on each other's comment.

Answers

(underlining = argument, italics = support)

Austin

<u>I think that saving children's lives just means more mouths to feed, more poverty, more children in the next generation</u> – *I've travelled a lot and seen the situation for myself.*

AndyT

That's very harsh! There have been *plenty of studies* showing exactly <u>the opposite is true</u>. Do a web search on UNICEF and you'll see for yourself.

Barbara

Of course <u>the population can double in a generation if couples have six children and four survive</u> – that's basic maths. Rosling's point is that <u>90 per cent child survival is the critical figure</u> and *he's based that on what's been happening in emerging economies.*

PRESENTATION SKILLS Using props

10

• Ask students to read about using props in the Presentation tips box. If necessary, clarify the meaning of:

   props – objects you use to create or enhance a desired effect, often used by actors and other performers

• ▶ 3.3 Play the clip so that students can identify the props Hans Rosling uses and decide which criteria from the Presentation tips box they meet.

The new thing is that we have the biggest pile of billions, the three billions here, which are also becoming emerging economies, because they are quite healthy, relatively well-educated, and they already also have two to three children per woman, as those have. And their aspiration now is, of course, to buy a bicycle, and then later on they would like to have a motorbike also.

> **Answers**
>
> His props: boxes, a bicycle (also a pair of shoes/sandals, and a toy car and plane)
>
> Students will probably agree that his props meet all the criteria.

• **Optional step.** Put students into pairs to discuss these questions: *What other props could/do presenters use? Would you use / Have you ever used props in a presentation? If yes, which ones? If no, why not? Could using props in a presentation have any negative effects?*

11

• Look at the photos with the class and elicit that these are examples of the four areas: a fax machine (*communication*), a burger (*food*), a games console (*games*) and a piggybank (*money*).

• Put students into pairs to decide on a recent trend involving one area which they would feel comfortable discussing. They then choose a prop or props which they could use to show the trend.

• Tell students to write a few sentences together to describe and to explain the chosen trend. If appropriate, ask them to do some online research to find out more detailed information and statistical data.

• Encourage students to see the writing stage as a time for research, reflection and organizing ideas, rather than the preparation of a 'script' to read out when they present their ideas.

• Ask students to take turns to practise presenting their ideas to their partner. They can make use of the sentences they've written at this stage, but they shouldn't just read them out. They should also give each other feedback on their use of the props and their presentation style.

• Students could do the presentation in the next lesson if they want to bring in prepared visuals or objects that they don't have access to.

12

• Put students into new pairs. They take turns to give their presentation and to give each other feedback on how well their props work.

• Conduct whole-class feedback. Gauge how well students think their props work. You could ask one or two of the best presenters to give their presentation again to the whole class.

▶ Set Workbook pages 24–25 for homework.

3.2 The next economic giant

GRAMMAR Present perfect simple and continuous

1

• Books open. Draw students' attention to the spread title: *The next economic giant*. Elicit that an *economic giant* is an economically powerful country. We also usually associate the term *economic giant* with countries that have a large population.

• Elicit names of countries that could be considered *economic giants*. Ask students to give reasons to support their answers. Possible countries could be: China, Germany, USA, India, etc. Write the names of the countries on the board as students mention them. Then ask students to divide the countries into those from the 'old West' and those which are 'emerging economies'. Compare the number of countries in each category.

• Look at the instructions with the class. Explain that abbreviations which use the initial letters of words are called *acronyms* in English. Elicit more acronyms, e.g. *UNICEF* (originally: United Nations International Children's Emergency Fund, now: United Nations Children's Fund), *NATO* (North Atlantic Treaty Organization), *FAQ* (frequently asked questions).

• Explain that one group of emerging economies is on the top line and the other on the bottom line. Ask students to match the acronyms BRIC and MINT with the two groups.

> **Answers**
>
> BRIC = Brazil, China, India, Russia
>
> MINT = Indonesia, Mexico, Nigeria, Turkey

• **Optional step.** Bring in students' own experiences. Ask: *Have you ever visited any of these countries? What were/are your impressions of them? What words come to mind when you think of them?* Write the names of the eight countries on the board and next to each name write the words that students suggest.

2

• Explain that the infographic is based on data from 2015 and that students need to read it as if it's now 2015.

• Ask students to look at the infographic. Elicit or explain that the letters *GDP* stand for 'Gross Domestic Product', i.e. the total value of goods produced and services provided in a country during one year. Then ask students to identify any BRIC or MINT countries. Establish that in 2002 two BRIC or MINT countries were among the world's largest economies (China and Mexico), but in 2015 there are four (China, Brazil, India and Russia).

- **Optional step.** Ask students to speculate on what they expect the world's ten largest economies to be in another thirteen years' time (2028). Ask: *Will there be any change between now and then? Will the BRIC and MINT countries become even more dominant?*

- Give students time to read the sentences. If necessary, clarify the meaning of:

  shrink – become or make smaller in size or amount (sentence 2)

- Students decide if the sentences are true or false, according to the information shown in the infographic.

> **Answers**
>
> 1 T
>
> 2 F (The UK economy has been growing: it has increased from $1.6 trillion to $3.0 trillion.)
>
> 3 F (France's economy has doubled since 2002 from $1.5 trillion to $3.0 trillion.)
>
> 4 T 5 T 6 T

3

- Look at the Grammar box with the class. If necessary, clarify the meaning of:

  emphasize – to give special importance to or to lay stress on something (question 2)

- Ask students to read the sentences in the Grammar box and to answer the questions. They can do this in pairs.

- Students can check their answers and overall understanding of the present perfect simple and continuous by turning to the Grammar summary on page 144.

> **Answers**
>
> 1 present perfect continuous 2 present perfect continuous 3 present perfect simple

- If you feel that students need more controlled practice before continuing, they could do some or all of the exercises in the Grammar summary. Otherwise, you could continue on to Exercise 4 in the unit and set the Grammar summary exercises for homework.

> **Answers to Grammar summary exercises**
>
> **1**
>
> 1 've been working 2 has been falling 3 has (your friend) been studying 4 haven't been making 5 Have (the development agencies) been planning 6 hasn't been doing
>
> **2**
>
> 1 I've visited 2 has been trying 3 hasn't replied 4 Has he saved 5 have had 6 haven't finished 7 Have you been listening 8 has run

3

1 've been having 2 Has (the proposal from the design department) arrived 3 've seen 4 haven't come 5 has known 6 haven't been sleeping 7 has been helping 8 has reached

4

1 have seen 2 have become 3 has been falling
4 've known 5 've been designing 6 's been
7 has (always) believed 8 has been going
9 has (that) meant 10 has shrunk

5

1 since 2011 2 *both* 3 *both* 4 just 5 yet
6 all morning 7 since 8 recently

6

1 ~~We're~~ **We've been** here since ten o'clock this morning.

2 In my opinion, spending habits ~~are changing~~ **have been changing** for many years.

3 ~~I work~~ **I've worked** (*or* **I've been working**) for this company for about three years.

4 ~~For a long time~~ I've been learning English **for a long time**.

5 How long ~~are you living~~ **have you been living** here?

6 I've just ~~been hearing~~ **heard** the news! Congratulations!

Extra activity

Describe the economy

Individual students take turns to choose a country from the infographic and to describe its economy. Remind them to talk as if it's now 2015. For example: *In 2002, Italy was in seventh position and its GDP was 1.2 trillion dollars. Since then, the economy has been growing and in 2015 its GDP is 2.3 trillion dollars. It is now in eighth position.*

4

- Ask students to read the conversations and to complete the replies with the present perfect continuous forms of the verbs.

- Elicit or explain that because the present perfect continuous is used for repeated or continuous activities, it is often combined with time expressions. These are the time expressions students need to identify and underline.

> **Answers**
>
> 1 've been replying (all morning)
>
> 2 haven't been waiting
>
> 3 has (she) been working (for the last few days)
>
> 4 've been talking (for weeks)
>
> 5 've been travelling (recently)
>
> 6 has been trying (all day)
>
> 7 haven't been reading
>
> 8 've been redesigning (this week)

- **Optional step.** Ask students to create and read out their own similar dialogues in pairs.

Creating dialogues

When students create their own dialogues, make sure they have a model to base them on. However, because these are their own dialogues, they should use contexts and examples that are relevant and meaningful for them. There are several ways in which students can prepare for their own dialogues:

1 Students write every word they want to say and then say it.

2 Students make notes on what they want to say and then say it.

3 Students decide what their scenario will be and then improvise the dialogue.

What will work best depends on the students' needs, speaking confidence levels and how familiar they are with the target language.

5

- Books closed. Write the time expressions from Exercise 4 on the board (*all morning*, *for the last few days*, *for weeks*, *recently*, *all day*, *this week*).

- Look at the example sentence with the class. Elicit that students will need to use the present perfect continuous in the sentences they write. You could also give an example of your own.

- Put students into pairs. They take turns to tell their partner about some of the things they've been doing recently, using a different time expression in each sentence.

- Monitor students while they're speaking, noting any examples of both good and incorrect use of the present perfect continuous.

- Conduct whole-class feedback, and draw students' attention to the examples of good and incorrect use that you collected.

6

- Look at the table with the class. If necessary, clarify the meaning of:

  groceries – food and household supplies (table)

  chunk – a large part or piece of something (line 3)

  year-on-year – year after year; for a number of years (line 14)

- Students use the information in the table to complete the text. Elicit or remind them that they should use the present perfect simple when the emphasis is on the result and the present perfect continuous when the emphasis is on the process.

- 🔊 **15** Play the recording so that students can check their answers.

Transcript

Trends in household expenditure have not shown great changes over the past ten years. The biggest chunk of household spending goes on housing and utilities, and this has jumped from 22 per cent to 26 per cent. Equally, transport costs have increased by 4 per cent. These numbers are not surprising, as fuel costs have been rising steadily over the ten-year period. As fast foods have become more and more popular, our spending on them has tripled. We've also been buying more health products – are we compensating for our poor eating habits? Unusually, given that clothes prices have been falling year-on-year, we still spend the same amount on clothes.

Answers

1 have not shown   2 has jumped
3 have increased   4 have risen   5 have become
6 has tripled   7 've/have also been buying
8 have been falling

7

- Ask students to estimate what percentage of their current household expenditure is spent on each of the ten categories in the table in Exercise 6.

- Put students into pairs to discuss how the changes shown in the table compare with changes in their own situations. Ask: *Have you also seen increases or decreases in the same areas? Were the increases and decreases on a similar or different scale?*

- Remind students to use the present perfect (simple or continuous, as appropriate) during their discussions.

- Conduct whole-class feedback to find out if changes in students' household expenditure are similar to or different from those shown in the table. Elicit possible reasons for the changes. For example: *Fuel prices have gone up and this has resulted in increased expenditure on transport.*

SPEAKING Popular brands

8   **21st CENTURY OUTCOMES**

- Before starting this exercise, refer students to the 21st CENTURY OUTCOMES at the foot of the page. You could get students thinking about personal and economic choices by asking: *What choices have you made so far today and what were the reasons for them?* Students could work in pairs to discuss their choices and the reasons for them. For example, a student could say: *This morning I chose to buy a small coffee instead of a large coffee at a coffee shop because it was cheaper and a small coffee is enough for me.*

- Ask students to look at the items of household expenditure in the box and to think of two brand names for each category. Encourage them to add more items and brands to their lists. They could do this in pairs and then work with a different partner in Exercise 9.

- If students are allowed to use mobile devices, such as smartphones and tablets, in your classroom, give them three minutes to take as many photos of brand images as they can. These brand images could be on items they have or other students have with them or any other items that are in the room. Tell students that the person who takes photos of the greatest number of brands will be the winner. Students can then decide which of the categories from Exercise 8 these brands belong to and refer to them during their discussion in Exercise 9.

Suggested answers

clothes – Gucci, Louis Vuitton, Zara

entertainment – Disney, Sky, Sony

fast food – McDonald's, Burger King

groceries – Lidl, Walmart, Nestlé

health products – Colgate, Gillette, L'Oréal

household goods – Ikea, General Electric

cars – BMW, Ford, Toyota,

computers and appliances – Apple, Samsung, IBM

9

• Put students into pairs to compare their lists from Exercise 8 and to discuss the questions. Remind students that they should try to use the present perfect in their answers.

• Conduct whole-class feedback. Invite individual students to tell the rest of the class about their experiences. If you have a multinational class, you can find out if the same brands are popular in different countries.

▶ Photocopiable communicative activity 3.1: Go to page 217 for practice of present perfect simple and present perfect continuous, and vocabulary for facts, studies and surveys. The teaching notes are on page 239.

▶ Set Workbook pages 26–27 for homework.

3.3 Personal development

READING What do you need?

1

• Books open. Draw students' attention to the spread title: *Personal development*. Elicit that *personal development* involves improving self-awareness and identity, developing talents and potential, and generally improving your quality of life.

• Bring in students' own experiences. Ask: *What have you done for your personal development? Can you think of any specific examples? What were the results of this personal development?*

• Elicit or explain that the link between the spread title (*Personal development*) and the section heading (*What do you need?*) is that we need personal development in order to fulfil our potential and achieve happiness.

• Look at the three diagrams with the class. Elicit that the most important things for the people who drew these diagrams are *chocolate*, *money* and *friends*.

• Ask students to work on their own to rank the three most important things that they need in their life. Direct them to the example diagrams for some ideas. They can choose abstract things, e.g. *love*, or material things, e.g. *my flat*. They then draw a diagram with the most important thing at the base of the pyramid.

• Put students into pairs to compare and discuss their diagrams.

• Conduct whole-class feedback to find out the most popular things that students need.

2

• Explain that students are going to match the four groups of words with their headings. If necessary, clarify the meaning of:

physiological – referring to the healthy or normal functioning of the body (heading 2)

shelter – a structure that protects or covers people or things, usually a place where people live (list A)

• Look at group A as an example with the class. Elicit that the heading for group A is *2 physiological needs*. If necessary, model and drill the pronunciation of *physiological* /ˌfɪziəˈlɒdʒɪkəl/.

• Ask students to match the other headings with the appropriate groups of words.

Answers

1 B   2 A   3 D   4 C

• Put students into pairs to discuss whether any of the three important things they discussed in Exercise 1 are in these groups.

3

• Look at the instructions with the class. You could ask students to predict the fifth 'need'. They then read the article to find out the order in which it mentions the four needs.

• Students could check their answers in pairs before you check with the whole class. If necessary, clarify that:

self-actualization – the realization and fulfilment of your own talents and potential (the fifth 'need')

Answers

1 A   2 D   3 B   4 C   5 self-actualization

4

• Give students time to read the sentences. They then read the article again to find out whether the sentences are true or false. They can do this in pairs.

Answers

1 F (Newer theories of human developmental psychology have largely replaced Maslow's original idea.)

2 F (Maslow didn't use the idea of the pyramid.)

3 T   4 T

- **Optional step.** Put students into groups and ask: *How relevant is Maslow's hierarchy to your lives?* Then conduct whole-class feedback to gauge the general feeling about its relevance. If the consensus is that students don't think the hierarchy is very relevant to their lives, ask them to design an alternative hierarchy that is more relevant.

5

- Look at question 1 as an example with the class. Students find a word in line 3 of the article which they can use to complete the question. Elicit that the missing word is *impact*.
- Ask students to complete the other questions with words from the lines of the article in brackets.
- Check answers with the class. Note that two words can be used to complete question 3. Elicit or explain that *belonging* in question 5 is the *-ing* form of a verb, whereas it is used as a noun in the article.

> **Answers**
> _____
> 1 impact   2 survival   3 admired (*or* respected)
> 4 goal   5 belonging   6 account

- Ask students to think of their own answers to the questions.

6

- Put students into pairs to discuss the questions from Exercise 5. Encourage students to ask follow-up questions. For example: *What kind of impact did the book have? Did it change your view of X? How?*

7

- Put students into pairs to discuss the questions. They could work with the same partner as in Exercise 6 or a different one.
- **Question 4.** Encourage students to give their own opinion and to give reasons or evidence to support it.

> **Answers**
> _____
> 1 The key idea is that we can't be successful in a given level of the pyramid unless we have fulfilled the needs in the previous level – or the ones lower down in the pyramid.
>
> 2 You can only achieve self-actualization when you have achieved your full potential.
>
> 3 For example, a pensions company may sell its products by appealing to our need for financial security or a social media service will target our 'level three' needs of social belonging.
>
> 4 Students' own answers, though they may agree that it will always be relevant.

VOCABULARY Personal growth: abstract nouns

8

- Draw students' attention to the section heading: *Personal growth: abstract nouns*. If necessary, clarify the meaning of:

  abstract noun – a noun for an idea, quality or state, rather than a concrete object

- Elicit that learning word pairs, e.g. adjective and noun pairs, or word families, e.g. verb, noun, adjective, adverb, is useful because it can help students to build and to widen their vocabulary. It can also draw their attention to patterns between words of the same type and within word families.
- Look at item 1 as an example with the class. Ask students to read the article until they find the noun linked to *motivated*. Elicit that *motivation* is in line 1 of the article.
- Ask students to complete the rest of the table with words from the article. They can do this in pairs.

> **Answers**
> _____
> 1 motivation   2 influential   3 safety   4 successful
> 5 growth   6 perfect   7 security   8 qualitative
> 9 quantitative

- Elicit that common endings for nouns in this table are *-tion* and *-ty,* and for adjectives are *-ed*, *-al*, *-ful* and *-ing*.

9

- Look at the sentences with the class. If necessary, clarify the meaning of:

  fulfilled – succeeded in developing abilities or qualities to their fullest degree; the noun is *fulfillment* (sentence 4)

- Put students into pairs to complete the sentences with words from Exercise 8. Tell students to look at the words that come before or after the gap to help them to decide whether they should use the noun or adjective. For example: after *the* or an adjective, they will need to use a noun.

> **Answers**
> _____
> 1 motivation   2 quality   3 success   4 safe
> 5 influence   6 successful

- Ask students to discuss whether the sentences are true for them. If students aren't yet in work, they can think about how they will feel when they are. Ask: *Do you think your salary will be your main motivation when you get a job?*

SPEAKING Are you satisfied?

10   21st CENTURY OUTCOMES

- Before starting this exercise, refer students to the 21st CENTURY OUTCOMES at the foot of the page. Exercise 10 encourages them to think about themselves and their needs, and to evaluate their needs based on Maslow's hierarchy.
- Put students into small groups to discuss the questions. Encourage students to give examples and reasons for their

opinions. Also encourage them to consider the causes of changes in people's priorities when answering question 3.

• Conduct whole-class feedback and focus on students' answers to question 3: how people's needs have changed, and why. Note that students may not feel completely comfortable discussing the extent to which their needs are met and what fulfils them the most. Students may currently be unemployed, suffering from health problems or having a difficult time in their private lives. Keep this in mind and don't push students to reveal too much in answer to questions 1 and 2 if they don't feel comfortable doing so.

▶ Photocopiable communicative activity 3.2: Go to page 218 for practice of survey language and sleep-related vocabulary. The teaching notes are on page 239.

▶ Set Workbook Exercises pages 28–29 for homework.

3.4 Could you call me back?

LISTENING Market research

1

• Books open. Draw students' attention to the spread title: *Could you call me back?* Elicit that we say this on the phone when we don't have time to talk to the other person.

• Draw students' attention to the section heading: *Market research*. Elicit or explain that market research is the activity of collecting information about consumers' preferences and buying habits. Ask students to brainstorm words they connect with market research, e.g. *questionnaire, survey, focus group*. Write words on the board as students mention them.

• Look at the instructions with the class. If necessary, clarify the meaning of:

    survey – a form of research where a group of people are all asked the same questions (line 2)

• Put students into pairs to discuss the questions.

• Conduct whole-class feedback to gauge how many students have previously taken part in a market research survey and what these surveys were about. Find out if any students have ever taken part in a survey about hotels.

2

• Look at the survey with the class. If necessary, clarify the meaning of:

    venue – a place where something happens, especially an organized event (final question)

• Put students into pairs to answer the questions from the survey. Tell them to use adverbs of frequency or frequency expressions in their answers, e.g. *occasionally, never* or *once a month*. They should then convert their answers into scores (1–5) in the survey.

• Ask students to discuss which area of the business they think the company is trying to grow.

Answers

The hotel wants to attract more business travellers, families, people looking for a wedding venue and people attending concerts nearby.

3

• Ask students to suggest who might call a hotel manager, e.g. people who are interested in staying at the hotel, people who sell or provide products or services that a hotel needs, people doing market research for the hotel. Don't confirm who the people leaving the voicemails are at this stage.

• Make sure that students are aware that they need to make notes – key words and phrases – from the voicemails. They don't need to write complete sentences.

• 🎧 16 Play the recording so that students can make notes.

Transcript

1

Hi there, Elaine. This is Louisa Redhill getting back to you about the licence for live music. I've got all the information you asked for – could you call me back before Friday as our office is closed all next week? Thanks.

2

Hi, Elaine. Matt here. I'm just getting back to you about the meeting with the bank manager that we talked about. It's confirmed for Wednesday 4th August at half past nine. Will you be able to make it? Let me know.

3

Good morning, this is a message for Elaine. This is Aziz from ATZ cars. I'm calling about using your venue for a company event, the weekend of 2nd and 3rd June. Could you email me your prices at Aziz at ATZ.com, please? That's A for apple, Z for zebra, I for Italy, Z for Zebra at A-T-Z.com.

4

Hi, Elaine. It's Nelson. I'm returning your call but … err … it looks like I've missed you. I can't make it on Friday, I'm afraid. Also, the report on the market research we did in February and March is ready and I'll email it to you. I'm out of the office for the rest of the week, but if you've got any questions, you can get in touch with me on 645 698 421.

• Students could compare their notes in pairs before you check with the whole class. You could play the recording again either before or after checking answers.

Answers

Message 1: Call Louisa Redhill back before Friday.

Message 2: Let Matt know if she can make it to the meeting with the bank manager on Wednesday 4th August at half past nine.

Message 3: Email Aziz her prices for company events.

Message 4: Get in touch with Nelson if she has any questions about the report on market research.

4

• Give students time to read the expressions in the Useful language box. You could ask them to predict the missing words based on what they can remember from the first time they listened to the voicemails.

• 🔊16 Play the recording again so that students can complete the expressions.

• Elicit that when you *get back* to someone, you call them to follow up on a previous conversation; when you *call someone back*, you call them after they've called you; when you *return a call*, you call someone who's called you; when you *get in touch* with someone, you contact them. Explain that these are fixed expressions.

Answers

1 back 2 back 3 for 4 about 5 me 6 call
7 touch

5

• Ask students to put the words in order. If necessary, they can refer to the Useful language box to help them to do this.

• Students could check their answers in pairs before you check with the whole class. Explain or elicit that these are all examples of requests you can make in a voicemail.

Answers

1 you call me back   2 you email me the details
3 get back to me on my   4 get in touch with you

Pronunciation Intonation in requests

6a

• If necessary, elicit that *intonation* is the rise and fall of the voice as we speak.

• 🔊17 Play the recording and ask students to pay attention to the intonation used in the requests. Elicit that the voice rises in the four requests.

Transcript

1   *Could you call me back before tonight?*
2   *Could you email me the details?*
3   *Can you get back to me on my mobile?*
4   *Do you have an email where I can get in touch with you?*

• Put students into pairs to practise saying the requests with the same intonation as in the recording.

6b

• Look at the requests with the class. Elicit or explain that *ring* (in request 3) has the same meaning as *call* – and the words can be used as both nouns and verbs.

• Put students into pairs to practise saying the requests. Elicit or remind them that their voice should rise at the end of the request.

• 🔊18 Play the recording so that students can check their intonation.

Transcript

1   *Could you get back to me?*
2   *Can you let me know?*
3   *Can you give me a ring?*
4   *Could you text me the prices?*

SPEAKING Leaving voicemails

7   21st CENTURY OUTCOMES

• Before starting this exercise, refer students to the 21st CENTURY OUTCOMES at the foot of the page. You could ask students to work in pairs and to discuss the features of effective speaking and listening before you conduct whole-class feedback. Possible features of effective speaking could include: *speaking clearly and at an appropriate speed (not too fast or too slow), speaking loudly enough so that you can easily be heard, not hesitating to the extent that it makes what you're saying difficult to follow, pronouncing words correctly, using the right words in the right place.* Possible features of effective listening could include: *giving your complete attention to what you're listening to, focusing on the key words a speaker uses and/or the words a speaker stresses, relaxing and not worrying if the speaker is speaking quickly or if you don't understand every word you hear.*

• Elicit that leaving a voicemail requires you to speak effectively to transmit information.

• Explain that students are going to work in pairs. Encourage them to think of something realistic to ask someone else (to do), i.e. something that they would actually want or need to ask someone (to do).

• Tell students to make notes on what they want to say to their partner. They should include specific details and dates, days and/or times.

• Alternatively, put students into pairs to prepare a voicemail. Each student will then work with a different partner in Exercise 8.

8

• Put students into pairs. If they are happy to give each other their phone numbers, they can actually leave a message on their partner's phone. Remind them to set the phone to voicemail before they make their call. Otherwise, they could use a voice-recording app on their own smartphone to record the message or just read their messages to each other.

• Ask students to take turns to leave, to record or to read their voicemails. Their partner should listen to the message and make notes.

• Tell students to prepare for the follow-up call. They need to think of a response to the request in the voicemail.

- Ask students to make the follow-up call. You could ask them to sit back-to-back so that they're unable to see each other, just as when you talk to someone on the phone.

- Conduct whole-class feedback. You could invite individual students to read out their messages to the rest of the class. Other students could then make an appropriate response.

WRITING Making notes from voicemails

9

- Look at the notes with the class. Elicit that when we want to make notes while listening to voicemails, it's usually easier to use abbreviations than to write words or expressions in full. This is what the writer of these notes has done.

- Look at item 1 as an example with the class. Tell students to imagine that they have written these notes. Ask: *Who left the voicemail?* Elicit that Anya left the message, which means that she would use *I* (not *Anya*) in her voicemail. Elicit the full forms of the abbreviations *Mon* (*Monday*), *Jul* (*July*) and *Aug* (*August*), and also that a name or pronoun is needed before *will*.

- Put students into pairs to read the notes and to discuss what the original voicemails said. Remind them to think about who left the voicemail and the full form of the abbreviations.

Answers

1 Hi, it's Anya. I can't do Monday. I'll send the budget for July and August.

2 Hi, it's x, your accountant. Can you confirm that you can meet me on Friday the second at 10.30 am / half past ten in the morning?

3 Hi, it's Nicole. Can you text me the days in September that you're available?

4 Hi, it's Jeff. Can you please return my call by 2 pm / two o'clock in the afternoon on Thursday?

Writing skill Abbreviations

10a

- Ask students to put the abbreviations into two groups: days and months. They can do this in pairs.

- Ask students whether abbreviations for days and months are also used in their own language.

Answers

Days = Fri, Mon, Sat, Sun, Thurs, Tues, Wed

Months = Apr, Aug, Dec, Feb, Jan, Jul, Jun, Mar, May, Nov, Oct, Sept

10b

- Elicit or explain that we usually say and write times and dates differently.

- Ask students to complete the spoken forms of the times and dates.

Answers

1 morning 2 two 3 forty-five 4 half past 5 ten, evening 6 three 7 twelfth 8 first, thousand 9 eleventh 10 twenty-second 11 third 12 thirtieth, April

- Explain that although the twenty-four hour clock is used in written times, the twelve-hour clock is used in spoken times. Elicit or explain that the dates in items 7–12 are used in British English: day / month / year. However, dates are written and said differently in North-American English: month / day / year. For example, in item 11: you could also say *the third of August* in British English, but a North American would read 3/8/2000 as either *the eighth of March* or *March the eighth*.

Extra activity

Abbreviations

Ask students to identify the full forms of some more work-related abbreviations, e.g. *HR* (Human Resources), *R&D* (Research and development), *asap* (as soon as possible), *FAO* (for the attention of), *CEO* (Chief Executive Officer), *eta* (estimated time of arrival), *tbc* (to be confirmed).

11

- Look at the voicemails with the class. Elicit or explain that *half two* (voicemail 4) is another way of saying *half past two*. Point out that you can't say *quarter four* – you must say *quarter past* or *quarter to*.

- Ask students to make notes from the voicemails. Remind them to use abbreviations. Alternatively, you could ask students to work in pairs. One partner reads out the voicemail while the other student, whose book is closed, listens and make notes. Remind students that listening to the message more than once would also be realistic.

Answers

1 Look at emailed sales projections – Janine. Get back by Thurs 10th.

2 Scott – talk about ideas for promotions, Jul + Aug. Tues.

3 Call Luigi before beg Dec.

4 Confirm Angela market research meeting 2.30 pm, Fri.

- **Optional step.** For further practice in making notes from voicemails, students could go back to the voicemails they prepared and/or left on their partner's phone in Exercise 7. They could either say or listen to the voicemail again and make notes using abbreviations.

▶ Set Workbook pages 30–31 for homework.

▶ Set Workbook Presentation 2 on pages 32–33 for homework.

4 Success and failure

LEAD IN

• Books open. Draw students' attention to the unit title, and to the photo on pages 40–41 and its caption. Ask: *What are the people in the photo doing? What is the link between what you can see in the photo, and the theme of success and failure?* Possible answers could be: *They're trapeze artists. If the man doesn't hold onto the woman's hands, she will fall – and they will fail.*

• To gauge students' prior knowledge of the unit vocabulary, ask them to decide on five criteria for what makes someone a success. Possible criteria could be: *wealth, fame, awards, whether they've made a positive difference to people's lives*. Then give students the names of five people you think they will already know who could be considered successful, e.g. businessmen, celebrities, scientists, politicians. (You could use photos too.) Put students into pairs to discuss how successful each person is according to the criteria. They should then agree on who they think is the most successful, giving an explanation for their decision. Conduct whole-class feedback. Write any words connected with success and failure on the board as students mention them, and, if necessary, clarify their meaning.

TEDTALKS

BACKGROUND

1

• Ask students to read the text about Richard St. John and his talk.

• **Question 1**. Put students into pairs to make a list of eight words they think could be in Richard St. John's summary of success.

• Ask: *How would you summarize what success means?* Conduct whole-class feedback, but don't confirm which words are actually in Richard St. John's list at this stage. Tell students that they will find this out later.

• **Question 2**. Ask students to think about real companies they know when making their lists of what makes businesses succeed or fail.

• **Question 3**. Elicit an example of an outside factor and a factor that is part of the business itself before students categorize the things on their list, e.g. an outside factor could be changes in demand for the business's product or service, a factor that is part of the business itself could be the management and leadership skills of those running the business.

• Conduct whole-class feedback on the two types of factors that can contribute to a business's success or failure. Write some of the factors on the board as students mention them.

Suggested answers

1 Students' own answers

2 Good management, capital, good location, planning – or lack of these things; competition, pricing

3 Management and planning are part of the business itself, while competition, for example, is an outside factor.

KEY WORDS

2

• Look at the instructions, the sentences and the definitions with the class. If necessary, clarify the meaning of:

  to be distracted – to lose focus on something you should be concentrating on and focus on something else instead (sentence 3)

  drive – a strong desire to succeed (definition d)

• Ask students to try to guess the meaning of the words in bold and then to match them with their definitions.

Answers

1 d 2 f 3 c 4 a 5 b 6 e

AUTHENTIC LISTENING SKILLS
Collaborative listening

3a

- Ask students to read the information about collaborative listening in the Authentic listening skills box. If necessary, clarify the meaning of:

   collaborative – involving two or more people working together

- Explain that students are now going to do some collaborative listening themselves.

- 🎧 **19** Play the recording and ask students to write down the words they can remember.

Transcript

Why do so many people reach success and then fail? One of the big reasons is, we think success is a one-way street. So we do everything that leads up to success, but then we get there. We figure we've made it, we sit back in our comfort zone, and we actually stop doing everything that made us successful. And it doesn't take long to go downhill. And I can tell you this happens, because it happened to me.

3b

- Put students into pairs to compare the words they wrote down in Exercise 3a. Ask: *Did your partner write down any words that you didn't?* If so, ask students to add these words to their original list in a different colour, and to highlight or underline them. Then elicit words from the whole class and write these on the board.

- **Optional step**. Ask students to use the words they wrote down to reconstruct and say or write in full sentences what Richard St. John said at the beginning of the talk.

- 🎧 **19** Play the recording again. Ask students to listen for the words they remembered and to add any other words that they didn't hear the first time.

- Students compare lists again. Ask: *Did you hear any more words when you listened to the recording the second time?*

- **Optional step.** Tell students to read the transcript on page 176 and to compare what Richard St. John actually said with the full sentences they wrote.

4.1 Success is a continuous journey

TEDTALKS

1

- Books open. Give students time to read the options. Tell them to focus on what Richard St. John talks about and not to become distracted by any specific details or unknown words or expressions as they listen.

- ▶ **4.1** Play the whole talk once. Then check the answer.

Transcript

0.14 *Why do so many people reach success and then fail? One of the big reasons is, we think success is a one-way street. So we do everything that leads up to success, but then we get there. We figure we've made it, we sit back in our comfort zone, and we actually stop doing everything that made us successful. And it doesn't take long to go downhill. And I can tell you this happens, because it happened to me.*

0.38 *Reaching success, I worked hard, I pushed myself. But then I stopped, because I figured, 'Oh, you know, I've made it. I can just sit back and relax.'*

0.46 *Reaching success, I always tried to improve and do good work. But then I stopped, because I figured, 'Hey, I'm good enough. I don't need to improve any more.'*

0.55 *Reaching success, I was pretty good at coming up with good ideas. Because I did all these simple things that lead to ideas. But then I stopped, because I figured I was this hot-shot guy and I shouldn't have to work at ideas, they should just come like magic. And the only thing that came was creative block. I couldn't come up with any ideas.*

1.13 *Reaching success, I always focused on clients and projects, and ignored the money. Then all this money started pouring in. And I got distracted by it. And suddenly I was on the phone to my stockbroker and my real estate agent, when I should have been talking to my clients.*

1.27 *And reaching success, I always did what I loved. But then I got into stuff that I didn't love, like management. I am the world's worst manager, but I figured I should be doing it, because I was, after all, the president of the company.*

1.39 *Well, soon a black cloud formed over my head and here I was, outwardly very successful, but inwardly* *very depressed. But I'm a guy; I knew how to fix it. I bought a fast car. (Laughter) It didn't help. I was faster but just as depressed.*

1.59 *So I went to my doctor. I said, 'Doc, I can buy anything I want. But I'm not happy. I'm depressed. It's true what they say, and I didn't believe it until it happened to me. But money can't buy happiness.' He said, 'No. But it can buy Prozac.' And he put me on anti-depressants. And yeah, the black cloud faded a little bit, but so did all the work, because I was just floating along. I couldn't care less if clients ever called. (Laughter)*

2.28 *And clients didn't call. (Laughter) Because they could see I was no longer serving them, I was only serving myself. So they took their money and their projects to others who would serve them better.*

2.39 *Well, it didn't take long for business to drop like a rock. My partner and I, Thom, we had to let all our employees go. It was down to just the two of us, and we were about to go under. And that was great. Because with no employees, there was nobody for me to manage.*

2.54 *So I went back to doing the projects I loved. I had fun again, I worked harder and, to cut a long story short, did all the things that took me back up to success. But it wasn't a quick trip. It took seven years.*

3.08 *But in the end, business grew bigger than ever. And when I went back to following these eight principles, the black cloud over my head disappeared altogether. And I woke up one day and I said, 'I don't need Prozac anymore.' And I threw it away and haven't needed it since.*

3.23 *I learned that success isn't a one-way street. It doesn't look like this; it really looks more like this. It's a continuous journey. And if we want to avoid 'success-to-failure-syndrome', we just keep following these eight principles, because that is not only how we achieve success, it's how we sustain it. So here is to your continued success. Thank you very much. (Applause)*

Answer

c

___

- Note the differences in North American English and British English shown at the foot of the spread. In this unit, these focus on vocabulary differences. See page 6 of the Introduction for ideas on how to present and practise these differences.

2

- ▶ **4.1** Play the first part (0.00–1.39) of the talk so that students can match the two halves.

- Check answers with the class. Elicit that when Richard St. John was pushing himself, trying to improve and doing what he loved, he experienced success; but when he thought that was good enough, he'd made it and he could relax, he experienced failure.

Answers

1 c   2 b   3 d   4 e   5 a

___

- **Optional step**. Bring in students' own experiences. Ask: *Have you ever experienced the causes of success and failure that Richard St. John sets out in this part of the talk yourselves? Or do you know anyone who has?*

3

- Give students time to read the sentences. Elicit or explain that *wealth* (sentence a) is a synonym for *money*.

- ▶ **4.1** Play the second part (1.39–3.08) of the talk so that students can put the events in order. They could check their answers in pairs before you check with the whole class.

Answers

1 d   2 a   3 e   4 b   5 c

___

4

- Elicit what students can remember about the two slides Richard St. John shows with the eight principles of success. Ask: *Do you remember which two metaphors he used for success?* (*a one-way street* and *a continuous journey*)

- ▶ **4.1** Play the third part of the talk (3.08 to the end) so that students can note the content of the two slides and the difference between them. They could check their answers in pairs before you check with the whole class.

Answers

The first slide shows success as one way – 'a one-way street' (a ladder); the second shows it as a continuous journey (a circle).

___

- **Optional step**. Put students into pairs to think of another metaphor for success and another one for failure which they think is appropriate. Students can then share and explain their metaphors, giving reasons why they think they're appropriate, with the whole class.

5

- **Question 1**. Encourage students to consider both sides of the argument, i.e. the ways in which money can bring happiness and the things that it can't buy.

- Conduct whole-class feedback to gauge whether or not students think that money can buy happiness. If students feel comfortable, ask them to share some of their personal criteria for success.

Extra activity

Debating

Put students into pairs and ask each pair to reach a consensus on whether they agree or disagree with the motion 'This house believes that money can buy happiness'. Find out which pairs agree and disagree, and then match up pairs who have different points of view. Ask these pairs to debate the motion. Students who don't have another pair to debate with can act as judges to decide the winner of some of the debates. As far as possible, make sure that there's a student judge to decide the winner of every debate.

Students take turns to present a point to support their view of the motion. They should also make counter-arguments in response to the other pair. The winner is the pair who makes the most convincing arguments and counter-arguments in the opinion of the judge. Monitor students while they're debating, noting any examples of interesting language use or areas for improvement in students' spoken English that you can then share in whole-class feedback.

VOCABULARY IN CONTEXT

6

• ▶ 4.2 Play the clips from the talk. When each multiple-choice questions appears, pause the clip so that students can choose the correct definition.

Transcript and subtitles

1 *we think success is a **one-way street**.*
   a a road where big companies have offices
   b a place where you can only work in one way
   c something that only goes in a single direction

2 *we **sit back in our comfort zone**, and we actually stop doing everything that made us successful.*
   a find a place to rest
   b relax in a chair
   c stop making an effort

3 *'Oh, you know, **I've made it**. I can just sit back and relax.'*
   a I finished it
   b I'm a failure
   c I'm a success

4 *But then I **got into stuff** that I didn't love, like management.*
   a liked new things
   b started doing things
   c stopped doing things

5 *I **couldn't care less** if clients ever called.*
   a had no interest
   b was worried
   c wasn't surprised

6 *I worked harder and, **to cut a long story short**, did all the things that took me back up to success*
   a to be completely honest
   b to explain the details
   c to give you a summary

Answers
1 b   2 c   3 c   4 b   5 a   6 c

7

• If you have a class where students feel comfortable talking about themselves, conduct whole-class feedback. Alternatively, you could ask students to work with another pair and share their answers.

CRITICAL THINKING Challenging assumptions

8

• Look at the section heading with the class. If necessary, clarify the meaning of:

   to challenge – to say that something may not be true or correct

   assumption – something someone believes to be true even if they don't necessarily have evidence to support it

• Put students into pairs to discuss the assumption Richard St. John says people normally have about the route to success

• Conduct whole-class feedback and ask students whether they agree that people assume success is a one-way street and that once they get to success, they've made it and can stop trying. Encourage students to give reasons and examples to support their points of view.

Answers
People usually assume it's a one-way street and that once we get to success, we've made it and stop trying

9

• Put students into pairs to discuss the questions.

• **Question 1.** Explain that students can use the transcript for the talk on page 176 and the information from Exercises 2 and 3.

• Conduct whole-class feedback to find out how successful students think Richard St. John was in achieving his purpose.

Answers
1 Roberto's comment
2 Students' own answers

• **Optional step**. Ask students to write a short reply to Janine's comment. They can then work in pairs or small groups and read each other's reply.

PRESENTATION SKILLS Repeating key phrases

10

• Ask students to read about repeating key phrases in the Presentation tips box. If necessary, clarify the meaning of:

   'take away' points – things the audience will remember after watching a talk (first bullet)

- ▶ **4.3** Play the three clips so that students can identify the two-word phrase Richard St. John uses to introduce each of his examples.

Transcript

1   Reaching success, I worked hard, I pushed myself. But then I stopped, because I figured, 'Oh, you know, I made it. I can just sit back and relax.'

2   Reaching success, I always tried to improve and do good work. But then I stopped, because I figured, 'Hey, I'm good enough. I don't need to improve any more.'

3   Reaching success, I was pretty good at coming up with good ideas. Because I did all these simple things that lead to ideas. But then I stopped, because I figured I was this hot-shot guy and I shouldn't have to work at ideas, they should just come like magic. And the only thing that came was creative block. I couldn't come up with any ideas.

Answers

1 Reaching success   2 Reaching success   3 Reaching success

11

- ▶ **4.1** Play the three clips again so that students can identify what Richard St. John repeats beginning with *But* … .

- Ask students if they think repetition helped Richard St. John to get his message across.

Answers

He repeats *But then I stopped, because I figured* … .

12

- Explain that students are going to write similar sentences to those Richard St. John used – sentences that repeat a pattern.

- Look at the example with the class. Write *worked hard / passed my exams easily* on the board, and elicit or explain that students should add *When I* and *I found I* to the three sets of words to make sentences with the same pattern.

Suggested answers

When I passed me exams, I found I had more job offers.

When I made friends at work, I found I enjoyed my job more.

When I changed jobs, I found I earned more money.

13

- Look at the photos with the class and ask students what is happening. Elicit that the student on the left has just passed an exam (perhaps English) and the student on the right is studying (perhaps English).

- Put students into pairs to write a few sentences to explain different consequences of learning English. Decide whether students should use the *When I … , I found* pattern or another

pattern of their choice, e.g. *If you … , you'll …* . Alternatively, they can decide for themselves. Encourage students to think about their own individual situation and what the consequences of studying English are or will be for them specifically.

- Ask students to take turns to practise presenting their sentences to their partner. Monitor students while they're practising, offering help where necessary.

14

- Put students into new pairs. They take turns to give their presentation and to give each other feedback on how well they got their message across. Monitor students while they're presenting, noting any examples of good sentences.

- Conduct whole-class feedback and invite individual students to share the example sentences that you have noted. Encourage discussion to get an overview of what students think the consequences of studying English are.

▶ Set Workbook pages 34–35 for homework.

4.2 Measures of success

GRAMMAR Narrative tenses

1

- Books open. Draw students' attention to the spread title: *Measures of success*. Ask students to brainstorm ways in which you can measure someone's success. Possible ways could be: *their personal wealth, the turnover of the company they run, their level in their company's or organization's hierarchy, how many prizes or awards they've won, how much they do to help other people, how good a work–life balance they have.*

- **Optional step.** If the class looked at certain well-known people and evaluated how successful they are as a lead-in to this unit, ask students to think about the person they decided was the most successful. Elicit what the 'measures' of this person's success are, referring back to the criteria they established.

- Put students into pairs and ask: *Is it easier or more difficult for anybody to achieve success today than it was fifty years ago?* Encourage students to consider all the areas in which people can become successful, from business to pop music.

- Look at the instructions with the class. Put students into pairs to discuss the questions. Point out that there is no right or wrong answer and students should give their own opinion.

- Conduct whole-class feedback. Elicit examples of jobs that you need to be either young or old to do and reasons why students feel that you need to be young or old to do these jobs.

- **Optional step.** Ask the class: *Do you think anything has changed in the last fifty years when it comes to the importance of age in the workplace? Are jobs more open to people of different ages now than they were fifty years ago?* Conduct whole-class feedback to gauge what students' opinions on these issues are.

2

- Ask students to look at the infographic and the jobs in the box. If necessary, clarify the meaning of:

  entrepreneur – someone who starts their own business (top right)

  magnate – someone who is dominant in a particular area, e.g. telecommunications or property, as a result of the large amount of assets he/she owns (bottom right)

- Ask students to find the people who do the jobs in the infographic. They can do this in pairs. It's unlikely that students will be able to recognize all the people, so encourage them to look for clues in the shorts texts if they're not sure.

Answers

Amancio Ortega – a fashion entrepreneur

Karren Brady – a sports executive

Sheryl Sandberg – a technology executive

James Dyson – an inventor

Carolyn McCall – an airline executive

Carlos Slim Helu – a telecoms magnate

- Elicit that the six people in the infographic 'really made it' when they were between 39 and 50 years of age.

3

- Look at the Grammar box with the class. Ask students to read the text, focusing on the verbs, and then to answer the questions. They can compare their answers in pairs.

- Students can check their answers and overall understanding of narrative tenses by turning to the Grammar summary on page 146.

Answers

1 a bought, worked   b was working   c 'd had (had had)
d had been trying
2 a past perfect continuous   b past continuous   c past simple   d past perfect simple

- If you feel that students need more controlled practice before continuing, they could do some or all of Exercises 1–3 in the Grammar summary. Otherwise, you could continue on to Exercise 4 in the unit and set the Grammar summary exercises for homework.

Answers to Grammar summary exercises

1

1 had been thinking   2 hadn't been working   3 hadn't been expecting   4 had (you) been discussing   5 Had (the business) been losing   6 hadn't been getting

2

1 came   2 They'd been living   3 wanted   4 they opened   5 hadn't run   6 had worked   7 was doing   8 there was   9 lost   10 had been saving   11 had

3

1 began   2 'd won   3 directed   4 was working   5 'd started   6 had met   7 'd been making   8 left   9 didn't want   10 closed   11 'd released

4

- If necessary, clarify the meaning of:

  chairman – in this context, a person who is the head of a company's board and, therefore, has ultimate control of it (paragraph 1)

  Chief of Staff – N AM ENG a person responsible for the day-to-day running of a governmental department or an administration (paragraph 2)

  graduate – to successfully complete a course of study at a university or equivalent institution (paragraph 3)

- Ask students to choose the correct option to complete the sentences. Remind them to refer to the Grammar box and/or the Grammar summary if they're unsure which tense is correct.

Answers

1 was operating, resigned, moved

2 joined, had been working, had risen

3 was doing, trained

5

- Look at the title and the photo with the class. If necessary, clarify the meaning of:

  philanthropist – someone who gives money to charity (first bullet)

- Elicit any facts students know about Oprah Winfrey and write key words on the board as they mention them, e.g. *American, talk show, interview, television, actress, politics.*

- Ask students to read the text to get a general understanding of what it says about Oprah Winfrey and to check if any of the words they mentioned are in it.

- Ask students to complete the biography of Oprah Winfrey with the correct forms of the verbs.

Extra activity

Writing a biography

Ask students to write a biography of one of the people in the infographic. They can use the text in Exercise 5 as a model and write roughly the same number of words. Students should use a range of narrative tenses in their texts.

6

• Remind students that it's not only wealthy, well-known figures such as the people in the infographic who are successful. We can all be successful.

• Give examples from your own life and/or give some examples of things people can be successful at, e.g. *winning a tournament with a sports team, getting promotion at work, renovating a house.*

• Ask students to think of something they were successful at. Then ask them to think about the events that led up to this success and what happened next.

• Put students into pairs to discuss the events that led up to this success and what happened next. Monitor students while they're speaking. Give help where necessary and note any good example sentences, which you can then share with the whole class.

GRAMMAR *used to* and *would*

7

• Explain that students are going to listen to an interview with Gina Desai, the founder of a children's charity. Elicit that you would expect such a person to be highly motivated, independent, and interested in helping others, but not particularly interested in becoming rich.

• Put students into pairs to discuss how the founder of the children's charity might measure her success.

• Conduct whole-class feedback on how students think Gina Desai would measure her success, but don't confirm students' ideas at this stage.

• If necessary, elicit or remind students of the meaning of *head up* ('to lead' or 'to be in charge of') which is recycled from Unit 1.

• 🔊 20 Play the recording so that students can choose the correct option.

Transcript

P = Presenter, G = Gina

P: *Welcome to the programme, Gina. Many listeners will know you as the founder of the children's charity, Places for Kids, which has worked with over 10,000*

vulnerable young people in London. You've just been named as one of the 100 most powerful women in the UK. How does that feel?

G: *Very odd, to be honest! I don't feel completely comfortable with the idea of power.*

P: *But your voice is listened to, certainly in the field of children's rights and education. Your charity is very large and successful.*

G: *I hope that it's successful in the sense that we make a difference. Size itself is not important.*

P: *How did your charity work begin?*

G: *I suppose you have to go right back to my childhood. We used to live in India – that's where my family is from originally. And so when we came to London and I went to school, I felt different.*

P: *Was that a difficult time?*

G: *It was, yes. Because the other girls wouldn't talk to me. Children can be very cruel. There used to be a girl called Alisha, and she would put my toys in strange places. It's hard to understand.*

P: *And I think you used to be dyslexic too?*

G: *Well, I still am dyslexic. I can't send texts or use a computer even now. I think I used to make it worse because I needed glasses, but I didn't use to wear them. So I really couldn't even see properly.*

P: *But somehow, you survived those experiences.*

G: *I did. And that was a success story. I got through those difficulties and from them I learned how I could help children.*

P: *So tell me more about how Places for Kids works …*

8

• Ask students to read the sentences. If necessary, check the meaning of:

  dyslexic – suffering from dyslexia, a learning disorder which makes reading and writing difficult (sentence 4)

• 🔊 20 Play the recording so that students can check their answers. Remind students that there is only one factual mistake in each sentence.

9

- Ask students to read the sentences in the Grammar box and to answer the questions. If necessary, check the meaning of:

- *habit* – something that we do repeatedly and/or on a regular basis (question 1)

- *state* – a situation, state of mind or something that happens in our lives (question 1)

- Students can check their answers and overall understanding of *used to* and *would* by turning to the Grammar summary on page 146.

Answers

1 used to   2 would

- If you feel that students need more controlled practice before continuing, they could do some or all of Exercises 4–6 in the Grammar summary. Otherwise, you could continue on to Exercise 10 in the unit and set the Grammar summary exercises for homework.

Answers to Grammar summary exercises

4

1 *both*   2 Did you use to have   3 used to be
4 *both*   5 *both*   6 *both*   7 *both*
8 didn't use to understand

5

1 used to live   2 used to take *or* would take
3 Did (you) use to wear   4 used to have *or* would have
5 didn't use to enjoy   6 did (your family) use to go *or* would (your family) go   7 used to miss *or* would miss
8 used to be

6

1 I met Jane yesterday and we ~~had~~ **talked** about the project.

2 Last year, the company ~~has~~ **opened** a new office.

3 I was very excited when I first ~~start~~ **started** my new job.

4 I ~~use~~ **used** to be a bad student because I never did my homework.

5 What did your boss ~~said~~ **say** to you?

6 The man gave me his business card and ~~was walking~~ **walked** away.

10

- Look at sentence 1 as an example with the class. Elicit that the correct option is *used to know* because 'knowing' someone is a past state and not a past habit.

Answers

1 used to know   2 Did Sue use to work
3 *both*   4 used to be   5 *both*

An object from the past

Ask students in advance to bring in an object that is connected with their childhood or youth, e.g. a teddy bear they were given as a child or a ticket for a concert they went to. Put students into small groups. They take turns to talk about the object, using *used to* and *would*. For example: *I used to love Bon Jovi. When I was thirteen or fourteen, I would listen to my Bon Jovi CDs every day.*

Pronunciation Elision of consonants *t* and *d*

11a

- If students have completed Unit 2, elicit that elision is the omission of certain sounds in words. If students haven't completed Unit 2, explain what elision is.

▶ Background information: Elision, Unit 2.2, page 30.

- Ask students to read the sentences and to predict which consonants will be omitted.

- 🔊 **21** Play the recording so that students can identify the omitted consonants.

Transcript

1   We **used to live** in India.

2   The other girls **wouldn't talk** to me.

3   She **would put** my toys in strange places.

4   I needed glasses, but I **didn't use** to wear them.

Answers

1 use~~d~~ to   2 wouldn'~~t~~ talk   3 woul~~d~~ put   4 didn'~~t~~ use

11b

- Ask students to practise saying the sentences in Exercise 8. They can do this in pairs. Tell students to give each other feedback on how successfully they used elision.

- Conduct whole-class feedback on how the sentences should be said with elision. If necessary, model and drill the correct pronunciation.

SPEAKING Old habits

12   `21st` **CENTURY OUTCOMES**

- Before starting this exercise, refer students to the 21st CENTURY OUTCOMES at the foot of the page.

- Give examples from your own life and invite students to say whether they're true or false.

- Ask students to read the list of things and to choose four of the things to write about. Decide how many sentences should be true and how many should be false. Alternatively, they can decide for themselves.

- Remind students to use *would* only for habits. Also, encourage students to use negative forms (*didn't use to* and *wouldn't*), where appropriate.

- Monitor students while they're writing, correcting any mistakes they make with *used to* and *would*.

- Elicit that we use *Did you use to* and *Would you* to ask questions.

- Put students into pairs. They take turns to read their sentences. The other student can then ask questions with *used to* or *would* to find out more information and discover which sentences are true and which are false. Encourage students to analyse the information their partner gives and then use this to draw conclusions in order to fulfil this 21st CENTURY OUTCOME.

- Monitor students to check that they're using questions with *used to* and *would* correctly.

▶ Photocopiable communicative activity 4.1: Go to page 219 for practice of Narrative tenses (past simple, past continuous, past perfect simple, past perfect continuous), and *used to* and *would*. The teaching notes are on page 240.

▶ Set Workbook pages 36–37 for homework.

4.3 Failure is not an option

READING Lessons for life

1

- Books open. Draw students' attention to the spread title: *Failure is not an option.*

- Put students into pairs to talk about people they know personally or well-known people they're familiar with for whom failure isn't or wasn't an option, i.e. people who kept on trying to achieve success no matter what. Ask: *Why was failure not an option for this person?* Remind students to give reasons for choosing their person or people, and possible explanations for why failure wasn't an option for them.

- Put students into pairs to discuss the questions. Encourage them to give more than a 'yes' or 'no' answer to these 'closed' questions. They should give a reason for their answer and support it with examples.

- Conduct whole-class feedback to establish the general consensus. Invite individual students to share the examples they used to support their opinions.

2

- Ask students to look at the article and to focus on the four quotations at the beginning. Tell them not to read the whole article at this stage.

- Tell students to complete the quotations. They can only use each word once. Students could check their answers in pairs before you check with the whole class.

Answers
failure, success, truth, nothing

- **Optional step.** Ask students if they're familiar with any of the people who said or wrote the quotations and, if they are, find out what they know about these people. Ask: *Could we say that the people who said or wrote these things are successful themselves? How do you know they are/aren't?*

Extra activity

Quotations and their meaning today

Put students into groups of four and assign each group member one of the four quotations. Ask students to focus on the meaning of their quotation and how we can use its message in our everyday lives. Students then each present the meaning of their quotation and how we can use its message.

3

- Explain that students are going to read the article and choose the main message or messages. Remind them that they should read the article quickly. They must decide whether it has one or more than one message. If necessary, clarify the meaning of:

  inevitable – cannot be prevented (message c)

- Students read the article to identify the main message(s).

Answer
c

- **Optional step.** Ask students whether they agree or disagree with the message that 'Mistakes are inevitable – it's what you do next that matters.' Encourage them to give reasons and/or examples to support their opinions.

4

- Look at the instructions and the three kinds of mistakes with the class. If necessary, clarify the meaning of:

  lack of – not a large enough amount of something (item 1)

- Draw students' attention to the glossary at the end of the article. Tell them to refer to the glossary if they're unsure about the meaning of these expressions.

- Ask students to read the article and to find an example of each kind of mistake.

- **Optional step.** Students could work in groups of three and do this activity as a collaborative reading exercise. Each member of the group focuses on finding an example of one kind of mistake. Once they've each found their example, they can tell the rest of the group about the mistake in their own words.

Answers
1 the printer cartridge had run out when Thomas Dowling was printing the handouts and he didn't have time to find a new one

2 someone Thomas Dowling knows found he owed a large sum in taxes after doing his own tax returns rather than pay an accountant

3 the 'New Coke' marketing disaster required, in theory, an in-depth analysis to work out who was to blame

5

• Look at extract 1 as an example with the class. Elicit that *one* and *other* refer to *success* and *failure.* Elicit or explain that the writer of the article has substituted the words here because there was no need for him to repeat them from the previous sentence. It is still clear to the reader what he's referring to.

• Ask students to find the other extracts in the article and to decide what the underlined words refer to.

Answers
1 success, failure   2 mistakes   3 printer cartridge
4 the fact that he owed a large sum in taxes   5 time you make a mistake

6

• Ask students to read the second to last paragraph of the article to remind themselves exactly what the 'New Coke' disaster was.

• Look at the instructions and the list of things with the class. Explain that *influenced* can mean 'led them to create New Coke' and 'led to the failure of New Coke'. Elicit the meanings of the expressions and some examples of their use. If necessary, clarify the meaning of:

   trialling – testing a product on a small scale before making it available to buy, or launching it (top right)

• Put students into small groups to discuss which of the things could have influenced the 'New Coke' disaster. They can also consider how and why the factors they've chosen influenced it.

• Conduct whole-class feedback on which factors influenced the 'New Coke' disaster, and how and why. Encourage students to use cause-and-effect statements to explain why they influenced the disaster.

Background information
'New Coke'

'New Coke' is the name given to a reformulation of Coca Cola which was launched in April 1985. The Coca Cola Corporation had decided to reformulate Coca Cola due to a drop in sales since the end of World War II and competition from Pepsi Co. Although the change was initially accepted by the majority of consumers in the USA, a small but negative and even hostile majority opposed the change. Protests and boycotts were organized. One factor that contributed to the discontent may have been the fact that Coca Cola didn't explain why the change had been made. In June 1985, Coca Cola announced that it would return to its original formula.

VOCABULARY Success and failure

7

• Elicit or explain that we can decide whether a noun is countable or uncountable by asking two questions: *Can you write a number directly in front of it? Does it have a plural form?* Explain that *coin* is a countable noun (*ten coins*), whereas *money* is uncountable. Make the point that some nouns can be used as both a countable and uncountable noun, and these usually have different meanings when they're used in these two ways.

• Look at item 1 as an example with the class. Students find *failure* in line 1 and work out from its context whether it is being used as a countable or uncountable noun. Elicit that it is being used as an uncountable noun here, but it can also be used as a countable noun. For example: *Many of the scientist's experiments were failures.*

• Tell students to find the other nouns in the article and to look at the context in which they're used, especially which word comes directly in front of them, to help to deduce what type of noun they are. Even if students think they already know whether a noun is countable or uncountable, encourage them to find the word in the article and to look at how it is being used.

Answers
1 B (U in article)   2 B (U in article)   3 C   4 U   5 U
6 U   7 C   8 B (C in article)   9 B (U in article)
10 U   11 U   12 B (C in article)   13 C

8

• Look at sentence 1 as an example with the class. Elicit that the missing word is *successes*.

• Ask students to complete the other sentences. Remind them that more than one word is possible in some sentences.

Answers
1 successes   2 failures   3 fault   4 catastrophe/disaster
5 experience/expertise   6 errors/mistakes, truth

- **Optional step.** Ask students to choose five nouns from Exercise 7 and to write sentences that are true for them / about their own life. Monitor students while they're writing, offering help where necessary. They can then share these sentences in pairs.

9

- Explain that students are going to put the words in the correct order to make questions. You can also point out that the questions use several different tenses and structures.

- Monitor students while they're ordering the words, offering help where necessary.

- Check answers with the class. Invite individual students to read out a sentence each.

> **Answers**
>
> 1 How good are you at planning?
>
> 2 What would you say are your areas of expertise?
>
> 3 Is knowledge or experience more useful for your job?
>
> 4 Do you mind making mistakes when you speak English?
>
> 5 Have you ever had a work-related disaster?
>
> 6 Do you ever take the blame for things that aren't your fault?

- Put students into pairs to ask and answer the questions. Encourage them to give answers that are true for them.

- Monitor students while they're asking and answering questions. Check how successfully they're using vocabulary connected with success and failure, and the world of work, and give students feedback on this when they've finished.

SPEAKING Passing on lessons learned

10 *21st* **CENTURY OUTCOMES**

- Before starting this exercise, refer students to the 21st CENTURY OUTCOMES at the foot of the page. You could ask students to reflect on how successful they are at reflecting critically on past experiences and using that reflection to inform their future actions and choices. Students can discuss this in pairs, giving examples where appropriate.

- Tell students that when they're talking about a mistake they've made, they should use the narrative tenses they looked at in Unit 4.2. Give an example so that they can see how they could use the narrative tenses. For example: *I'd been planning our holiday in Greece for months. I'd booked the flights and hotel, and I'd read several guidebooks about the country. Finally, our departure date arrived, and we got up and drove to the airport. While we were driving up to Departures, my friend John looked for his passport in his bag. He couldn't find it anywhere! Then he remembered that he'd left it on the roof of the car! We drove back home and found John's passport lying in the middle of our road where it had fallen off the car. Of course, by that time, we'd missed our flight!*

- Advise students to start with the past continuous or past perfect continuous to give some background information and set the scene. They should then use the past simple for a sequence of events and the past perfect to say that one event happened earlier than another – this sequence could be the reason for the mistake, as in the example above.

- Put students into pairs to tell a story about a mistake they've made and to say what advice they would give someone in the same situation in order to help them to avoid making that mistake.

- Monitor students while they're telling their stories, offering help with the use of narrative tenses where necessary.

▶ Set Workbook pages 38–39 for homework.

4.4 How did it go?

LISTENING Reviewing an event

1

- Books open. Draw students' attention to the spread title: *How did it go?* Elicit or explain that this is a question you would ask someone after they'd done something. Then elicit things the person could have done. Encourage students to use verb + noun collocations and the past simple. Possible answers could be: *had a job interview, given a presentation or talk, taken part in a meeting, pitched a product idea to a potential investor.*

- Explain that students are going to look at things that happened at a company open day. Elicit or explain that a company open day is an event where a company opens its doors to the public and lets them look around. There's usually some kind of entertainment programme for the visitors too.

- Put students into pairs to brainstorm events they think could happen at an Open Day, e.g. games, competitions, treasure hunts, live music, demonstrations. Then conduct whole-class feedback and ask students to share their ideas.

- Ask students to read the list of things that happened at the Open Day and decide which ones are successes and which are problems. If necessary, clarify the meaning of:

  suffer minor injuries – hurt yourself, but not seriously (item 7)

  litter bins – containers, normally made of plastic, that you put paper, cans and bottles into (item 10)

- Put students into pairs. They take turns to explain why they think the things are successes or problems.

> **Answers**
>
> 1 P   2 P   3 S   4 P   5 P   6 S   7 P   8 P
> 9 S   10 P   11 S

2

• Put students into pairs to discuss how to avoid repeating the problems. Don't conduct whole-class feedback at this stage: students will focus on the suggestions made in the meeting in Exercise 3.

• 🔊 22 Play the recording so that students can identify the points from Exercise 1 that the people talked about.

Transcript

J = Jason, T = Tamara, A = Andy

J: OK, so let's move on now to looking at last summer's Open Day. I think we all agree that it was a great success and we made a good profit on the day, but we still need to talk about how to avoid some of the things that went wrong.

T: Well, we can't do anything about the weather, unfortunately!

J: No, I know. And it hadn't rained for weeks before that day! Oh well. Why don't we think about setting up another covered area?

T: OK, let's look into that. I can do that. But I think the most important thing we need to sort out is the problem with the food. Two people said they'd got food poisoning from the burger stall.

J: Well, that may or may not be true.

T: It doesn't matter – it's a risk we can't afford to take. We should be careful here.

A: I couldn't agree more; that's our priority. We ought to check all the caterers more carefully and see what their certification is, and of course, I don't think we should have that burger stall back.

T: I heard that they went out of business! We made a big mistake getting them in the first place.

J: I think you're right. Actually, I don't think we need to have a burger stall.

T: I'm not sure I'm with you on that. Burgers are really popular and everyone expects them at this kind of thing.

A: OK, so we need to find a new burger stall and also we need to check the whole list of caterers and their certificates. I'll do that. What else?

J: Well, by the end of the day all the litter bins were overflowing and it looked terrible.

T: And I think that's connected to another point – we didn't really have enough volunteer helpers, did we? How about putting something out on Twitter to get more volunteers?

A: I like the sound of that. We got loads of coverage last year so obviously it's a good way of getting a message out.

T: And we could consider other ways of getting more followers on Twitter. I can have a look into that.

J: Yes, that's a good idea. Let's talk more about that next time.

T: It's a shame we ran out of T-shirts. We'd better get more printed this time.

A: OK ... or I could look at the prices first, they were quite a big cost and I think it's better to sell out than to be left with unsold T-shirts.

T: Yes, I think you're right, actually. That's a good point.

J: Now, the other major thing was the children that got hurt ...

Answers

They talk about the following points in this order:

it rained in the afternoon

two people got food poisoning

the litter bins overflowed

there weren't enough volunteer helpers

they ran out of T-shirts to sell

3

• Ask students to read the suggestions and the responses to suggestions in the Useful language box. Draw students' attention to the structures used for making suggestions, especially: Why don't we + infinitive, How about + -ing form, and We'd (We had) better + infinitive.

• Ask students to predict which responses could follow each of the suggestions based on what they think and what they can remember from the first time they listened to the recording.

• 🔊 22 Play the recording so that students can match the suggestions with the responses.

• Conduct whole-class feedback and then direct students to the transcript on page 167. Ask students to identify the phrases for making and responding to suggestions.

Answers

1 e 2 a 3 c 4 b 5 f 6 d

Pronunciation Intonation and meaning

4a

• 🔊 23 Look at an example with the class. Play the recording and pause after the first response. Ask students to listen and notice whether the speaker sounds enthusiastic or unsure. Elicit that the speaker says this response enthusiastically.

Transcript

1 I couldn't agree more.

2 I like the sound of that.

3 I'm not sure I'm with you on that.

4 OK ... or I could look at the prices first.

5 Let's look into that.

6 That's a good idea.

- Play the rest of the recording and ask students to decide if the speakers sound enthusiastic or unsure. Students could check their answers in pairs.

- Conduct whole-class feedback and ask students what features of the speakers' speech helped them to decide if they sounded enthusiastic or unsure. Possible answers could be: *speed, pitch, pace, rhythm, voice variety and the words the speakers stress*. Explain that Jason says sentence 6 quite enthusiastically, but it's what he says after sentence 6 (*Let's talk more about that next time*) which suggests he's unsure and unenthusiastic.

Answers

1 enthusiastic   2 enthusiastic   3 unsure   4 unsure
5 enthusiastic   6 unsure

- **Optional step.** Puts students into pairs. They take turns to say the responses in either an enthusiastic or an unsure tone. The listener's task is to decide whether the other student sounds enthusiastic or unsure. If necessary, model and drill one example response in an enthusiastic tone and one in an unsure tone before students start.

4b

- 🔊 **23** Play the recording and pause after each response so that students can listen and repeat.

SPEAKING Making and responding to suggestions

5   *21st* CENTURY OUTCOMES

- Before starting this exercise, refer students to the 21st CENTURY OUTCOMES at the foot of the page.

- Put students into small groups to look at the problems in the list in Exercise 1 and then to work together to make suggestions for the problems that weren't mentioned in the recording.

- Remind students to use the expressions from the Useful language box. Monitor students while they're making suggestions, offering help where necessary.

- Conduct whole-class feedback and ask students to share their suggestions.

- Students then work together again in their groups to think of and agree on two more activities or ideas for a company open day. Encourage students to focus on prioritizing, planning and managing their groupwork in order to fulfil this 21st CENTURY OUTCOME.

- Explain that everyone should make notes on the discussion. One person will need the notes in Exercise 6 and everyone will need them in Exercise 11.

6

- Ask students to choose a spokesperson from their group to present the ideas and activities they thought of in Exercise 5 to the rest of the class. Students should keep these presentations very simple, i.e. a maximum of two minutes.

- Remind the spokespeople to present their suggestions in an enthusiastic tone.

- The spokespeople present their group's ideas to the rest of the class. Write each of the suggestions they make on the board. Then ask the class to vote for the best two suggestions.

WRITING Minutes (1)

7

- Draw students' attention to the section heading: *Minutes (1)*. Elicit or explain that *minutes* are a written record of what happened during a meeting.

- Bring in students' own experiences. Ask: *Have you ever written or read meeting minutes? If so, can you remember what was in them?*

- Ask students to read the email that was sent out before the meeting in Exercise 2 and to identify the point which deals with the Open Day. They can compare their answers in pairs.

Answer

2

- Students may not be familiar with the term *AOB*, but don't clarify or confirm its meaning at this stage as students will look at this in Exercise 9.

8

- Tell students to read the extracts and to identify which points from the email in Exercise 7 are referred to in these extracts. Students can check their answers in pairs before you check with the whole class.

Answer

2 A

9

- Look at item 1 as an example with the class. Elicit that *agenda* refers to what is going to be discussed at a meeting.

- Ask students to look at the email and minutes again, and to work out the meaning of the other items from their context.

> **Answers**
>
> 1 the list of things to be discussed at the meeting
>
> 2 any other business – anything else to be talked about that isn't on the agenda
>
> 3 people who attended the meeting
>
> 4 people who have apologized for not being able to attend

Writing skill Bullet points

10a

- Elicit or explain that bullet points are usually short sentences or phrases. We use bullet points to organize pieces of information, e.g. action points from a meeting, in list form and they can help us to present information more clearly. Elicit that there are five bullet points in the agenda.

- Look at the questions with the class. If necessary, clarify the meaning of:

> *initials* – the first letters of a name or word, usually of a person's name (question 2)

> **Answers**
>
> 1 imperative   2 the initials of the person who will be responsible for the action

10b

- Elicit that if the action points are written as complete sentences, the first words will be the name of the person who is going to do the task. Also elicit that the verb form will change from imperative to *will* + infinitive.

- Ask students to write the action points as complete sentences. They can do this in pairs.

> **Answers**
>
> Tamara Watson will look into setting up an additional covered area.
>
> Andy Carhill will check the caterers' certificates.
>
> Andy Carhill will find a different burger stall to hire
>
> Tamara Watson will use Twitter to get more volunteers.
>
> Andy Carhill will check the prices of the T-shirts

10c

- Look at sentence 1 as an example with the class. Elicit that this could be written as *find a new venue for next open day.*

- Students write the other sentences as bullet points. They can either work on their own and then compare their sentences with a partner, or they can work in pairs to write the bullet points. Remind them to include the bracketed initials of the person who is going to do the task.

- Conduct whole-class feedback and invite six students to write one of the bullet points each on the board. Elicit that no one person is responsible for the first action.

> **Answers**
>
> find a new venue for our next open day
>
> get a quote for a children's entertainer (AC)
>
> check the latest health and safety regulations (TW)
>
> find a new company to design the promotional material (AC)
>
> send everyone a new budget outline (JL)
>
> investigate collaborations with other charities (TW, JL)

11

- Put students into groups so that they work with the people they worked with in Exercise 5. Ask students to look at the notes they made in their discussion in Exercise 5.

- Tell students to use their notes to write sections 2B and 3 from the agenda. They can do this either as a group or in pairs.

- Remind student to use bullet points for their action points.

12

- Ask students to exchange their minutes with another group.

- Tell students to read the questions and to use these to evaluate the minutes of the other group.

- Tell students to make notes on the feedback they want to give the other group or pair. Their feedback should include the extent to which the minutes have fulfilled the objectives in the questions, and reasons and evidence from the minutes to support their opinions.

- Ask students to give their feedback on the minutes to the other group. Encourage students to respond to and possibly disagree with the feedback, where appropriate.

- Conduct whole-class feedback and ask students to tell the class about any ideas they have read about that they think would work.

▶ Photocopiable communicative activity 4.2: Go to page 220 for practice of making and responding to suggestions, and writing a plan of action after a meeting. The teaching notes are on page 240.

▶ Set Workbook pages 40–41 for homework.

▶ Set Workbook Writing 2 on pages 42–43 for homework.

REVIEW 2 | UNITS 3 AND 4

READING Krochet Kids

1

> ### Answers
> 1 Kohl, Travis, Stewart   2 Uganda   3 wool   4 150
> 5 Peru

2

> ### Answers
> 1 It wasn't a typical 'boy' skill.
>
> 2 They wanted to crochet their own unique and
> personalized hats to wear when snowboarding and skiing
> at the weekend.
>
> 3 It was a name used in a local newspaper headline about
> the boys.
>
> 4 He was working with people who had been living in
> government camps for more than twenty years.
>
> 5 Krochet Kids has expanded its operation to employ
> 150 women in Uganda and more in Peru.
>
> 6 a The women's personal income has increased as
> much as ten times.
>
> b They are able to save up to 25 times more money than
> before.
>
> c Their children are 25 times more likely to have
> increased their school attendance.
>
> d Families are five times healthier than they used to be.
>
> e The incidence of domestic abuse has fallen by 40 per
> cent for these women and they have become more
> involved in decision-making in the home.

GRAMMAR

3

> ### Answers
> 1 has increased   2 have been fighting   3 has given
> 4 have developed   5 has been looking   6 have been
> making

4

> ### Answers
> 1 had moved   2 found   3 didn't have   4 had been
> struggling   5 used to take   6 was working   7 heard
> 8 had   9 needed   10 didn't have to   11 provided

VOCABULARY

5

> ### Answers
> 1 influential   2 qualitative   3 security   4 growing
> 5 success   6 motivated   7 safety   8 perfect

6

> ### Answers
> 1 success   2 failure   3 expertise   4 planning
> 5 mistake   6 truth   7 knowledge   8 experience

DISCUSSION

7

> ### Suggested answers
> 1 Commercial companies usually measure success in
> terms of profit. *Krochet Kids* is more likely to measure
> success in terms of how many women it can help to earn
> money and to become independent.
>
> 2 Students' own answers, though they may mention that
> hard work, identification of a market and good promotion
> are keys to their success.
>
> 3 Students' own answers, though they may say that in
> the West possessions and lifestyle are used to measure
> success.

SPEAKING

8

> ### Answers
> 1 How about looking at the Krochet Kids website?
> 2 I like the sound of that.
> 3 We'd better book a restaurant for a meal.
> 4 Or we could do something different this year.
> 5 Why don't we think about changing
> 6 Yes, that's a good idea.
> 7 I'm not sure I'm with you on that.
> 8 I don't think we need to completely change.

WRITING

9

> ### Suggested answers
> 1 Upload website content Mon morn.
>
> 2 Return Fairtrade call before 12.00. Set up meeting
> Thurs/Fri.
>
> 3 Confirm sales figures Oct–Dec. Forward to Marta Thurs
> latest.
>
> 4 Look into new venue children's festival. Call Mike
> Wed 3.30.

5 Exercise

LEAD IN

• Books open. Draw students' attention to the unit title, and to the photo on pages 52–53 and its caption. If necessary, clarify the meaning of:

lap – swimming from one end of the pool to the other (caption, top line)

• Bring in students' own experiences. Ask: *Do you like swimming? Is swimming good exercise? What types of exercise do you do? How often do you exercise? How does it make you feel?* This could be a whole-class discussion or students could discuss the questions in pairs.

• To gauge students' prior knowledge of the unit vocabulary, draw a Venn diagram with two intersecting circles on the board. Write *business* in one of the circles and *sport* in the other. Put students into pairs to discuss what business and sport have in common with each other, i.e. things that are important in the business world which are also important in the world of sport. These are the things which fit into the overlapping parts of the two circles in the Venn diagram. If students are unsure about where the two areas converge, give an example: teamwork – it is important in both business and sport. Other things that business and sport include: hierarchy, management, sponsorship, advertising, league tables / ranking, uniforms, negotiations, multi-million deals, etc. Ask students to complete a Venn diagram and then show it to another pair. They take turns to present the words they've chosen, giving reasons for their choices.

• Conduct whole-class feedback on the words students chose. If necessary, elicit the meaning of any words that are unknown to some members of the class.

TEDTALKS
BACKGROUND

1

• Ask students to read the text about Nilofer Merchant and her talk. If necessary, clarify the meaning of:

humanistic approach – an approach which assumes that every person has their own way of perceiving and understanding the world (line 6)

• Put students into pairs to discuss the questions. They can then compare their answers with another pair.

• **Question 2.** Remind students to recycle *used to* and *would* to compare the fitness of previous generations with those or people today. See Unit 4.2.

> **Suggested answers**
>
> 1 Students' own answers
>
> 2 Students' own answers
>
> 3 We can all be healthier, more productive and more creative if we have 'walking meetings'.

KEY WORDS

2

• Ask students to try to guess the meaning of the words in bold and then to match them with their definitions.

> **Answers**
>
> 1 c 2 a 3 e 4 b 5 f 6 d

AUTHENTIC LISTENING SKILLS Rising intonation

3a

• Ask students to read the information about rising intonation in the Authentic listening skills box.

• Explain that it's better for non-native speakers to use standard intonation, i.e. to only use rising intonation in questions, in order to minimize misunderstandings. However, it's good to be aware of the fact that native speakers may also use rising intonation in statements. This should reduce the chances of students misunderstanding them.

• Remind students that focusing on the grammatical structure of the extracts they hear should be helpful when they're deciding whether they're questions or statements. Elicit that the subject and auxiliary verb will be inverted in questions.

• 🔊 24 Play the recording so that students can decide whether the extracts are questions or statements.

Transcript

1 *Nowadays people are sitting 9.3 hours a day, which is more than we're sleeping …*

2 *Sitting is so incredibly prevalent, we don't even question how much we're doing it …*

3 *Of course there's health consequences to this, scary ones, besides the waist.*

4 *'I have to walk my dogs tomorrow. Could you come then?'*

• Check answers with the class. If necessary, play the recording again.

Answer

The intonation is rising in each extract, so it could be said that they sound like questions.

Background information

Rising intonation

Rising intonation in statements can be found in a wide range of English accents. Accents where it tends to be most frequently used include: Australian, New Zealand, Californian, Northern Irish, English West Midlands and Liverpudlian. Some commentators have been critical of the use of rising intonation in statements and see it as an example of inappropriate use of English.

3b

• Ask students to read the phrases and to decide whether they expect them to have a rising or falling intonation.

• 🔊 25 Play the recording so that students can check their answers.

Transcript

5 *Now, any of those stats should convince each of us to get off our duff more …*

6 *I've learned a few things …*

7 *First, there's this amazing thing about actually getting out of the box …*

• Conduct whole-class feedback. Elicit or explain that we can use rising intonation to indicate to our listeners that there is still more information to come and they, therefore, need to keep listening. We can also use rising intonation to add emphasis to a word or expression, as Nilofer Merchant does in extract 7 with 'amazing thing' and 'out of the box'.

Answers

The intonation in each sentence is:

5 rising   6 falling   7 two rising intonations, on 'amazing thing' and 'out of the box'

• Ask students to practise saying all the extracts (1–7) with falling intonation.

TEACHING TIP

Mumble drill

A 'mumble drill' involves saying phrases or sentences under your breath – in other words, mumbling them. Doing a 'mumble drill' can help students to prepare for saying phrases or sentences out loud with other students. You could ask students to do mumble drills with the extracts so that they can practise saying them with falling intonation before they practise saying them in pairs.

5.1 Got a meeting? Take a walk

TEDTALKS

1

• Books open. Ask students to complete the summary with five of the words in the box. They can do this in pairs.

• ▶ 5.1 Play the whole talk once so that students can check their answers.

Transcript

0.15 *What you're doing, right now, at this very moment, is killing you. More than cars or the Internet or even that little mobile device we keep talking about, the technology you're using the most almost every day is this, your tush. Nowadays people are sitting 9.3 hours a day, which is more than we're sleeping, at*

7.7 hours. Sitting is so incredibly prevalent, we don't even question how much we're doing it, and because everyone else is doing it, it doesn't even occur to us that it's not OK. In that way, sitting has become the smoking of our generation.

0.55 *Of course there's health consequences to this, scary ones, besides the waist. Things like breast cancer and colon cancer are directly tied to our lack of physical activity. Ten per cent in fact, on both of those. Six per cent for heart disease, seven per cent for type 2 diabetes, which is what my father died of. Now, any of those stats should convince each of us to get off our duff more, but if you're anything like me, it won't.*

1.22 *What did get me moving was a social interaction. Someone invited me to a meeting, but couldn't manage to fit me in to a regular sort of conference room meeting, and said, 'I have to walk my dogs tomorrow. Could you come then?' It seemed kind of odd to do, and actually, that first meeting, I remember thinking, 'I have to be the one to ask the next question,' because I knew I was going to huff and puff during this conversation. And yet, I've taken that idea and made it my own. So instead of going to coffee meetings or fluorescent-lit conference room meetings, I ask people to go on a walking meeting, to the tune of 20 to 30 miles a week. It's changed my life.*

2.03 *But before that, what actually happened was, I used to think about it as, you could take care of your health, or you could take care of obligations, and one always came at the cost of the other. So now, several hundred of these walking meetings later, I've learned a few things.*

2.19 *First, there's this amazing thing about actually getting out of the box that leads to out-of-the-box thinking. Whether it's nature or the exercise itself, it certainly works.*

2.30 *And second, and probably the more reflective one, is just about how much each of us can hold problems in opposition when they're really not that way. And if we're going to solve problems and look at the world really differently, whether it's in governance or business or environmental issues, job creation, maybe we can think about how to reframe those problems as having both things be true. Because it was when that happened with this walk-and-talk idea that things became doable and sustainable and viable.*

3.00 *So I started this talk talking about the tush, so I'll end with the bottom line, which is, walk and talk. Walk the talk. You'll be surprised at how fresh air drives fresh thinking, and in the way that you do, you'll bring into your life an entirely new set of ideas.*

3.18 *Thank you.*

3.19 (Applause)

Answers _____

1 smoking   2 physical   3 life   4 office   5 ideas

• Note the differences in North American English and British English shown at the foot of the spread. In this unit, these focus on vocabulary, pronunciation and spelling differences. See page 6 of the Introduction for ideas on how to present and practise these differences.

• **Optional step.** Put students into small groups to discuss their opinions. Ask: *How unhealthy do you think sitting really is? Would you agree that serious illnesses are tied to a lack of physical activity? Are we more capable of out-of-the-box thinking when we're outside the office than inside it?* Then conduct whole-class feedback.

2

• ▶ **5.1** Play the first part (0.00–1.22) of the talk so that students can complete the notes.

• Conduct whole-class feedback and, if necessary, clarify the meaning of:

   breast – the upper front part of the body (answer 3)

   colon – a part of the large intestine (answer 3)

• Draw students' attention to the use of the full stop as a decimal point in English. A comma may be used instead of a full stop in students' L1.

Answers _____

1 9.3   2 7.7   3 breast, colon   4 six   5 seven

3

• ▶ **5.1** Give students time to read the extracts and the questions. Then play the second part (1.22–2.19) of the talk without pausing. Use the activity as a test of how much students can recall. Conduct whole-class feedback on the answers to the questions. Ask students to put their hands up if they know the answer to a question to avoid stronger students dominating the feedback session.

• **Optional step.** Alternatively, you could pause the recording after each extract and give students time to make notes on their ideas. Students can then compare their notes in pairs and check their answers during whole-class feedback.

Answers _____

1 having a meeting with someone who was walking their dogs

2 she asks people to go on walking meetings with her

3 obligations

4

• Play the third part (2.19 to the end) of the talk so that students can check whether the sentences are true or false.

Answers _____

1 T   2 T

5

• Put students into pairs to discuss the questions. Monitor students while they're speaking and collect examples of interesting language. You can then share these examples with the whole class at the end of the exercise.

> **Answer**
> She means that getting exercise outside while you work makes you think in a different way.

• **Optional step.** After a few minutes' discussion, invite volunteers to share their opinions on what Nilofer Merchant means by *fresh air drives fresh thinking*. Encourage students to tell the class about a time when this has been true for them.

VOCABULARY IN CONTEXT

6

• ▶ **5.2** Play the clips from the talk. When each multiple-choice question appears, pause the clip so that students can choose the correct definition.

• Note that Nilofer Merchant actually and mistakenly says *inactivity* in the first clip. Elicit or explain, if necessary, that a *mile* (clip 3) is about 1.6 kilometres.

Transcript and subtitles

*1   Things like breast cancer and colon cancer are directly **tied** to our lack of physical activity.*
   a causing
   b connected
   c equal with

*2   It seemed **kind of odd** to do*
   a a bit strange
   b quite generous
   c perfectly reasonable

*3   I ask people to go on a walking meeting, **to the tune of** 20 to 30 miles a week.*
   a listening to music
   b to the amount of
   c exercising

*4   Because it was when that happened with this walk-and-talk idea that things became **doable** and sustainable and viable.*
   a difficult
   b clear
   c possible

*5   so I'll end with **the bottom line***
   a the lowest level
   b a new idea
   c the key thing

> **Answers**
> 1 b   2 a   3 b   4 c   5 c

7

• Review the meaning of the expressions *doable*, *tied to* and *kind of odd* with the class.

• Ask students to read the statements and to decide whether they agree or disagree with them.

• Put students into pairs to share their opinions. Encourage students to support their opinions with reasons.

• Monitor students while they're speaking. Make a note of which students agree and disagree with the statements. Allow 5–10 minutes for discussion.

• Invite individual students with differing views to share their opinions and reasons for them with the class.

CRITICAL THINKING Reflecting on experiences

8

• Elicit or explain that reflection involves recalling what happened, analysing the causes and consequences of your actions or feelings in that situation, and then considering how you could have done things more successfully and what changes you could make if you find yourself in that situation again.

• Ask students to read the options. If necessary, clarify the meaning of:

   mutually exclusive – not able to exist at the same time or directly contradictory to each other (option a)

• Ask students to identify what Nilofer Merchant realized when she reflected on her experience of walking meetings.

• Conduct whole-class feedback, and establish that Nilofer Merchant believes that health and work can be combined, i.e. they don't have to be mutually exclusive.

> **Answer**
> a

• **Optional step.** Invite students to suggest other pairs of things which they see as mutually exclusive, e.g. playing video games and learning, eating a lot and being healthy, travelling a lot and having a full-time job. Write a list on the board. Ask students to reflect on whether the pairs of things on the board really are mutually exclusive. Ask: *Can you imagine scenarios where the two things could be combined?* A possible answer with the example of playing video games and learning could be: *Some video games can help us to learn.*

9

• Ask students to read the comments about the TED Talk. Put students into pairs to discuss the question.

• Tell students that they can refer to the transcript for the talk on page 176 while answering the question.

• Conduct whole-class feedback on students' responses to the question.

• **Optional step.** Ask students to write their own comment in which they say what they've learned from their experience, and what they've learned from the Ted Talk about links between moving around and getting fresh air on the one hand and productivity at work on the other. When they've finished writing, put students into pairs or small groups to read and to give feedback on each other's comment.

PRESENTATION TIPS Beginning with a strong statement

10

• Ask students to read about beginning with a strong statement in the Presentation tips box. Explain that a strong statement used at the start of a presentation can also be called a 'hook.' Elicit that a strong statement is designed to hook the audience, i.e. get their attention and make them want to carry on listening.

• Look at the opening sentence with the class. You could ask students to complete the opening sentence based on what they can remember from watching the talk. They can do this in pairs.

• ▶ 5.3 Play the clip so that students can complete the opening sentence. Then conduct whole-class feedback to confirm the completed opening sentence.

Transcript

What you're doing, right now, at this very moment, is killing you.

• Put students into pairs to discuss which technique Nilofer Merchant is using. They can also discuss how successfully she uses this technique and whether it would have been more appropriate to use another technique to begin this particular presentation. Encourage students to give reasons for their answers.

Answers

is killing you

This opening sentence is surprising – unless you have heard that sitting isn't good for you before.

• **Optional step.** Ask students: *Can you remember any examples of strong statements used at the start of other presentations you've seen? If so, which technique did the speaker use?*

11

• Draw students' attention to the statistics. Elicit or explain that statistics can sometimes be quite dry, i.e. boring. It is, therefore, especially important that presenters are able to present them in a way that gets and keeps the audience's attention.

• Give students 10–15 minutes to prepare opening statements and the first few lines of a presentation for each of the statistics.

• Encourage students to try out all three techniques from the Presentation tips box and to consider which technique would work best for each of the statistics they're going to present.

• Direct students to the illustrations for the statistics – they may be able to find some inspiration for their opening statements there.

• Tell students to follow their opening statements with a sentence explaining what the statistic means, e.g. *So … , Which means … , Therefore … , As a result … ,* and then a comment on the statistic. Their comment could be their opinion on the reason for the problem, or they could recycle language for suggestions (see Unit 4.4) and make suggestions for how the issue can be resolved.

• **Optional step.** Put students into pairs. They take turns to give the opening of the three presentations. The other student should give feedback on how successfully their partner got and kept their attention.

12

• Put students into pairs. They take turns to give their presentation. Note that each student can give more than one presentation.

• Remind students to focus on getting their partner's attention at the start of the presentation. The other student should give feedback on how successfully their partner got and kept their attention.

• Monitor students while they're presenting and collect interesting examples of opening statements, which you can share with the whole class afterwards.

- **Optional step.** Students modify their opening statements in response to their partner's feedback and do their presentation again for another student.

▶ Set Workbook pages 44–45 for homework.

5.2 Overcoming challenges

GRAMMAR Modals and related verbs: past forms (1)

1

- Books open. Draw students' attention to the spread title: *Overcoming challenges*. Elicit or explain that when you overcome a challenge, you successfully deal with it and don't let it stop you doing what you want to do.

- Bring in students' own experiences. Put students into small groups to discuss challenges that they have overcome in their lives and what they did in order to overcome them.

- Conduct whole-class feedback on the challenges students have overcome, and how. Write any useful vocabulary connected to the theme of overcoming challenges on the board. Elicit or explain the meaning of any unknown vocabulary.

- Look at the instructions with the class. Put students into pairs to make a list of as many different sports as they can think of. You could do this activity as a timed task and give students two minutes to write their list. They should also agree on an order for the sports according to how dangerous they think they are.

- Conduct whole-class feedback and try to agree on a class order for the sports. Revise associated vocabulary, such as team/individual sports, names for places where sports take place, and people who do sports.

2

- Ask students if tennis was on their list of sports and what rank they gave it in their ranking of dangerous sports. Ask: *How dangerous is tennis really? Are there any dangers or problems that you could encounter when playing it?* Students can discuss these questions in pairs.

- Ask students to look at the infographic and to compare the information about tennis injuries with what they had thought. If necessary, clarify the meaning of:

  wrist – the joint between your arm and your hand (top left)

  ankle – the joint between your leg and your foot (bottom left)

- Conduct whole-class feedback on how surprised students were by the information in the infographic and whether there was anything they found particularly surprising.

Answers

Students' own answers, but the infographic shows that tennis is perhaps more dangerous than we imagine.

- Bring in students' own experiences. Ask: *Have you heard of these tennis players mentioned in the questions? If so, what do you know about them?*

3

- 🎧 26 Play the recording so that students can choose the correct option to complete the sentences.

Transcript

A: We don't normally think of tennis as being a particularly risky or dangerous sport, and yet looking back over the last few years, almost all the top players seem to have been injured at some time. Was it always like this?

B: No, I don't think so. There are several reasons why professional tennis is so demanding these days. One is simply the huge number of tournaments there are. In the past, players could rest between big matches, but nowadays players don't get time to get over injuries. Like Juan Martin del Potro – he hurt his hip early in 2011 and he wasn't able to recover until the 2011 season ended. He said that he'd considered retiring several times and it was only the encouragement of his friends that kept him going.

A: Ah yes? I remember Novak Djokovic saying something similar in 2013. He had an ankle injury and said he managed to keep going with his teammates' support, despite the pain. But not everyone has been so lucky, have they? It was a tragedy that Rafael Nadal couldn't defend his Wimbledon title in 2009 because of recurring problems with his left knee.

B: Nadal suffers a lot. He had to miss the US Open in 2014 because of a wrist injury too. It's interesting that he doesn't like to blame injury when he loses, though. Remember Steve Darcis? He succeeded in beating Nadal in a first-round match in 2013, but unfortunately it left him with a damaged shoulder.

A: Yes, he dropped out injured before the second round.

B: And what about Andy Murray? When he was younger, he could play five-set matches easily, but I think his back injury has changed things.

A: Oh yes …he had to have surgery on his back and it's definitely affected his stamina.

B: But what about age? Do you think that's a factor too?

Answers

1 b   2 c   3 b   4 a

4

- Ask students to read the sentences in the Grammar box. You could ask them to predict who *He* in each sentence refers to based on what they can remember from the first time they listened to the recording. They can do this in pairs.

- ⒜ 26 Play the recording again so that students can check who *He* refers to. Alternatively, students can look at the transcript on page 168.

> **Answers**
>
> Rafa Nadal couldn't defend his Wimbledon title in 2009.
>
> Juan Martin del Potro wasn't able to recover until the 2011 season ended.
>
> Juan Martin del Potro / Novak Djokovic managed to keep going with his teammates' support, despite the pain.
>
> Steve Darcis succeeded in beating Nadal in a first-round match.
>
> Andy Murray had to have surgery on his back.

5

- Ask students to read the sentences again, focusing on the words in bold. If necessary, clarify the meaning of:

  ability – what someone or something can do (question 1b)

  necessity – the need to do something (question 1c)

- Tell students to answer the questions and then compare their answers in pairs.

- **Optional step.** Ask students to use the information in the infographic and to write one or more sentences about Roger Federer using one of the modals or related verbs. For example: *Roger Federer was able to defend his Wimbledon title in 2004. In fact, he succeeded in winning five times in a row. He didn't manage to beat Novak Djokovic in the 2015 Wimbledon final.*

- Students can check their answers and overall understanding of modals and related verbs by turning to the Grammar summary on page 148.

> **Answers**
>
> 1 a *can (not)* + infinitive without *to*
>
> b *can (not)* + infinitive without *to*, *to (not) be able to* + infinitive, *manage to* + infinitive, *succeed in* + *-ing*
>
> c *must* + infinitive without *to* / *have to* + infinitive
>
> 2 *couldn't, wasn't able to, managed to, succeeded in*
>
> 3 He couldn't defend his Wimbledon title in 2009. = He wasn't able to …
>
> He managed to keep going with his teammates' support, despite the pain. = He succeeded in keeping going …
>
> He succeeded in beating Nadal in a first-round match. = He managed to beat …

- If you feel that students need more controlled practice before continuing, they could do some or all of Exercises 1–4 in the Grammar summary. Otherwise, you could continue on to Exercise 6 in the unit and set the Grammar summary exercises for homework.

> **Answers to Grammar summary exercises**
>
> **1**
>
> 1 were able to talk 2 was able to give 3 *both*
> 4 Were you able to find 5 was able to pass 6 *both*
>
> **2**
>
> 1 c 2 b 3 d 4 f 5 e 6 a
>
> **3**
>
> 1 succeeded in getting 2 managed to fit 3 wasn't able to take 4 Did (you) manage to get 5 were able to beat 6 didn't succeed in reaching
>
> **4**
>
> 1 had to think about 2 was able to make 3 succeeded in coming up with 4 could do 5 weren't able to use 6 managed to deal with 7 didn't have to hire

6

- Look at the instructions with the class. Ask: *What does being a triathlete involve? What qualities or characteristics would you expect a triathlete to have?* Write a list of words on the board as students mention them.

- **Optional step.** Bring in students' own experiences. Ask: *Have you ever watched a triathlon on TV or seen one live? Do you know anyone who's done a triathlon? Do you think you would have what it takes?* Students can discuss the questions in pairs.

- Draw students' attention to the photo. Ask students to read the text and to choose the correct options to complete it.

> **Answers**
>
> 1 had to 2 couldn't 3 were able to 4 was able to
> 5 managed to

7

- Ask students to complete the comments with verbs from the Grammar box. Explain that they can use some of the verbs more than once. Students could check their answers in pairs before you check with the whole class.

> **Answers**
>
> 1 succeeded in 2 couldn't 3 couldn't, had to, managed to 4 had to, wasn't able to, managed to

- Students can discuss in pairs whether they can relate to any of the comments.

- Conduct whole-class feedback and encourage students to say which comments they can and can't relate to, giving reasons for their answers.

- **Optional step.** Put students into small groups. They take turns to share an anecdote about a sport or fitness challenge that they or someone they know has experienced. Remind them to use appropriate narrative tenses. The other students in the group can then say how much they can relate to the anecdotes.

SPEAKING Getting motivated

8 21st **CENTURY OUTCOMES**

- Tell students that in this exercise they're going to establish some personal health goals and they can then monitor their progress towards these goals afterwards in order to fulfil the 21st CENTURY OUTCOME. If possible, you could ask students to report back on how much progress they've made towards achieving these goals a week or a month later in order to motivate them to monitor this.

- Put students into groups to read the list of excuses and discuss whether they've ever used any of them. Students could also explain why they made these excuses and/or what were the real reasons they didn't want to exercise.

- Ask students to brainstorm different activities that people can do to get fit. Encourage them to think beyond the obvious, and to come up with some more unusual and original ideas.

- **Optional step.** Ask each group, or a spokesperson from each group, to present their ideas to the rest of the class.

9

- Put students into pairs and get them to decide who is Student A and who is Student B.

- Look at an example conversation with the class. Begin: *I don't take exercise. I haven't got time.* Encourage students to look at the ideas and to suggest an activity for someone who hasn't got time. Encourage individual students to make suggestions.

- Give students time to prepare for the conversation. Student A can prepare by choosing an excuse from Exercise 8 and thinking about how to convince their partner that it's a valid one. Student B should look at the ideas, and think about how you can motivate and encourage someone to do more sport or to get fit when they don't want to.

- Encourage students to use language for making and responding to suggestions, which they looked at in Unit 4.4.

- Students take turns to choose an excuse. Monitor students while they're speaking, noting any examples of good conversations. Then ask students whose conversation you have noted to repeat the conversation for the rest of the class.

▶ Photocopiable communicative activity 5.1 Go to page 221 for further practice of modals and related verbs: past forms, and making excuses. The teaching notes are on page 241.

▶ Set Workbook pages 46–47 for homework.

5.3 The bottom line

READING What's in a name?

1

- Books open. Draw students' attention to the spread title: *The bottom line.* Remind the class that *the bottom line* was used in the TED Talk to mean 'the most important point'. In this spread title, it has the more common meaning of 'the amount of profit'.

- Ask: *What links are there between 'sport' and 'profit'?* Possible answers could be: *sport clubs and associations are run for profit, professional sports people can make a lot of money from sport, a lot of merchandise is produced and sold at a profit by sports clubs and associations.* Students can discuss these questions in pairs.

- Conduct whole-class feedback and write on the board any useful vocabulary connected to the theme of sport and profit that students mention. Elicit or explain the meaning of any unknown vocabulary.

- Ask students to read the news headlines, and to identify the sport and the sponsor in each one. Students could check their answers in pairs before you check with the whole class.

Answers

football, Adidas

Formula 1 racing, Casio

cycling, Sky

- **Optional step.** Put students into pairs to rank the sports teams or events and the sponsors according to the general public's level of awareness of them. They should give reasons for their ranking. Then conduct whole-class feedback.

Background information

Sport and sponsorship

Manchester United is a world-famous English football club.

Adidas is a Germany-based sports equipment company that sponsors sports teams and events.

Red Bull Racing is an Australian Formula One racing team based in Milton Keynes, UK, which is owned by the Red Bull beverage company.

Casio is a Japanese electronics company which produces calculators, cameras, mobile phones and watches.

Sky is a British telecommunications company that provides satellite television and internet access. The company is known for spending large amounts of money on buying the rights to sporting events, especially football.

Extra activity

Sports sponsorship headlines

Ask students to go online and to find some recent sport-related headlines in English. They could start by searching for 'sports news'. Ask students to specifically look for headlines which mention sponsorship deals or other relationships between sports and corporations. Students can search individually and then share the headlines they've found in pairs or small groups, explaining what the connection is between the sports and the companies.

2

• Put students into pairs to brainstorm other sport sponsorship partnerships that they know. Then conduct whole-class feedback.

• Ask students to focus on the sports in the box and to discuss what companies might sponsor them, and why. Then conduct whole-class feedback.

• **Optional step.** Ask students: *Which sport do you think attracts the most and the least sponsorship, and why?*

3

• Put students into pairs to discuss the questions.

• Conduct whole-class feedback. Don't confirm whether any of these ideas are mentioned in the article at this stage. If necessary, introduce and clarify the meaning of:

   brand awareness – the extent to which consumers know about the existence of a product (perhaps needed in students' answers)

4

• Students read the article quickly to check their ideas from Exercise 3. Then conduct whole-class feedback.

Answers

1 Sponsorship brings in money.

2 They get the company's name known and raise brand awareness.

3 Sponsorship, unlike advertising, doesn't focus on the features or aspects of specific products.

4 The most typical partnerships are between sports products (clothing, equipment, etc.) and teams.

5

• Ask students to read the article again and to find the answers to the questions.

Answers

1 The club's owner was looking for a new sponsorship deal and estimated that a new name for the stadium would bring in up to £10 million a year.

2 They reacted with anger.

3 The sponsor restored the original stadium name.

4 On a global scale, sports sponsorship is estimated to be worth tens of billions of dollars a year.

5 Media companies are eager to sign up the rights to show events because television reaches massive national and international audiences.

6

• Ask students to find the expressions in the article and to write the preposition that completes each one.

Answers

1 with   2 over   3 for   4 to   5 on   6 across
7 behind   8 in

7

• Put students into pairs to brainstorm examples of minority-interest sports, e.g. base jumping, body building, taekwondo. If students have access to the Internet, they could go online and search for examples of minority-interest sports too. Write the sports on the board as students mention them.

• Ask students to discuss how the difficulties minority-interest sports have in attracting sponsorship affects them. Then conduct whole-class feedback.

• **Optional step.** Put students into small groups to brainstorm ways in which minority-interest interest sports could attract more sponsorship.

VOCABULARY Finance

8

• Draw students' attention to the section heading: *Finance*. Ask students to brainstorm words that they connect with *finance*. Write a list of words on the board as students mention them.

• Ask students to look at the nouns in the box. If necessary, clarify the meaning of:

   debt – something that is owed to someone, typically money (fourth word, top row)

• Elicit or explain that *debt* is pronounced /det/ with a silent /b/. If necessary, model and drill its pronunciation.

• Look at item 1 as an example with the class. Elicit that *balance the* should be followed by *books*.

• Ask students to complete the expressions with the nouns and then to check their answers in the questions in Exercise 9.

Answers

1 balance the books   2 charge a fee   3 control your finances   4 form a partnership   5 get into debt
6 invest money   7 make an offer   8 make a deal
9 sponsor an event   10 work out a budget

- **Optional step.** Ask students to create more verb + noun collocations connected with finance using the words that they brainstormed. These could include: *take out a loan, pay interest, make a loss/profit, grow/expand a business, borrow money.*

9

- Put students into pairs to discuss the questions.

- Encourage students to use the finance-related verb + noun combinations from the questions in their answers.

SPEAKING A sponsored event

10   **21st CENTURY OUTCOMES**

- Before starting this exercise, refer students to the 21st CENTURY OUTCOMES at the foot of the page. This 21st CENTURY OUTCOME also featured in Unit 4.4.

- Put students into groups (4–5 students). Explain that they are going to organize a sponsored event.

- **Optional step.** Tell students to assign each group member a specific role within the event organization project, e.g. team leader, secretary, finance representative, sponsorship representative. Students can then make an agenda for the group's meeting based on the points they have to make decisions on.

- Students have a meeting in which they brainstorm and discuss ideas for the event. They should reach a consensus on what kind of event of it should be, who will benefit and where they can get sponsorship.

- **Optional step.** In order to give students further practice in writing minutes, the secretary (or possibly secretaries) in the group could make notes on what is discussed and decided on during the group discussion and then write these up as minutes. See Unit 4.4.

11

- Students could choose one spokesperson from their group to present the plans or they could do a team presentation where two, three or even all four or five students each present part of their plans.

- Give students about five minutes to prepare their presentation.

- **Optional step.** Students could prepare slides and use them as visual aids to present their plans to the class.

- When all the groups have presented their plan, ask students to vote for the best plan(s). Students can do this by a show of hands. Conduct whole-class feedback and ask students to explain why they voted for the plans that they did.

▶ Set Workbook pages 48–49 for homework.

5.4 Who funded you?

LISTENING Young entrepreneurs

1

- Books open. Draw students' attention to the spread title: *Who funded you?* Ask: *Where do new businesses get the money to start up? Who funds them?*

- Ask students to read the words in the box. They match the terms with the definitions and then complete the sentences.

Answers
___

1 banks   2 private loan   3 personal savings
4 shareholders   5 angel investors   6 crowd funding

Background information

Funding

The UK-produced BBC television programme *Dragon's Den* gives young inventors the opportunity to pitch their business ideas to angel investors. Students may have seen the original version or a locally produced version in their home country, so you might want to use the 'dragons' from the programme as an example of angel investors.

Kickstarter is a company launched in 2009 in order to give people an online crowdsourcing platform for creative projects. Inventors and entrepreneurs post details of their projects online and visitors to the Kickstarter website can donate money to help fund them. Kickstarter could, therefore, be used as an example of crowdsourcing.

Extra activity

Kickstarter projects

If possible, students could visit the Kickstarter website and look at some example projects. Put students into groups to choose a selection of about five different projects. They agree on criteria to use to decide which project would be the best one to invest in, e.g. how innovative, unique, potentially profitable, marketable a project is. Then students use these criteria to decide which one of the projects they would invest in if they were angel investors. They could then present the chosen project and their reasons for deciding to invest in it to the rest of the class.

2

- Explain that students are going to listen to part of a radio programme about young inventors with new business ideas.

- Put students into pairs to speculate on possible business ideas that a young inventor could have and the sources of investment a young inventor could raise funds from. Encourage students to use the vocabulary from Exercise 1 in their discussion. Then conduct whole-class feedback.

- 🔊 27 Play the recording so that students can answer the questions.

Transcript

P = Presenter, R = Ryan

P: *So, Ryan, you're going to tell us about your amazing 'smart' cushion that should help us keep fit at our desks, aren't you?*

R: *Yes, I am. Basically it monitors your body and sends a message to your phone when to take a break and move around.*

P: *Where did the idea come from?*

R: *From my final-year project at college, actually. I was working on something completely different but spending so long in front of the computer that I could feel the effect on my body – and I'm only 22!*

P: *So tell us about how you got the money to develop your idea into an actual product. Who funded you? Did you go to a bank?*

R: *No, we didn't. My partner suggested asking my parents for a loan, but I didn't want to. Actually, we worried that it would be hard to find investors, but it wasn't. We managed to raise about £60,000 which all came from Kickstarter, and that was about three times our target!*

P: *That's impressive! So, can we buy this wonderful cushion in the shops?*

R: *Not yet. We're still developing it and we haven't got a name yet. People keep telling us a brand name is really important, so we're giving it as much thought as we can.*

P: *Well, Ryan, good luck and I for one can't wait to get myself one of your cushions.*

- Check answers with the class. If necessary, play the recording again.

Answers

1 It monitors your body and sends a message to your phone when to take a break and move around.

2 He was working on something completely different for his final-year project at college, but spending so long in front of the computer that he could feel the effect on his body.

3 about £60,000.

4 Kickstarter

5 They're still developing it.

3

- 🔊 27 Play the recording again so that students can complete the extracts. Check answers with the class. If necessary, play the recording again.

Answers

1 're going to tell us   2 come from   3 Did you go
4 asking my parents   5 find investors   6 can we buy
7 're giving

4

- Look at the Useful language box with the class. Check that students understand the meaning of *ellipsis*. (See Background information.) You could give an example to clarify. For example: *I've never had a private loan, but my brother has (had a private loan).* Elicit that it is not necessary to repeat *had a private loan*.

- Ask students to identify the questions in Exercise 3 (these are items 1, 2, 3 and 6) and to match the four answers with these questions.

- Ask students to match the statements with the remaining extracts (items 4, 5 and 7). They could then check their answers in the transcript on page 168 before you check with the class.

- Put students into pairs. Ask students to focus on which words the speaker omits in each expression in the Useful language box.

- Conduct whole-class feedback on which words could be omitted. Elicit that these words could be missed out because you don't need them in order to understand the meaning of what the speaker wants to say.

Answers

1 d   2 a   3 b   4 e   5 f   6 c   7 g

1 Yes, I am (going to tell you about my amazing 'smart' cushion).

2 (I got the idea) from my final-year project at college.

3 No, we didn't (go to a bank).

4 I didn't want to (ask my parents).

5 it wasn't (hard to find investors)

6 (You can) not yet (buy this wonderful cushion in the shops).

7 we can (give it)

Background information

Ellipsis

Ellipsis is the omission of information by a speaker or writer either because this information is superfluous or because the speaker or writer thinks that their message will still be clear for their audience when it is omitted. Ellipsis can help us to avoid the unnecessary repetition of words or expressions. It tends to be used more frequently in spoken than written English, particularly when answering questions. Using ellipsis can help students to make their English sound more natural.

Pronunciation Stress in ellipsis

5a

• If necessary, elicit or remind students that stress is the placing of more emphasis on some syllables within words or on some words in a sentence. Stressed words are usually the most important words, e.g. nouns and verbs.

• Tell students that they're going to listen and focus on which words in the Useful language box are stressed in ellipsis.

• Ask students to look at the matched items in Exercise 4 and to predict which words in the Useful language box will be stressed.

• ▣ 28 Play the recording so that students can check which words are stressed.

Transcript and answers

(underlining = stressed words)

P = Presenter, R = Ryan

1	P:	*So, Ryan, you're going to tell us about your amazing 'smart' cushion that should help us keep fit at our desks, aren't you?*
	R:	*Yes, I <u>am</u>.*
2	P:	*Where did the idea come from?*
	R:	*<u>From</u> my final-year project at college.*
3	P:	*Did you go to a bank?*
	R:	*No, we <u>didn't</u>.*
4	R:	*My partner suggested asking my parents for a loan, but I didn't <u>want to</u>.*
5	R:	*Actually, we worried that it would be hard to find investors, but it <u>wasn't</u>.*
6	R:	*People keep telling us a brand name is really important, so we're giving it as much thought as we <u>can</u>.*

• Conduct whole-class feedback and check that students noticed which words were stressed. If appropriate, play the recording again so that students can confirm their choices.

• **Optional step.** Ask students to look at the transcript on page 168. Put students into pairs to practise saying the exchanges with the same word stress they heard in the recording. Monitor students while they're practising to check that they're using word stress appropriately.

5b

• Ask students to read the questions and to think of their answers, using ellipsis. Remind students to decide which words in their answers should be stressed.

• Put students into pairs. They take turns to ask and answer the questions.

• Monitor students while they're speaking to check that they're using ellipsis and word stress appropriately.

SPEAKING Asking questions

6

• Elicit that *Q&A* stands for 'Question and Answer' and that an *online Q&A* is an online interview or live-chat session in which people can put their questions to someone who will then answer them.

• Ask students to read the information about Maya Penn and to think of three questions that they would send to the online Q&A session.

• **Optional step.** Give each student three cards or strips of paper. Ask students to write one of their questions on each card or strip of paper. Make sure they write their questions clearly so that other students will be able to read them in Exercise 7.

• Encourage students to think of original, interesting questions such as *How would your best friend describe you?* instead of more predictable ones such as *Where are you from? What do you do in your free time?*

• **Optional step.** Students can look at the TED website to find answers to the questions and watch Maya Penn's TED Talk.

7

• Put students into small groups to look at the questions they have written.

• Explain that they should identify whether any of the questions are similar or the same and group any such questions together. They should then organize their questions according to whether they think that they're very interesting, quite interesting or not very interesting.

• Encourage students to give reasons for their choices and to agree or disagree with each other's opinions, where appropriate. They should also make a final decision about which three questions are the most interesting.

• Monitor students while they're speaking, noting examples of good questions.

• Conduct whole-class feedback and ask students to share the questions which you have noted with the rest of the class.

Extra activity

Find out about it

Give students the name of a person, company, organization, etc. that is unknown to them and ask them to do an online search to find out more about this person or thing. For example, you could write the name Maya Penn on the board. If students have internet access, ask them to search for 'Maya Penn' and to find out as many facts as they can about her in five minutes. Conduct whole-class feedback on the facts students found.

WRITING An email (1)

8

• Ask students to read the email from Jake to Andy and to identify where the sections in italics come from. Students can compare their answers in pairs.

• Conduct whole-class feedback and make sure that students are clear about the fact that we sometimes include the original text of the email we received in our reply. Elicit that we include the original text so that our responses to the points made in the original email are very clear. Ask: *Have you ever done this when replying to an email?*

> **Answer**
> They come from Andy's original email.

9

• Ask students to read the email again and to focus on what Andy's original email was about.

• Tell students to choose the correct option. They can then check their answers in pairs.

• Conduct whole-class feedback on what Andy's original email was about. Ask students to give evidence from the email to support their choice.

> **Answer**
> b

Writing skill Questions

10a

• Look at each type of question in turn with the class. Elicit or explain that: *Don't* is a negative question word; an indirect question begins with a short phrase such as *I wonder* and is followed by the statement form of the verb; a tag question is a statement followed by a 'tag' – usually an affirmative statement followed by a negative tag, or a negative statement followed by an affirmative tag.

• Tell students to look at the email again and to decide why Jake used these question types. They can then discuss their answers in pairs.

• Conduct whole-class feedback. Discourage the more confident students from always giving the answer by asking people to raise their hand if they think they know.

• Students can check their answers and overall understanding of questions by turning to the Grammar summary on page 148.

> **Answers**
> 1 (And) wouldn't it be better to start with just one or two activities?
> 2a Can you explain exactly what activities you're thinking about?
> 2b I wonder if you could start off just using Twitter?

3 That's a bit soon, isn't it?

He asked questions 1, 2b and 3 in this way because the content words of his sentences reflected his opinion. He *thought it would be better to start off with one or two activities*, for example.

He used an indirect question in 2a to be less direct than asking *What activities are you thinking about exactly?*

• If you feel that students need more controlled practice before continuing, they could do some or all of Exercises 5–7 in the Grammar summary. Otherwise, you could continue on to Exercise 10b in the unit and set the Grammar summary exercises for homework.

> **Answers to Grammar summary exercises**
>
> **5**
> 1 Don't you want to come with us?
> 2 Isn't that Suzanne over there?
> 3 Wouldn't you prefer to meet on Friday?
> 4 Can you tell me how much it costs?
> 5 I was wondering if you've got any free time tomorrow?
> 6 Do you know why this machine doesn't work?
>
> **6**
> 1 You don't understand, do you?
> 2 It's a fantastic idea, isn't it?
> 3 You've read the document, haven't you?
> 4 They aren't coming until later, are they?
> 5 The plane arrived late again, didn't it?
> 6 You couldn't give me a hand, could you?
>
> **7**
> 1 When I was at school, we ~~must~~ **had** to work in groups quite often.
> 2 On our trip, we ~~could~~ **managed to** (*or* **were able to**) visit every capital city in South America.
> 3 I was so tired, but I ~~could~~ **was able to** make it to the end of the race.
> 4 I tried to tell you, but I ~~didn't could~~ **couldn't** find you.
> 5 The team succeeded ~~to win~~ **in winning** in the final minute.
> 6 We weren't able ~~to~~ finish the race.
> 7 I wonder what time ~~is it~~ **it is**?
> 8 You didn't phone the office, ~~isn't it~~ **did you**?

10b

• Draw students' attention to the fact that Jake chose not to use direct questions in his email. Elicit that this is because not using direct questions gives an impression of politeness and respect and is, therefore, more likely to result in a positive response.

- Ask students to rewrite the questions from the emails as direct questions. Students could check their answers in pairs before you check with the whole class.

Answers

1 What activities are you thinking about exactly?

2 Would it be better to start with just one or two activities?

3 Could you start off just using Twitter?

4 Is that a bit soon?

10c

- Look at question 1 as an example with the class. Elicit that this should be rewritten as the indirect question: *Could you tell me what time it is?*

- Ask students to rewrite the other questions to make them into the question types in brackets.

- If necessary, students can refer to the example questions in Exercise 10a and/or the email from Jake in Exercise 8 to remind themselves how to form the question types in brackets.

- Students could check their answers in pairs before you check with the whole class.

Answers

1 Could you tell me what time it is?

2 You aren't busy today, are you? / You're busy today, aren't you?

3 Shouldn't we wait?

4 Sue remembered to phone the bank, didn't she? / Sue didn't remember to phone the bank, did she?

5 I wonder if they know the price of the tickets?

6 Don't you think this is a bad idea?

11 `21st` `CENTURY OUTCOMES`

- Before starting this exercise, refer students to the 21st CENTURY OUTCOMES at the foot of the page. You could get students to think about how to express their thoughts and ideas clearly in writing. Ask: *What are the features of 'clear' writing? How can you recognize that someone has written something clearly?* Students could discuss these questions in pairs. Possible answers could be: *You have no problem understanding what the writer wanted to say, The writer has avoided vague language, The writer has avoided long and complicated sentences, The writer has used linking expressions to give the text greater coherence.*

- Put students into pairs and tell them to decide who will be Student A and who will be Student B.

- Ask the A students to write Andy's full original email to Jake, adding more detail and including at least two questions. Ask the B students to write Andy's reply to Jake's email, answering Jake's questions and adding at least two more.

- Encourage students to spend some time planning what they're going to include in their emails, especially the questions and/or answers that they need to add before they start writing. Also, remind students to use the same informal tone as in the email in Exercise 8.

- Students should write clearly so that their partner will be able to read their email when they exchange emails in Exercise 12.

- Monitor students while they're writing, offering help where necessary.

12

- Ask students to exchange emails with their partner from Exercise 11.

- Tell students to read their partner's email and check that he/she has used question forms correctly.

- Ask students to decide whether they would invest in Andy's business if they were Jake and to think of reasons or evidence from the email to support their decision.

- Ask students to work in pairs and to tell each other whether they would invest in Andy's business if they were Jake, giving reasons for their decision.

- Conduct whole-class feedback on whether students would invest in Andy's business, and why or why not.

> **TEACHING TIP**
>
> ### Displaying students' writing
>
> Assuming that your students will have been working together now for some time by this stage, they will probably feel comfortable with displaying their emails for other students to read at the end of a lesson. Students could either do this directly after they've exchanged emails in pairs or after making changes to their emails in response to their partner's feedback. You could use the walls or noticeboards in your classroom to display the emails and space the texts out around the room so that students have to move around to read them. Just remind students before they start writing that they will need to write legibly, clearly and large enough so that other students will be able to read their emails when they're displayed. Or, if you're familiar with how to set up blogs, you could start a class blog and let your students post their writing there for other students to read.

▶ Photocopiable communicative activity 5.2: Go to page 222 for further practice of finance vocabulary, funding and entrepreneurial vocabulary, and negative, indirect and tag questions. The teaching notes are on page 241.

▶ Set Workbook pages 50–51 for homework.

▶ Set Workbook Presentation 3 on pages 52–53 for homework.

6 Values

LEAD IN

• Books open. Draw students' attention to the unit title, and to the photo on pages 62–63 and its caption. Ask: *What adjectives come to mind when you look at the photo?* Possible answers could be: *amazing, scary, breath-taking, brave.*

• To gauge students' prior knowledge of the unit vocabulary, ask: *What do you think of when you hear the word 'awesome'?* Possible answers could be: *a beautiful sunset, a new pair of designer shoes, a band you like.* Tell students to make a list of the things that come to mind. They can do this in pairs. Ask students to share their lists with the class. Write some of the things they mention on the board. Then ask students to divide these things into two groups according to whether they're things you can or can't buy, e.g. you can't buy a beautiful sunset, but you can buy a new pair of shoes.

• Bring in students' own experiences. Ask: *Which of the items on the board do you think really deserve to be described as 'awesome', and which don't?* Students can discuss this question in pairs. Then conduct whole-class feedback.

Background information

Danny MacAskill and his climb

The photo shows Scottish street trials cyclist Danny MacAskill on the Cuillin Ridgeway. Students can watch a video showing MacAskill climbing up to the peak in the photo and then cycling along the Cuillin Ridgeway on Youtube.

TEDTALKS
BACKGROUND

1

• Ask students to read the text about Jill Shargaa and her talk. If necessary, clarify the meaning of:

   awe – a feeling of wonder or amazement that you get when you see or experience extraordinary things; adjective: *awesome* (line 7)

• Ask students whether they agree with Jill Shargaa that the word *awesome* is used too much. Encourage them to give reasons or evidence to support their point of view.

• Put students into pairs to discuss the questions. Then conduct whole-class feedback.

• **Question 1.** If appropriate, bring in students' own experiences of humour in a foreign language during feedback. Ask: *Have you ever heard jokes or watched comedians from other countries or in other languages? Did you find them funny?*

• **Question 2.** Elicit or introduce the idea of people using the same slang or fashionable words or phrases in order to strengthen a sense of group identity during feedback. Ask: *Have you ever experienced people using slang or fashionable words to strengthen group identity first-hand?*

• **Question 3.** Remind students to recycle language for describing trends, e.g. for upward movement: *increase, rise, grow, improve, climb, jump*; for downward movement: *decrease, fall, drop, sink, decline, plummet.*

• **Question 3.** If appropriate, elicit reasons for the popularity of words or expressions students identified, e.g. their use in a popular TV programme, film or advertisement.

▶ Teaching tip: Language for describing trends, Unit 3 Opener, page 38

Suggested answers

1 It can be difficult to understand humour in a foreign language: foreigners don't necessarily know the cultural background, they don't understand the slang words.

2 People can feel connected to each other, if they: are the same nationality, come from the same part of a country, have the same interests, have the same political beliefs, are from the same age group.

3 Students' own answers

Extra activity

Popular new words

Write the words below, all of which have recently become popular, on the board. Ask students to discuss where these words came from and what factors played a role in their popularity:

vaguebooking – posting deliberately vague Facebook updates in order to get attention from your friends

selfie – a photo you take of yourself

big data – large data sets that can be analysed by computers to demonstrate patterns and trends

fracking – the controversial practice of injecting liquid into rocks at high pressure in order to extract gas

freegan – someone who tries to help the environment by reusing food and other products that people don't want

crowdfunding – raising funds for a project from the public, usually via the Internet

KEY WORDS

2

• Ask students to try to guess the meaning of the words in bold and then to match them with their definitions.

• Draw students' attention to the use of *astonished* in sentence 5 (for describing a person) and *astonishing* in sentence 6 (for describing a thing).

Answers

1 d   2 a   3 f   4 b   5 c   6 e

AUTHENTIC LISTENING SKILLS Listening for gist

3a

• Ask students to read the information about listening for gist in the Authentic listening skills box. Ask students to identify synonyms for *gist*, i.e. *the overall idea, the general sense of the message*.

• Bring in students' own experiences. Ask: *Have you ever had a conversation with a native speaker? Were you able to understand every word they said, or did you focus on getting*

the gist of what they were saying? If you focused on getting the gist, what strategies did you use to help you do that? You could put students into pairs to discuss these questions and then conduct whole-class feedback.

• 🔊 29 Play the recording. Ask students to focus on the general sense of what Jill Shargaa says and to confirm the order in which she does the three things.

Transcript

How many times have you used the word 'awesome' today? Once? Twice? Seventeen times? Do you remember what you were describing when you used the word? No, I didn't think so, because it's come down to this, people: You're using the word incorrectly, and tonight I hope to show you how to put the 'awe' back in 'awesome'.

Answers

1 b   2 c   3 a

3b

• Explain that students are going to listen to another short extract from the talk. Again, they should focus on the general sense. Give students time to read the three options.

• 🔊 30 Play the recording so that students can choose the correct option.

Transcript

Recently, I was dining at an outdoor café, and the server came up to our table, and asked us if we had dined there before, and I said, 'Yes, yes, we have.' And she said, 'Awesome'. And I thought, 'Really? Awesome or just merely good that we decided to visit your restaurant again?'

Answer

c

6.1 Please, please, people. Let's put the 'awe' back in 'awesome'

TEDTALKS

1

• Books open. Ask students to read the list of things Jill Shargaa mentions in the TED Talk.

• Bring in students' experiences. Ask: *Have you ever been to any of the places in the list? Have you ever done any of the activities in the list?* This could be a whole-class discussion or students could discuss the questions in pairs.

- If students have internet access, they could search for information and/or images of any things that they're not familiar with, e.g. the Wright Brothers, Rolling Stone Magazine.

- If necessary, clarify that *the Allied invasion of Normandy* was the entry into German-ruled France by the armed forces of the countries that opposed Germany during World War II, also called the Allies, in 1944.

- ▶6.1 Play the whole talk once so that students can tick the things Jill Shargaa says are *awesome*. If necessary, play the recording twice. You could put students into pairs to check answers before you check with the whole class.

Transcript

0.14 *How many times have you used the word 'awesome' today? Once? Twice? Seventeen times? Do you remember what you were describing when you used the word? No, I didn't think so, because it's come down to this, people: You're using the word incorrectly, and tonight I hope to show you how to put the 'awe' back in 'awesome'.*

0.34 *Recently, I was dining at an outdoor café, and the server came up to our table, and asked us if we had dined there before, and I said, 'Yes, yes, we have.' And she said, 'Awesome.' And I thought, 'Really? Awesome or just merely good that we decided to visit your restaurant again?'*

0.55 *The other day, one of my co-workers asked me if I could save that file as a PDF, and I said, 'Well, of course,' and he said, 'Awesome.' Seriously, can saving anything as a PDF be awesome?*

1.13 *Sadly, the frequent overuse of the word 'awesome' has now replaced words like 'great' and 'thank you'. So Webster's dictionary defines the word 'awesome' as fear mingled with admiration or reverence, a feeling produced by something majestic. Now, with that in mind, was your Quiznos sandwich awesome? How about that parking space? Was that awesome? Or that game the other day? Was that awesome? The answer is no, no and no. A sandwich can be delicious, that parking space can be nearby, and that game can be a blowout, but not everything can be awesome. (Laughter)*

1.57 *So when you use the word 'awesome' to describe the most mundane of things, you're taking away the very power of the word. This author says, 'Snowy days or finding money in your pants is awesome.' (Laughter) Um, no, it is not, and we need to raise the bar for this poor schmuck. (Laughter)*

2.21 *So in other words, if you have everything, you value nothing. It's a lot like drinking from a firehose like this jackass right here. There's no dynamic, there's no highs or lows, if everything is awesome.*

2.35 *Ladies and gentlemen, here are ten things that are truly awesome.*

2.39 *Imagine, if you will, having to schlep everything on your back. Wouldn't this be easier for me if I could roll this home? Yes, so I think I'll invent the wheel. The wheel, ladies and gentlemen. Is the wheel awesome? Say it with me. Yes, the wheel is awesome!*

2.58 *The Great Pyramids were the tallest man-made structure in the world for 4,000 years. Pharaoh had his slaves move millions of blocks just to this site to erect a big freaking headstone. Were the Great Pyramids awesome? Yes, the pyramids were awesome.*

3.16 *The Grand Canyon. Come on. It's almost 80 million years old. Is the Grand Canyon awesome? Yes, the Grand Canyon is.*

3.24 *Louis Daguerre invented photography in 1829, and earlier today, when you whipped out your smartphone and you took a shot of your awesome sandwich, and you know who you are – (Laughter) – wasn't that easier than exposing the image to copper plates coated with iodized silver? I mean, come on. Is photography awesome? Yes, photography is awesome.*

3.48 *D-Day, June 6, 1944, the Allied invasion of Normandy, the largest amphibious invasion in world history. Was D-Day awesome? Yes, it was awesome.*

4.00 *Did you eat food today? Did you eat? Then you can thank the honeybee, that's the one, because if crops aren't pollinated, we can't grow food, and then we're all going to die. Bees are awesome. Are you kidding me?*

4.15 *Landing on the moon! Come on! Apollo 11. Are you kidding me? Sixty-six years after the Wright Brothers took off from Kitty Hawk, North Carolina, Neil Armstrong was 240,000 miles away. That's like from here to the moon. (Laughter) That's one small step for man, one giant leap for awesome! You're damn right, it was.*

4.42 *Woodstock, 1969: Rolling Stone Magazine said this changed the history of rock and roll. Was Woodstock awesome? Yes, it was awesome.*

4.52 *Sharks! They're at the top of the food chain. Sharks have multiple rows of teeth that grow in their jaw and they move forward like a conveyor belt. Some sharks can lose 30,000 teeth in their lifetime. Does awesome inspire fear? Oh, hell yeah, sharks are awesome!*

5.12 *The Internet was born in 1982 and it instantly took over global communication, the Internet is awesome.*

5.22 *And finally, finally some of you can't wait to come up and tell me how awesome my PowerPoint was. I will save you the time. It was not awesome, but it was true, and I hope it was entertaining, and out of all the audiences I've ever had, y'all are the most recent. Thank you and good night.*

5.40 *(Applause)*

Answers

These things are awesome:

the wheel, the Great Pyramids, the Grand Canyon, photography, the Allied invasion of Normandy, bees, sharks

- Note the differences in North American English and British English shown at the foot of the spread. In this unit, these focus on vocabulary differences. See page 6 of the Introduction for ideas on how to present and practise these differences.

- **Optional step.** Ask students if they agree with what Jill Shargaa says about whether or not the items in the list are *awesome* and why / why not. Students could also suggest other things, not in the list, which they think deserve to be described as *awesome*.

Extra activity

Put the X into Y

In the very first section of the talk, Jill Shargaa tells her audience that she hopes to show them *how to put the 'awe' back in 'awesome'*. Write these expressions on the board: *1 put the service back into customer service, 2 put the fast back into fast food, 3 put the power back into empowerment, 4 put the work back into workout*.

Put students into pairs to discuss the meaning of the expressions. Possible answers could be: *1 focus on providing a good service to customers, 2 produce fast food more quickly than normal, 3 empower people by giving them more power, 4 work out in a more strenuous way / work harder when you're working out*.

2

- ▶ 6.1 Play the first part (0.00–2.35) of the talk so that students can check whether the sentences are true or false.

- Conduct whole-class feedback. Elicit or explain that Jill Shargaa omits the words *producing feelings of* in her definition of *awesome*, but these words have actually been added in sentence 4.

Answers

1 F (Jill Shargaa thought that visiting the outdoor café again was 'merely good'.)

2 T

3 T

4 T

5 F (She says that when we use *awesome* to describe the most mundane of things, we're taking away the very power of the word.)

6 T

3

- Ask students to read the list of six things and the possible reasons for describing them as *awesome*. If necessary, clarify the meaning of:

pollinate – to give a plant pollen from another plant of the same kind so that seeds will be produced (item 4)

jaw – the upper and lower bony structures in the head that border the mouth (item 6)

- You could ask students to predict the reason Jill Shargaa gives for the things being described as *awesome* based on what they can remember from the first time they watched this part of the talk.

- ▶ 6.1 Play the second part (2.35 to the end) of the talk so that students can check their answers.

- Conduct whole-class feedback. Elicit that the information in the other option is not incorrect: it's just not the reason Jill Shargaa gave for the thing being described as *awesome*.

Answers

1 a 2 b 3 a 4 a 5 b 6 a

4

- Put students into pairs to discuss the questions. Conduct whole-class feedback for question 1 before moving on to question 2.

- **Question 1.** Students share other things which they think are awesome, giving reasons why.

- **Question 2.** Conduct whole-class feedback on the situations students thought of.

- **Optional step.** Write the situations students suggested on the board. Assign a different situation to each pair and ask students to develop short exchanges that could take place in that context. Students can then present their exchanges to the class.

VOCABULARY IN CONTEXT

5

- ▶ 6.2 Play the clips from the talk. When each multiple-choice question appears, pause the clip so that students can choose the correct definition.

Transcript and subtitles

*1   No, I didn't think so, because **it's come down to this**, people*
    a   my idea is this
    b   the truth is this
    c   we are so low

*2   Webster's dictionary defines the word 'awesome' as fear **mingled with** admiration*
    a   much more than
    b   mixed together with
    c   rather than

*3   Now, **with that in mind**, was your Quiznos sandwich awesome?*
    a   considering what I've just said
    b   have you thought about this
    c   what are your thoughts

*4   when you **whipped out** your smartphone and you took a shot*
    a   removed something quickly from your pocket or bag
    b   quickly looked at something
    c   tried to switch something on too quickly

5 *and you **took a shot** of your awesome sandwich*
  a *had a bite*
  b *got a photo*
  c *made a video*

6 *Landing on the moon! Come on! Apollo 11. **Are you kidding me**?*
  a *I don't believe you*
  b *it's just obvious*
  c *that can't be true*

Answers

1 b 2 b 3 a 4 a 5 b 6 b

6

• Ask students to underline the words from Exercise 5: *mingled with*, *whip out* and *take shots*. Elicit the meaning of the three expressions.

• Put students into pairs to discuss the questions. Encourage them to use the target expressions in the questions in their answers too. Also encourage students to share their own experiences and to relate the questions to their own context. Monitor students while they're speaking to check that they are doing these two things. Then conduct whole-class feedback.

CRITICAL THINKING Reading between the lines

7

• Elicit or explain that *reading between the lines* means 'looking beyond the surface meaning of what someone says or writes in order to understand what they really want to say'.

• Elicit that the main point of Jill Shargaa's message was that people overuse the word *awesome* and that the instructions express another part of her message. Give students time to read the three statements which could also be part of her message. If necessary, clarify the meaning of:

  be conscious of – be aware of or know about something or someone (statement c)

• Put students into pairs to discuss which of the statements (a–c) could also be part of Jill Shargaa's message. Explain that they can choose one or more options. This isn't a test of memory, so students can refer to the transcript on page 177 if they want to.

• Conduct whole-class feedback. Ask students to give reasons or evidence from the transcript to support the option(s) that they think could also be part of Jill Shargaa's message.

Answers

b, c

Reading between the lines

Exercise 7 requires students to practise reading between the lines, but the idea that someone wouldn't say 'what they really mean' could be surprising and unfamiliar for some students who come from cultures where more direct communication styles are commonly used (low-context cultures). Students may also see people who don't directly say 'what they really mean' as being dishonest and deceitful. If this is the case for your students, reassure them that in high context cultures, such as Anglo-Saxon culture, it's common for people to not say exactly what they mean and for the statements they make to have several layers of meanings. Even if students don't use this communication style themselves, they need to be aware of the fact that other people they communicate with in English may do and be able to work out what these people really mean.

8

• **Optional step.** Elicit expressions for expressing degrees of understanding, e.g. complete understanding: *completely understand*; general understanding: *on the whole*, *generally*, *largely*; some understanding: *to some extent/degree*; little understanding: *understand little*, *not really understand*.

• Ask students to read the comments and to decide the extent to which the writers have understood Jill Shargaa's message. Students can do this in pairs. Then conduct whole-class feedback.

Answers

Jaycee has completely understood the message.

Kristen hasn't understood the message She herself uses 'awesome' to describe the talk – which Jill Shargaa would disagree with completely. It is true that we should celebrate brilliant things, but the point Jill Shargaa is making is that we should limit our use of 'awesome' to things that are truly awesome.

Andreas seems to have understood the message. He acknowledges that he uses 'awesome' without really thinking about it.

PRESENTATION SKILLS Being authentic

9

• Ask students to read about being authentic in the Presentation tips box and to identify which points are most concerned with 'personality'. Explain that students are going to consider Jill Shargaa's personality and how authentic her presentation is.

- ▶ 6.3 Play the clip so that students can decide if the presentation reflected Jill Shargaa's personality and which adjectives they think describe her.

Transcript

Landing on the moon! Come on! Apollo 11. Are you kidding me? Sixty-six years after the Wright Brothers took off from Kitty Hawk, North Carolina, Neil Armstrong was 240,000 miles away. That's like from here to the moon. (Laughter) That's one small step for man, one giant leap for awesome! You're damn right, it was.

- Put students into pairs to compare the adjectives they chose and to say why they chose them. Students can also use other adjectives which aren't in the box to describe Jill Shargaa's personality. Then conduct whole-class feedback.

> #### Answers
> Students' own answers, although they will probably agree that all the adjectives describe Jill Shargaa.

- **Optional step.** Ask: *How important do you think is it for a presentation to reflect the speaker's personality? How can a speaker ensure that their presentation reflects their personality?* Students can discuss these questions in pairs or as a whole class.

10

- Ask students to each think of an interest they have. Point out that even if students don't see themselves as having any fixed interests, we all have something that we like more than other things and could talk about. The prompts in the instructions (*A hobby? A book? An issue?*) may give students ideas. You could also give students an example of an interest you have to get them started, e.g. a country, a pet a television programme, or something more abstract, e.g. helping others.

- Give students 5–10 minutes to prepare their short (2–3 minute) presentation. Remind students that their aim is to express their personality through their presentation, so they should also consider this while preparing.

- Discourage students from writing out their presentations word for word as their aim is to try to speak naturally. They can, however, write notes to help organize their ideas.

- **Optional step.** If appropriate, ask students to look for photos on their phones that they can use while presenting. Explain that they need to think about what points they can use these photos to make and what order they will show them in.

11

- Put students into pairs. They take turns to give their presentation. Remind students to try to speak naturally and, if appropriate, to show their partner the photos they selected.

- When both students have given their presentation, they can reflect on what their own presentation style was and share this in pairs. Students can then say whether they had the same perception of each other's presentation style.

- **Optional step.** Students could consider which adjectives they would use to describe their partner's personality based solely on the presentation they've just given. They could then share this with their partner before you conduct whole-class feedback on the adjectives students chose. During feedback, ask students to give reasons or evidence for choosing the adjectives they chose. You could also use this as an opportunity to elicit other adjectives for describing personality. The vocabulary focus in Unit 9 and Unit 12 is on adjectives for describing personality, so students will be able to recycle and expand on this vocabulary then.

▶ Set Workbook pages 54–55 for homework.

6.2 Getting value for money

GRAMMAR Zero, first and second conditionals

1

- Books open. Draw students' attention to the spread title: *Getting value for money.* If necessary, clarify the meaning of:

  value for money – a good return on the money you pay for something

- Elicit that *getting value for money* is something people usually hope to do when they're shopping or buying things.

- Look at statement 1 as an example with the class. Elicit or explain that in order to find out if the sentence is true for another person, students will have to convert the statement into a question beginning *Do you … ?* Elicit the question: *Do you ever buy things if you think they aren't value for money?*

- If necessary, clarify the meaning of:

  bargain – something you buy at a lower price than normal (sentence 4)

- Put students into pairs to discuss the statements.

- Conduct whole-class feedback on what students learned about their partners. Encourage students to use adverbs of frequency in their responses, e.g. *always, usually, occasionally.*

2

- Ask students to look at the infographic. Explain or elicit that this is a *flowchart*.

- **Question 1.** Ask: *Have you seen a flowchart like this before? What was it about?*

- **Question 2.** Look at the example with the class. Note that this example includes the zero conditional, which is part of the focus of this grammar section. Invite students to say whether they shop in the same way.

- Conduct whole-class feedback. If students don't usually follow the steps in the infographic when shopping, encourage them to say what they do instead.

Answers

1 It helps you get value for money when you are shopping.

2 Students' own answers

3

- Ask students to look at the photos of the four items. Ask: *Do you own any of these items?*

- Elicit or explain the possible uses of the items.

- 🎧 **31** Play the recording so that students can identify what the shoppers are interested in buying.

Transcript

1

S = Shopper, A = Assistant

S: *It's so hard to decide, really. My old laptop is five years old, and it's really slow.*

A: *Well, if laptops slow down like that, there's not much you can do to fix them.*

S: *I guess not. But I'm wondering about a tablet. It's more in my price range.*

A: *Aha. Well, let me show you these particular laptops first. They're excellent value for money because they're last year's models. And we've got a great deal on at the*

moment – if you decide to buy before the end of the month, we'll extend the guarantee for two years.

S: *Oh, that's interesting. So can I have a look at this one?*

A: *Of course. It's already switched on, so feel free.*

S: *Thanks. It's quite heavy, isn't it? And I'm just not sure that I can afford to spend that much. If it wasn't so pricey, I'd be really tempted.*

A: *Well, I can show you some tablets if that's more what you're looking for.*

S: *Yes, I think so.*

2

S = Shopper, F = Friend

S: *Oh, look at this drill! It's great, and it's just what I need.*

F: *Really? Look how much it costs! Didn't you want to buy a new toolbox?*

S: *But this is a really good quality brand. It's fantastic value for money.*

F: *Well, I suppose so. But if you got that drill, how often would you use it, really? And what about those other tools you wanted? You wouldn't be able to afford them if you got this drill.*

S: *Yes, I would. I could put everything on my credit card.*

F: *Haven't you reached the limit on that?*

S: *Well, if I've gone over my limit already, it won't make any difference.*

F: *Listen, we've been in this place for hours. If you don't make up your mind soon, I'm going to get a coffee.*

S: *OK, I'll take it.*

F: *Oh no …*

Answers

1 tablet   2 drill

- **Optional step.** Write *cheap* and *expensive* on the board. Ask students whether these words have a positive or negative meaning for them. Then ask students to consider whether they could have the opposite meaning in other cultures. Elicit that in some cultures or languages *cheap* has a positive meaning, but in others it has a negative meaning. The same is true for *expensive*. Ask: *What consequences could different interpretations of the meanings of these words have in the context of inter-cultural communication? Can you think of any misunderstandings it could cause?*

4

- Explain that students are going to listen to the recording again. This time they're listening for specific information.

- Ask students to read the questions. They can then discuss what they remember in answer to them in pairs. Remind students of the value of collaborative listening that they worked on in Unit 4: Authentic listening skills.

- **A 31** Play the recording again so that students can listen and answer the questions.

Answers

1 It's really slow.

2 They're excellent value for money.

3 It's quite heavy. She's not sure that she can afford to spend that much.

4 It's a really good quality brand.

5 He decides to pay with his (credit) card.

5

- Look at the Grammar box with the class. Ask students to read the sentences – which are from the recording – and to answer the questions. They can do this in pairs.

- Students can check their answers and overall understanding of conditional sentences by turning to the Grammar summary on page 150.

Answers

1 zero conditional: present simple, present simple

first conditional: present simple, future simple; present simple, *going to* + infinitive; present perfect, future simple

second conditional: past simple, *would* + infinitive (x 2)

2 a zero conditional, b first conditional, c second conditional

- If you feel that students need more controlled practice before continuing, they could do some or all of Exercises 1–4 in the Grammar summary. Otherwise, you could continue on to Exercise 6 in the unit and set the Grammar summary exercises for homework.

Answers to Grammar summary exercises

1

1 *both*   2 a   3 b   4 b   5 *both*   6 *both*

2

1 will buy   2 there are   3 pay   4 Would   5 don't want 6 didn't have to   7 we'd be   8 will be   9 would you go 10 lose

3

1 would happen   2 joined   3 would be   4 would (the shop assistants) do   5 wouldn't be able to   6 had to 7 owned   8 came   9 'd give   10 wanted   11 'd be 12 wouldn't close

4

1 'll buy   2 sound   3 had to   4 are   5 wouldn't be 6 loses

6

- Look at sentence 1 as an example with the class. Elicit that *If I see some clothes I can't afford,* is followed by *I look for something cheaper* and that this is an example of a zero conditional sentence. Tell students that we write a comma in between these two sentence halves.

- Ask students to match the two parts of the other sentences, focusing on their general sense.

- Ask students to identify whether the sentences describe things that are generally true (zero conditional), something that the speaker thinks is likely to happen (first conditional), something that is the opposite of the real situation (second conditional) or something that the speaker thinks is unlikely to happen (second conditional).

Answers

1 e zero conditional   2 c second conditional   3 d first conditional   4 a second conditional   5 b first conditional

7

- Look at the instructions with the class. If necessary, clarify the meaning of:

  bid – offer a certain amount of money for something you'd like to buy (line 3)

- Elicit examples of unusual gifts that students could buy or have bought for friends online.

- Look at sentence 1 as an example with the class. Elicit possible endings. For example: *We're only going to bid if … the price isn't too high / another friend will contribute towards the gift too.*

- Look at sentence 5 with the class. Elicit that *unless* is the equivalent of *if not*. For example: *I won't go out unless it stops raining* has the same meaning as *I won't go out if it doesn't stop raining.*

- Put students into pairs to complete the sentences.

- Conduct whole-class feedback and encourage individual students to share their completed sentences.

Suggested answers

1 we see something we like.

2 we'll stop bidding.

3 then we mustn't spend more than that amount.

4 then we won't buy something we don't want.

5 it's absolutely perfect.

6 then we won't be able to buy it.

7 you want us to buy something.

8 we'll have to stop.

8

- Look at the example with the class. Elicit or explain that conditional sentences don't always have to start with *if*. As in this example, *if* can be used in the middle of a sentence instead. Elicit that when *if* is in the middle of a sentence, there is no comma. Explain that it's sometimes necessary to change the wording slightly if you want to begin the sentence the other way. For example, in this case, it is preferable to say *If the tablet was better value for money, I'd buy it* rather than *If it was better value for money, I'd buy the tablet.*

• Look at the sentences with the class. If necessary, clarify the meaning of:

  keep on – continue (sentence 1)

  be tempted – have a desire to buy or do something because it's attractive (sentence 6)

• Look at sentence 1 as an example with the class. Elicit that *I might need to look for a new one* is a situation which is likely to happen in the future, so we have to use the first conditional. Elicit that the conditional sentence is: *If my car keeps breaking down, I'll need to look for a new one.*

• Ask students to write conditional sentences using the words in brackets. They can do this in pairs. Encourage them to use the words in brackets in the first part of the sentence.

• Check answers with the class. Accept sentences with *if* in either the first or second clauses as correct.

Suggested answers

1 If my car keeps on breaking down, I'll need to look for a new one.

2 If a product is advertised on TV, it doesn't influence me.

3 If I had more self-control, I wouldn't have so much stuff.

4 If I make more food at home, I'll save money on takeaways.

5 If there was less packaging on everything, our recycling bin wouldn't always be full.

6 If the shops didn't have so many special offers, I wouldn't be so tempted.

9

• Put students into pairs. Ask them to look at their rewritten sentences in Exercise 8 again and to discuss whether they could imagine saying these sentences.

• If students disagree with the sentences, they can formulate and say alternative conditional sentences on the same topic which are relevant to them.

• Conduct whole-class feedback and ask individual students to tell the class any alternative conditional sentences that they formulated.

SPEAKING Consumerism and the economy

10 **21st CENTURY OUTCOMES**

• Before starting this exercise, refer students to the 21st CENTURY OUTCOMES at the foot of the page.

• Look at the photo with the class. Elicit that the man is mending or trying to mend a computer.

• Look at the first situation as an example with the class. Elicit possible consequences of electrical goods and gadgets still working after a few years. Elicit that electrical goods and gadgets do generally stop working after a few years, so this situation is one that's unlikely to become a reality in the future and that's why we use the second conditional. Students will also need to use the second conditional when discussing the consequences of the other situations.

• Put students into groups (4–5 students) to discuss the consequences of each situation.

• **Optional step.** You could add a game-like element to this activity. One student in each group starts by asking *What would happen if … ?* The other students then take turns to say a possible consequence of that situation. If students can't think of a possible consequence or hesitate too much, they're out. The winner is the student who can say the most possible consequences. Demonstrate how the activity works with the whole class first. Choose a different *What would happen if … ?* sentence – something relevant to your students' lives – and go around the class, asking students to give you possible consequences.

• Conduct whole-class feedback and invite groups to share the possible consequences they discussed for the second and third situations.

Suggested answers

Electrical gadgets and goods: If these didn't stop working, we wouldn't need to buy any more / we'd only buy new ones if we wanted a new model / we'd spend less money on such items / electrical stories would go out of business / millions of people would lose their jobs

New clothes: If people didn't buy any more new clothes, they'd get tired of wearing the same things / their clothes would lose their colour through washing and get holes / their clothes would look awful / lots of clothes shops would close / the fashion industry would die

TV advertising: If there was no TV advertising, television would be much better than today / the price of the TV licence would go up / people wouldn't find out about new products

---

• **Optional step.** Ask students to think of other situations which are unlikely to become a reality in the future, e.g. young people could have a say in the running of the country, and discuss the possible consequences of these. Conduct whole-class feedback, and ask students to share the situations they talked about and the possible consequences of them.

▶ Photocopiable communicative activity 6.1: Go to page 223 for practice of zero, first and second conditionals. The teaching notes are on page 242.

▶ Set Workbook pages 56–57 for homework.

6.3 Is it worth it?

READING Ethical consumption

1

• Put students into pairs to make a list of three things they each bought this week. Tell students that they should choose objects rather than services.

• Tell students to ask and answer the questions about each of the things. If students are unsure about the answers to any of the questions, encourage them to speculate based on what they do know about the items.

• Monitor students while they're speaking and listen for the items students discuss.

• Conduct whole-class feedback and ask individual students who talked about different interesting examples to each share the information about a thing they bought. If possible, choose examples that contrast items that are ethically and locally produced, e.g. a piece of jewellery made by a local craftsman, with items that are less ethically produced, e.g. a T-shirt produced under unethical conditions in Bangladesh. Elicit the meaning of the section heading: *Ethical consumption*.

Background information

Ethical practices

When we talk about ethical practices, there are usually three constituents that we consider: human factors, the physical environment and transparency. Human factors covers how a company treats their employees: Are they paid fairly? Do they have acceptable working conditions? The physical environment includes the company's interaction with the natural world: How much pollution and environmental damage does the company create? Transparency covers how willing a company is to let the public know about their activities and whether it's involved in secret illicit or illegal activities.

2

• Look at the article with the class. Elicit that this is divided into three parts, and that each part contains a heading, and a question section (Q) and an answer section (A). Give students time to read the headings and the question sections. If necessary, clarify the meaning of:

disposable – describes something you can throw away after using it once (first heading)

• Elicit that the use of the word *evil* in the question *Are disposable cups evil?* is designed to have an emotional impact.

• Ask students to combine the heading and what it says in the question section to make a question for each section. Some possible questions are: *Isn't using disposable cups incredibly wasteful? Is buying fake fashion really unethical?*

Buying imported fruit: do the benefits for a healthy diet outweigh the effect of CO_2 emissions and climate change? If necessary, clarify the meaning of:

CO_2 emissions – amounts of the gas carbon dioxide (CO_2) that are released into the atmosphere (third question section)

• Students continue to work in pairs. Ask them to tell each other what they would reply to the questions. Remind students to give reasons or evidence to support their point of view.

• Ask students to make notes on their own and their partner's replies to the questions so that they can compare these with the responses given in the article.

3

• Ask students to read the whole article to find out whether it contains the answers they gave to the questions in Exercise 2.

• Conduct whole-class feedback. Invite individual students to say if the article gave the same or different answers to those they gave in Exercise 2. Alternatively, leave this discussion until the end of Exercise 4 – since the options include some of the main points to be considered.

Suggested answers

Section 1: Disposable cups are as eco-friendly (or unfriendly) as any other cups.

Section 2: Fake items are often associated with organized crime and they deprive companies of income, thus affecting costs and ultimately the price of goods.

Section 3: Experts are undecided on this. The reduction in carbon emissions would only be 0.1 per cent, and there would be an enormous knock-on effect on producers if we all ate only seasonal and locally-produced food. (The water and pesticide footprints that growing produce creates are likely to have a greater impact on the environment than the carbon emissions produced by transporting them.)

4

• Ask students to read the questions and the options. If necessary, clarify the meaning of:

humanitarian – connected with promoting human welfare (question 2, option c)

• **Optional step.** Ask students to predict the answers to the questions based on what they already know about the content of the article. They can do this in pairs.

• Students read the article and focus on finding information that answers the questions.

Answers

1 b   2 c   3 a

5

• Invite students to discuss whether they would change their buying habits after reading the article, giving reasons or evidence to support their answers. Encourage students to use first and second conditionals where appropriate. You could put students into small groups to do this.

• If students have worked in small groups, conduct whole-class feedback to gauge the number of students who would and wouldn't change their buying habits. Ask individual students who said they would change and individual students who said they wouldn't to give reasons for their decisions.

6

• Ask students to look at the list of words (1–6). Reassure them that it doesn't matter if they don't know the meaning of all the words because they don't need to at this stage.

• Look at word 1 as an example with the class. Elicit that *single-use* is an adjective because it describes *cup* and that it means: *intended for use once only*.

• Tell students to find the other words in the article, to decide if they're nouns, verbs or adjectives, and to work out their meaning. They can do this in pairs.

• Check answers with the class. Elicit or explain that the stress is on the first syllable of *produce* (word 5) because it is a noun; the stress is on the second syllable when it is a verb. Make the point that working out the meaning of words from their context is something students can do in all their reading activity.

> **Answers**
> _____
> 1 adjective – intended for use once only
>
> 2 adjective – can be used again
>
> 3 verb – improving something so that it is of a higher quality or it is a newer model
>
> 4 verb – take away or remove access to
>
> 5 noun – food that is grown in large quantities to be sold
>
> 6 adjective – related to or happening during a particular period of the year

VOCABULARY Consumerism: phrasal verbs

7

• Elicit or explain the meaning of *phrasal verb*: a verb + preposition or adverb, which has a different meaning from those of its separate parts.

• Look at item 1 as an example with the class. Elicit or explain that the phrasal verb *take away* means 'to remove something or take it somewhere else' and, more specifically in the case of food and drink, 'to buy a ready-made item from a café/restaurant and to take it home to eat or drink'. Elicit that *takeaway* in line 8 is an adjective.

• Ask students to find the other phrasal verbs in the article and to decide what they mean.

> **Answers**
> _____
> 1 to buy a ready-made item from a café/restaurant and to take it home to eat or drink
>
> 2 to get rid of something that has no use or that you no longer need
>
> 3 to be discovered to be, to prove to be
>
> 4 to stop working because of a fault
>
> 5 to explode
>
> 6 to reduce

8

• Look at sentence 1 as an example with the class. Elicit that the missing phrasal verb is *cut back* and that the form doesn't need to change in order to complete this sentence.

• Ask students to complete the other sentences with forms of the phrasal verbs from Exercise 7. They can do this in pairs.

> **Answers**
> _____
> 1 cut back   2 turned out   3 blew up   4 take away
> 5 threw (it) away   6 break down

SPEAKING Ethical awareness

9   *21st* **CENTURY OUTCOMES**

• Before starting this exercise, refer students to the 21st CENTURY OUTCOMES at the foot of the page. Explain that students now have the opportunity to think about their impact on the natural world.

• Look at the quiz with the class. Ask if anyone in the class is vegetarian or vegan; if so, they should tick YES for question 5 – even though they may not eat chicken.

• **Optional step.** Before students do the quiz, they can say whether they think they are an ethical consumer.

• Put students into pairs to match the statements with the areas (a–e). If necessary, clarify the meaning of:

> *sustainability* – the degree to which something causes little or no damage to the environment and therefore is able to continue for a long time (area d)

> **Answers**
> _____
> 1 d   2 c   3 e   4 b   5 a

• Students do the quiz on their own, choosing YES or NO answers. Encourage students to be honest in their answers.

• Ask students to read the key and to find out if they are an ethical consumer. They can discuss this in pairs. They can also tell each other whether the results of the quiz are the same as what they thought about themselves.

- If appropriate, conduct whole-class feedback to gauge the results students got in the quiz. Ask students whose result was that they could be more ethical whether this will make them change their habits.

▶ Set Workbook pages 58–59 for homework.

6.4 Shopping around

LISTENING Sales talk

1

- Books open. Draw students' attention to the spread title: *Shopping around*. Elicit or explain that this means 'comparing the prices and quality of the same or a similar object in different shops before you decide which one to buy'.

- Look at the instructions and the questions with the class. If necessary, clarify the meaning of:

    on contract – a situation where you make a contract with a company that provides you with a service for which you pay a certain amount of money every month (question 1)

    landline – a phone connected to the power supply in your home (question 1b)

- **Question 3: Optional step.** Focus on different ways of talking about making payments. Write these words in list form on the board: *cash, credit card, cheque, bank transfer* and *standing order*. Elicit the words that could come in front of these words when we're talking about making payments, e.g. *pay in cash, pay by credit card, pay by cheque, make a bank transfer, set up a standing order*. Encourage students to use the appropriate collocation.

- Put students into pairs to discuss the questions.

- Conduct whole-class feedback. Write any useful words on the board as students mention them.

2

- Explain that students are going to listen to a conversation between a customer and a sales assistant about mobile phone contracts. If necessary, clarify the meaning of:

    tariff – money that you have to pay as part of an agreement with a service provider (question 2)

- Elicit possible answers to questions 1 and 2. Ask: *What enquiries do people make about their mobile phone contracts? What types of mobile phone tariffs do you know of?*

- ▣32 Play the recording so that students can answer the questions. Note that the assistant mistakenly said *if* before *you're on the unlimited tarriff* in her third speech.

Transcript

A = Assistant, C = Customer

A: Good morning. How can I help you today?

C: Hello there. I've got some queries about my phone bill and I was wondering if you could explain why my bill is usually higher than I expect.

A: OK, let's have a look at your contract details, just bear with me a moment. Right, yes, you're on the basic tariff which has a set charge per unit, when probably you should be on the unlimited tariff.

C: And what's the difference between those two tariffs?

A: OK, so if you just take a look at this sheet … if you're on the unlimited tariff – that's this one here.

C: So if I changed to unlimited, would that be more economical?

A: Possibly yes. If your phone use stays as it is now. Let me put it another way: you would pay more but you would also get more minutes, more free calls and more data use.

C: Did you say I would pay more?

A: Yes, that's correct. You would pay more than your current contract, but less than the additional charges you pay at the moment.

C: And what was my current contract again?

A: As I said, you're on the basic tariff at the moment. But really that's not the most logical tariff for you because you use your phone so much.

C: OK. Well if it's going to be cheaper in the long run to upgrade to the unlimited rate, then I suppose I'll do that.

Answers

1 his phone bill and why it is usually higher than expected

2 basic tariff, unlimited tariff

3 upgrade to the unlimited rate/tariff

3

- Look at the Useful language box with the class. If necessary, clarify the meaning of:

    clarification – an explanation of the meaning of something when it is unclear

- Ask: *Can you remember hearing any of these expressions when you listened to the conversation? If so, which ones? Can you remember the words that were used to complete the expressions?*

- ▣32 Play the recording so that students can identify which expressions are used in the conversation. Elicit and write a list of the full expressions on the board.

- **Optional step.** Focus on the intonation used in the expressions: rising intonation in the expressions for requesting clarification and downward intonation in those for giving clarification. Model and drill the intonation patterns, and ask students to practise saying the expressions.

Pronunciation Words beginning with *u*

4a

- Explain that students are going to listen to the pronunciation of four words beginning with *u*. Students will hear two different sounds for the letter *u*.

- ◼ 33 Play the recording and pause after each word so that students can listen and repeat.

- Conduct whole-class feedback and establish that the two sounds for the letter *u* are /ʌ/ and /juː/.

- **Optional step.** Tell students that we don't use *an* in front of all words that start with *u*, only those that start with the /ʌ/ sound. For example, we say *an upgrade* but *a unit*.

Transcript

unit   unlimited   upgrade   usually

4b

- Ask students to read the words in the box and to predict which *u* sounds they are pronounced with. You could put students into pairs to practise saying the words as they do this. Don't confirm which *u* sounds the words are pronounced with at this stage.

- ◼ 34 Play the recording and pause after each word so that students can check which sounds are used.

Transcript

umbrella   unfriendly   unique   utilities

- Conduct whole-class feedback on which *u* sounds are used. If necessary, model and drill the pronunciation of the four words and ask students to practise saying them.

Optional step. Ask students if they know any other words beginning with these sounds. Examples include: /ʌ/ *ugly, under, unpredictable up-to-date*; /juː/ *uniform, United (States), universal, use.*

SPEAKING Consumer to consumer

5 *21st* CENTURY OUTCOMES

- Before starting this exercise, refer students to the 21st CENTURY OUTCOMES at the foot of the page.

- Put students into small groups to read the questions and to share their knowledge of these areas in order to fulfil this 21st CENTURY OUTCOME.

- Remind students to use expressions for requesting and giving clarification from the Useful language box during their discussion when they need clarification about something or another member of their group is asking them for clarification.

- Conduct whole-class feedback and ask students to share any interesting knowledge they have about smartphones, internet connections and tablets.

WRITING A consumer review

6

- Ask students to look at the product photos and to read the feedback comments. Explain that the comments are all about the same product.

- Ask students to decide which product the comments are about. They can do this in pairs.

- Check the answer with the class. Ask: *Which words or phrases helped you to identify the product?* Possible answers could be: *listen to music, sound quality, get the volume up, plug in my phone, earphones.*

Writing skill Intensifiers

7a

- Look at the instructions and the questions with the class. Ask students to look at the sentences and to decide which adjective is stronger: *poor* or *appalling*. Elicit or explain that both *poor* and *appalling* have the same meaning, i.e. 'bad or negative', but *appalling* is stronger than *poor*. Also elicit that *very* is used with the weaker adjective *poor*.

- Ask students to look at the comments and to find word combinations with *very* and then to find other intensifier + adjective combinations. If students are unsure about how to recognize intensifiers, you can say that they usually end in *-ly* and come in front of adjectives.

Answers

We use *very* with adjectives that are not strong (*poor* but not *appalling*).

Fred Q

We bought these to take away on holiday with us to listen to music in our hotel room. They were <u>amazingly cheap</u>, so we didn't expect much. But the sound quality was <u>incredibly good</u>!

B Ferry

<u>Very disappointing</u>. You can't get the volume up at all. <u>Totally useless</u>. What a waste of money.

Dinah

I use these to plug in my phone in the kitchen when I'm cooking – I find earphones <u>really annoying</u>. I'm <u>completely satisfied</u> with this product – it's <u>absolutely brilliant</u> value for money.

• **Optional step.** Check understanding of the meaning of the intensifiers by asking students to organize the ones they looked at in this exercise into the following groups: intensifiers that mean 100% (*absolutely, completely, totally*), higher intensity: (*amazingly, incredibly*) and lower intensity: (*very, really*).

• Students can check their answers and overall understanding of intensifiers by turning to the Grammar summary on page 150.

• If you feel that students need more controlled practice before continuing, they could do some or all of Exercises 5–7 in the Grammar summary. Otherwise, you could continue on to Exercise 7b in the unit and set the Grammar summary exercises for homework.

Answers to Grammar summary exercises

5

1 really 2 incredibly 3 completely 4 very
5 absolutely 6 extremely

6

1 good 2 delicious 3 big 4 slow 5 awful
6 wonderful

7

1 If I ~~would have~~ **had** enough money, I'd buy a new phone.

2 What ~~you will~~ **will you** say if they offer you the job?

3 If I were you, I would ~~to~~ **ask** for help.

4 If we all ~~will~~ **pass** the exam, we'll go out for a meal.

5 If you ~~would be~~ **were** younger, you'd have better opportunities at work.

6 We're going to China next year if ~~we'll~~ **we have** enough money.

7 We had ~~an absolutely good~~ **a very good** (*or* an absolutely brilliant/fantastic, etc.) weekend in the mountains.

8 The exam was ~~very~~ **absolutely/totally**, etc. impossible for me to finish on time.

7b

• Look at sentence 1 as an example with the class. Elicit that all three options are possible.

• Ask students to read the other sentences and to cross out any words that aren't possible. Students could do this in pairs.

• Conduct whole-class feedback and clarify any uncertainties about how to use intensifiers.

Answers

1 I was incredibly / totally / really disappointed with the sound quality.

2 This is a very interesting / ~~excellent~~ app.

3 The DVD player was really / very / ~~totally~~ expensive.

4 The picture on this player was really / ~~very~~ / particularly awful.

5 I am very ~~disgusted~~ / unhappy with the after-sales service.

6 I found this function to be completely / really / ~~very~~ useless.

• **Optional step.** Ask students to write similar sentences of their own. Students can then work in pairs and exchange their sentences for their partner to decide which words are not possible.

8

• Explain that students are going to write a review of a product they bought recently. Ask them to choose the product.

• Tell students to use the comments from Exercise 6 as models for their reviews. Remind them to use at least two intensifier + adjective combinations in their reviews.

9

• Ask students to stand up and mingle to find another student who's written a review of a similar product.

• Students read each other's review and ask follow-up questions. Encourage students to develop this into a discussion about their experiences with the product.

• Conduct whole-class feedback. Ask a spokesperson from each pair to give the rest of the class a summary of how they felt about the product.

▶ Photocopiable communicative activity 6.2: Go to page 224 for practice of requesting and giving clarification. The teaching notes are on page 242.

▶ Set Workbook pages 60–61 for homework.

▶ Set Workbook Writing 3 on pages 62–63 for homework.

LISTENING FooARage

1

• Explain that students are going to read a short introduction about a skateboard company and then listen to an interview connected with it. Ask: *Have you ever had a skateboard? If you have, where did you buy it? Do you know who made it?*

• You could put students into pairs to discuss the questions.

Answers

1 how to design and build professional skateboards

2 to teach life and employment skills to young people

3 young people who do less well in traditional academic situations

2

• [🔊 35] Play the recording so that students can decide whether the sentences are true or false.

Transcript

I = Interviewer, J = Jamila

I: Jamila, tell us how you got involved with the FAR Academy and their skateboard company.

J: Well, I run a club for kids who have problems at school. Most of them left traditional education some time ago because they couldn't fit in. So I'm always looking for ways to get these kids interested in learning, and sport is one of the things that often gives us good results. Our first skateboard workshop was a good example of that.

I: How did it work in practice?

J: Basically, the kids built their own skateboards over a series of sessions. None of them had any of the skills they needed at the beginning, but almost all of them managed to make a skateboard.

I: And what did they learn from that?

J: It was easy to combine the project with some of the traditional school subjects like science or design. At the same time, the fact that the kids were able to commit to coming to workshops over a period of time was a huge step forward for many of them. When they realize that they can do this, it gives them confidence for the future.

I: How are the workshops funded?

J: Well, the skateboard company is a charity which is funded by sponsors, donations and partnerships. They are supported by local councils, corporate partners and individuals. They also work with volunteers – if I had more time, I'd probably become a volunteer myself. I've always loved skateboarding!

I: Why is the company so important to you?

J: I think it's because it brings people together in a very relaxed way – and that's something which this company promotes too. They helped us to organize a community action day and we were able to improve an old skateboard park in our area. Skateboarding is an activity that anyone can do. You don't have to pay a lot to join a club and you can do it anywhere. It keeps you fit and you can make some great friends.

Answers

1 F (Jamilia runs a club for young people who have problems at school.)

2 F (Workshop participants build their own skateboards.)

3 T

4 F (Jamilia doesn't say that everyone is a volunteer – she says that they also work with volunteers.)

5 T

3

• [🔊 35] Play the recording again so that students can complete the sentences.

Answers

1 sport   2 step   3 sponsors   4 fit

GRAMMAR

4

• Ask students to look at the modals and related verbs in the box and elicit that they are all past forms.

• Ask students to complete the sentences with six of the eight verb forms from the box. Tell students that they can only use each one once. Students can do this in pairs.

Answers

1 weren't able to   2 had to   3 could   4 succeeded in
5 couldn't   6 managed to

5

• Explain that students are going to complete these conditional sentences with the appropriate forms of the words in brackets. Remind students to pay attention to the verb forms used in the completed clause (only sentence 8 doesn't have one) and use these to help them to decide how they should complete the other clause.

Answers

1 didn't have   2 reach   3 aren't   4 have   5 Would
(so many kids) have   6 won't   7 're going to offer
8 enjoys (making skateboards, he) brings

VOCABULARY

6

• Look at item 1 as an example with the class. Elicit that *event* goes in the first gap and draw students' attention to the collocation *sponsor an event*.

- Ask students to complete the rest of the text with finance expressions. The first letter of each noun is given.

> **Answers**
> 1 event 2 finances 3 budget 4 money 5 fee
> 6 books 7 debt 8 partnership

7

- **Optional step.** Elicit the meanings of the phrasal verbs in the box.

- Ask students to complete the text with five of the phrasal verbs. Remind them that they may have to change the form of the phrasal verbs.

> **Answers**
> 1 throw away 2 cut back 3 turned out 4 blowing up
> 5 take away

DISCUSSION

8

- Put students into small groups to discuss the questions.

- **Question 1.** If students don't know how some of the sportspeople in the list have combined their sporting careers with successful businesses, they could look this information up online.

- **Question 2.** Students think of other people they know who've moved from success in one field to be successful in business. These could be individuals who aren't internationally known, but are well-known in the country students come from. If the other students in the class aren't aware of who these people are and what they've done, students can explain this to each other.

> **Suggested answers**
> 1
>
> David Beckham: atftershave and fragrances
>
> George Foreman: endorsement of the George Foreman Grill (for cooking)
>
> Tony Hawks: acting; launched the online YouTube Channel, RIDE Channel
>
> Michael Jordan: owner of the Charlotte Hornets, an American professional basketball team
>
> Cristiano Ronaldo: opened a fashion boutique on the island of Madeira (where he's from) and another in Lisbon, has his own fashion brand
>
> Venus Williams: CEO of her own interior design firm; has her own fashion line; part-owner of the Miami Dolphins, a professional American football team
>
> 2
>
> Actors are often successful in other fields. For example, Kevin Costner owns a company that specializes in separating oil and water; Clint Eastwood has a golf club and a dairy farm; several actors own restaurant chains; some Indian actors own or co-own cricket teams.

SPEAKING

9

- Ask students to read the whole conversation first to get a feel for what the sports instructor and teacher are talking about.

- Ask students to use the word prompts to write complete sentences and questions. They could check their sentences and questions in the Useful language box in Unit 6.4.

- You could check answers by asking a stronger pair to read out the conversation to the rest of the class.

> **Answers**
> 1 Did you say you run kids' courses?
>
> 2 What's the difference between Gold and Platinum?
>
> 3 Yes, that's correct.
>
> 4 Can you tell me about the beginners' course again?
>
> 5 What would happen if you had a mixture of kids with different experiences?
>
> 6 So can I just check that the kids

WRITING

10

- Ask students to read the email from Rob. You could elicit that this is an example of an informal email.

- Ask students to imagine that they are Matt and to write a reply to Rob. Remind them to use an informal register. Students use the question forms in the box to ask Rob about the underlined information.

> **Suggested answer**
> Hi Rob
>
> Archery sounds like an interesting idea! Can you explain exactly how many classes you've arranged? Year 4 kids are a bit young for archery, aren't they? Or perhaps the classes are designed for this age group – it's not clear. I wonder if there's enough time in the lunch hour for the kids to eat and do this activity? Wouldn't it be better to find out the cost before we email the parents? I think it would help to give them as much information as we can.
>
> Next month is perhaps a bit soon, isn't it? Let's look at this again when we have all the details of cost, number of classes, and so on.
>
> Matt

11

- Put students into pairs to read each other's email and compare the questions they used.

7 Innovation and technology

LEAD IN

• Books open. Draw students' attention to the unit title, and the photo and its caption on page 74. Ask: *Does anything surprise you about what you can see in the photo?* The expected answer would be: *someone who has lost the bottom part of his legs and feet is rock climbing.*

• Write the words *amputee* and *prosthetic limb* on the board. Explain or elicit that the connection between these two items and the photo is that the man in the photo is an amputee, which means he has had part of his legs or arms removed, and he is using prosthetic limbs – artificial arms or legs.

• Focus on the pronunciation of *amputee* /ˌæmpjʊˈtiː/, *prosthetic* /prɒsˈθetɪk/ and *limb* /lɪm/. Model and drill the pronunciation of these words.

• Explain that Hugh Herr, the man in the photo, is mentioned in the TED Talk.

Background information

Hugh Herr

By the age of 17, Hugh Herr was acknowledged to be one of the best climbers in the United States. In 1982, both of his legs had to be amputated below the knee after an accident in which he suffered frostbite. Months later, he was climbing again. While studying at MIT (Massachusetts Institute of Technology), he began working on leg prostheses.

• Bring in students' own experiences. Ask: *Do you know anyone who is an amputee? If so, what do they use to help them get around? Do they have any difficulties?*

TEDTALKS
BACKGROUND

1

• Ask students to read the text about David Sengeh and his talk.

• Put students into pairs to discuss the questions.

• **Question 1.** Students brainstorm problems amputees might face in everyday life.

• **Question 2.** Students discuss how the areas could help solve the problems they brainstormed and come up with suggestions for things that could be done in these areas. For example: *Make more housing accessible to wheelchair users.*

• **Question 3.** Tell students to think about someone they know personally or know of, i.e. someone in the public eye, who's good at solving problems. Ask: *What skills does this person have?*

• Conduct whole-class feedback. Write any useful words connected to the topic of solving problems that amputees experience on the board as students mention them.

Suggested answers

1 difficulty in mobility, e.g. getting into buildings, inability to move quickly; inability to work in some professions; prejudice

2 housing – flat with lift not house with stairs; transport – marked seats near doors; access to information / legal changes / financial aid – all making support more easily available

3 methodical, determined, able to think outside the box / consider the bigger picture, innovative, resourceful, creative

KEY WORDS

2

• Ask students to try to guess the meaning of the words in bold and then to match them with their definitions.

• If necessary, model and drill the pronunciation of *prosthesis* /ˈprɒsθɪsɪs/ (sentence 1).

> **Answers**
>
> 1 a 2 d 3 b 4 e 5 c 6 f

AUTHENTIC LISTENING SKILLS Dealing with accents

3a

• Ask students to read the information about dealing with accents in the Authentic listening skills box.

• **Optional step.** Elicit what types of spoken English students have heard. Write these on the board and categorize them according to where students have heard them: 1 face-to-face, or 2 on TV, in films, online, etc. Ask: *Are you used to hearing these types of spoken English?* Students can discuss this question in pairs or as a whole class.

• 🎧 36 Play the recording.

Transcript

I was born and raised in Sierra Leone, a small and very beautiful country in West Africa, a country rich both in physical resources and creative talent.

However, Sierra Leone is infamous for a decade-long rebel war in the '90s when entire villages were burnt down. An estimated 8,000 men, women and children had their arms and legs amputated during this time.

• Ask students to work in pairs and to tell each other which aspects of David Sengeh's English were different from the spoken English they're used to.

• Conduct whole-class feedback on the aspects of David Sengeh's speech that are different from the spoken English students are used to. Ask: *Did these aspects make it more difficult to understand David Sengeh? If so, did some aspects make it more difficult to understand him than others? Which ones?*

> **Suggested answers**
>
> He stresses 'mate' in *estimated* and 'tate' in *amputated*.
>
> He says everything at the same pace, without the natural stress of a native-speaker.

3b

• Give students time to read the transcript of the beginning of the talk before they listen.

• 🎧 36 Play the recording again so that students can underline the parts of the transcript that are different from what they expected. They are likely to find different parts unexpected depending on their backgrounds and world knowledge.

• Conduct whole-class feedback on which parts were unexpected for students.

• **Optional step.** Elicit what students had expected. Ask students to link these two pieces of information together with a contrast linker, e.g. expectation + contrast linker: *but, whereas, yet* + the information David Sengeh gave.

3c

• Put students into pairs. They take turns to read the beginning of the talk to each other.

• Ask students to reflect on and give each other feedback on the differences they notice between their stress, rhythm and intonation, and David Sengeh's.

• Conduct whole-class feedback on the differences students noticed and elicit possible reasons for them, e.g. the influence of students' first language.

TEACHING TIP

Discussion about pronunciation

Students are all likely to find the same aspects of David Sengeh's English different to the English they're used to hearing. He comes from Sierra Leone and his pronunciation is typical of a native of that country. Students may not be used to hearing African accents such as this one. However, at times his pronunciation is also very similar to British English pronunciation, e.g. his pronunciation of *beautiful* /ˈbjuːtəfʊl/ (*a small and very beautiful country*) is typical for British English. (Contrast this with the North American pronunciation: /ˈbjutəfəl/.) This could be explained by having English teachers at school who used British English. When it comes to David Sengeh's use of vocabulary, the influence of the time he has spent in the USA is evident and he uses words such as *custom* (BE: *custom-made*) and *figure it out* (BE: *work it out*). This could suggest that we're more likely to modify the vocabulary we use than our pronunciation as we travel and come into contact with other varieties of English.

You could use the features of David Sengeh's speech as the basis for discussion on students' own pronunciation and use of vocabulary especially with multilingual classes. For example, you could ask: *How would other people characterize your pronunciation and use of vocabulary? When you speak English, is your accent typical of people from your home country or with your first language? How strong is your accent? Are there also elements of British or North American English pronunciation in your speech? And what about vocabulary? Which do you use more often: British English or North American English? Or do you combine words from both varieties?* Students could discuss these questions either as a whole class or in small groups.

7.1 The sore problem of prosthetic limbs

TEDTALKS

1

- Books open. Draw students' attention to the photo. Ask: *What are these men doing? How many legs do they have? Do they have prosthetic limbs?* Possible answers could be: *They are playing football. They have one leg only and are using crutches.*

- Give students time to read the sentences. Remind them to focus on listening for the pieces of information needed to complete the sentences and not to worry about understanding every word David Sengeh says.

- ▶ 7.1 Play the whole talk once.

Transcript

0.13 *I was born and raised in Sierra Leone, a small and very beautiful country in West Africa, a country rich both in physical resources and creative talent.*

0.27 *However, Sierra Leone is infamous for a decade-long rebel war in the '90s when entire villages were burnt down. An estimated 8,000 men, women and children had their arms and legs amputated during this time. As my family and I ran for safety when I was about twelve from one of those attacks, I resolved that I would do everything I could to ensure that my own children would not go through the same experiences we had. They would, in fact, be part of a Sierra Leone where war and amputation were no longer a strategy for gaining power.*

1.07 *As I watched people who I knew, loved ones, recover from this devastation, one thing that deeply troubled me was that many of the amputees in the country would not use their prostheses. The reason, I would come to find out, was that their prosthetic sockets were painful because they did not fit well. The prosthetic socket is the part in which the amputee inserts their residual limb, and which connects to the prosthetic ankle. Even in the developed world, it takes a period of three weeks to often years for a patient to get a comfortable socket, if ever. Prosthetists still use conventional processes like moulding and casting to create single-material prosthetic sockets. Such sockets often leave intolerable amounts of pressure on the limbs of the patient, leaving them with pressure sores and blisters. It does not matter how powerful your prosthetic ankle is. If your prosthetic socket is uncomfortable, you will not use your leg, and that is just simply unacceptable in our age.*

2.20 *So one day, when I met professor Hugh Herr about two and a half years ago, and he asked me if I knew how to solve this problem, I said, 'No, not yet, but I would love to figure it out.' And so, for my PhD at the MIT Media Lab, I designed custom prosthetic sockets quickly and cheaply that are more comfortable than conventional*

prostheses. I used magnetic resonance imaging to capture the actual shape of the patient's anatomy, then use finite element modelling to better predict the internal stresses and strains on the normal forces, and then create a prosthetic socket for manufacture. We use a 3D printer to create a multi-material prosthetic socket which relieves pressure where needed on the anatomy of the patient. In short, we're using data to make novel sockets quickly and cheaply. In a recent trial we just wrapped up at the Media Lab, one of our patients, a US veteran who has been an amputee for about 20 years and worn dozens of legs, said of one of our printed parts, 'It's so soft, it's like walking on pillows.' (Laughter)

3.45 *Disability in our age should not prevent anyone from living meaningful lives. My hope and desire is that the tools and processes we develop in our research group can be used to bring highly functional prostheses to those who need them. For me, a place to begin healing the souls of those affected by war and disease is by creating comfortable and affordable interfaces for their bodies. Whether it's in Sierra Leone or in Boston, I hope this not only restores but indeed transforms their sense of human potential.*

4.29 *Thank you very much.*

4.31 *(Applause)*

Answers

1 boy 2 didn't wear 3 painful 4 doing his PhD
5 cheap 6 anywhere

- David Sengeh doesn't speak with a North American accent, but as some of his words are North American and he did his research at MIT (Massachusetts Institute of Technology), North American versions are listed first at the foot of the spread. In this unit, the differences in North American English and British English focus on spelling, vocabulary and pronunciation.

2

- Ask students to complete the sentences with five of the words and expressions in the box.

- ▶ 7.1 Play the first part (0.00–2.20) of the talk so that students can check their answers.

Answers

1 as a result of 2 promised himself 3 fit
4 find 5 acceptable

3

- Give students time to read the list of events.

- **Optional step.** Ask students to predict the correct order. They could do this in pairs.

- ▶ 7.1 Play the second part (2.20–3.45) of the talk so that students can put the events in order.

- Check answers with the class. Students can refer to the transcript on page 177.

Extra activity

Narrating David Sengeh's story

Books closed. Put students into pairs to narrate David Sengeh's story. Ask students to take turns to give each other an overview of the sequence of events. Encourage students to use sequencers and linking words, e.g. *after that*, *subsequently*, *as a result*, *which meant*, to link the events.

4

• ▶️ **7.1** Play the third part (3.45 to the end) of the talk so that students can decide whether the sentences represent David Sengeh's views.

• Put students into pairs to discuss and to give reasons for their answers.

• Conduct whole-class feedback and ask students if they can suggest any other sentences that represent David Sengeh's views. Students could refer to the transcript on page 177 to help them to do this. For example, another possible sentence could be that David Sengeh wants a society where war is no longer used to gain power: *I resolved that I would do everything I could to ensure that my own children would not go through the same experiences we had. They would, in fact, be part of a Sierra Leone where war and amputation were no longer a strategy for gaining power.*

5

• Look at the questions with the class. If necessary, clarify the meaning of:

   ramp – a sloping surface that connects two different levels (question 1, item 1)

   braille – a system of writing for blind people which they can read by touch (question 1, item 4)

• **Question 1.** Encourage students to think about how they've seen technology or design helping people with disabilities.

• **Question 2.** Students brainstorm ideas for other technologies or changes that would make life better for disabled people in their own community.

• Conduct whole-class feedback and ask students to tell the rest of the class the ideas they brainstormed in response to question 2.

Extra activity

An accessible workplace

Put students into small groups. Ask them to think about the accessibility of their school, institution or workplace. Ask: *How easy is it for disabled people, including the visually and hearing impaired, to enter and move around in the building and do the things they need to do there?* Students think about what things make it already accessible for disabled people, e.g. *There's a ramp to the front entrance of the building*, and what could be done to make it more accessible, e.g. *Add braille to the lifts*. Students then do a team presentation for the rest of the class on how accessible their place is and how it could be made (even) more accessible.

VOCABULARY IN CONTEXT

6

• ▶️ **7.2** Play the clips from the talk. When each multiple-choice question appears, pause the clip so that students can choose the correct definition.

Transcript and subtitles

1   one thing that deeply **troubled** me was that many of the amputees in the country would not use their prostheses
   a angered
   b pleased
   c worried

2   If your prosthetic socket is uncomfortable, you will not use your leg, and that is **just simply** unacceptable in our age.
   a almost
   b sadly
   c totally

3   he asked me if I knew how to solve this problem, I said, 'No, not yet, but I would love to **figure it out**.'
   a calculate the cost
   b find the answer
   c help you with it

4   I used magnetic resonance imaging to capture the **actual** shape of the patient's anatomy
   a current
   b imagined
   c real

5   In a recent trial we just **wrapped up** at the Media Lab, one of our patients, a US veteran
   a finished
   b published
   c started

6   Whether it's in Sierra Leone or in Boston, I hope this not only restores but **indeed** transforms their sense of human potential.
   a already
   b possibly
   c really

7

- Ask students to underline the words from Exercise 6: *troubles, simply* and *figure (it) out*. Elicit the meaning of the three expressions. Explain that you don't have to use *just* before *simply*. Students might remember that *figure (it) out* was also in Vocabulary in context in Unit 1.

- Ask students to complete the sentences so that they're true for them.

CRITICAL THINKING Asking significant questions

8

- Ask students to read the comment about the TED Talk.

- Ask students to identify 'the right question' that David Sengeh asked. They can refer to the transcript on page 177 if they need to. They can do this in pairs.

9

- Put students into pairs to discuss the questions. Monitor students while they're speaking and encourage them to refer to the transcript where necessary. Encourage students to give reasons for their answers. Then conduct whole-class feedback.

PRESENTATION SKILLS Taking the audience on a journey

10

- Ask students to read about taking the audience on a journey in the Presentation tips box.

- Ask students to identify what David Sengeh did in the beginning, middle and end of his talk. They could refer to the transcript to do this or to check their answers.

11

- Explain that students are going to watch three clips from the TED Talk, one from each of the three parts. Elicit what David Sengeh did in each part of the talk. Tell students that they have to decide which clip is from the beginning, which is from the middle and which is from the end of the talk.

- ▶ 7.3 Play the clips so that students can match them with the parts of the talk (B, M, E).

- Conduct whole-class feedback and ask students to explain how they knew which part of the talk the clip was from.

Transcript

1 *And so, for my PhD at the MIT Media Lab, I designed custom prosthetic sockets quickly and cheaply that are more comfortable than conventional prostheses.*

2 *As my family and I ran for safety when I was about twelve from one of those attacks, I resolved that I would do everything I could to ensure that my own children would not go through the same experiences we had.*

3 *If your prosthetic socket is uncomfortable, you will not use your leg, and that is just simply unacceptable in our age.*

12

- Put students into pairs to choose one of the innovations they discussed in Exercise 5 and to prepare a short (about two minutes long) presentation together.

- **Optional step.** You could discuss one of the innovations in Exercise 5 with the whole class and elicit the points that you could communicate about this situation in a presentation. Students could then discuss one of the three other situations in pairs.

- Tell students to follow the model that David Sengeh used to structure his TED Talk when they're planning their presentation.

- Encourage students to see this preparation stage as a time for research, reflection and organizing ideas, rather than the preparation of a 'script' to read out when they present their ideas.

13

- Put students into new pairs. They take turns to give their presentation. Monitor students while they're speaking.

- Ask students to give each other feedback on whether the three parts of their presentation are clear, giving reasons why they are or aren't. Then conduct whole-class feedback.

- You could ask one or two of the best presenters to give their presentation again to the rest of the class.

▶ Set Workbook pages 64–65 for homework.

7.2 New technology

GRAMMAR Passives

1

- Books open. Tell students to read the list of inventions and to tick the ones that they're familiar with. If necessary, clarify the meaning of:

  stem cell therapy – the use of stem cells (cells from which a variety of other cells can develop) to treat or to prevent a disease or illness (last item)

- Look at an example with the class. Elicit that 3D printers were invented in the 2000s.

- Ask students to match the inventions with the dates.

> **Answers**
>
> electric car 1880s, solar cells 1950s,
> computer mouse 1960s, fibre optics 1970s,
> stem cell therapy 1980s, driverless car 1980s,
> smartphone 1990s, 3D printer 2000s

- **Optional step.** Ask students to brainstorm other important inventions from the last 150 years and add these. If you have internet access, they can check the dates of their development online.

> **TEACHING TIP**
>
> ### How to say the names of decades
>
> Elicit or clarify the pronunciation of the names of decades in English. We say: 1950s (nineteen fifties), 1960s (nineteen sixties), 1970s (nineteen seventies), 1980s (nineteen eighties), 1990s (nineteen nineties). However, we call the first decade of the twenty-first century the 2000s (the two thousands) and the second decade the 2010s (the twenty tens). The third decade of the twenty-first century is then known as the 2020s (the twenty twenties) and so on, following the same pattern used for the decades in the twentieth century.

Extra activity

Students' personal technology timelines

Ask students to think about when they first owned pieces of personal technology, e.g. a desktop computer, a Walkman (if students are old enough to remember them), a laptop, a mobile phone, an MP3 player, a smartphone, a tablet. Students make a timeline with the years. Tell students that it's OK if they don't remember the exact years when they owned the piece of technology, they can estimate them. Put students into small groups to share and present their technology timelines, saying something about each type of technology and the effect it had on their lives. Students give each other feedback on their presentation and ask follow-up questions.

2

- Ask students to look at the infographic. You could put students into pairs to discuss and decide together whether the inventions from Exercise 1 were the result of the research and development process they can see in the infographic.

- Conduct whole-class feedback and elicit that the development of all these inventions could have been the result of the process in the infographic.

3

- Tell students that they're going to read a text about fibre optics. Ask: *What do you know about developments in the area of fibre optics?*

- Ask students to read the text in the Grammar box and to answer the questions. They can do this in pairs. Remind students that they have already done some work with present simple and present continuous passives in Unit 1.

- Students can check their answers and overall understanding of passives by turning to the Grammar summary on page 152.

> **Answers**
>
> Fibre optics is a technology which allows information <u>to be transmitted</u> along a flexible, transparent fibre. The technology <u>was initially researched</u> in the mid-20th century. The term <u>was made</u> popular in 1960 following an article in *Scientific American* by Narinder Singh. By the 1970s, the first commercially successful optical fibre <u>had been developed</u>. Since then, many uses for fibre optics in telecommunications and medicine <u>have been identified</u>. New applications <u>are being tested</u> all the time and it's clear that fibre optics <u>will be used</u> in a wide range of contexts in the future.
>
> 1 *be*   2 d

- If you feel that students need more controlled practice before continuing, they could do some or all of the exercises in the Grammar summary. Otherwise, you could continue on to Exercise 4 in the unit and set the Grammar exercises for homework.

> **Answers to Grammar summary exercises**
>
> **1**
>
> 1 A 3D printer was taken to the International Space Station (by an astronaut).
>
> 2 When was the computer mouse invented?
>
> 3 Was stem cell therapy being used in the 1990s (by doctors)?
>
> 4 Fibre optic cables weren't installed in my area until last year.
>
> 5 Which company are driverless cars being manufactured by?
>
> 6 Were electric cars being demonstrated at the exhibition?

2

1 have been prescribed   2 had been examined
3 has been contacted   4 hasn't been spoken
5 had (the results of the tests already) been given
6 has (the patient) been taken

3

1 should be accompanied   2 won't be implemented
3 must be notified   4 will (the building checks) be
completed   5 shouldn't be used   6 should (these
boxes) be delivered   7 Can (the invitations) be sent
8 mustn't be seen

4

1 a   2 b   3 b   4 a   5 b   6 b

5

1 by   2 for   3 by   4 for   5 by   6 for

6

1 The emails were ~~send~~ **sent** yesterday.
2 Too many changes ~~are~~ **have** been made too quickly.
3 The faulty device was sold ~~for~~ **by** most shops.
4 The report will ~~publish~~ **be published** next week.
5 Many people ~~was~~ **were** questioned in the survey.
6 All of this work has **been** done by our group.

4

- Explain that students are going to read a text about nanotechnology. Ask: *Have you heard of nanotechnology? If so, what do you know about nanotechnology and its development?*

- Ask students to complete the paragraph about nanotechnology with the passive verbs.

- Check answers and draw students' attention to the use of the structure *be* + past participle in passive forms with modal verbs (*can't, should, need, will*).

Answers

2 can't be seen   3 has been used   4 should be handled
5 needs to be regulated   6 will be disposed of

Extra activity

Write about an invention

Students write about the development of an invention (not fibre optics or nanotechnology). They can use the text in the Grammar box as a model and include a range of passive forms. Students exchange texts in pairs and give each other feedback on how successfully they've used passives.

5

- Elicit that we usually use active forms when the focus is on the person or agent doing the activity and passive forms when the focus is on the process or activity itself.

- Students choose the correct form of the verbs to complete the text.

Answers

1 have been developed   2 are caused   3 are delivered
4 can stop   5 are given   6 haven't been kept
7 is being tested   8 have been working   9 will make

6

- Ask students to read the article in Exercise 5 again and to look for examples of *by* and *for*. Elicit that these are in lines 2, 4 and 6.

- Students use the examples of *by* and *for* in the article to decide what they're used to say.

Answers

1 for   2 by

7

- Ask students to read the sentences and to decide whether they're giving information about *why* or *how* something happens. Elicit that we use *for* with *why* and *by* for *how*.

- Students complete the sentences and then compare their answers in pairs.

Answers

1 by   2 by   3 by   4 for   5 for   6 by

SPEAKING Technology in everyday life

8   **21st CENTURY OUTCOMES**

- Tell students that in this exercise they're going to look at two inventions, and focus on how successfully they have achieved their goals and how important they are in order to fulfil the 21st CENTURY OUTCOME.

- Look at the list of inventions with the class. If necessary, clarify the meaning of:

  biodegradable – capable of being broken down by bacteria or other living organisms (item 6)

- Put students into small groups to discuss what they know about each invention. They should discuss what problem each invention solves and what purpose it has.

- Students discuss and reach a consensus on which two inventions they think are the most important. Encourage them to think of reasons or evidence to support their choices.

- **Optional step.** Students do a group presentation about the two inventions they think are the most important. In the presentation, students should include the following: some background information about the invention and its development, the influence the invention has had on the world, why it's one of the most important inventions in the list.

▶ Photocopiable communicative activity 7.1: Go to page 225 for practice of passives. The teaching notes are on page 243.

▶ Set Workbook pages 66–67 for homework.

7.3 Innovative approaches

READING The real value of digital tools

Extra activity

Digital tools

Ask students to brainstorm any digital tools they know. Encourage students to include both objects, e.g. smartphones and tablets, and online platforms, e.g. online learning, digital or interactive whiteboards, social media. Then ask students to rank these according to their value. They can do this in pairs. Then conduct whole-class feedback, and ask students to present their rankings.

1

• Books open. Put students into pairs to talk about their experiences of using digital technology as students or adult learners and how digital technology has changed since they first started school. Encourage them to use the examples in the box as a starting point for their discussion, but to also talk about any other types of digital technology which they have used.

• Conduct whole-class feedback and ask as many students as possible to share their experiences of digital technology.

• **Optional step.** Individual students make recommendations to the class for types of digital technology which they think are worth buying.

2

• Ask students to read the article quickly and to identify which examples of digital technology in Exercise 1 are mentioned. They can then compare their answers in pairs.

• Check answers with the class and confirm which forms of digital technology are mentioned in the article.

Answers
tablets, online learning

• **Optional step.** Students read the article again quickly and identify the other types of digital technology mentioned in it. These are: digital or interactive whiteboards, computer coding and programming, social networking sites, computers and mobile devices.

3

• Explain that students are going to read the article again. This time they're going to read for detail.

• Ask students to read the article to find out which sentences are true and false.

• **Optional step.** Put students into pairs to discuss whether they agree or disagree with the true statements in sentences 4, 5 and 6. Then conduct whole-class feedback.

Answers
1 F (According to the European Commission, young people are not necessarily competent in the skills needed to work in the digital economy.)

2 F (Traditional chalkboards have been replaced by digital whiteboards in classrooms across Europe. There's been a massive investment in both hardware and software in education.)

3 F (Experts are in favour of this being taught in the same way as other traditional subjects, which suggests that is not currently taught traditionally.)

4 T   5 T   6 T

4

• **Optional step.** Encourage students to look at only the words in bold that they don't know, to find them in the text and to try to work out their meaning from the context. They can use the three options to help them to do this.

• Ask students to choose the correct meaning for the words from the article.

Answers
1 b   2 a   3 b   4 b   5 b   6 a   7 c   8 b

• **Optional step.** Ask students to identify the nouns in the list of eight words and then decide if they are countable or uncountable. Answers: *recreation* (uncountable), *hardware* (uncountable), *shortage* (countable), *access* (uncountable), *device* (countable), *flexibility* (uncountable).

5

• **Optional step.** Ask students to identify the parts of the article where the suggestions are made. They could use the information in those parts to inform their decisions about whether they agree or disagree with them.

• Put students into pairs to discuss whether they agree or disagree with the suggestions made in the article. Then conduct whole-class feedback.

VOCABULARY Innovation: verbs

6

• Look at item 1 as an example with the class. Elicit that *replaced by* is a synonym for *changed for*.

• Ask students to read the other sentences and to match the words in bold with the synonyms in the box.

• Check answers with the class. Ask individual students to read out a sentence each, replacing the words in bold with the synonyms. Elicit or explain that they may need to change the verb form.

Answers
1 replace(d) by   2 introduce(d)   3 exploit(ed)
4 improve   5 enable(s)   6 inspire(d)   7 got round
8 put into practice

7

- Elicit that *exploit your time* means to make use of your time (first bullet).

- Put students into pairs to tell each other about three things in the list. Students don't have to limit themselves to three, they can talk about more than three of the things. Remind them to talk about their own experiences or things that are true for them. Then conduct whole-class feedback.

SPEAKING New ideas for unexpected problems

8 21st CENTURY OUTCOMES

- Explain that students are going to think about a problem and then discuss it in small groups in Exercise 9 in order to fulfil the 21st CENTURY OUTCOME.

- Ask students to read the beginning of the news item. Elicit or explain that a primary school is for children aged 5–11.

- Put students into pairs to discuss what answer they think the teachers expected to get and possible reasons why the pupil gave the answer that he/she did.

- Conduct whole-class feedback and confirm that the expected answer was 'from cows' or something similar, but this wasn't the answer given because nowadays young people are used to getting all their food and drink from supermarkets and aren't so aware of where food and drink comes from.

> **Suggested answer**
>
> from cows

- **Optional step.** Bring in students' own experiences. Ask: *What answer do you think young people you know would give to the same question? Do you think the news item is a fair representation of young people's views about food in the place where you live?*

9

- Put students into small groups to discuss what they would do to help schoolchildren to understand more about where their food comes from, how it's produced and how it gets to their plates. Tell students to think about what they want to achieve, how to do it and what results they would like to see.

- Monitor students while they're speaking, offering help where necessary. Encourage students to think of concrete and specific suggestions for how to educate schoolchildren.

- **Optional step.** Ask students to present their proposals to the rest of the class. If appropriate, students could also create a PowerPoint presentation. Students can then vote on which proposal they think is the best.

▶ Photocopiable communicative activity 7.2: Go to page 226 for practice of innovation: verbs, and revision of passives. The teaching notes are on page 243.

▶ Set Workbook pages 68–69 for homework.

7.4 It can all be done online

VOCABULARY Online operations

1

- Books open. Put students into pairs to discuss which of the operations in the list they do online, whether they feel safe when doing online operations, and why or why not.

- Conduct whole-class feedback to gauge how safe or unsafe students feel when doing online operations and the reasons for this. Ask: *Have you or anyone you know ever had problems as a result of doing operations online?*

2

- Ask students to choose the correct option to complete the sentences.

> **Answers**
> ___
> 1 PIN number   2 security question   3 log in with
> 4 e-tickets   5 password

- **Optional step.** Students write similar sentences about online security that include the words that weren't the correct options, i.e. *email address, username, save, touchscreens, bank account number.* Conduct whole-class feedback and invite individual students to write one of their sentences on the board.

LISTENING New ways of doing things

3

- Ask students to look at the operations in Exercise 1 again. Explain that they're going to listen to three conversations, each of which is about one of the online operations in Exercise 1.

- 🎧 37 Play the recording so that students can match the situations with the operations.

Transcript

1

TS = Ticket seller, C = Customer

TS: *… and here are your tickets. Did you know that you can now get e-tickets for all our local bus journeys?*

C: *No, I didn't. How does that work?*

TS: *Just go to our website and choose the kind of ticket you want, and they'll be downloaded to your phone.*

C: *And will I have to download an app to use them?*

TS: *Yes, but there are several apps you can choose from. Our tickets work with them all.*

C: *What about paying for them? How would I do that?*

TS: *All the main cards are accepted and there's no extra charge for paying by card.*

C: *Well, it sounds simple enough. Maybe I'll have a go next time.*

2

C = Customer, BE = Bank employee

C: *Excuse me, I wonder if you could help. How do I pay my electricity bill with the self-service machine?*

BE: *Yes, of course. Let me show you how to do it. OK, so after you've put in your card and your PIN number, choose 'make a payment' on the touchscreen.*

C: *Right. And what do I need to do now?*

BE: *Now you key in your account number – the one from the bill – and the amount to be paid.*

C: *OK. And how will I know if it's been paid correctly?*

BE: *You can print out a receipt by choosing that option on the screen, or you can see your account details. It's updated immediately.*

C: *Thanks for all your help.*

3

C = Customer, SA = Shop assistant

C: *I shop here quite regularly, so I'm interested in getting your store credit card.*

SA: *Yes, I can do that for you. If you have your bank details with you, it's easy to arrange today.*

C: *OK, could I just ask a couple of questions about how it works? When would the money be taken from my account?*

SA: *The payments are monthly, on the first day of the month, and you can see all the details on your credit card statement.*

C: *How often are the statements sent out?*

SA: *They're also monthly.*

C: *And where do they go? To my home address?*

SA: *No, they're sent by email.*

C: *And is there a minimum amount I need to spend?*

• Conduct whole-class feedback and encourage students to identify the speakers and to say in detail what they are talking about. For example: *1 a ticket seller is explaining to an elderly customer about getting e-tickets for local bus journeys.*

Answers

1 buying travel tickets   2 paying bills
3 using credit cards

4

• Explain that the numbers (1–3) in the Useful language box refer to the three conversations and that the customer in each conversation asked the questions.

• Ask students to read the questions in the Useful language box. When students listen to the recording again, they have to put themselves in the position of the ticket seller, bank employee and shop assistant, and answer the questions. Tell students to focus on writing down key words and phrases which they can then use to reconstruct the complete answers.

• [▲37] Play the recording so that students can answer the questions. They can then compare their answers in pairs.

Answers

1

you download the tickets from the website to your phone

yes

by credit card

2

key in the account number and the amount

by printing a receipt or looking at your account details

3

monthly

monthly

to your email address

Pronunciation Linking with /w/

5a

• [▲38] Play the recording and ask students to focus on how the underlined words are linked with the /w/ sound at the end of the first underlined word.

Transcript

1   *How will I <u>know if</u> it's been paid correctly?*

2   *Could I just ask a couple of questions about <u>how it</u> works?*

3   *<u>How often</u> are the statements sent out?*

• Check that students noticed the way the two words become linked, i.e. the /w/ sound becomes the first sound in the second word. Play the recording again if necessary.

• Explain that linking with /w/ is an example of connected speech, which is regularly used by native English speakers.

• **Optional step.** Ask students if they know any other words ending in /w/, e.g. *draw/drew, flew, low, new, now, saw, show.*

Background information

Connected speech

Connected speech is the linking of adjacent words by a speaker. It results in the pronunciation of words being affected by those that surround them as the boundaries between words shift. Individual sounds change and new sounds are added. Being aware of these changes helps students to understand native speakers and also helps their own speech to sound more natural and fluent.

5b

- Ask students to read the sentences. Elicit that the underlined words don't include the letter /w/, but the sound linking the first underlined word to the second is /w/.

- 🔊 **39** Play the recording and ask students to focus on how the underlined words are linked with the /w/ sound at the end of the first underlined word.

Transcript and answers

1 There's <u>no extra</u> charge for paying by card.

2 How <u>do I</u> pay my electricity bill?

3 Let me show you how to <u>do it</u>.

4 <u>the one</u> from the bill

5 <u>So I'm</u> interested in getting your store credit card.

6 It's easy <u>to arrange</u> today.

- Check that students noticed the way the two words become linked, i.e. the /w/ sound is added in between the two underlined words. Play the recording again if necessary.

- Elicit that in these examples the /w/ sound is added to link the two words.

Background information

Intrusion

Intrusion involves inserting additional sounds in between two words that are said together in connected speech. The insertion of the /w/ sound between two adjacent words is a typical example of intrusion.

5c

- You could put students into pairs to practise saying the sentences. Encourage students to correct each other's pronunciation of the inserted /w/ sound where necessary.

6 *21st* CENTURY OUTCOMES

- You could ask students to evaluate their English oral and written skills, and decide which they think are stronger and what the reasons for this could be. They could then discuss this in pairs. Tell students that in this exercise they're going to practise using their oral skills to articulate ideas and information effectively in order to fulfil the 21st CENTURY OUTCOME.

- Elicit or give students example operations that they could choose, e.g. making a bank transfer online or buying something online. Tell students that they shouldn't choose an operation which is too simple, i.e. one that only involves one or two steps, or one which is too complicated, e.g. setting up a website.

- Put students into pairs to explain the process involved in the operation they've chosen. Students then ask each other questions to clarify details of the process or to find out more.

WRITING A formal online message

7

- **Optional step.** Tell students to take a quick look at the online message from a bank to its customers. Ask: *Have you ever received a similar message from your bank? If so, what was the purpose of the message(s)?*

- Students read the message and identify its purpose. They can then check their answer in pairs before you check with the whole class.

Answer

c

8

- Ask students to read the list of features of formal communication. Explain that not including the recipient's name doesn't always indicate a formal style as this can also happen in informal communication. Elicit that using a title (*Mr, Ms*, etc.) and a surname is the way that people usually write their name in formal communication.

- Ask students to identify and to underline the parts of the message where they can see evidence of the features. They can do this in pairs.

Answers

a Important changes to our online banking service

b Online Services Director

c Dear Customer

d Pauline Harris

e You will receive, You do not need

Writing skill Being clear and precise

9a

- Ask students to read the message again and to underline the parts that provide the answers to the questions.

- Students can then work in pairs. They take turns to ask and answer the questions, using the information from the message.

Answers

(2) From November of this year the system for logging in to your bank account online will change.

(1) The existing security questions will be replaced by a secure number system. (3) You will receive instructions on how to generate your personal secure number by letter to your home address.

(4) These changes will ensure that our online banking service is safer than ever and will enable you to access your account more easily when you are mobile.

(5) You do not need to do anything at this time.

9b

- Elicit or explain that although writing clearly and precisely may be more challenging, it makes your message easier to understand.

- Look at comment 1 as an example with the class. Elicit that the writer doesn't make it clear when the person will send the letter. The comment is also longer than it needs to be: instead of *put in the post* we can say *send*, for example. Elicit that the clearer and more precise version of this comment would be: *I will send you the form as soon as possible.*

- Ask students to use the verbs in brackets to rewrite the other sentences in a clear and precise way.

- Conduct whole-class feedback and elicit or explain that the sentences students have written are more formal in style than the original comments. Students may actually find the less formal original comments easier to understand. Ask: *Which sentences do you actually find easier to understand? Why?*

Answers

1 I will send you the form as soon as possible.

2 From next month, airport check-in will not be available.

3 New charges now apply.

4 Due to lack of space, bikes are no longer allowed on trains.

5 You have to contact the insurance company with your change of address.

6 Our new opening hours will improve our service to customers.

10 *21st* CENTURY OUTCOMES

- Before starting this exercise, refer students to the 21st CENTURY OUTCOMES at the foot of the page. Elicit that students had the opportunity to articulate their ideas using oral skills in Exercise 5 and now they can do this in writing.

- Ask students to read the description of their problem.

- Tell students to write a message which they could send to their bank's 'Send us a message' space which explains the problem and asks for help. They should focus on explaining the problem, and on writing in a clear and precise way.

- Monitor students while they're writing. Focus on whether students are writing in a clear and precise way. Offer suggestions for how they could make their writing clearer or more precise where appropriate.

11

- Put students into pairs and ask them to exchange messages. They then read each other's message, and check that this explains when and how the problem happens. They could underline the parts of the message where the writer has explained these things.

- Students give the message back, and give each other feedback on how successfully the message has explained when and how the problem happens.

- Monitor students while they're giving each other feedback. Where appropriate, ask students questions to prompt them to give more detail in their feedback and add your comments to students' feedback. Make a note of which students have written some of the strongest messages.

- Ask the students who've written the strongest messages to read out their messages to the rest of the class.

Suggested answer

I have a problem that I hope you can help me with: I can't get into my online account. When I type in my details, they are accepted. However, the screen then always freezes.

I look forward to hearing from you.

Yours sincerely

TEACHING TIP

Peer feedback

It's important that students don't only get feedback from you, but also from their peers. Firstly, other students may spot things that you miss or bring a different perspective to yours. Secondly, the giving and receiving of peer feedback helps to build and strengthen a supportive and collaborative learning environment in your classroom. Students may, however, not be familiar with how to give constructive feedback to their peers.

By this stage, students will have had several opportunities to give feedback to each other and you will have had the chance to observe how they do it. Students are likely to have a tendency to give feedback which is too positive and too general, but positive and general feedback isn't always very helpful. Tell students that it's OK for them to mention things that weren't so good as long as they frame them as suggestions for improvement – this is what feedback is, after all. Also, encourage students to be specific when giving feedback, for example, by using specific things a student wrote or said or didn't write or say to support the points they want to make. Making notes or underlining words while they're reading something their partner has written or making notes on what their partner says while they're listening to them should help students to collect those specific examples.

▶ Set Workbook pages 70–71 for homework.

▶ Set Workbook Presentation 4 on pages 72–73 for homework.

8 Balance

LEAD IN

• Books open. Draw students' attention to the unit title, and to the photo and its caption on page 84. Elicit or explain that *slacklining* involves balancing on a piece of rope which is slack, i.e. the rope is loose or not held tightly in position. Ask: *Have you or anyone you know every tried slacklining? What skills or qualities do you think you need to have in order to be good at slacklining?* Possible answers could be: *a good sense of balance, courage, muscular strength.*

• Ask: *What do we have to balance in our lives?* Possible answers could be: *eating healthily and eating things we prefer, being active and relaxing, the amount of money you have coming in and going out, spending time with your family and time with your friends.* Bring in students' own experiences. Ask: *Do you find any of these things difficult to balance and, if so, why? What would make it easier for you to balance them?*

• Students will most likely mention that they have to balance time for work or study with time for relaxation. To gauge students' prior knowledge of the unit vocabulary, write all the letters of the alphabet on the board and ask students to think of a word for or connected with something you can do to relax or enjoy yourself that starts with each letter. Students can do this in pairs. For example, for *a* students could have *angling, archery* or *abseiling.* When students have words for every letter of the alphabet, or as many as they can think of, ask individual students to write a few of their words on the board until there is a word next to every letter.

TEDTALKS
BACKGROUND

1

• Ask students to read the text about Nigel Marsh and his talk. Elicit that *work–life balance* is being able to balance your working life with the rest of your life. If necessary, clarify the meaning of:

vastly improve – improve a lot (line 8)

• Ask students whether they agree with Nigel Marsh that you don't need to make a dramatic change in your lifestyle in order to achieve a good work–life balance, you can do this by focusing on the 'small things'.

• Put students into pairs to discuss the questions. Then conduct whole-class feedback.

• **Question 1.** Students could talk about people they know who have and don't have a work–life balance.

• **Question 2.** Point out that relationships don't only have to be romantic, they can also be any connection we have with the people in our lives.

• **Question 3.** Encourage students to focus on the positive effects relationships can have on someone's quality of life and also to think about what factors can have a negative effect on those relationships, e.g. the amount of time we spend at work or away from home.

KEY WORDS

2

• Ask students to try to guess the meaning of the words in bold and then to match them with their definitions.

Answers
1 e   2 c   3 b   4 f   5 d   6 a

AUTHENTIC LISTENING SKILLS Elision: dropped vowels

3a

• If students have completed Unit 2 and/or Unit 4, elicit that elision is the omission of certain sounds in words. If students haven't completed Unit 2, explain what elision is.

▶ Background information: Elision, Unit 2.2 on page 30

- Ask students to read the information about dropped vowels in the Authentic listening skills box. If necessary, clarify the meaning of:

  compressed syllable – a syllable in the middle of a word that isn't pronounced (line 3)

- Elicit that in the word *comfortable*, the second syllable (comf**or**table) isn't pronounced.

- Ask students to read the phrases from the TED Talk and to focus on the words in bold. They should practise saying the words and predict which syllable will not be pronounced.

- ⬛ **40** Play the recording so that students can listen to the phrases and cross out the syllable that isn't pronounced in the words in bold.

Transcript

1   your **miserable** existence

2   classic **corporate** warrior

3   neglecting the **family**

Answers
1 miserable   2 corporate   3 family

Background information

Syllabic compression

Syllabic compression is the omission of a mid-word unstressed syllable while speaking. When it occurs, the consonant sound blends with the preceding or following syllable. The use of syllabic compression is almost always optional and the result of speaker preference, but it is more commonly used in some words than others and more commonly used by native than non-native English speakers.

3b

- Ask students to read the phrases from the TED Talk and to predict which syllables in the words in bold are pronounced and which are not pronounced.

- ⬛ **41** Play the recording so that students can listen and check their predictions.

Transcript

4   **especially** when the money runs out

5   enforcing the **boundaries**

6   I've got no mates or **interests** left

Answers
4 three   5 two   6 two

3c

- ⬛ **42** Play the recording so that students can listen and repeat. It shouldn't be necessary to pause the recording for students to repeat. However, as the words have been extracted from the TED Talk, they are quite 'clipped'. You might prefer to say the words yourself for students to repeat.

Answers
1 miserable   2 corporate   3 family   4 especially
5 boundaries   6 interests

8.1 How to make work–life balance work

TEDTALKS

1

- Books open. Give students time to read the list of possible observations. They could try to predict which four they think Nigel Marsh will make.

- ▶ **8.1** Play the whole talk once so that students can identify which observations Nigel Marsh makes.

Transcript

0.14   What I thought I would do is I would start with a simple request. I'd like all of you to pause for a moment, you wretched weaklings, and take stock of your miserable existence. (Laughter)

0.31   Now that was the advice that St. Benedict gave his rather startled followers in the fifth century. It was the advice that I decided to follow myself when I turned 40. Up until that moment, I had been that classic corporate warrior – I was eating too much, I was drinking too much, I was working too hard and I was neglecting the family. And I decided that I would try and turn my life around. In particular, I decided I would try to address the thorny issue of work–life balance. So I stepped back from the workforce, and I spent a year at home with my wife and four young children. But all I learned about work–life balance from that year was that I found it quite easy to balance work and life when I didn't have any work. (Laughter) Not a very useful skill, especially when the money runs out.

1.30   So I went back to work, and I've spent these seven years since struggling with, studying and writing about work–life balance. And I have four observations I'd like to share with you today. The first is: if society's to make any progress on this issue, we need an honest debate. But the trouble is so many people talk so much rubbish about work–life balance. All the discussions about flexitime or dress-down Fridays or paternity leave only serve to mask the core issue, which is that certain job and career choices are fundamentally incompatible with being meaningfully engaged on a day-to-day basis with a young family. Now the first step in solving any problem is acknowledging the reality of the situation you're in. And the reality of the society that we're in is there are thousands and thousands of people out there leading lives of quiet, screaming desperation, where they work long, hard hours at jobs they hate to enable them to buy things they don't need to impress people they don't like. (Laughter) (Applause) *It's my contention that going to work on Friday in jeans and [a] T-shirt isn't really getting to the nub of the issue.*

3.02   (Laughter)

3.06   *The second observation I'd like to make is we need to face the truth that governments and corporations aren't going to solve this issue for us. We should stop looking outside. It's up to us as individuals to take control and responsibility for the type of lives that we want to lead. If you don't design your life, someone else will design it for you, and you may just not like their idea of balance. On the one hand, putting childcare facilities in the workplace is wonderful and enlightened. On the other hand, it's a nightmare – it just means you spend more time at the bloody office. We have to be responsible for setting and enforcing the boundaries that we want in our life.*

3.57   *The third observation is we have to be careful with the time frame that we choose upon which to judge our balance. We need to be realistic. You can't do it all in one day. We need to elongate the time frame upon which we judge the balance in our life, but we need to elongate it without falling into the trap of the 'I'll have a life when I retire, when my kids have left home, when my wife has divorced me, my health is failing, I've got no mates or interests left.'* (Laughter) *A day is too short; 'after I retire' is too long. There's got to be a middle way.*

4.42   *A fourth observation: we need to approach balance in a balanced way. A friend came to see me last year – and she doesn't mind me telling this story – a friend came to see me last year and said, 'Nigel, I've read your book. And I realize that my life is completely out of balance. It's totally dominated by work. I work ten hours a day; I commute two hours a day. All of my relationships have failed. There's nothing in my life apart from my work. So I've decided to get a grip and sort it out. So I joined a gym.'* (Laughter) *Now I don't mean to mock, but being a fit ten-hour-a-day office rat isn't more balanced; it's more fit.* (Laughter) *Lovely though physical exercise may be, there are other parts to life – there's the intellectual side; there's the emotional side; there's the spiritual side. And to be balanced, I believe we have to attend to all of those areas – not just do 50 stomach crunches.*

5.51   *I truly understand how that can be daunting. But an incident that happened a couple of years ago gave me a new perspective. My wife, who is somewhere in the audience today, called me up at the office and said, 'Nigel, you need to pick our youngest son' – Harry – 'up from school.' Because she had to be somewhere else with the other three children for that evening. So I left*

work an hour early that afternoon and picked Harry up at the school gates. We walked down to the local park, messed around on the swings, played some silly games. I then walked him up the hill to the local café, and we shared a pizza for tea, then walked down the hill to our home, and I gave him his bath and put him in his Batman pyjamas. I then read him a chapter of Roald Dahl's *James and the Giant Peach. I then put him to bed, tucked him in, gave him a kiss on his forehead and said, 'Goodnight, mate,' and walked out of his bedroom. As I was walking out of his bedroom, he said, 'Dad?' I went, 'Yes, mate?' He went, 'Dad, this has been the best day of my life, ever.' I hadn't done anything, hadn't taken him to Disney World or bought him a Playstation.*

7.07   *Now my point is the small things matter. Being more balanced doesn't mean dramatic upheaval in your life. With the smallest investment in the right places, you can radically transform the quality of your relationships and the quality of your life. Moreover, I think, it can transform society. Because if enough people do it, we can change society's definition of success away from the moronically simplistic notion that the person with the most money when he dies wins, to a more thoughtful and balanced definition of what a life well lived looks like. And that, I think, is an idea worth spreading.*

7.54   (Applause)

Answers

a, c, d, f

• **Optional step.** Ask students if they agree with what Nigel Marsh says about how to achieve a good work–life balance. You could also ask students whether they think Nigel Marsh might be likely to make the other two observations.

• Note the differences in North American English and British English shown at the foot of the spread. In this unit, these focus on vocabulary and spelling differences. Nigel Marsh moved from Britain to Australia in 2001, so he uses British English in this TED Talk. See page 6 of the Introduction for ideas on how to present and practise these differences.

2

• Give students time to read the sentences. If necessary, clarify the meaning of:

  the root of the problem – the cause of or real reason for the problem (sentence 4)

• ▶ 8.1 Play the first part (0.00–3.06) of the talk so that students can complete the sentences with the words and expressions Nigel Marsh uses.

Answers

1 life   2 easy   3 rubbish   4 jeans and T-shirt

3

• ▶ 8.1 Play the second part (3.06–5.51) of the talk so that students can decide whether the sentences are true or false.

• Students can refer to the transcript on page 178 to check their answers before you check with the whole class.

Answers

1 T

2 T

3 F (A friend whose life was out of balance told Nigel Marsh that she had joined a gym. He thinks that to be balanced involves more than just being fit.)

4 T

• **Optional step.** Put students into pairs to discuss whether they agree or disagree with the true sentences (1, 2 and 4). Then conduct whole-class feedback.

4

• Put students into pairs. Explain that they're going to watch the third part of the talk again and then retell the events from the afternoon Nigel Marsh spent with his son Harry. Advise students to make notes or create a timeline to help them remember what happened.

• ▶ 8.1 Play the third part (5.51 to the end) of the talk. Students work in pairs and retell the story.

• Monitor students while they're speaking and identify students who are the most confident at retelling the events. You can then ask these students to retell all or part of the story during whole-class feedback.

Suggested answer

Nigel Marsh and his son did nothing special on the afternoon they spent together (they walked down to the local park, messed around on the swings, played some silly games, walked up the hill to the local café, shared a pizza for tea, walked down the hill to their home, then Nigel gave Harry his bath, put him in his Batman pyjamas, then read him a chapter of Roald Dahl's *James and the Giant Peach*, then put him to bed, tucked him in, gave him a kiss on his forehead, said 'Goodnight' and walked out of his bedroom). But his son said, 'Dad, this has been the best day of my life, ever.' The important thing to Harry was that they had spent time together.

TEACHING TIP

Retelling stories

Retelling stories in their own words can help students to develop spoken fluency. However, they may lack confidence in retelling stories if they haven't had a lot of or any experience of doing it. Make sure that students do retelling activities with a partner they feel comfortable with and reassure them that they won't have to retell the events in front of the rest of the class if they feel uncomfortable with that.

We usually use mental imagery to help us retell a story, so you could encourage students to draw a short series of sketches to map the events as they listen. If students don't feel comfortable sketching, encourage them to write key words and create a timeline of events when they've finished listening. Students can then use their sketches or timelines as visual prompts when they're retelling.

5

• Give students time to read the extract from Nigel Marsh's concluding comments. If necessary, clarify the meaning of:

   upheaval – a major period of change which can cause conflict, confusion and anger (second line)

• Put students into small groups to discuss whether they agree with Nigel Marsh. Remind them to give reasons for their opinions and then to share examples of the 'small things' they could focus on in their lives. Encourage students to think of some examples of 'small things' even if they disagree with Nigel Marsh. Then conduct whole-class feedback.

Extra activity

Nigel Marsh's hand movements and gestures

Draw students' attention to the photo montage of Nigel Marsh on page 86. Elicit that Nigel Marsh uses different hand movements and gestures in each photo from the TED Talk. Ask: *How important is it to use hand gestures and body language to express yourself when you're presenting?* You could put students into pairs to discuss what message they think Nigel Marsh could be communicating or what he could be saying in the photos. For example, in the photo which is second from the right in the second row, Nigel Marsh's body language suggests thinking about something; in the photo which is second from the left in the bottom row, he seems to be talking about how much of something there is or how long something is. Then conduct whole-class feedback. Students will look at hand movements and gestures in presentations in Unit 10.

VOCABULARY IN CONTEXT

6

• ▶8.2 Play the clips from the TED Talk. When each multiple-choice questions appears, pause the clip so that students can choose the correct definition.

• You could elicit the meaning of *elongate* (item 2) by writing the word *long* on the board and asking students what they think the verb *elongate* means.

Transcript and subtitles

1   we need to **face the truth** that governments and corporations aren't going to solve this issue for us
    a   accept
    b   demand
    c   explain

2   we need to elongate it without **falling into the trap of** the 'I'll have a life when I retire'
    a   tripping over
    b   hurting ourselves
    c   making the mistake

3   A day is too short; 'after I retire' is too long. There's got to be **a middle way**.
    a   alternative
    b   compromise
    c   ending

4   So I've decided to **get a grip** and sort it out.
    a   hold
    b   start again
    c   take control

5   We walked down to the local park, **messed around** on the swings
    a   played some games
    b   made a mess for no reason
    c   spent time with no purpose

> **Answers**
>
> 1 a   2 c   3 b   4 c   5 c

7

• Ask students to complete the sentences in their own words. Elicit or explain that in sentence 2, *of* has to be followed by a verb in the *-ing* form.

• Fast finishers could work in pairs and take turns to complete the sentences in different ways. This could have a competitive element as students try to make more sentences than their partner.

CRITICAL THINKING Convincing the listener

8

• Ask students to read the comments about the TED Talk and to identify which technique each comment refers to.

> **Answers**
>
> Jamila – first-hand experience
> Frank – general observations

9

• Put students into pairs to discuss the questions.

• **Optional step.** After a few minutes' discussion in pairs, invite volunteers to share their opinions on how convincingly Nigel Marsh explained his ideas.

PRESENTATION SKILLS Pace and emphasis

10

• Ask students to look at the Presentation tips box. Explain that they are going to focus on which of the three techniques Nigel Marsh uses in a clip from the TED Talk.

• ▶8.3 Play the clip so that students can decide which techniques Nigel Marsh uses.

Transcript

As I was walking out of his bedroom, he said, 'Dad?' I went, 'Yes, mate?' He went, 'Dad, this has been the best day of my life, ever.' I hadn't done anything, hadn't taken him to Disney World or bought him a Playstation.

Now my point is the small things matter. Being more balanced doesn't mean dramatic upheaval in your life.

> **Answers**
>
> Nigel Marsh varies his speed and he pauses for emphasis.

• If students say that they think Nigel Marsh speaks very quickly, then say that they are right: both non-native and native speakers would most likely find that he speaks quickly.

11

• Ask students to each choose a topic from the list or an idea of their own. Explain that anything that happens to us could be turned into an interesting anecdote.

• Give students about five minutes to prepare their anecdote. Discourage them from writing out their anecdotes word for word as their aim is to try to speak naturally. They can, however, write notes to help to organize their ideas.

• Put students into pairs to practise telling their story. Encourage them to give each other feedback on how well they used the techniques in the Presentation tips box.

What makes a good anecdote?

This may be the first time that students have told an anecdote in English, but anecdote-telling is an important component of presentations and informal conversation. Here are some tips for telling anecdotes which you could share with the class:

1 Think about the purpose of your anecdote.

2 Consider your audience and tailor your anecdote to this group as far as possible.

3 Humour helps, but remember that humour doesn't always translate.

4 Set up the anecdote in an interesting way, but don't make the build-up too long.

5 Use pace and timing effectively.

6 Make sure your anecdote has a beginning, a middle and an end

7 Include relevant and appropriate details.

8 Have a memorable 'punch-line' at the end, i.e. a statement of what happened at the end of the story which illustrates the point you wanted to make with your anecdote.

12

• Put students into new pairs. They take turns to tell their anecdote. Remind students to focus on using the techniques from the Presentation tips box.

• When both students have given their presentation, they can tell each other how well they used the techniques from the Presentation tips box and how they think their presentations differ. Students could then work with a different partner and give their presentation again.

▶ Set Workbook pages 74–75 for homework.

8.2 Can we 'have it all'?

GRAMMAR Verb patterns with -ing and infinitive

1

• Books open. Draw students' attention to the spread title: *Can we 'have it all'?*

• Put students into pairs to discuss the questions. Ask students to look at each question in turn, conducting whole-class feedback after each one.

• **Question 1.** Students tell each other how common the expectation that we can 'have it all' is in their countries. Encourage students to give possible reasons for the

prevalence of this expectation. Students can also consider and discuss whether the number of people who expect to 'have it all' has increased over time in their countries.

• **Question 2.** If students are currently working adults, they can bring in their own life experiences here. If they're not, they can think about the lives of working adults they know, e.g. family members or friends.

• **Question 3.** Encourage students to consider a range of different people they know in their country, e.g. young and old, those in jobs with minimal responsibility and those in high-pressure jobs, when they're considering how much of an issue stress is.

• **Optional step.** If appropriate, students could go online and do some research into the proportion of people in their country who describe themselves as stressed. Students could then either write up their findings as a report or present them verbally. Ask: *Were the results what you'd expected?*

2

• Ask students to look at the infographic and to say what they can see in the picture. Invite individual students to read out what the people in the office are saying and the other students to show whether they have done each thing by raising their hand.

• Alternatively, students could work in pairs to discuss whether they've ever done any of these things. Encourage them also to say what effect doing these activities has had on their lives and how often they do them, where appropriate.

• Conduct whole-class feedback to find out which activities students have done. Ask students: *Do you think any of the activities you haven't tried would help you? Would you try them?*

3

• Ask students to read the sentences in the Grammar box and to find sentences in the infographic that have the same patterns. You may need to point out that it won't be immediately obvious from the sentences in the infographic which sentence has the same pattern as sentence 5.

• Check the answers with the class. Invite one student to read out the sentence from the Grammar box and another student to read out the sentence from the infographic.

Answers

1 I avoided checking work emails when I was at home.

2 I learned to say no more often.

3 I asked my boss to give me more feedback.

4 I made myself find new hobbies.

5 I started spending more time with friends and family (*also* I started to spend …)

6 I stopped working through my lunch break.

7 I stop to take regular breaks.

• Students can check their answers to the questions in the Grammar box and overall understanding of the verb patterns with -ing and infinitive by turning to the Grammar summary on page 154.

Answers

1

1 verb + -ing   2 verb + infinitive + to   3 verb + object + infinitive + to   4 verb + object + infinitive without to

2 remember

• If you feel that students need more controlled practice before continuing, they could do some or all of the exercises in the Grammar summary. Otherwise, you could continue on to Exercise 4 in the unit and set the Grammar summary exercises for homework.

Answers to Grammar summary exercises

1

1 speaking   2 working   3 to look   4 not living
5 to give up   6 to reach   7 losing   8 having

2

1 e   2 b   3 c   4 f   5 a   6 d

3

1 to book … to do   2 play … to win   3 to come … say
4 use … to have

4

1 giving up   2 to stop   3 learning   4 to find   5 to give
6 to do   7 to set   8 to get   9 go off   10 being

5

1 checking   2 staying   3 to talk   4 to buy
5 eating   6 to be

6

1 Sorry, I forgot **to** tell the neighbours about our party!

2 I recommend ~~to~~ **you to read** this book – it's great.

3 Taking a break can help you to avoid ~~get~~ **getting** stressed.

4 My company doesn't allow **us** to do flexitime.

5 My friend asked me ~~to not~~ **not to** phone him too early.

6 I didn't tell you because I didn't want ~~that you know~~ **you to know**.

4

• Look at sentence 1 as an example with the class. Ask students to complete the sentence with the -ing form or infinitive of the verb in brackets. Encourage them to refer to the Grammar summary if they are unsure of the answer. Elicit that the verb *meet* should be in the infinitive form because it follows the verb *arrange*.

• Students complete the sentences.

Answers

1 to meet   2 to come   3 having   4 working   5 to do
6 not to take   7 reading   8 to see   9 bringing   10 to feel

5

• Ask students to look at the example and elicit that the underlined verb (*arrange*) is the verb from sentence 1 in Exercise 4. Encourage students to underline the verbs in the sentences in Exercise 4 that they must use in their sentences and questions.

• Put students into pairs so that they know who the questions should be relevant for. Tell them to write a new sentence or question with each verb in Exercise 4. Tell students that they should write sentences which are true for them or questions that they could ask another student. They should also write a mixture of questions and sentences unless you would prefer them to write only sentences or only questions. Remind students that the focus of this activity is on using -ing and infinitive verb forms correctly.

6

• Put students into pairs to compare their sentences and to ask their questions from Exercise 5.

• Ask students to give each other feedback on the accuracy of these sentences and questions, focusing on the use of -ing and infinitive verb forms, and offering help where necessary.

• Students should give their answers in full sentences so that they can also practise using -ing and infinitive verb forms while answering.

• Conduct whole-class feedback and ask students to read out to the rest of the class any interesting sentences or questions that their partners wrote.

7

• Look at the conversation with the class. Elicit that the verbs before the gaps are all verbs that when followed by the -ing form and infinitive either have similar or different meanings. This means that in some cases, both forms are possible.

• Ask students to complete the conversation with the correct form of the verbs in brackets.

• Ask students to compare their answers in pairs. They could also read out their completed conversation in pairs in order to get a sense of how natural their completed sentences sound.

• Check answers with the class. You could do this by asking two of the more confident students to read out the conversation to the rest of the class.

Answers

1 getting / to get   2 leaving / to leave   3 keeping
4 to pick up   5 finding   6 to have   7 saying
8 being / to be

LISTENING Adjusting the balance

8

- Ask students to complete the sentences with the verbs.
- 🔊 43 Play the recording so that students can check their answers. If necessary, play the recording twice.

Transcript

P = Presenter, E = Business editor

P: *We've got our business editor in the studio with us today. So Edwina, what has caught your eye in the business news this week?*

E: *Well, I've been reading about Max Schireson, who's featured in several magazines following his viral blog post.*

P: *Tell us more.*

E: *The blog has gone viral because Schireson decided to give up his job as the CEO of a big database company and spend more time with his family. Quite an unusual step for a career businessman.*

P: *That certainly sounds like a brave thing to do for a CEO. Doesn't he risk limiting his career opportunities in the future?*

E: *Maybe – not everyone thinks it's a wise choice. But apparently he doesn't miss travelling continually back and forwards from New York to San Francisco and doesn't regret slowing down his career.*

P: *What was the reaction of his colleagues?*

E: *Well, it turns out that he hasn't actually left the company altogether: he's still the vice-chairman, so his colleagues encouraged him to do what he felt was right for him.*

P: *So what benefits has this change brought him?*

E: *Well, he says he now works a 'normal' full-time schedule instead of a 'crazy' one. This means he now enjoys being involved in the day-to-day care of his three kids and he says he loves helping them with their homework.*

P: *OK. And what else does he say? Does he recommend following in his footsteps if you're a working parent too?*

E: *Not exactly. He says he realizes that he's in a privileged position and that it's easier for him than for most parents. What he says is that everyone needs to find the right balance for themselves.*

P: *And if you're lucky enough to be able to change the way you work …*

E: *Exactly!*

Answers

1 to give up	2 limiting	3 travelling	4 slowing
5 to do	6 being	7 helping	8 following	9 to find

- **Optional step.** You could also ask students to think about and discuss the situation outlined in the recording. Ask: *In your country, would people give up their jobs in this situation?*

SPEAKING Making the most of your time

9 **21st** **CENTURY OUTCOMES**

- Before starting this exercise, refer students to the 21st CENTURY OUTCOMES at the foot of the page. Elicit or explain that being aware of how much time you spend on different activities every day can help to raise your awareness of where you waste time or of how little time you spend doing the things you enjoy doing and, therefore, help you to reduce your physical and mental stress. Ask: *Have you ever analysed how you spend your time? If so, what did you learn about yourself as a result?* Students can discuss these questions in pairs or as a whole class.

- Ask students to look at the diagram and elicit that it shows how someone spends their day. Elicit that 90 degrees (one quarter of the circle) is the equivalent of six hours. Ask questions about how this person spends his/her time, for example: *How much time do they sleep (about 7½ hours) / do leisure and sports (about 5 hours) / work (about 2½ hours) / study (about 3 hours) / eat and drink (about 1 hour) / socialize (about 1½ hours) / do other things (about 3½ hours)?* Draw students' attention to the additional activities outside the diagram too. You could also ask: *Does this person seem to have a lot of physical and mental stress in their day? (no)*

- Ask students if their day is similar to that in the diagram. Tell students to draw their own diagram and to complete it with the hours they spend on each activity every day. They should also any additional activities they do which aren't in the diagram. If students aren't sure of the exact amount of time they spend on each activity, tell them to estimate.

10

- Put students into small groups to compare diagrams, and to find the main similarities and differences in the way they spend their day. Ask: *Is there anything you'd like to change about how you spend your time? What?*

- Students make suggestions for how the other students in their group could implement the changes they'd like make. Then conduct whole-class feedback.

> **TEACHING TIP**
>
> **How students spend their time**
> Bear in mind that the subject of how students spend their time might be a sensitive one for them. Ensure that students don't feel that judgements are being made about how they spend their time, e.g. if they spend a lot of time sleeping. Present this activity as an exercise in optimizing how they use their time.

▶ Photocopiable communicative activity 8.1: Go to page 227 for further practice of verb patterns with *-ing* and infinitive. The teaching notes are on page 244.

▶ Set Workbook pages 76–77 for homework.

8.3 Taking it easy

READING Leisure time around the world

1

- Books open. Draw students' attention to the spread title: *Taking it easy.* Elicit or explain that this is an idiom or idiomatic expression and elicit or clarify that it means 'to relax'.

- Put students into small groups to discuss what they do when they want to *take it easy*. Again, if you have students from a range of different countries, they can also compare how people from different countries spend their leisure time and discuss possible reasons for any differences. Conduct whole-class feedback on the leisure activities students like to do when they're taking it easy and write the activities on the board so that students can refer to them while they are working in pairs later.

- Put students into pairs to read the list of activities and to discuss the questions. If necessary, clarify the meaning of:

  heritage centre – a building where visitors can get information about a place and its people which has some historical value (third item)

- If you made a class list of leisure activities on the board, students can compare the list of activities on the board with the list of activities here.

- Conduct whole-class feedback and, if you have a monolingual class, seek to establish a class consensus on which activities are the most popular in the students' country. Students could also agree on a class ranking of the activities in terms of their popularity. If you have a class with students from several different countries, ask a student or students from each one to share the activities that are popular in their home country and to compare these as a class.

2

- Ask students to read the article quickly to find and underline or highlight as many leisure activities as they can. Point out that they don't need to understand the article at this stage: their focus should be on identifying leisure activities.

- Put students into pairs to compare the leisure activities they found in the article.

Answers

hiking (line 2), shopping (line 4), visiting family (line 5), entertaining friends (line 6), eating and drinking (lines 25–26), listening to live music (line 27), dancing (line 27), watching TV (line 30), using the Internet (line 30), visiting historic sites (lines 41–42), online activities such as gaming, chatting or watching videos (lines 46–47)

3

- Ask students to read the article again more closely and decide whether the statements are true or false, or the information is not given in the article. They can do this in pairs.

Note that students met the verb *fulfil* in Unit 3.3, but you may still need to clarify the meaning of:

  fulfilment – a sense of satisfaction you experience when you achieve your goals (sentence 2)

Answers

1 T   2 T

3 NG (The OECD carried out research – or published their results – in 2009. Only France and Mexico are mentioned, so this suggests that the research was not 'extensive'.)

4 T

5 NG (The article says that: 'An American theme park developer, for example, can't assume that the Western leisure model will be automatically successful in another culture.' It doesn't specifically say whether theme parks have or have not been shown to be successful all over the world.)

6 F (The article says that gender is one of the things that affects the actual leisure activities that people engage in [lines 18–20]. The end of the article says that what really determines the kind of activities that people choose is age: gender is not mentioned in this part of the article.)

4

- Ask students to find the expressions in the article. Encourage them to work out the meaning of any unknown expressions from the context in which they're used.

- Students complete the sentences with the expressions.

- **Optional step.** Students could read out their completed sentences as this should help them decide whether they've chosen the correct expressions.

Answers

1 What's interesting is   2 Things like   3 the key question is   4 on the contrary   5 The idea is that
6 In other words

5

- Put students into pairs to discuss the questions. Encourage them to use the expressions from Exercise 4 in their answers, where appropriate.

- Conduct whole-class feedback on what students learned from the article.

VOCABULARY Relaxation

6

- Look at the pairs of expressions with the class. If necessary, clarify the meaning of:

  quality time – time when you give your undivided attention to the people who are important to you in your life (item 5)

  unwind – relax (item 8)

- Elicit or explain that in some cases the two expressions in each pair have the same or similar meanings, but there may be a difference in register between the two. For example, in item 8, *unwind* has a more formal register than *chill out*.

- Ask students to match the expressions with their definitions. They can do this in pairs.

Answers

1 b 2 c 3 e 4 g 5 a 6 d 7 f 8 h

7

- Look at item 1 as an example with the class. Elicit possible endings to the sentence, e.g. *my family and friends*.

- Ask students to complete the sentences in their own words.

- Students then compare their sentences with a partner and ask each other follow-up questions to find out more about how they each spend their time. They could also give each other feedback on how good a work–life balance they have and, if appropriate, advice on how they could improve the balance.

SPEAKING Giving advice

8 *21st* **CENTURY OUTCOMES**

- Before starting this exercise, refer students to the 21st CENTURY OUTCOMES at the foot of the page. If you think that students will feel comfortable discussing more personal aspects of their lives in class, you could ask: *What health-related decisions have you made during the course of your life and what effects did they have on you?* You could give an example from your own life. For example: *I started going to the gym a year ago and now I have a lot more energy than I used to have.* Students can discuss this question in pairs or as a whole class.

- Review language for giving advice about other people, e.g. *He should/shouldn't … , He could … , Why doesn't he … ? How about … ?*

- Put students into small groups to read the quotes from the three people and to discuss what advice they would give them. For example, *I think Andy should … , He could … .* Alternatively, students could work in groups of three and each take the role of one of the people. Students take turns to read out their problem and the other two students give them advice. For example, *I think you should … , You could … .* Students could then develop this into a conversation.

- Conduct whole-class feedback and ask students to write on the board the pieces of advice they discussed in their groups. Encourage students to use a range of structures when they give advice.

- **Optional step.** Ask: *Have you ever experienced any of the things that the writers of the quotes have experienced?* Students can discuss this question in their groups or as a whole class.

▶ Set Workbook pages 78–79 for homework.

8.4 I need a break!

LISTENING Taking a break

1

- Books open. Draw students' attention to the spread title: *I need a break!* and to the section heading: *Taking a break.* Elicit or explain that *a break* is a short period of rest and that it can be used to refer to a period of a few days' rest.

- Draw students' attention to the photo and ask: *Who are these people? What are they doing?* Possible answers could be: *They're a group of friends. They're enjoying a day / a weekend / a short break in the mountains where they're skiing and snowboarding.* You could then ask students if they like skiing and/or snowboarding.

- You could put students into pairs to discuss what people in their country do on a national holiday or a long weekend. Ask: *Do shops and other businesses close on a public holiday? Do people have particular traditions for different public holidays or particular events that happen on them?*

- If you have a class with students from different countries, they can compare and ask each other questions about public holidays in their respective countries.

2

- If necessary, clarify the meaning of:

    budget city break – a short, low-price holiday in a city (perhaps needed in students' answers)

- 🎧 **44** Play the recording so that students can write down the options that the two colleagues discuss for the long weekend.

Transcript

C = Carla, S = Steve

C: *I haven't had a day off for six months! I need a break! I want to go somewhere new, exciting and not too expensive.*

S: *Oh, Carla! You don't want much, then!*

C: *I know, but there's a long weekend coming up and it would be a shame not to make the most of it.*

S: *Well, you could fly to Rome or Budapest or somewhere on one of those budget city breaks.*

C: *Yeah, that's a possibility. Although I'd prefer not to deal with airports on a long weekend.*

S: *OK, you don't want to go abroad. So what are the alternatives? London? There's always something going on there.*

C: *That's very true, Steve. On the other hand, I've been to London so many times … I'd rather do something new than visit the same old places.*

S: *And as you said, you have to think about the expense – London's not cheap you know, Carla. Perhaps you'd be better off looking at another option.*

C: *Yes, but what?*

S: *Have you thought about an activity weekend? You know, going kayaking or rock climbing? That kind of thing is exciting. And not only that, you'd be doing something totally new.*

C: *Hmm. I can see your point. But, Steve, I haven't done any sports for years.*

S: *There are loads of weekends like that for people like you. The only problem would be choosing which one to do.*

C: *Well, I'd better make my mind up soon if I want to book something.*

• Check answers and ask students which option they think Carla is most likely to take up for her long weekend.

> **Answers**
> _____
> fly to Rome or Budapest or somewhere on a budget city break
>
> go to London
>
> go on an activity weekend – going kayaking or rock climbing

• **Optional step.** Elicit that when Carla and Steve talk about visiting London, they're talking about visiting their own capital city. Ask: *Have you ever tried any of the options mentioned in the conversation? Which option would you choose, and why?* Make the point that the second option would be visiting students' own capital city.

3

• Ask students to look at the Useful language box and to read the expressions. Explain that they are listed in the order in which they are spoken in the conversation. Ask: *Can you remember hearing any of these expressions when you listened to the conversation? If so, which ones?* You could then ask students to predict who says each expression based on what they can remember from the first time they listened to the recording.

• 🔊 **44** Play the recording so that students can identify which speaker says each expression.

• **Optional step.** Focus on the intonation used in the expressions, e.g. downward intonation in *That's a possibility* and *I'd prefer (not) to …* and rising intonation in *What are the alternatives?* and *Not only that … .* Model and drill the intonation patterns and ask students to practise saying the expressions.

> **Answers**
> _____
> 1 C 2 C 3 S 4 C 5 C 6 S 7 S 8 S 9 C
> 10 S 11 C

Pronunciation Stress in expressions

4a

• If students have completed Unit 5, elicit that stress is the placing of more emphasis on some words than others in a sentence. Stressed words are usually the most important words.

• **Optional step.** Ask students to read the sentences and to predict which words are stressed. They can read out the sentences to help them to do this.

• 🔊 **45** Play the recording and ask students to listen and underline the stressed words.

> **Transcript and answers**
> _____
> 1 That's a *possibility*.
> 2 What are the *alternatives*?
> 3 I can see your *point*.

4b

• **Optional step.** Students can predict which of the words in bold are stressed. They can read out the sentences to help them to do this.

• 🔊 **46** Play the recording so that students can listen and underline the stressed words.

• Conduct whole-class feedback and elicit possible reasons why the speaker decided to stress these words.

> **Transcript and answers**
> _____
> 1 **I'd prefer <u>not</u> to** deal with airports on a long weekend.
> 2 **On the <u>other</u> hand**, I've been to London so many times.
> 3 **I'd rather do something <u>new</u>** than visit the same old places.
> 4 **You <u>have</u> to think about** the expense – London's not cheap.

Extra activity

Stress and meaning

In order to illustrate how meaning is reinforced by stress, you could write the expression *You never buy me red roses anymore* on the board and ask students to practise saying it in pairs, putting stress on a different word each time. Ask students to reflect on the different meanings the expression has when different elements are emphasized. Conduct whole-class feedback and elicit what the speaker intends to convey by stressing different words.

4c

• 🔊 **46** Play the recording again and pause after each sentence so that students can listen and repeat.

• Ask students to complete the expressions in bold with their own endings. Encourage students to write sentences which are true for them.

• Put students into pairs to exchange their sentences. They take turns to read out their partner's sentences.

SPEAKING A day off

5

• Put students into small groups to discuss the things they could do, either together or individually, on a day off. Encourage students to think of things that they could realistically do and be as specific as possible.

- Remind students to use expressions for discussing options during their discussions.

- Encourage students to agree on what they would all be happy to do together on a day off. Then conduct whole-class feedback.

WRITING An email (2)

6

- Ask students to look quickly at the email and to say what it is about. Elicit that it is about an end-of-year social event organized by a sports and social committee.

- You could put students into pairs or small groups to brainstorm key words they expect to read in the email or key points they expect it to make.

- Give students time to read the questions and the email. If necessary, clarify the meaning of:

  premises – a building and, where appropriate, land that surrounds a building which belongs to a business, company or organization (paragraph 2)

  drawback – disadvantage (paragraph 4)

- Ask students to answer the questions. They can then compare their answers in pairs.

> **Answers**
>
> 1 the Sports and Social Committee
>
> 2 all staff
>
> 3 an end-of-year social event
>
> 4 an office party held on the premises, a meal out and a day trip
>
> 5 an office party held on the premises
>
> 6 let the Sports and Social Committee know what he/she thinks of their decision to have an office party

Writing skill Linking expressions

7a

- Elicit or explain that linking expressions are words or expressions which we use in order to link ideas and signpost the structure of the text to the reader.

- Ask students to look at the categories of linking expressions and the examples in each one. Draw attention to the fact that some linking expressions are followed by a comma.

- Students read the email again and underline the linking expressions. They then add the underlined expressions to the seven groups.

> **Answers**
>
> 1 Firstly,; Finally,; In addition, 2 such as,; for example
> 3 The main advantage of 4 On the other hand, 5 due to; therefore 6 One argument against; The main drawback of 7 Taking all of the points into consideration,

7b

- Look at sentence 1 as an example with the class. Elicit that the second sentence shows a contrast to the first, so the correct option is *Despite this,*.

- Ask students to choose the correct option to complete the sentences. Encourage students to look at the words that come before and after the options when they're deciding which option to choose.

- Conduct whole-class feedback, and clarify any uncertainties about the meaning and use of the linking expressions.

> **Answers**
>
> 1 Despite this,   2 To conclude,   3 All in all,
> 4 For this reason,   5 Many people argue that   6 like
> 7 The main disadvantage of

8   *21st* CENTURY OUTCOMES

- Before starting this exercise, refer students to the 21st CENTURY OUTCOMES at the foot of the page. Explain that students are now going to take part in a discussion and that they should participate actively in it in order to fulfil the 21st CENTURY OUTCOME.

- Put students into pairs to discuss the advantages and disadvantages of each option. Encourage students to use language for talking about advantages and disadvantages from the email, e.g. *the main advantage is … , the main drawback is … .*

- Ask students to choose one of the other two options and to work on their own to write a report using the structure of the email in Exercise 6 as a model.

9

- Ask students to exchange emails with a new partner. They can stand up and mingle to find a new partner.

- Students read each other's email and check that the ideas in the email flow well, i.e. they're presented in a logical way and there are links between them, and that the student's choice logically follows from the reasons given.

- Students give each other feedback on their emails. Monitor students while they're doing this, adding your input or asking questions where appropriate.

▶ Photocopiable communicative activity 8.2: Go to page 228 for further practice of discussing options, and linking expressions. The teaching notes are on page 244.

▶ Set Workbook pages 80–81 for homework.

▶ Set Workbook Writing 4 on pages 82–83 for homework.

READING Enova

1

Answers
1 B 2 A 3 C

2

Answers

1 The Tech Museum of Innovation

2 Mexico

3 Jorge Camil Starr and two of his oldest friends

4 economics

5 looked at the failure of the existing systems

6 1: each educational centre would be run by only one person with full responsibility

2: they would use video games to deliver educational content

7 the children's mothers also wanted to play the games

8 1: Enova follows the students who graduate.

2: and those who drop out. Students who abandon their studies are asked why and the information is used to try and improve the programmes.

3: Enova also measures students' success on the external government exams, which gives an independent assessment of its impact.

GRAMMAR

3

Answers

1 are designed   2 can be found   3 has been visited
4 was set up   5 have been played   6 is being accessed
7 will be developed   8 can be used

4

Answers

1 to monitor   2 choose   3 checking   4 to use
5 starting   6 showing   7 to come   8 to fund

VOCABULARY

5

Answers

1 inspired   2 put into practice   3 enabled   4 were
replaced   5 get round   6 exploit

6

Answers

1 quality time   2 day off   3 catch up   4 switch off
5 take (it) easy   6 recharge (your) batteries
7 put (your) feet   8 change (of) scene   9 chilling out
10 get away from

DISCUSSION

7

Answers

1 Students' own answers, though they may agree that this has not happened. Technological innovations have often meant that things can be ready sooner, so this just means more pressure (rather than less) for workers.

2 Students' own answers. Advantages are that you can study when you like and work at your own pace. Disadvantages are that you have no personal or academic contact with either a teacher or other students.

SPEAKING

8

Answers

1 I'd prefer not to go   2 you'd be better off doing
3 How does that work?   4 Will I have to download
5 You have to think about   6 The only problem would be
speaking   7 I'd rather speak face to face than on Skype
8 I'd better make my mind up.

WRITING

9

Suggested answer

Dear colleagues

We're writing to ask about your interest in joining a new social and educational association for Blackthorn employees. The association would offer activities such as social events, a cinema group, language classes, etc. In addition, it would organize trips to places of interest.

We'd love to hear your views and for this reason we have set up a page where you can join in the discussion. There's also a quick survey to see the level of interest. Please let us know your opinion using the links below.

Best wishes

Anya Waite

Jess Lynn

9 Creative thinking

UNIT AT A GLANCE

THEME: Creativity

TED TALK: *Doodlers, unite!* In this TED Talk, Sunni Brown proposes that while doodling is usually frowned upon and discouraged, it can, in fact, help us to unlock our creativity.

AUTHENTIC LISTENING SKILLS: Understanding fast speech

CRITICAL THINKING: Supporting arguments

PRESENTATION SKILLS: Supporting key points with slides

GRAMMAR: Relative clauses

VOCABULARY: Personality adjectives (1)

PRONUNCIATION: Stress and meaning

READING: The left-brain–right-brain debate

LISTENING: Launching a new product

SPEAKING: Are you persuaded?, Boosting your creativity, Co-operating in a discussion: turn taking (Organizing a campaign)

WRITING: A personal account

WRITING SKILL: Informal language

LEAD IN

• Books open. Draw students' attention to the photo on page 96 and its caption. Elicit or explain that trash means 'rubbish'. Ask: *What is your reaction to the 'Trashmen'? What adjectives would you use to describe them?* Write any interesting adjectives on the board as students mention them, dividing them into two groups, if appropriate: adjectives with a positive meaning and adjectives with a negative meaning.

• Draw students' attention to the unit title: *Creative thinking*. Tell students that brainstorming is one way in which we can facilitate creative thinking. Put students into small groups and ask them to brainstorm what 'creative thinking' means to them. You could give each group an A3 piece of paper to write their ideas on.

• Conduct whole-class feedback and, if appropriate, ask groups to show and present the ideas they brainstormed on their pieces of paper to the rest of the class.

• Bring in students' own experiences. Ask: *Can you think of a time when creative thinking has helped you to solve a problem, to create an opportunity, or to generate new ideas?* Students could discuss their answers in pairs before you conduct whole-class feedback. Write the situations where creativity helped students on the board.

TEDTALKS
BACKGROUND

1

• Ask students to read the text about Sunni Brown and her talk. If necessary, clarify the meaning of *doodle* by drawing some doodles on the board or showing some images.

• Put students into pairs to discuss the questions. Conduct whole-class feedback for questions 1 and 2 before moving on to question 3.

• **Question 1.** If appropriate, bring in students' own experiences of learning and making decisions during whole-class feedback.

• **Question 3.** Clarify the meaning of:

mind map – a diagram used to organize information with a central idea or concept and lines linked to connected ideas branching out from the centre

flow chart – a diagram showing a sequence of events or actions, which usually uses connected lines and symbols

concept map – a type of graphic organizer used to organize and represent knowledge of a subject which begins with a main idea (or concept) and then branches out to show how that main idea can be broken down into specific areas

• **Optional step.** You could bring in real examples of the four different ways of drawing ideas mentioned in this question, in either print or digital form, and distribute them so that students have a clearer idea of what the four ways look like and how they can be used.

• Conduct whole-class feedback to gauge how familiar students are with the four ways of drawing ideas from question 3 and whether they've ever used them.

• **Optional step.** If appropriate, elicit examples of situations or ways in which students could use the four ways of drawing ideas to help them in their studies or working life.

KEY WORDS

2

• Ask students to try to guess the meaning of the words in bold and then to match them with their definitions.

Answers
1 c 2 a 3 f 4 b 5 d 6 e

AUTHENTIC LISTENING SKILLS
Understanding fast speech

3a

• Bring in students' own experiences. Ask: *Have you ever listened to English speakers, especially native speakers, who speak fast? If so, how much do you think you understood? Can you identify what specifically made the fast speech difficult to understand? Possible reasons include: listening comprehension skills not being developed enough to process language when it is produced at a fast pace; connected speech is more likely to be used in fast speech, which means that sounds in some words will be omitted; simply not being used to hearing fast speech.* Students can discuss the answers to these questions in pairs.

• Conduct whole-class feedback to find out more about students' experiences.

• Ask students to read the information about understanding fast speech in the Authentic listening skills box.

• ⌂ 47 Play the recording so that students can write down the words that are stressed. Elicit that there are two opening sentences.

• Put students into pairs to compare the words they wrote down and to work together to reconstruct the sentences that they heard.

• Conduct whole-class feedback. Invite individual students to read out and write their sentences on the board. Get the rest of the class to amend the sentences if necessary. You can then refer students to the transcript on page 179 so that they can confirm the complete sentences. Then get other students to underline the words on the board that they think are stressed.

Transcript and answers

(underlining = stressed words)

So I just want to tell you my <u>story</u>. I spend a lot of <u>time teaching adults</u> how to use <u>visual language</u> and <u>doodling</u> in the <u>workplace</u>.

3b

• Put students into pairs to read out the sentences to each other, first slowly and then quickly.

• Students listen to their partner and to how they say the sentences themselves, and notice which parts 'disappear' and which parts are stressed.

• Conduct whole-class feedback. Invite individual students to read out the sentences. Don't confirm answers at this stage, however: tell students that they will listen to Sunni Brown saying the sentences so that they can compare.

3c

• ⌂ 48 Play the recording so that students can listen to the sentences from Exercise 3b and confirm which words are stressed.

Transcript and answers

(underlining = stressed words)

1 <u>So</u> I <u>discovered</u> some very interesting <u>things</u>.

2 <u>Additionally</u>, I've heard <u>horror stories</u> from people whose <u>teachers scolded</u> them, of course, for <u>doodling</u> in <u>classrooms</u>.

3 And they have <u>bosses</u> who <u>scold</u> them for <u>doodling</u> in the <u>boardroom</u>.

9.1 Doodlers, unite!

TEDTALKS

1

• Draw students' attention to the title of the talk: *Doodlers, unite!* Elicit or explain that this is a call to people who doodle to come together. Ask: *Why would doodlers feel the need to do this? Possible answers could be: because they're criticized for being lazy or easily distracted, because doodling isn't seen as a productive and valuable activity.*

• Bring in students' own experiences. Ask: *Do you doodle? If so, when and why do you do it? Do you have any examples of your doodles with you? If you don't doodle, are there any specific reasons why you don't?* Students can discuss these questions in pairs and, if they doodle, show each other any doodles that they have with them.

• Conduct whole-class feedback. Ask: *Do people's doodles say anything about them and how they think?*

• Give students time to read the list of key points that Sunni Brown makes in the TED Talk. Explain that she may or may not show all these points in her slides.

• ▶ 9.1 Play the whole talk once so that students can tick the key points that Sunni Brown shows in her slides.

Transcript

0.13 *So I just want to tell you my story. I spend a lot of time teaching adults how to use visual language and doodling in the workplace. And naturally, I encounter a lot of resistance, because it's sort of considered to be anti-intellectual and counter to serious learning. But I have a problem with that belief, because I know that doodling has a profound impact on the way that we can process information and the way that we can solve problems.*

0.39 *So I was curious about why there was a disconnect between the way our society perceives doodling and the way that the reality is. So I discovered some very interesting things. For example, there is no such thing as a flattering definition of a doodle. In the 17th century, a doodle was a simpleton or a fool – as in Yankee Doodle. In the 18th century, it became a verb, and it meant to swindle or ridicule or to make fun of someone. In the 19th century, it was a corrupt politician. And today, we have what is perhaps our most offensive definition, at least to me, which is the following: to doodle officially means to dawdle, to dilly dally, to monkey around, to make meaningless marks, to do something of little value, substance or import, and – my personal favourite — to do nothing. No wonder people are averse to doodling at work.*

1.32 *Additionally, I've heard horror stories from people whose teachers scolded them, of course, for doodling in classrooms. And they have bosses who scold them for doodling in the boardroom. There is a powerful cultural norm against doodling in settings in which we are supposed to learn something. And unfortunately, the press tends to reinforce this norm when they're reporting on a doodling scene – of an important person at a confirmation hearing and the like – they typically use words like 'discovered' or 'caught' or 'found out', as if there's some sort of criminal act being committed.*

2.02 *And additionally, there is a psychological aversion to doodling – thank you, Freud. In the 1930s, Freud told us all that you could analyse people's psyches based on their doodles. This is not accurate.*

2.15 *And here is the real deal. Here's what I believe. I think that our culture is so intensely focused on verbal information that we're almost blinded to the value of doodling. And I'm not comfortable with that. And so because of that belief that I think needs to be burst, I'm here to send us all hurtling back to the truth. And here's the truth: doodling is an incredibly powerful tool, and it is a tool that we need to remember and to relearn.*

2.40 *So here's a new definition for doodling. Doodling is really to make spontaneous marks to help yourself think. That is why millions of people doodle. Here's another interesting truth about the doodle: people who doodle when they're exposed to verbal information retain more of that information than their non-doodling counterparts. We think doodling is something you do when you lose focus, but in reality, it is a pre-emptive measure to stop you from losing focus. Additionally, it has a profound effect on creative problem-solving and deep information processing.*

3.14 *There are four ways that learners intake information so that they can make decisions. They are visual, auditory, reading and writing, and kinaesthetic. Now in order for us to really chew on information and do something with it, we have to engage at least two of those modalities, or we have to engage one of those modalities coupled with an emotional experience. The incredible contribution of the doodle is that it engages all four learning modalities simultaneously with the possibility of an emotional experience. That is a pretty solid contribution for a behaviour equated with doing nothing.*

3.50 *This is so nerdy, but this made me cry when I discovered this. So they did anthropological research into the unfolding of artistic activity in children, and they found that, across space and time, all children exhibit the same evolution in visual logic as they grow. In other words, they have a shared and growing complexity in visual language that happens in a predictable order. And I think that is incredible. I think that means doodling is native to us and we simply are denying ourselves that instinct. And finally, a lot a people aren't privy to this, but the doodle is a precursor to some of our greatest cultural assets. This is but one: this is Frank Gehry the architect's precursor to the Guggenheim in Abu Dhabi.*

4.31 *So here is my point: under no circumstances should doodling be eradicated from a classroom or a boardroom or even the war room. On the contrary, doodling should be leveraged in precisely those situations where information density is very high and the need for processing that information is very high. And I will go you one further. Because doodling is so universally accessible and it is not intimidating as an art form, it can be leveraged as a portal through which we move people into higher levels of visual literacy. My friends, the doodle has never been the nemesis of intellectual thought. In reality, it is one of its greatest allies.*

5.10 *Thank you. (Applause)*

> **Answer**
> Sunni Brown shows all the points in her slides.

• Note the differences in North American English and British English shown at the foot of the spread. In this unit, these focus on pronunciation and spelling differences. Note the British English spelling *kinaesthetic* in the transcript and Exercise 4: the North American spelling is *kinesthetic*.

2

• Ask students to read the questions. If necessary, clarify the meaning of:

tell someone off – a phrasal verb which means to criticize someone in an angry way; a synonym for *scold* (question 2, option c)

• ▶ 9.1 Play the first part (0.00–2.02) of the talk so that students can choose the correct option to answer the questions.

• **Optional step.** Conduct whole-class feedback and ask: *Why do you think Sunni Brown shared these definitions? What point is she trying to make?* A possible answer could be: *Doodles have been seen, for hundreds of years, as things which don't have any value. Sunni Brown wants to make the point that we've been wrong to see doodles in this way and instead we should look at the benefits doodling can bring us.*

> **Answers**
>
> 1 a 19th century b 17th century c today
>   d 18th century
> 2 a bosses b journalists c teachers

3

• ▶ 9.1 Play the second part (2.02–3.14) of the talk so that students can check their answers.

• Conduct whole-class feedback, and ask students whether they agree with Sunni Brown's belief and her new definition of doodling.

> **Answers**
>
> 1 c 2 a

4

• Ask students to complete the summary with the words. If necessary clarify the meaning of:

  auditory – related to the sense of hearing (line 3)

• ▶ 9.1 Play the third part (3.14 to the end) of the talk so that students can check their answers.

> **Answers**
>
> 1 decisions 2 two 3 all 4 children 5 anyone
> 6 thought

• **Optional step.** Ask students whether they think they process more information in one of the four ways – visual, auditory, reading and writing, and kinaesthetic – than in the others. Elicit examples from students' experiences which demonstrate that this either is or isn't the case.

5

• Put students into pairs to discuss the questions. Encourage students to bring in their own experiences and/or to share examples that they're familiar with. They could then discuss the questions with another pair.

VOCABULARY IN CONTEXT

6

• ▶ 9.2 Play the clips of the talk. When each multiple-choice questions appears, pause the clip so that students can choose the correct definition.

Transcript and subtitles

1 *And naturally, I **encounter** a lot of resistance*
   a oppose
   b meet
   c expect

2 *And today, we have what is perhaps our most **offensive** definition, at least to me*
   a aggressive
   b confusing
   c insulting

3 *There is a powerful cultural norm against doodling in **settings** in which we are supposed to learn something.*
   a meetings
   b situations
   c schools

4 *And here is the **real deal**. Here's what I believe.*
   a agreement
   b best suggestion
   c truth

5 *We think doodling is something you do when you **lose focus***
   a feel tired
   b start paying attention
   c stop concentrating

6 *That is a pretty **solid** contribution for a behaviour equated with doing nothing.*
   a strong
   b small
   c unusual

> **Answers**
>
> 1 b 2 c 3 b 4 c 5 c 6 a

• Elicit or explain that in item 6 *solid* has the meaning of a firm foundation for something, rather than the more frequently used meaning of 'a state of a material which isn't a liquid or gas'.

7

• Put students into pairs to discuss the questions. Encourage them to use the target expressions in the questions in their answers too. Encourage students to share their own experiences and opinions. Then conduct whole-class feedback.

CRITICAL THINKING Supporting arguments

8

• You could put students into pairs to discuss which of the sentences describes Sunni Brown's argument. This isn't a test of memory, so students can refer to the transcript on page 179 if they want to.

• Conduct whole-class feedback on which sentences describe Sunni Brown's arguments. Ask students to give reasons or evidence from the talk to support their choice.

9

• Put students into pairs to discuss which of the comments support(s) Sunni Brown's arguments. Elicit or explain that one or more of the comments could support her arguments. Then conduct whole-class feedback.

• **Optional step.** Ask students to write their own comment in which they give their opinion on and experience of doodling. When they've finished writing, put students into pairs to read and to give feedback on each other's comment.

PRESENTATION SKILLS Supporting key points with slides

10

• Ask students to read about supporting key points with slides in the Presentation tips box.

• **Optional step.** Elicit any other possible tips for creating or using slides which students can think of. For example: *use background and text colours which will make it easier for people to read the information on the slides, use animations to show one point or image after another, align the pace at which you show your slides with the pace of your presentation, move more quickly or slowly from one slide to the next as appropriate.*

• ▶ 9.3 Play the clips so that students can identify the techniques from the Presentation tips box that Sunni Brown uses.

Transcript

1   For example, there is no such thing as a flattering definition of a doodle. In the 17th century, a doodle was a simpleton or a fool – as in Yankee Doodle. In the 18th century, it became a verb, and it meant to swindle or ridicule or to make fun of someone. In the 19th century, it was a corrupt politician.

2   To doodle officially means to dawdle, to dilly dally, to monkey around, to make meaningless marks, to do something of little value, substance or import, and – my personal favourite – to do nothing.

• Conduct whole-class feedback on which techniques Sunni Brown uses and how effectively students think she uses them.

11

• Put students into pairs to choose one of the ideas. Encourage them to choose one that they're interested in or can relate to.

• Give students 5–10 minutes to prepare a slide that supports the idea they've chosen and to write a few sentences to explain the idea. Remind students that their aim is to create a slide that supports what they want to say and to use it effectively while they're speaking.

• **Optional step.** If appropriate, students could use a programme such as PowerPoint or Keynote to (re)create their slide.

• Students practise presenting the idea to each other with their slide.

▶ Teaching tip: Using slides to create visuals, Unit 1.1, page 13

12

• Put students into new pairs. You could choose to put students into pairs with someone who has chosen the same idea in Exercise 11 – or with someone who has chosen a different idea. Students take turns to use their slide to present the idea they've chosen.

• Monitor students while they're presenting, and focus on how well students' slides support the ideas and how effectively they use them.

- Students can then give each other feedback on how effectively they think their partner's slide supported their words.

- **Optional step.** Students modify their slides in response to their partner's feedback and do their presentation again for another student.

- Conduct whole-class feedback and ask students who've created the best slides to demonstrate them to the rest of the class.

▶ Set Workbook pages 84–85 for homework.

9.2 Looking for inspiration

GRAMMAR Relative clauses

1

- Books open. Draw students' attention to the spread title: *Looking for inspiration*. Ask: *What do you do or where do you go when you need to 'look for inspiration'?* Students can discuss the question in pairs.

- Conduct whole-class feedback and write key words connected to the topic of looking for inspiration on the board as students mention them.

- Put students into pairs to discuss the questions. Conduct whole-class feedback for question 1 before moving on to question 2.

- **Question 1.** Other examples of organizations that use advertising include: charities, non-governmental organizations (NGOs), non-profits, newspapers, magazines, broadcasting corporations.

- If appropriate, ask students to go online, to do an image search for the names of organizations that fall into these categories and to find examples of their advertising.

- **Question 2.** Encourage students to focus on what advertising can help organizations to do and how or whether different types of organizations have different aims for advertising. For example: advertising can make consumers aware of certain products, make them associate certain things with products, e.g. energy, style, youthfulness, time with the family, or help to make products memorable for consumers; it can also shock consumers or make them feel good about themselves because they've understood the reference(s) an advertisement is making.

2

- Ask students to look at the infographic and to read the information about the different parts of the creative process. Encourage students to deduce the meaning of any unknown vocabulary from its context and the visuals.

- ⋒ 49 Play the recording so that students can number the sections of the infographic in the order the creative consultant mentions them. Students can then check their answers in pairs.

Transcript

I = Interviewer, C = Chris

I: *Chris, you've been in the advertising industry for twenty years now, first as a graphic designer, then you were the art director for one of the biggest advertising agencies in Australia, responsible for adverts seen by millions. Now you run your own business as a consultant.*

C: *That's right.*

I: *So you're the best person to explain to us just how the creative process works in advertising. Do you use a different approach according to who the client is?*

C: *Not really, no. The basic process is the same whether it's a product like soap powder or an NGO like Oxfam. We start with the big picture. That's the basic idea that describes what we're going to do – say, a TV ad to boost sales. And connected to this, we need to know what the overall goal is – something which tells us what the organization wants to achieve. This could be raising their public profile, for example. Then you need to look at the competitors operating in the same areas. It would be disastrous to make an ad that was the same as your client's main business competitor! And then what you really need to know before you can start to come up with ideas is the people who you want to reach with the message. In other words, the target audience.*

I: *So this is all the background information you need before you can start to think about ideas.*

C: *Yes, basically. Then we aim for two main things, one is visual and the other is words. So the visuals could be a single photo or video. That's the part of the process that I most enjoy. I just love finding interesting visual ways of representing ideas. And then you need some words too. The slogan, which is a phrase or a sentence, should be short and memorable.*

I: *And I suppose what a lot of people listening are really interested in is where the ideas come from. How do you come up with them?*

- Check answers with the class. If necessary, play the recording again. Elicit that the consultant mentions the terms *the big picture*, *the target audience*, *the visuals* and *the slogan*, but he doesn't specifically mention the other two: instead he talks about *the overall goal* (rather than *the objective*) and *the competitors operating in the same area* (rather than *the background*).

Answers

1 The big picture   2 The objective   3 The background
4 The target audience   5 The visuals   6 The slogan

Extra activity

Guess the product

Students choose a product they know, e.g. the sports shoes they like to wear, and think about the steps in the creative process involved in its creation, i.e. its objective, target audience, slogan, etc. Students then work in small groups and take turns to talk about the product without saying what the product is. The other members of the group have to guess what the product is.

3

• Explain that students are now going to listen to the recording again. This time they're going to answer specific questions about what Chris, the consultant, said.

• ⌂ 49 Play the recording again so that students can answer the questions.

4

• Elicit or explain that a *relative clause* is part of a sentence which starts with a relative pronoun and it defines a person, thing, time or place.

• Ask students to read the sentences in the Grammar box and to answer the questions. They can do this in pairs.

• Students can check their answers and overall understanding of conditional sentences by turning to the Grammar summary on page 156.

Answers

1 that, which, who   2 defining   3 non-defining
4 a reduced relative clause

• If you feel that students need more controlled practice before continuing, they could do some or all of Exercises 1–6 in the Grammar summary. Otherwise, you could continue on to Exercise 5 in the unit and set the Grammar summary exercises for homework.

Answers to Grammar summary exercises

1

1 which   2 who   3 whose   4 which
5 where   6 who   7 which   8 which

2

1 The artists who I like

2 Most people that object

3 The books which I used

4 These are the pictures that I drew

5 The magazine that published

6 The time when I doodled

7 Doodling is something which everyone does

8 The drawings that Picasso did

3

1 My favourite 20th century artist is Picasso, who had several different styles.

2 In the 1880s, when Picasso was born, Claude Monet was a successful painter.

3 Central Saint Martins is a famous art college, where many famous designers studied.

4 Advertising, which is a relative new industry, is a mix of creativity and sales.

5 My friend, who loved art at school, is now a graphic designer.

6 Holiday adverts, which appear on TV every winter, make you think of summer.

7 I work for TPQ magazine, which is only published online.

8 I lost my phone, which has hundreds of my photos on it, last week.

4

1 The ideas suggested by the new team were great.

2 Young artists seeking experience are welcome here.

3 The candidates interviewed yesterday were excellent.

4 Students enrolling on this course must be over 18.

5 Adverts paid for in advance get a discount.

6 Clients needing personal attention should make an appointment.

7 Customers paying a deposit are given priority.

8 The applications processed yesterday are on file.

5

Many charities [1] **which** depend on donations from the public use advertising. Adverts, [2] **which** make the public more aware of a charity's activities, are a good way of raising money. One style of advertising [3] **which** has recently become more common is using shocking scenes. Charities [4] **who** use this style say it is effective. However, many viewers [5] **seeing** the latest campaign from a children's charity have complained. The UK Advertising Standards Authority, [6] **whose** job it is to monitor adverts, surveyed the public. As a result, the Authority is considering changing the time [7] **when** such adverts can be shown on TV until after 10 pm.

6

1 The DVD what **that** (*or* **which**) you lent me was really interesting. (Or omit *what*.)

2 The actor, ~~that~~ **who** was in the Nike advert, is famous now.

3 The people ~~which~~ **who** (or **that**) we spoke to helped us a lot. (Or omit *which*.)

4 The film, ~~which~~ **whose** director is French, has won an Oscar.

5 I have two jobs ~~where~~ **that** (or **which**) take up all my time.

6 I ate melon, ~~that~~ **which** is quite unusual in winter, at the restaurant.

5

• Look at part 1 as an example with the class. Elicit that *Advertising agencies who listen to their clients* matches b *get the best results*. Elicit or explain that *who* is used here because an advertising agency is seen as the sum of the people who work for it. It would also be possible to replace *who* with *that* or *which* in this example.

• Ask students to match the two parts of the other sentences.

> **Answers**
> _____
> 1 b 2 e 3 d 4 f 5 a 6 c

• **Optional step.** Ask students to start making an advertising vocabulary list containing all the advertising terms in the sentences. They can add any other terms in advertising that they know or they can add new terms they encounter later.

6

• Ask students to look at the sentences in Exercise 5 again and to identify the sentence(s) where the relative pronoun could be replaced with *that*.

• Check answers with the class. Elicit that sentences 1 and 5 contain defining relative clauses, and that *that* can only be used in defining relative clauses.

> **Answers**
> _____
> You can replace the relative pronoun with *that* in sentences 1 and 5.

7

• Look at item 1 as an example with the class. Elicit that this pair of sentences can be rewritten as: *The CLIO Awards, which are given annually, celebrate creative and inventive thinking.* Elicit or explain that *which are given annually* is a non-defining relative clause and this is why we use commas before and after it.

• Ask students to rewrite the other pairs of sentences as one sentence containing a defining or non-defining relative clause. Students could do this in pairs.

• Check answers with the class. Elicit or explain that *that* or *which* can be used in sentences 3, 5 and 7. Also draw students' attention to the way in which *a place* in item 6 becomes *the place* in the rewritten sentence and *An advert* in item 7 becomes *The advert* in the rewritten sentence.

> **Answers**
> _____
> 1 The CLIO Awards, which are given annually, celebrate creative and inventive thinking.
>
> 2 A graphic designer whose style is really original won the design award.
>
> 3 Adverts which are too entertaining don't help the audience to remember the product.
>
> 4 Outdoor adverts, which need to have visuals with a big impact, use large billboards.
>
> 5 Talented people who work for big agencies can earn a lot of money.
>
> 6 The Internet is the place where the most creative advertising ideas are found.
>
> 7 The advert which was voted for by most people won the top prize.
>
> 8 Viral videos, which appear on the Internet, can be a form of advertising.

8

• Students decide which of the sentences can be rewritten with reduced relative clauses. They could do this in pairs.

• Check answers, and elicit or explain that sentences 5 and 7 can be rewritten as reduced relative clauses because these sentences still make sense without the relative pronouns.

• **Optional step.** You could also elicit or explain that we are able to use reduced relative clauses in sentences 5 and 7 because they contain non-defining relative clauses and the relative pronouns are the subject of the relative clauses.

> **Answers**
> _____
> 5 Talented people working for big agencies can earn a lot of money.
>
> 7 The advert voted for by most people won the top prize.

9

• Look at the first sentence with the class. Elicit that *which* or *that* could be used before *I've ever seen*, but this is not essential (as *memorable adverts* is the object) and is not one of the ten missing relative pronouns. Elicit that *whose* is missing before *name*. Make sure that everyone agrees that no commas need to be added to this sentence.

• You could look at the second sentence with the class too or get students to read the rest of the description, and add ten relative pronouns and eight commas. They can do this in pairs.

• Remind students to use commas only in non-defining relative clauses, and that in some cases either *that* or *which* is possible.

- Conduct whole-class feedback. If possible, you could do this by writing the text on the board or projecting it onto a screen, and asking students to come up to the front and to add the relative pronouns and commas into that text.

- Ask students to underline the three examples of relative clauses that could be reduced. They can also do this in pairs.

Answers

One of the most memorable adverts I've ever seen was for a bank **whose** name I can't even remember. But the advert, **which was promoting some kind of savings product**, was very funny. You see two bank employees **(who are) working** at their desks. They're both answering phone queries. The office **(that)** they are in looks grey and boring. Then one of the employees, **who is very serious**, says something **that** sounds like a line from a pop song. It's a song **(which/that is) heard** a lot on the radio. The other one, **(who is) sitting** next to him, starts to sing and dance. She's trying to make him laugh. The idea, **which is simple**, is good, but it's the actors **who** make it really funny.

10

- Ask students to read the description of the advert in Exercise 9 again quickly and to consider whether they think the advert was successful. Encourage them to think of reasons or evidence to support their point of view.

- Put students into pairs to discuss whether they think this advertisement was successful, giving reasons or drawing examples from the description to support their point of view. Possible reasons could be: *it's memorable, funny, simple, it includes a pop song which is heard a lot on the radio and it includes the element of contrast and surprise, i.e. the contrast between the boring setting of the bank and the surprise when the bank workers start to sing and dance.*

- Conduct whole-class feedback on whether the advertisement was successful, and why / why not.

- Ask students to tell their partner about an advert they can remember.

- Conduct whole-class feedback and ask students to share some general ideas about what makes an advert memorable.

TEACHING TIP

Using adverts

Students talk about their own favourite memorable adverts. They could talk about adverts they see on billboards or posters on public transport in their day-to-day lives. If they have access to YouTube or other video-sharing platforms and, if appropriate, they could find adverts online and show them in class.

SPEAKING Are you persuaded?

11 21st CENTURY OUTCOMES

- Before starting this exercise, refer students to the 21st CENTURY OUTCOMES at the foot of the page. Ask students whether they think their own beliefs and behaviour have been influenced by the media, and encourage them to think of some specific examples. For example: *Since I started watching … , I've thought … ; Since I saw a video with … online, I've felt … .* This kind of awareness of how media influence works will help students when they analyse the influence of five TV adverts in this exercise.

- Put students into small groups to brainstorm a list of TV adverts and then to rate them. Tell students that they should use their answers to the five questions about the advert to help to decide what rating to give each one. Monitor students while they're doing this.

- If you have a multinational class and you want to focus on adverts shown in the country where the English course is taking place, you could ask students in advance to prepare for this activity by watching local TV or finding examples of local TV adverts online.

- Conduct whole-class feedback and ask students to present their ideas about which adverts are successful, and why.

▶ Photocopiable communicative activity 9.1: Go to page 229 for further practice of relative clauses. The teaching notes are on page 245.

▶ Set Workbook pages 86–87 for homework.

9.3 Agreeing to differ

READING The left-brain–right-brain debate

1

- Draw students' attention to the spread title: *Agreeing to differ*. Elicit that when you *agree to differ* with someone, you accept the fact that you will not agree about something. Ask: *Can you think of a situation where you agreed to differ with someone?* Put students into pairs to tell each other what happened in this situation and what the outcome was.

- Elicit or explain that scientists believe the two different sides of the brain are responsible for different functions. Put students into small groups to brainstorm what they think the functions and characteristics of the right brain and left brain could be. Then conduct whole-class feedback and ask the groups to present their ideas to the rest of the class.

- Put students into pairs to discuss the questions. Encourage them to give examples of anyone they know who fits the descriptions and to give some details about their personalities.

- Monitor students while they're discussing the questions. Listen to check that they're using appropriate personality adjectives and collect any interesting examples which they use. You can then share these examples with the rest of the class during whole-class feedback.

2

- Put students into pairs to look at the descriptions in Exercise 1 again and to predict whether they refer to 'left-brain' or 'right-brain' thinkers.

- Encourage students to give reasons for their choices. For example: *I think right-brain thinkers paint and draw a lot because they're more creative.*

- Ask students to read the article and to confirm which descriptions refer to 'left-brain' thinkers and which refer to 'right-brain' thinkers.

> **Answers**
>
> A 'left-brain' thinker:
>
> never makes decisions in a hurry.
>
> is great with words and can express themselves well.
>
> has a good head for numbers and can keep track of their finances.
>
> A 'right-brain' thinker:
>
> paints and draws a lot.
>
> plays a musical instrument.
>
> is sensitive and acts according to their feelings.

3

- Give students time to read the sentences. If necessary, clarify the meaning of:

  species – a group of plants or animals which share similar characteristics (sentence 1)

- Ask students to read the article again to identify whose views they represent: Cary Wilson's or Kirk Monroe's. They can do this in pairs.

> **Answers**
>
> 1 KM   2 CW   3 CW   4 KM   5 KM

- **Optional step.** Ask students which sentences they agree with, giving reasons for their answers where appropriate. They can discuss this in pairs.

4

- Encourage students to find the words (1–8) in the article to help deduce their meaning from context.

- Students match the words with their meanings (a–h).

> **Answers**
>
> 1 c   2 b   3 h   4 a   5 f   6 e   7 d   8 g

5

- Put students into pairs to discuss the questions.

- Conduct whole-class feedback on whether students have done the tests mentioned in the article and which ones, whether they think they have more 'left-brain' or 'right-brain' skills and why, and whose views – Cary Wilson's or Kirk Monroe's – students find more convincing, and why.

VOCABULARY Personality adjectives (1)

6

- Elicit that learning word pairs, e.g. contrasting adjectives, or word families, e.g. verb, noun, adjective, is useful because it can help students to build and to widen their vocabulary. It can also draw their attention to patterns that exist between words of the same type and within word families.

- Ask students to complete the table with the adjectives. They can do this in pairs.

- Conduct whole-class feedback and elicit that adjectives can have either a negative prefix, e.g. *-un*, or a negative suffix, e.g. *-less*. Draw students' attention to the fact there is no affirmative adjective that includes the base word *fool*. You could also draw students' attention to the range of negative prefixes and suffixes that exist, e.g. *il-, un-, ir-, in-, im-, -less*.

- **Optional step.** Ask students to think of other adjectives that include each of the negative prefixes and suffixes above.

> **Answers**
>
> 1 analytical   2 careful   3 emotional   4 unimaginative
> 5 illogical   6 irrational   7 realistic   8 sensible
> 9 sensitive

7

- Ask students to read the sentences and elicit that the two options are contrasting adjectives.

- Tell students to choose the best option to complete the sentences.

> **Answers**
>
> 1 sensible   2 irrational   3 precise   4 unrealistic
> 5 emotional   6 sensitive

8

- Ask students to think about whether their job or area of study attracts people with any of the personality types in Exercise 7, and which ones. Tell students that they shouldn't feel limited to the personality adjectives from Exercises 6 and 7. Encourage students to also bring in any other personality adjectives or vocabulary for personality types which they know.

- Students could then discuss the personality type(s) they've thought of in pairs. They can compare and contrast the personality type(s) they've thought of.

- Conduct whole-class feedback and ask students to share the personality types they chose and their reasons for choosing these.

- **Optional step.** Students write their own sentences about personality types using the unused options in Exercise 7. They could then work in pairs and read out their sentences saying *beep* instead of the adjective: their partner has to supply the correct adjective.

Dealing with personality types associated with students' jobs or areas of study

Exercise 8 does require a degree of generalization and students may be reluctant to associate seemingly negative personality types with their job or area of study. Focus on the fact that these are just stereotypes and even if a more negative personality type is associated with their job or area of study, this doesn't necessarily mean that they also have that negative personality type. You could inject some humour into Exercise 8 and encourage students to not take it too seriously.

SPEAKING Boosting your creativity

9 21st **CENTURY OUTCOMES**

- Before starting this exercise, refer students to the 21st CENTURY OUTCOMES at the foot of the page. Elicit other possible idea-creation techniques such as mind-mapping, role-playing scenarios, looking at images or using random input, e.g. picking a word at random from the dictionary. Encourage students to use one of these techniques to generate ideas in answer to question 2.

- Put students into small groups and give them 5–10 minutes to discuss the questions.

- Conduct whole-class feedback and focus on students' answers to question 2. Ask: *What does 'being creative' mean to you? Possible* answers could be: *self-expression, communication with other people, mental stimulation, identity creation.*

10

- Look at the diagram with the class. Explain that this shows six things that would be impossible for a particular person to do. Ask students to identify the six things. Then explain or elicit that imagining how to do the six impossible things is a way to boost your creativity.

- You could put students into pairs to discuss which of the suggestions they've tried and also which ones they would like to try. Encourage students to brainstorm any other suggestions of their own for boosting your creativity.

- Conduct whole-class feedback to gauge which of the suggestions students have tried or would like to try. Ask: *Do you have any other suggestions for boosting your creativity?* Some possible suggestions could be: *read a book, try a new hobby, watch a TV programme you've never watched before, go to bed an hour earlier.*

11

- Put students into groups to choose one of the activities from Exercise 10 that they're all going to try out now in class. Encourage students to choose one of the activities which it will be possible to do within the constraints of the classroom environment, i.e. not the second and fifth.

- Students then choose another activity which they will try out outside the classroom before the next lesson.

- In the next lesson, students will work in the same groups and compare experiences of trying out the activity they chose.

Self-study activities

Some sensitivity is required when assigning self-study activities to students. It's important to gauge students' willingness and ability to complete self-study activities in their own time. Forcing students to do activities outside of class may prove counter-productive. Even where students agree to undertake activities in their own time, keep in mind the fact that, due to various factors, they may not actually manage to complete them. In Exercise 11, don't assume that all students will have been able to try out the activity by the next lesson. Ask those students who have done the activity to share their experiences nonetheless and this may inspire students who haven't done it. Give students additional time to try out the activity and then report back on their experiences, where appropriate.

▶ Set Workbook pages 88–89 for homework.

9.4 It's a great idea

LISTENING Launching a new product

1

- Draw students' attention to the section heading: *Launching a new product*. Elicit that when you *launch a product*, you make it available for people to buy for the first time.

- Direct students' attention to the photo and ask: *Which company is launching a new product in this photo?* (The company is Apple.) You could tell students that the photo shows: *20-year-old Marcel Gaisbachgrabner from Gmunden in Austria cheering as he steps out of an Apple store holding two new iPhone 6's.*

- Put students into pairs to discuss their own experiences of queuing to buy something or pre-ordering online. If necessary, clarify the meaning of:

  gadget – a mechanical device or tool which we use to make our lives easier (third item)

- Encourage students to start by talking about any of the four items in the box that they've had experience with and then, if appropriate, to go on to discuss any other items they've queued up to buy or had an experience with.

- Monitor students while they're speaking. Encourage students to give reasons for queuing up to buy something or pre-ordering something online and to say what the effects of doing this were. Ask: *Were you one of the first to get the product or tickets? Did you get a superior version of the product or better seats at the event?*

2

- Bring in students' own experiences. Ask: *Have you ever queued up to buy a new video game or experienced the launch of a new video game first-hand?*

- **Optional step.** Ask students to brainstorm what you would have to think about and decide on if you were organizing a video game product launch. Possible answers could be: *date, time, venue, how many people you expect to come, how you're going to publicize the event, food and drink, entertainment.*

- ⏹ 50 Play the recording so that students can answer the questions.

Transcript

N = Nina, G = Greg, J = Joanna

N: OK, welcome everyone. As you know, we're here to talk about the launch of the Series 7 game. Basically we need to agree on a date and a time when Series 7 will go on sale. Greg, what are your thoughts on the date?

G: Well, we obviously want to make the most of the Christmas market, so I think mid-December is best. How about you, Nina?

N: Middle of December – yes, I agree.

J: If I could say something here. I think mid-December might be a little late. I think the beginning of December would be better.

G: It depends what kind of campaign we are going to run, really. I mean, are we thinking about a midnight release with a big build-up?

N: Joanna, would you like to say anything about that?

J: Erm, well there aren't any signs that the public is getting tired of big spectacular launches. So I think opening the stores for a midnight release is still an interesting idea. It creates a lot of excitement around the product.

N: Let me just say that we've got a smaller budget for advertising this year, so we really need to come up with ways of making the launch date memorable.

G: So that would suggest a midnight launch is still a great idea.

3

- Ask students to look at the Useful language box and to read the expressions. Ask: *Can you remember hearing any of these expressions when you listened to the conversation? If so, which ones?*

- ⏹ 50 Play the recording for students to tick the expressions which are used in the conversation.

Pronunciation Stress and meaning

4a

- If students have completed Unit 5 and/or Unit 8, elicit that stress is the placing of more emphasis on some words than others in a sentence. Stressed words are usually the most important words, i.e. nouns and verbs.

- ⏹ 51 Play the recording so that students can listen and write the word they think is stressed in each case.

- Ask students to check their answers in pairs. Then check answers with the class.

- ⏹ 51 Play the recording again, pausing after each sentence to confirm which word is stressed each time.

- **Optional step.** Elicit the questions and ask students to practise saying them with the stress on the words that were stressed in the recording. They could do this in pairs.

4b

- Ask students to identify which questions in Exercise 4a show that the person's opinion is more important and which show that the topic is more important.

- Conduct whole-class feedback and elicit that words which refer to the topic are stressed (*date*, *that*) in 1a and 2b and this suggests that the topic is more important than the person's opinions in these contexts. Words which refer to people are stressed in 1b and 2a (*your*, *you*) and this suggests that a person's opinion is more important than the topic in these contexts. You could point out that whether we choose to stress words connected with a person or a topic will also depend on the context we're speaking in and who we're speaking to. For example: if we're in a situation where we're talking to someone who has more power than us, we're likely to stress words such as *you* and *your* to show that person how much we're focused on them. However, if we're in a context where we're talking to someone who has less power than us, we're likely to stress words connected with the topic instead.

Answers

1a topic, 1b person's opinion

2a person's opinion, 2b topic

4c

- Ask students to complete the questions which end ... ? in the Useful language box with their own ideas.

- Students can work in pairs and practise saying their completed questions with the two different stress patterns.

- Monitor students while they're saying the questions, offering help with their use of word stress if necessary.

- **Optional step.** Put students into pairs to create mini-conversations in which the stressed word within the question would be completely natural.

SPEAKING Organizing a campaign

5

- Ask students to form groups (4–5 students). Explain that they are going to discuss ideas for an advertising campaign for their English course.

- Students make notes on some ideas on their own and then discuss these with the rest of the group. Tell students to use at least four expressions from the Useful language box as they give their opinions and ask other students for their opinions.

- Monitor students while they're speaking and, where appropriate, prompt them to use the expressions from the Useful language box.

WRITING A personal account

6

- Look at the title of the article with the class. Explain or elicit that a *lightbulb moment* is a moment of inspiration.

- Draw students' attention to the photo in the article and elicit the name of the woman in the photo and her job.

- Students read the article to find the answers to the questions.

Answers

1 apps

2 for Leanne Jones to explain where she gets her lightbulb moments (her ideas) and to pass on her tips about what to do to be successful

3 a She got frustrated buying something online, so she asked herself if she could do it better – and created one of her most successful apps.

b She was flying off on holiday, dreaming about lying on the beach, and an idea for a flight-checking app just popped into her head.

Writing skill Informal language

7a

- Ask students to look at the list of features of written language. If necessary, remind students that they worked with *phrasal verbs* (two-part verbs which usually consist of a verb and a preposition or prepositions) in Unit 6.3 and clarify the meaning of:

  imprecise terms – vague or ambiguous words or expressions (item 5)

  exclamation mark – a punctuation mark (!) which indicates exclamation (item 12)

- Ask students to decide which features are used in formal writing and which are used in informal writing. They can do this in pairs. Remind students that something that is a feature of formal writing in their own first language may actually be a feature of informal writing in English, and vice versa: for example, it's acceptable to use exclamation marks in both formal and informal writing in German.

- Conduct whole-class feedback and ensure that students have correctly identified the features of formal written English. Elicit or give examples of the features, where appropriate, avoiding the examples given in the text.

- Ask students to find and underline examples of the features of informal writing in the article.

- Conduct whole-class feedback, and discuss with the class which features of formal and informal writing they currently use and whether they use these features in the appropriate context. Ask: *Is your formal writing formal enough and your informal writing informal enough? How do you know?*

7b

• Look at sentence 1 as an example with the class. Elicit that *lead* could be replaced by the phrasal verb *head up* and the adverb *highly* could be replaced by a more informal adverb such as *very* or *really*.

• Ask students to rewrite the other sentences in a more informal style by making the changes in brackets. Remind students that their rewritten sentences should still communicate the same message as the original sentences.

• **Optional step.** Put students into pairs to write three or four formal sentences on a topic of their choice, which they then exchange with another pair who rewrite them as informal sentences.

8 *21st* CENTURY OUTCOMES

• Before starting this exercise, refer students to the 21st CENTURY OUTCOMES at the foot of the page. Tell students that they will need to incorporate input and feedback into the writing they do in this exercise. You could ask students to reflect on how they usually behave when they're working collaboratively in a group. For example, you could ask: *Are you the natural leader who likes to dominate and talk the most? Or are you a more reserved team member who says as little as possible? How easy do you find it to incorporate ideas that other people have suggested into your work?*

• Put students into groups (4–5 students). Explain that each group should decide on a popular product they all know about.

• Ask students to brainstorm ideas and vocabulary that they could use to write a paragraph about the experience of being involved in the development of the product they have chosen. Students can refer back to the infographic of the creative process on page 100 while they're doing this if necessary.

• Monitor students while they're brainstorming and discussing ideas. Encourage all group members to take an active part in the activity and to incorporate everyone's feedback into the opening sentences as far as possible.

• **Optional step.** Ask each group, or a spokesperson from each group, to present their opening sentence to the rest of the class, who could then give them feedback. Students could either read out the sentences or write them on the board.

9

• Students work on their own to complete the paragraph. You can monitor students while they're writing, but don't offer any corrections as students will give feedback to each other on what they've written.

• Ask students to exchange paragraphs with someone else in their group. They read each other's paragraph and focus on possible areas for improvement in the other student's writing. Encourage students to focus on whether the writer of the paragraph they're reading has used the correct register. Other areas that students could give each other feedback on are: content, structure, vocabulary, grammar, spelling and punctuation. Another relevant point for feedback could also be how interesting the paragraph is to read.

• Students give the paragraph back and make two suggestions to improve their partner's writing.

• Monitor students while they're making suggestions about how each other's writing could be improved and let them know if you disagree with what they're saying, e.g. if a student suggests that another student hasn't used the appropriate register when you think that they have.

▶ Photocopiable communicative activity 9.2: Go to page 230 for further practice of turn-taking expressions and personality adjectives. The teaching notes are on page 245.

▶ Set Workbook pages 90–91 for homework.

▶ Set Workbook Presentation 5 on pages 92–93 for homework.

10 Connections

THEMES: Listening, making connections with people

TED TALK: *5 ways to listen better*. In this TED Talk, Julian Treasure points out that we don't consciously listen to most of what we hear; focusing on what he calls 'conscious listening' can help us to build more meaningful relationships with the people around us.

AUTHENTIC LISTENING SKILLS: Dealing with unknown vocabulary

CRITICAL THINKING: Identifying problems and solutions

PRESENTATION SKILLS: Body movement and gesture

GRAMMAR: Reported speech

VOCABULARY: Customer service

PRONUNCIATION: Sounds and meaning

READING: Cross-cultural awareness

LISTENING: Two sides to every story, Helplines

SPEAKING: Two sides to every story, Leaving tips, Taking part in a meeting: RASA (Comparing experiences)

WRITING: Minutes (2)

WRITING SKILL: Reporting verbs

LEAD IN

• Books open. Draw students' attention to the unit title, and to the photo on pages 106–7 and its caption. Ask: *What is the link between the unit theme of connections and the photo?* A possible answer could be: *the people in the photo are making nets by sewing material together, so they're connecting pieces of material to create something useful.*

• Bring in students' own experiences. Ask: *In what situations in your life is it important that you listen effectively? Why?* Possible answers could be: *When my boss is talking to me so that he knows that I'm paying attention to him, When I'm having a job interview and want to make a good impression, When my friends are talking to me about their day and I want to show them that I'm genuinely interested in what they're doing.*

TEDTALKS
BACKGROUND

1

• Review the differences between *to listen (to)* and *to hear*, and between *sound* and *noise* with the class. Elicit that *listening* involves paying attention to someone or something, whereas *hearing* is just being aware of a sound through your ears. A *sound* is something that you hear whereas a *noise* is often something unpleasant.

• Ask students to read the text about Julian Treasure and his talk. If necessary, clarify the meaning of

conscious – describing a state of being aware of something or aware that something is happening (line 8)

• Put students into pairs to discuss the questions.

• Conduct whole-class feedback. Elicit what kind of advice students think that Julian Treasure's company gives, but don't reveal the answer at this stage. Invite students to talk about the types of situations in which they find it easier or more difficult to listen to and understand English, and the reasons.

Suggested answers

1 soft background music or pop music; announcements in a supermarket asking members of staff to go to a till, or announcements about what's happening in a particular shop department; the general buzz of conversation

2 It will advise companies on how sound can increase retail sales and improve employee performance.

3 Students will probably find one-to-one conversation the easiest since this is two-way communication and they can ask a question if something is unclear; the same applies to the classroom. Radio may be the most difficult in that the speaker and the situation is not visible.

KEY WORDS

2

• Ask students to try to guess the meaning of the words in bold and then to match them with their definitions.

Answers

1 d 2 a 3 b 4 f 5 c 6 e

• Put students into pairs to ask and answer the questions.

AUTHENTIC LISTENING SKILLS Dealing with unknown vocabulary

3a

• Ask students to read the information about dealing with unknown vocabulary in the Authentic listening skills box.

• Look at the instructions with the class. Draw students' attention to the term *pattern recognition*. Ask them to try to predict what this could involve, but don't confirm answers at this stage.

- ⋒ 52 Play the recording so that students can complete the extract. You could play the recording again either before or after checking answers. Confirm that *pattern recognition* involves using patterns in your speech in order to get your audience's attention. Elicit or explain that the missing words in the extract help to make clear the meaning of *pattern recognition*.

> ### Transcript and answers
>
> *We use some pretty cool techniques to do this. One of them is pattern recognition. So in a cocktail party like this, if I say, 'David, Sara, pay attention,' some of you just sat up. We recognize patterns to distinguish noise from signal, and especially our name.*

3b

- ⋒ 53 Play the recording so that students can complete the extracts. Elicit or explain that the missing words in the extracts help to make clear the meaning of the words in bold.

> ### Transcript and answers
>
> 1   *differencing is another <u>technique</u> we use*
>
> 2   *filters take us from all sound down to what we <u>pay attention</u> to*

- **Optional step.** You could look at another example of dealing with unknown vocabulary in the transcript. Ask students if they know the meaning of the word *intention*, but don't confirm answers at this stage. Ask them to find *intention* in the transcript (in the section starting 1.05). Elicit or explain that if students didn't know the word *intention*, then the sentence that follows give an example of the term: *When I married my wife, I promised her that I would listen to her every day as if for the first time.*

10.1 5 ways to listen better

TEDTALKS

1

- Books open. Give students time to look at the parts of the talk and the things. If necessary, clarify the meaning of:

  mundane – describing something which is very ordinary and usually also boring (a, third item).

- Don't explain what the acronym *RASA* stands for at this stage. Explain that students will focus on what the letters stand for in Exercise 4. This is a supporting task designed to help students to understand the main messages Julian Treasure wants to communicate in this TED Talk rather than a comprehension task.

- Tell students to focus on matching the three parts of the talk (1–3) with the things Julian Treasure talks about (a–c) while they're watching. You could encourage them to match the parts with the things before they watch the talk.

- ▶ 10.1 Play the whole talk once so that students can match the parts with the things.

Transcript

0.13   *We are losing our listening. We spend roughly 60 per cent of our communication time listening, but we're not very good at it. We retain just 25 per cent of what we hear. Now not you, not this talk, but that is generally true. Let's define listening as making meaning from sound. It's a mental process, and it's a process of extraction.*

0.36   *We use some pretty cool techniques to do this. One of them is pattern recognition. (Crowd noise) So in a cocktail party like this, if I say, 'David, Sara, pay attention,' some of you just sat up. We recognize patterns to distinguish noise from signal, and especially our name. Differencing is another technique we use. If I left this pink noise on for more than a couple of minutes, you would literally cease to hear it. We listen to differences, we discount sounds that remain the same.*

1.05   *And then there is a whole range of filters. These filters take us from all sound down to what we pay attention to. Most people are entirely unconscious of these filters. But they actually create our reality in a way, because they tell us what we're paying attention to right now. Give you one example of that: intention is very important in sound, in listening. When I married my wife, I promised her that I would listen to her every day as if for the first time. Now that's something I fall short of on a daily basis. (Laughter) But it's a great intention to have in a relationship.*

1.43   *But that's not all. Sound places us in space and in time. If you close your eyes right now in this room, you're aware of the size of the room from the reverberation and the bouncing of the sound off the surfaces. And you're aware of how many people are around you because of the micro-noises you're receiving. And sound places us in time as well, because sound always has time embedded in it. In fact, I would suggest that our listening is the main way that we experience the flow of time from past to future. So, 'Sonority is time and meaning' – a great quote.*

2.17   *I said at the beginning, we're losing our listening. Why did I say that? Well there are a lot of reasons for this. First of all, we invented ways of recording – first writing, then audio recording and now video recording as well. The premium on accurate and careful listening has simply disappeared. Secondly, the world is now so noisy, (Noise) with this cacophony going on visually and auditorily, it's just hard to listen; it's tiring to listen. Many people take refuge in headphones, but they turn big, public spaces like this, shared soundscapes, into millions of tiny, little personal sound bubbles. In this scenario, nobody's listening to anybody.*

3.00 *We're becoming impatient. We don't want oratory anymore, we want sound bites. And the art of conversation is being replaced – dangerously, I think – by personal broadcasting. I don't know how much listening there is in this conversation, which is sadly very common, especially in the UK. We're becoming desensitized. Our media have to scream at us with these kinds of headlines in order to get our attention. And that means it's harder for us to pay attention to the quiet, the subtle, the understated.*

3.33 *This is a serious problem that we're losing our listening. This is not trivial. Because listening is our access to understanding. Conscious listening always creates understanding. So I'd like to share with you five simple exercises, tools you can take away with you, to improve your own conscious listening. Would you like that?*

3.57 *(Audience: yes) Good.*

3.59 *The first one is silence. Just three minutes a day of silence is a wonderful exercise to reset your ears and to recalibrate so that you can hear the quiet again. If you can't get absolute silence, go for quiet, that's absolutely fine.*

4.13 *Second, I call this the mixer. (Noise) So even if you're in a noisy environment like this – and we all spend a lot of time in places like this – listen in the coffee bar to how many channels of sound can I hear? How many individual channels in that mix am I listening to? You can do it in a beautiful place as well, like in a lake. How many birds am I hearing? Where are they? Where are those ripples? It's a great exercise for improving the quality of your listening.*

4.41 *Third, this exercise I call savouring, and this is a beautiful exercise. It's about enjoying mundane sounds. This, for example, is my tumble dryer. (Dryer) It's a waltz. One, two, three. One, two, three. One, two, three. I love it. Or just try this one on for size. (Coffee grinder) Wow! So mundane sounds can be really interesting if you pay attention. I call that the hidden choir. It's around us all the time.*

5.16 *The next exercise is probably the most important of all of these, if you just take one thing away. This is listening positions – the idea that you can move your listening position to what's appropriate to what you're listening to. This is playing with those filters. Do you remember, I gave you those filters at the beginning. It's starting to play with them as levers, to get conscious about them and to move to different places. These are just some of the listening positions, or scales of listening positions, that you can use. There are many. Have fun with that. It's very exciting.*

5.47 *And finally, an acronym. You can use this in listening, in communication. If you're in any one of those roles – and I think that probably is everybody who's listening to this talk – the acronym is RASA, which is the Sanskrit word for juice or essence. And RASA stands for Receive,*

which means pay attention to the person; Appreciate, making little noises like 'hmm', 'oh', 'OK'; Summarize, the word 'so' is very important in communication; and Ask, ask questions afterward.

6.18 *Now sound is my passion, it's my life. I wrote a whole book about it. So I live to listen. That's too much to ask from most people. But I believe that every human being needs to listen consciously in order to live fully – connected in space and in time to the physical world around us, connected in understanding to each other, not to mention spiritually connected, because every spiritual path I know of has listening and contemplation at its heart.*

6.47 *So I invite you to connect with me, connect with each other, take this mission out and let's get listening taught in schools, and transform the world in one generation to a conscious listening world – a world of connection, a world of understanding and a world of peace.*

7.01 *Thank you for listening to me today.*

7.03 *(Applause)*

Answers _____

1 c   2 b   3 a

• Note the differences in North American English and British English shown at the foot of the spread. In this unit, these focus on spelling, pronunciation and vocabulary differences.

2

• ▶10.1 Play the first part (0.00–2.17) of the talk so that students can check whether the sentences are true or false.

Answers _____

1 T

2 T

3 F (It's not that most people don't use filters – they are entirely unconscious of them.)

4 T

3

• Ask students to complete the sentences with four of the words. They can do this in pairs. Remind students to look carefully at the words that come before and after – especially before – the gaps to help them to decide which type of word (adverb, adjective or noun) should go in the gaps.

• ▶10.1 Play the second part (2.17–3.57) of the talk so that students can listen and check their answers.

Answers _____

1 carefully   2 tiring   3 headlines   4 understanding

4

• ▶10.1 Play the recording so that students can answer the questions. Encourage them to make notes as they listen.

Answers

1 three   2 coffee bar   3 tumble dryer, coffee machine
4 listening positions   5 receive, appreciate, summarize, ask

• **Optional step.** Ask students: *How many minutes of silence each day do you think you have? What noisy environments are you in during a typical day? Which 'mundane sounds' do you hear during a typical day? Which technique, if any, are you now going to start using?*

5

• Put students into pairs to write a one-sentence summary of the Authentic listening skills sections in Units 1–9. For example: Unit 1 *Be aware of how key words in your area of work or study are pronounced by native speakers*; Unit 2 *Listen out for signposting sentences or phrases*; Unit 3 *If you get advance information about what you're going to listen to, your listening will be more focused because you will be listening to check that the ideas you formed before you listened are correct*; Unit 4 *Different people will understand different parts of a message, so working together with other people can help you to understand more of a message*; Unit 5 *A rising intonation at the end of a sentence usually means that the speaker is asking a question, but speakers with some accents may also use a rising intonation at the end of sentences which aren't questions*; Unit 6 *When you're listening to a native speaker, relax and focus on getting the gist of what they're saying*; Unit 7 *It's a good idea to expose yourself to a wide range of native and non-native speaker accents*; Unit 8 *Be aware that some words are pronounced with compressed syllables, which means that there's a difference between how we write them and how we say them*; Unit 9 *Focus on the stressed words in fast speech.*

• Students discuss the similarities and differences between the techniques from previous units and Julian Treasure's techniques. Ask students to think about the aim of the techniques that Julian Treasure proposes and whether this aim is similar to or different from the aim of the Authentic listening skills sections. Ask: *Do we need to use the same or different listening skills when we're listening to people speaking a foreign language and people speaking our first language?*

• Monitor students while they're speaking, noting any examples of good points.

• Conduct whole-class feedback. Invite individual students to tell the rest of the class the good points that you have noted.

Answers

Julian Treasure's perspective is a more general, monolingual one, but it is aimed at improving overall listening skills and awareness.

The specific techniques of conscious listening and active/passive listening also apply to foreign language learning. Learning to filter out the unknown words that aren't essential to understanding also applies.

VOCABULARY IN CONTEXT

6

• ▶10.2 Play the clips from the TED Talk. When each multiple-choice question appears, pause the clip so that students can choose the correct definition.

Transcript and subtitles

1   *We spend **roughly** 60 per cent of our communication time listening, but we're not very good at it.*
    a approximately
    b an average of
    c precisely

2   *Now that's something I **fall short of** on a daily basis.*
    a manage to do
    b fail to do
    c try to do

3   *We don't want oratory anymore, we want **sound bites**.*
    a slogans
    b meaningful speeches
    c short comments

4   *If you can't get absolute silence, **go for** quiet, that's absolutely fine.*
    a aim for
    b ask about
    c demand

5   *And RASA stands for Receive, which means pay attention to the person; **Appreciate**, making little noises like 'hmm', 'oh,' 'OK'*
    a ask questions
    b interrupt
    c show understanding

Answers

1 a 2 b 3 c 4 a 5 c

7

• Look at the sentences with the class. If necessary, clarify the meaning of:

I reckon … – I think … / in my opinion … (sentence 3)

• Give students a few minutes to complete the three sentences on their own. Monitor students while they're writing, offering help where necessary.

• Put students into pairs or small groups to compare their sentences. You could then invite individual students to read out a sentence each to the rest of the class.

CRITICAL THINKING Identifying problems and solutions

8

• Check that students noticed that Julian Treasure structured his talk by pointing out a problem and then offering some solutions. Ask students to think about what Julian Treasure said during his talk and what the problem was. They can discuss this in pairs.

• Ask students to discuss whether they think the structure of the talk was effective. Encourage them to give reasons for their opinions. Then conduct whole-class feedback.

Suggested answers

The problem is that we're losing the ability to listen.

The structure was effective because Julian Treasure set out the problem, clarified what the problem is and then clearly set out five techniques which we can use to help us solve this problem.

9

• Ask students to read the comment and to think about what Jerome's problem could be and which of the techniques from the talk would help him. They can discuss this in pairs. Encourage students to give reasons for their answers. Then conduct whole-class feedback.

Suggested answers

Jerome's problem is that he sometimes misunderstands what people he's listening to are saying.

The techniques which could help him are: the second technique: the mixer; the fourth technique: use listening positions; the fifth technique: the RASA technique.

PRESENTATION SKILLS Body movement and gesture

10

• You could remind students of the gestures Nigel Marsh used in the photo montage from his talk in Unit 8.1 on page 86.

• Ask students to read about body movement and gesture in the Presentation tips box. If necessary, clarify the meaning of:

pace the floor – to walk up and down (first bullet)

palm – the inner surface of the hand (fourth bullet)

• Give students time to read the questions and the extracts from the first two clips.

• Draw students' attention to […] in the middle of the second extract. Explain that they needn't focus on this part of the clip. Note that this middle part of the clip includes the words *what we pay attention to* whereas students should focus on *what we're paying attention* to *right now,* which comes at the end of the clip.

• ▶10.3 Play the first two clips. Tell students to focus on what Julian Treasure does with his hands.

• Pause after the second clip and check students' answers to question a. Then show the third clip so that students can answer question b.

Transcript

1   *Now not you, not this talk, but that is generally true.*

2   *And then there is a whole range of filters. These filters take us from all sound down to what we pay attention to. Most people are entirely unconscious of these filters. But they actually create our reality in a way, because they tell us what we're paying attention to right now.*

3   *But that's not all. Sound places us in space and in time. If you close your eyes right now in this room, you're aware of the size of the room from the reverberation and the bouncing of the sound off the surfaces.*

• Check students' answers to question b and elicit the full list of the gestures that Julian Treasure uses. Write these on the board for students to refer to in Exercise 12.

Answers

a 1 **you:** He stretches his arms forward and indicates the audience with his outstretched fingers.

this talk: He points his fingers towards the floor.

that: He stretches his arms out to the right and left with fingers open.

2 **whole range of filters:** He holds his arms and hands up and out wide.

we're paying attention: he puts his hands almost together and pointing forward

b He uses outstretched hands, with the palms out and open, and facing both up and down.

11

• Look at the instructions with the class. If necessary, clarify the meaning of:

decibel – the unit of measurement for noise (line 2)

• Put students into pairs to look at the slide about different levels of noise, and to prepare sentences to present the information and to decide what gestures to use. Remind them to use the techniques in the Presentation tips box. Students then take turns to practise their presentation.

12

• Put students into new pairs. They take turns to give their presentation and to give each other feedback on how well their sentences and gestures work.

▶ Set Workbook pages 94–95 for homework.

10.2 How can I help?

GRAMMAR Reported speech

1

• Books open. Put students into pairs to discuss an experience they've had with a Customer Service department and to rate their level of satisfaction. Encourage students to choose a recent experience which is still fresh in their memory and to give reasons for the ranking they've chosen.

• Conduct whole-class feedback and gauge how satisfied or dissatisfied students were with the customer service they experienced. Ask a student who rated their satisfaction at 1 to summarize their experience, then a student who rated it at 2 to summarize their experience, and so on up to 5.

2

• Tell students to look at the infographic. Get them to identify the two questions in the survey: *Think of a customer service experience you had. Was it good or bad? How many people did you share that customer service experience with?*

• Explain that students should think about the experience they talked about in Exercise 1 when they answer these questions. They should also think of a quote – something to say – after their good/bad experience.

• You could put students into pairs to ask and answer the questions, and to give a quote about their good/bad experience.

• **Optional step.** If students chose a bad experience in Exercise 1, they could also answer the questions in the survey and think of something to say about a good experience, and vice versa.

• Conduct whole-class feedback and ask individual students to summarize their experience of customer service.

3

• Look at the Grammar box with the class. If necessary, clarify the meaning of:

respondent – a person who answers a request for information (first reported statement)

• Look at the first two reported statements with the class. Elicit that *I remember* and *I told* in the infographic have become *they remembered* and *they had told* in the reported statements.

• You could put students into pairs to compare the other three reported statements in the Grammar box with the statements in the infographic. Encourage them to report the two quotes after a good experience: *55% said (that) they **would** consider using the company again, 25% said they **would** recommend the company to others.*

• Students can check their answers and overall understanding of reported speech by turning to the Grammar summary on page 158.

Answers

1 remember → remembered, told → had told, have used → had used, won't use → wouldn't use, was → had been, did you share → had shared (might *stays the same*)

2 I → they, you → they (in a question)

3 tell

4 *yes/no* questions

• If you feel that students need more controlled practice before continuing, they could do one or more of Exercises 1–3 in the Grammar summary. Otherwise, you could continue on to Exercise 4 in the unit and set the Grammar summary exercises for homework.

Answers to Grammar summary exercises

1

1 phoned   2 were thinking   3 had gone   4 hadn't had
5 'd write   6 might request

2

1 if I knew

2 what we'd said

3 if I'd be (at work) the next day

4 where they'd decided to go

5 if I could finish (the work) that day

6 how long we had all worked there

3

1 Mark said (that) he'd heard a great song on the radio that morning.

2 Anya asked (him) which station he was listening to.

3 Mark said (that) he didn't know its name. He'd been in a café.

4 Anya asked (him) why he hadn't asked one of the waiters.

5 Mark said (that) It had been too busy to interrupt them.

6 Anya said (that) he could go back there the following day.

4

• Find out if students use Twitter and, if they do, ask: *What do you use it for? What does it help you to do?*

• Give students time to read the text without completing the comments. Look at items 1 and 2 as examples with the class. Elicit that the missing verbs are *were using* and *had decided*.

• Ask students to read the news item and to complete the other reported comments with the verbs.

• Check answers with the class and clarify any remaining uncertainties about how to form reported comments.

Answers

1 were using   2 had decided   3 could deal with
4 was going to be   5 wouldn't bother   6 was
7 didn't mean   8 were   9 had   10 had been travelling
11 had tweeted

5

• Explain that students are going to read a news item about a hotel review. Ask: *Do you ever write reviews of hotels you stay in? If you do, what do you usually comment on?* For example: *location*, *cleanliness*, *service*, *food*, *comfort*.

• Ask students to read the news item and to find the first quote. Look at this quote and the example sentence with the class.

• Students find and rewrite the other sentences with quotes. Remind them to change the verbs, pronouns and adverbs in the quotes where necessary. They can do this in pairs.

• Check answers with the class. Draw students' attention to the fact that there is more than one way to start some of the sentences.

Answers

2 He told the reporter / the newspaper / Bruce Shield (that) they had introduced the policy because some customers had been abusing feedback websites.

3 The reporter / the newspaper / Bruce Shield asked the owner how their policy had improved customer relations.

4 He said (that) the situation was difficult since customers would threaten them with a bad review because they wanted a discount.

5 The couple said (that) they had found an extra charge of £100 on their credit card bill.

6 The couple asked their bank if that was legal.

6

• Look at the first situation and the example with the class. Ask: *Have you ever had an experience like this?* Then invite individual students who have had an experience like this to complete the final sentence with what happened to them.

• Put students into pairs. Ask students to read the rest of the list of situations and to think about whether they've ever been in any of them. Students take turns to tell each other about what happened when they were in these situations. Remind students that they will need to use narrative tenses and reported speech to recount what happened and what was said. Encourage students to ask each other questions to find out more information about the scenario they're talking about, as in the example for the first situation.

• Monitor students while they're speaking, offering help where necessary and noting any examples of good use of reported speech.

• Conduct whole-class feedback. For each situation, invite one pair of students to tell the rest of the class what happened, what was said and how the situation ended. Encourage other students to say whether their situation ended in a similar way.

Suggested answers

A delivery man once brought a parcel to my door. It contained a present I'd bought for my mother's birthday. He rang the bell, I opened the door and I was horrified to see that the cardboard box the present was in had holes in it and was coming apart. I asked the delivery driver what had happened to my parcel and why it was so damaged. He told me that he'd had to slam down on the brakes to avoid a driver who came out of nowhere while he was driving here and there wasn't anything he could do about my damaged parcel.

I once went for a job interview at a big multi-national company. While I was sitting at reception waiting to be called up for my interview, I saw a woman smoking a cigarette at the reception, even though there was a no-smoking sign there for everyone to see. The receptionist noticed the woman and told her very firmly that smoking was prohibited inside the building and that she would have to go outside if she wanted to carry on smoking. The woman said she wasn't going anywhere, so the receptionist called security and had her removed from the building.

Last weekend I went out for dinner with my family because it was my mother's birthday. As she was sixty, we decided to go somewhere and we were really looking forward to the meal. My mother ordered blackcurrant juice. The waiter brought her drink, together with all the others, over to our table on a tray. There were so many drinks, I was afraid he was going to spill one. Then he did just that. The blackcurrant juice my mother had ordered went all over her brand-new white dress. My mother was so angry that she yelled at the waiter and told him to bring her a wet towel to try to mop the mess right away. The waiter said how sorry he was, but that didn't seem to calm her down at all. Then the restaurant manager came and told us that we wouldn't have to pay for our meals, which made us feel a bit better about the situation.

I went on holiday to Spain last summer and when I arrived at the airport there was an enormous queue at the check-in and bag drop for the airline I was flying with. I made my way to the end of the queue and had been waiting for about twenty minutes when I finally got closer to the check-in desks. Then someone just strolled in front of me and tried to slip into the queue. I asked him where he was flying to, he told me he was flying to Alicante and that they'd just announced that passengers for Alicante could go to the front of the queue. I corrected him and said that in fact it was only passengers for Madeira who could go to the front of the queue and he should go and join the back of the queue!

LISTENING AND SPEAKING Two sides to every story

7 **21st CENTURY OUTCOMES**

• Before starting this exercise, refer students to the 21st CENTURY OUTCOMES at the foot of the page. Ask students why listening effectively is important. Make the point that only half of oral communication involves speaking – students must be able to understand what is said to them in response to what they say.

• Look at the instructions and the photo with the class. Elicit or explain that the photo shows a *kettle* and that kettles play an important role in British life because they're used to boil water for cups of tea. Ask students to predict what the problem could be based on the scenario, but don't confirm answers at this stage.

• 🔊 **54** Play the recording so that students can identify the problem and what the tourist asks for.

• Direct students to the transcript on page 171. Elicit that James Rutter's use of the phrase *Are you crazy?* is rude and inappropriate in this situation. Elicit more appropriate alternatives that James Rutter could have said here. For example: *That can't be right*, *What do you mean?*

Transcript

J = James, F = François

J: Hi, could I speak to François Bartolone, please? This is James Rutter.

F: Speaking. Hello, Mr Rutter. Is everything all right with the house?

J: Well, actually it isn't. There's no kettle. How are we going to boil water? What are we supposed to make tea with?

F: Hmm, there's a microwave in the kitchen. Is it broken?

J: A microwave? That's no good for making tea. Are you crazy? The house isn't properly equipped.

F: Well, I'm sorry that you feel that way …

J: Look, we're on holiday. We need to relax. I really think we deserve some sort of a refund.

F: A refund? I don't think so!

Answers

There's no kettle in the house. The tourist asks for a refund.

8

• Ask students to predict how the sentences end based on what they can remember from the first time they listened to the recording. They can do this in pairs.

• Explain that students are going to listen to the recording again. They may not be able to write down every word that they hear, so they should focus on writing down the key words they hear. They can then use these to reconstruct the complete sentences.

• 🔊 **54** Play the recording again and ask students to complete the sentences.

Answers

1 François asked if <u>everything was all right with the house</u>.

2 James asked how <u>they were going to boil water</u> and what <u>they were supposed to make tea with</u>.

3 François then asked if <u>the microwave (in the kitchen) was broken</u>.

4 James asked François if <u>he was crazy</u>.

9

• Put students into small groups to discuss the questions. Encourage students to use reported speech where appropriate while they're discussing the questions. Monitor students while they're speaking, offering help where necessary and collecting interesting examples of language use. Then conduct whole-class feedback.

1 François probably told the owner of the house that James called to complain because there wasn't a kettle in the house and he didn't want to use the microwave instead. François also probably said that James asked for a refund, but he told him that this wouldn't be possible.

2 James probably told the owner of the house that François was very unhelpful when he called him to complain that there wasn't a kettle in the house and that François had stupidly told him to use the microwave instead. He would also have said that he was unhappy about the fact that François had said that he wouldn't give him a refund.

3 Both François and James were rude to each other. For example: François said: 'A refund? I don't think so!' and James said 'Are you crazy?' Neither of them handled the situation well.

4 Both François and James should have shown more politeness, respect and understanding for each other's situation. François shouldn't have suggested the microwave as an alternative for the kettle and he also shouldn't have immediately ruled out a refund.

5 Students' own answers, though they may think that James was being unreasonable.

TEACHING TIP

The pragmatics of politeness

In the recording students listen to in Exercise 9, both speakers could be described as rude. We could interpret the phrases *A refund? I don't think so!* and *Are you crazy?* as being rude because of how direct they are and because they could have unfriendly, even aggressive, overtones. However, your students may not interpret these utterances in this way, especially if they come from a culture where communicating directly and bluntly is the norm. You may want to draw students' attention to the fact that when we speak, we're constantly negotiating and constructing meaning with the people we speak to because different utterances can be interpreted in different ways. The context in which this negotiation takes place also plays a crucial role in determining its outcome. Within the context of an informal conversation with friends, for example, the phrase 'Are you crazy?' may be seen as indicative of friendly teasing, rather than rudeness.

10

• Put students into pairs to prepare and have their conversation. They could change roles or work with different students and have the conversation more than once. Monitor students while they're speaking.

• Conduct whole-class feedback and check that students' conversations all had an outcome that was satisfactory for both people. Ask students to tell the class how they managed to achieve that outcome.

▶ Photocopiable communicative activity 10.1: Go to page 231 for further practice of reported speech. The teaching notes are on page 246.

▶ Set Workbook pages 96–97 for homework.

10.3 The customer is always right

READING Cross-cultural awareness

1

• Books open. Draw students' attention to the spread title: *The customer is always right.* Elicit that this expression would usually be used by people who have contact with customers at work, e.g. people working in a hotel, restaurant or a call centre, and that it is usually used to show the importance a business places on the customer – no matter what situation arises, a service provider will always agree with what the customer says and do what the customer wants. Ask: *Have you heard this expression before? Do people working in customer service in your home country also believe that the customer is always right, or do they have a different attitude?*

• Ask students to look at the service industries in the box. If necessary, clarify the meaning of:

> *utilities* – water, electricity, gas, telecommunications (last item)

• Give students time to think about which of these service industries are most likely to be used by foreign visitors in their country and which areas they've experienced problems in when travelling abroad. You could put students into pairs to discuss the questions.

• Conduct whole-class feedback. If you have a multinational class, you could invite individual students to tell the rest of the class about the situation in their country.

They are all likely to be used – but some more than others, for example: banking, restaurants, transport, travel, tourism.

2

• **Optional step.** If students are studying at a college or university, ask if their institution also has a website where students can give their feedback on the courses it offers. If it does, ask: *Do you ever write comments on there? What do students usually comment on? Are the comments anonymous?*

• Ask students to read the feedback from four students on a college website and to find the information. Students could then work in pairs to check their answers. To facilitate the use of reported speech, tell students to assume that the four students who wrote the comments were all female.

- Ask students to discuss whether they would do either of these units, giving reasons for their answers. They can do this in pairs before you conduct whole-class feedback.

Extra activity

A course review

Ask students to choose a course which they've taken recently – either at a college or university, or at work – and to write a review based on the comments they've just read. Students can then exchange and compare their reviews and give each other feedback on their use of English in pairs.

Answers

1 HC2.2 Cross-Cultural Awareness module

2 Cross-cultural misunderstandings, Cross-cultural communication

3/4

Student 1: (3) On the whole, I think the course was excellent and that it has prepared me very well for working with both colleagues and customers from different cultural backgrounds.

Student 2: (4) The only thing I would say is that the tutor could have given more specific information about different cultures and what they regard as unacceptable so that we can avoid giving offence. (3) On the other hand, I now know greetings and basic terms in six languages, which is great as I've always been unable to learn a foreign language. I was amazed at how easy this was and how confident I now feel using the greetings. It was a very enjoyable class too.

Student 3: (3) But using video really helped us to see what our body language looks like to others. This was invaluable given that most of what we communicate is actually non-verbal. I also found the active listening workshops useful. These were ideas that were completely new to me. Following on from this, watching the videos, we were able to really understand how frequently we interrupted the other person and how we hardly ever gave them feedback during the conversation. (4) I would have liked more time to practise the effective questioning techniques, as I am still unclear on how to use reflective questions and paraphrasing. I think that this is one aspect of the unit that could be improved.

Student 4: (3) I'd just like to say that the tutors on the Cross-Cultural Awareness module were among the best I've had at this college. They gave us lots of positive feedback. They were also sensitive in helping us to understand that sometimes we aren't aware of how negative our own behaviour can be.

3

- Ask students to read the feedback again and to complete the headings in the syllabus of the Cross-Cultural Awareness module.

- **Optional step.** Put students into pairs. Ask students to discuss how useful they would find the content of this course based on its syllabus. Ask: *Is it similar to any courses that you've done? Would you add anything to or remove anything from the syllabus?* Then conduct whole-class feedback.

Answers

Cross-cultural misunderstandings: 1.1 religion, 1.3 ways of dressing, 1.4 formality, 2.2 basic terms in other languages

Cross-cultural communication: 1.2 active listening, 1.3 effective questioning, 2.1 body language

4

- The meaning of most, if not all, of the words in this list should already be known to students, but check and clarify the meaning of any unknown words.

- Look at item 1 as an example with the class. Elicit that *misunderstandings* has a negative meaning. Elicit or explain that *mis-* is a prefix.

- Ask students to work out whether the other words have negative, positive or neutral meanings and to underline the prefixes. They can do this in pairs.

- Check answers with the class. Explain that students shouldn't assume that all words with the prefixes in this exercise have negative meanings as not all of them do. Elicit that *invaluable* is an example of a word with a prefix which has a positive meaning (*invaluable* means 'extremely useful'). Elicit other examples of adjectives with prefixes which have positive meanings, e.g. *indescribable, unlimited, impressive*. Draw students' attention to the range of negative prefixes used in this list of words: *im-, in-, mis-, un-*. You could also elicit other examples of negative prefixes, e.g. *ir-* (*irrational*), *dis-* (*dissatisfied*).

Answers

Positive: invaluable
Negative: misunderstandings, unaware, inappropriate, unfriendly, impolite, unacceptable, unable, uncomfortable, unclear
Neutral: informal, non-verbal

- **Optional step.** You could draw students' attention to ways in which adjectives and prefixes are used. Compare how context can change the meaning of words such as the ones in this list. For example, *informal* has a neutral meaning, but using informal language in the context of a text which should be formal, e.g. a piece of academic writing, is seen as negative. Then draw students' attention to the fact that we don't always create a word with the opposite meaning to the original word when we add a prefix to it. For example, you can add the prefix *mis-* to *understanding*, but *misunderstanding* isn't the opposite of *understanding*. Also point out that the prefix *non-* is used to mean *without* and other combinations with *non-* include: *non-alcoholic, non-academic, non-stick*.

- Ask students to underline the prefixes of the words in Exercise 4.

5

- Look at sentence 1 as an example with the class. Elicit that the missing word is *clear*.

- Ask students to complete the other sentences with words from Exercise 4 (with or without the prefix).

- Check answers and elicit that the link between all six sentences is customer service.

> **Answers**
>
> 1 clear   2 unaware   3 formal   4 misunderstandings
> 5 unacceptable   6 invaluable

6

- Put students into pairs to discuss the questions. Draw students' attention to the use of the structure *might have helped* in the third question in item 1. Elicit that we use structures with modal + present perfect like this one to talk about situations in the past that didn't happen (in this case, students didn't study the cross-cultural units) and encourage students to also use *might have helped* in their answers to this question. For example: *They might have helped me to appreciate other cultures more.* Explain that students will work with this structure in Unit 12.4.

- If students have always lived in the same country, they may feel that they don't have any cross-cultural experience. However, reassure them that even if this is the case, they can also reflect on any contact they've had with people from other cultures in their own country or during trips abroad.

- Monitor students' while they're discussing the questions. Check that they are giving reasons for their opinions and examples to support them.

- Conduct whole-class feedback to establish the general consensus. Ask students to share the examples they used to support their opinions.

> **Suggested answers**
>
> 1 Students' own answers
>
> 2 In order to avoid difficulties arising from cross-cultural misunderstandings, you can inform yourself about the culture of people you encounter, and respect and accept it. You can also avoid making judgements about other cultures, and comparisons between your own culture and other people's, and show flexibility and the ability to adapt to different situations. Difficulties could be resolved by apologizing, where appropriate, giving an explanation for the reason for the misunderstanding, e.g. the fact that things are done differently in your own culture, and reaffirming your respect for and appreciation of the person from another culture who you're encountering.

VOCABULARY Customer service

7

- Look at expression 1 as an example with the class. Elicit that you can *behave appropriately*, *behave politely*, *behave professionally*, *behave badly* and *behave offensively*. Encourage students to give examples of each kind of behaviour and to say who behaves in this way.

- Ask students to complete the other expressions with the verbs. They can do this in pairs.

- Check answers with the class and ask students to identify who would usually do these things – the customer or the service provider.

> **Answers**
>
> C = customer, SP = service provider, B = both
>
> 1 behave: appropriately (SP) / politely (B) / professionally (SP) / badly (B) / offensively (B)
>
> 2 pay: a service charge (C) / bill (C)
>
> 3 give: a tip (C) / a refund (SP)
>
> 4 leave: a tip (C)
>
> 5 offer (SP) / provide (SP) / charge for (SP) / pay for (C): a service / extras
>
> 6 make: a mistake (SP) / an apology (SP)
>
> 7 ask for: an apology (C) / a refund (C)

- **Optional step.** Put students into small groups to discuss the last time they experienced any of the things or took part in any of the transactions in the expressions themselves. Encourage students to focus on the context of customer service as they do so. For example: *The last time I gave a waiter a tip was when I was … , The last time someone in customer service apologized to me was when … .*

8

- Ask students to read and to complete the conversation with some of the expressions from Exercise 7. Remind students that they may have to change the verb forms.

- Check answers. Invite individual students to read out one part of the conversation each.

- **Optional step.** Ask students to read out the conversation in pairs and then role-play a similar conversation. One student starts the conversation by saying how comfortable or uncomfortable they feel about complaining; the other student responds by agreeing or disagreeing with their point of view. Students can then go on to give examples of times that they've complained about customer service.

> **Answers**
>
> 1 behave politely   2 made a mistake   3 charging for a service   4 ask for a refund   5 given/left a tip   6 pay a bill

SPEAKING Leaving tips

9 21st **CENTURY OUTCOMES**

• Before starting this exercise, refer students to the 21st CENTURY OUTCOMES at the foot of the page. Elicit ways in which getting a better understanding of other nations and cultures can be valuable. Possible ways include: *It helps us to gain a better understanding of our own nation and culture, It helps us to build relationships with other people which could be beneficial, It enables us to be more open-minded and less prone to prejudice against people who are different to us, It teaches us a lot about the rest of the world and how it works, It can help to humble us and make us appreciate what we have when we encounter people from other nations or cultures whose lives aren't as easy as our own.*

• Look at the comment with the class. If necessary, clarify the meaning of:

   the States – a common abbreviation for the United States of America (first line)

• Ask students to say whether or not they think the comment is an accurate representation of tipping behaviour in the USA, and why / why not. Then ask: *What is the reaction of the British student to what his/her friend has said?*

• Put students into groups of three to discuss the British student's reaction and normal tipping behaviour in their country. If you have a multinational class, ensure that students from a range of countries are grouped together. If you have a monolingual class, students can first discuss what normal tipping behaviour is in their country and then discuss their experiences of tipping behaviour in other countries.

10

• Ask students to decide who is Student A, Student B and Student C. Students then read their information on page 164.

• Ask students to give the other students in their group a summary of what they read, without reading out the information if possible. Students then discuss what they would say to the British student in light of what they've read and reach a consensus on how to respond to his/her question.

Extra activity

Write a response

Students write a response to the student's comment in which they advise him/her about how to tip in the USA based on what they've read and discussed in Exercise 10.

▶ Photocopiable communicative activity 10.2: Go to page 232 for further practice of customer service vocabulary and cross-cultural awareness vocabulary, and revision of reported speech. The teaching notes are on page 246.

▶ Set Workbook pages 98–99 for homework.

10.4 Any other business?

LISTENING Helplines

1

• Books open. Draw students' attention to the spread title: *Any other business?* Elicit or remind students that they met this term and its abbreviation (*AOB*) in Unit 4.4.

• Put students into pairs to read the list of options and to discuss what they value most when they deal with a company's helpline. Encourage students to give reasons or talk about their own experience to support their choices.

2

• Explain that students are going to listen to a meeting of a customer care team. Elicit what customer care teams do. Possible answers could be: *give information to customers and answer their questions, deal with customers' complaints, make changes to orders for customers where necessary.*

• 🔊 55 Play the recording so that students can choose the correct option.

Transcript

N = Neil, P = Pat, R = Rory

N: *OK well if there's nothing else to add, let's move on to item 2, the helpline. Pat?*

P: *Yes. Thanks, Neil. OK. Well as you know, at the moment the customer helpline is an 0845 number.*

R: *And is that a premium rate line, Pat?*

P: *It is, yeah. The latest feedback shows that people are really unhappy about this, probably since they're using mobiles more.*

N: *Yeah …*

R: *Hmm …*

P: *I really think the best solution is to change to a free phone number.*

N: *You're absolutely right. We'll have to think about this sooner or later. Most of our competitors are moving across to free phones.*

R: *So, what you're saying is that you think we need to do this too? OK then, why don't I take a look at this? It will mean an additional cost to us, but it's worth looking into. I'll get back to you next week.*

N: *Great, Rory, thanks. Any other business? … No? OK, thanks. By the way, next month the office is being redecorated, so we'll have to meet somewhere else. I'll email you, so remember to keep an eye out for that.*

• Check answers and pick up on the use of the expression *keep an eye out* in the sentence *I'll email you, so remember to keep an eye out for that* at the end of the conversation. Elicit that the meaning of this expression is *look out for.*

Answer

c

3

• Explain that students are now going to listen to the recording again. This time they're going to listen for detail and make notes.

• You could put students into pairs to tell each other what they can remember about the problem, a suggestion, the reaction and an offer.

• 🎧 55 Play the recording again so that students can make notes. Check answers with the class. If necessary, play the recording again.

Answers

1 The helpline is a 'premium rate' line and that is expensive for customers.

2 to change to a free phone number

3 total agreement

4 Rory will look into changing the premium rate line to a free phone number.

Pronunciation Sounds and meaning

4a

• Look at the Useful language box with the class. Draw students' attention to the acronym *RASA* used in the TED Talk and what the letters stand for. Then focus on the expressions for showing understanding. Ask students to practise saying these expressions. Note that *uhuh* is pronounced /u-huh/.

• 🎧 56 Tell students that they're now going to listen to people saying the expressions in the Useful language box with different intonation. Play the recording so that students can decide what the speaker's intonation shows. If necessary, play the recording twice.

Transcript

1 oh	*3 uhuh*	*5 OK*	*7 hmm*	*9 yeah*
2 oh	*4 uhuh*	*6 OK*	*8 hmm*	*10 yeah*

• Students can check their answers in pairs before you check answers with the whole class.

Answers

1 surprise   2 understanding   3 disagreement
4 understanding   5 understanding   6 disagreement
7 understanding   8 disagreement   9 surprise
10 understanding

4b

• Explain that students are going to listen again and repeat the different intonations.

• 🎧 56 Play the recording and pause after each response so that students can listen and repeat.

• **Optional step.** Ask students to choose an intonation and an expression and say the expression with that intonation to their partner without telling him/her which intonation they've chosen. Students have to make it sufficiently clear which intonation they've chosen so that their partner can identify which one it is.

SPEAKING Comparing experiences

5   *21st* **CENTURY OUTCOMES**

• Explain that students are going to interact with the other members of their group during a discussion in order to fulfil the 21st CENTURY OUTCOME. If you have students from different cultures in your class, you could remind them to be aware of the differences in communication styles that are likely to exist between the students. For example, students from some cultures are likely to be more reserved and less comfortable saying what they think than other students who may talk a lot and not see a need to wait until someone has finished their turn before they start theirs.

• Look at the instructions with the class. Elicit one or more questions for each option in Exercise 2 that students should discuss. For example, option a: *Which do you prefer, helplines or websites? Why?* option b: *Do you think response times on helplines are fast enough?* option c: *Do you think charges on helplines are fair? Why? / Why not?* Also elicit examples of language students can use to talk about their experiences and give their opinions. For example: *You* + present simple (for experiences in general), *I've / I've never* + present perfect, *Once I* + past simple, *I think/feel … , Don't you think/feel … ?, In my opinion/view, … .*

• Put students into small groups to discuss their experiences and opinions of the options in Exercise 2. Remind students to use the expressions from the Useful language box. Encourage them to focus on interacting effectively with the other members of their group during their discussion, e.g. by listening to each other, taking turns and ensuring that everyone is able to speak.

• After about fifteen minutes, ask students to bring their discussions to a close and to spend two more minutes making notes which summarize the key points from the discussion they've just had. Remind students that they will then need to use these notes in Exercise 8.

WRITING Minutes (2)

6

• Remind students of the work they did on minutes in Unit 4, where they looked at how to organize information into bullet points.

• Ask students to read the minutes of the meeting they listened to in Exercise 2 and to compare these with the notes they made in Exercise 3.

Writing skill Reporting verbs

7a

• Elicit that *say* and *tell* are the most common reporting verbs, but that other verbs give more information about the speaker's intention. For example, you can report *The service isn't very good. Don't give a tip.* as *The service wasn't very good. I recommended not giving a tip.*

• Ask students to look at the groups of reporting verbs and to underline five reporting verbs in the minutes in Exercise 6 that have the same patterns. They should then add the five verbs to the groups. Students can do this in pairs.

• Students can check their answers and overall understanding of reporting verbs by turning to the Grammar summary on page 158.

> **Answers**
>
> 1 suggest   2 offer   3 remind   4 agree   5 inform

• If you feel that students need more controlled practice before continuing, they could do some or all of Exercises 4–6 in the Grammar summary. Otherwise, you could continue on to Exercise 7b in the unit and set the Grammar summary exercises for homework.

> **Answers to Grammar summary exercises**
>
> **4**
>
> 1 explained that   2 suggested waiting   3 told the company that   4 promised to give   5 persuaded the customer not to complain   6 asked us to stay   7 denied starting   8 realized that
>
> **5**
>
> 1 recommended   2 advised   3 told   4 admitted 5 agreed   6 offered
>
> **6**
>
> 1 Our teacher explained ~~us the homework~~ **the homework to us**.
>
> 2 I asked them where ~~had they been~~ **they had been**.
>
> 3 My friend ~~told that~~ **told me** (*or* **said**) **that** he'd bought a new car.
>
> 4 The manager ~~said them~~ **said that** (*or* **told them that**) they could have a refund.
>
> 5 I asked the woman ~~to not phone~~ **not to phone** me before lunchtime.
>
> 6 I recommend that you ~~doing~~ **do** this course.

7b

• Look at sentence 1 as an example with the class. Elicit that the correct option is *told* because the word after the gap is *me* and, of the two options, *told* is the only one that we can use before personal pronouns.

• Ask students to choose the correct option to complete the other sentences.

• Check answers with the class. You could ask individual students to rephrase the reported speech as direct speech.

> **Answers**
>
> 1 told   2 proposed   3 explained   4 asked   5 warned 6 has invited   7 promised   8 refused
>
> Direct speech: suggested answers
>
> 1 Your complaint is being looked into.
>
> 2 We think we should wait for the results of the survey.
>
> 3 There is a way to speak to an agent immediately on the phone. Don't press any of the keys when you're told to: just hang on.
>
> 4 Could you send me proof of your identity?
>
> 5 Please note that all deliveries will be delayed by two days.
>
> 6 Would you like to write about your experience on our website?
>
> 7 Don't worry! I won't get angry when I complain about the food.
>
> 8 We will not give you your money back.

8

• Ask students to use their notes to write the minutes of their discussion in Exercise 5. Tell them to use at least three reporting verbs in their minutes.

• Remind student to use bullet points for their action points if they include any.

• Monitor students while they're writing. Offer help, especially with the use of reporting verbs, where necessary.

9

• Ask students to exchange their minutes with someone from their group in Exercise 5. Students compare the points they remember. They can also check that their partner has used reporting verbs correctly.

• Ask students to give each other feedback on the minutes. Encourage students to respond to and possibly disagree with the feedback given to them where appropriate.

• Conduct whole-class feedback and ask students to tell the class about any ideas they have read about that they think would work.

▶ Set Workbook pages 100–101 for homework.

▶ Set Workbook Writing 5 pages 102–103 for homework.

LISTENING Alpha Communication

1

- Explain that students that are going to read a short introduction about a company called Alpha Communication, and then listen to an interview connected with it.

- Ask students to read the text about Alpha Communication.

> **Answers**
> _____
> 1 a co-operative social enterprise   2 marketing

2

- 🎧 **57** Play the recording so that students can decide whether the sentences are true or false.

Transcript

P = Presenter, E = Business editor

P: *Today we're having a closer look at the world of co-operative businesses. These are businesses which are owned and run by people who are equal members of the co-op. Members are involved in the way the co-op is run and they also share the profits of the business. In the UK, there are over 6,000 businesses set up as co-ops, and they cover the whole range of products and services from supermarkets to web designers. One typical co-op is Alpha Communication, based in the north of England. Our business editor Edwina Jones visited them recently.*

E: *The marketing sector isn't one that most people associate with co-ops, but Alpha is one of many communications companies operating on co-operative principles. They're a really dynamic group of three designers, two writers and an accountant. The team are all equal owners – directors – of the company. Once they have been paid and all the business costs have been covered, the surplus earnings are returned to the company. The benefit of this approach is that they can grow the business and create more employment opportunities locally.*

P: *And what about the benefits for the co-op members themselves?*

E: *Well, on a personal level, job satisfaction levels are reported as being much higher among people working in a co-op. One of the directors explained to me that Alpha has been in operation for 25 years now and that the creative team has changed several times over the years. However, she said that the co-op's core values haven't changed in this time. The company is guided by the values of co-operation, honesty, equality, fairness and respect. And these values are often shared by Alpha's clients.*

P: *That's interesting. What kind of clients do they work with?*

E: *In many cases they are voluntary or community organizations, social enterprise and of course other co-operatives. While I was there, two of the designers offered to show me a social-media campaign they were developing for a local Fairtrade partnership. As they said, the Internet didn't exist when Alpha began, but*

now online work is the largest part of their business. They do still work on market research, videos, brand development and traditional print materials, of course.

P: *It's not the usual image we have of marketing and advertising, is it, Edwina?*

> **Answers**
> _____
> 1 F (In the UK, co-ops cover the whole range of products from supermarkets to web designers.)
> 2 F (Alpha Communication is one of many communications companies operating on co-operative principles.)
> 3 T
> 4 F (The creative team has changed several times.)
> 5 T

3

- 🎧 **57** Play the recording again so that students can complete the sentences.

> **Answers**
> _____
> 1 owners   2 services   3 dynamic   4 equality
> 5 partnership

GRAMMAR

4

- Ask students to read through the text to get a feel for what it's about.

- Look at the first sentence with the class. Elicit that *based* is a reduced relative clause, so *which is* could be added after the word *co-operatives*. Look at the second sentence with the class and elicit that *where* goes after *town*.

- Ask students to add relative pronouns and commas to the rest of the text, and to underline the other three reduced relative clauses.

> **Answers**
> _____
> The Mondragon Corporation is a collection of worker co-operatives (**which is**) **based** in northern Spain, in the Basque Country. The name comes from the town **where** the first co-op was founded. The co-op was started in 1956 by a group of people **who** had studied locally. The first product (**which was**) **made** by the co-op was a heater. Now the Mondragon Corporation is the biggest business group in the region. In the first twenty years, the Corporation grew quickly with the addition of companies **whose** business models followed co-operative principles. The Mondragon Corporation, **which** now includes more than 250 companies, operates in four sectors: finance, industry, retail and knowledge. The sector (**which is**) **growing** most rapidly is probably knowledge. There are fifteen technology centres **which** together have more than 1,700 employees (**who are**) **working** in research and development.

5

• Ask students to read the sentences and then rewrite them as reported speech. Students can do this in pairs.

Answers

1 Tyne Co-op said (that) Alpha had come up with a highly original campaign that they were really pleased with.'

2 Bill Rylands told us (that) he was very happy with Alpha and he wouldn't use any other company.'

3 KidCare asked how much a typical website cost.

4 Sandra Brown asked if/whether she could change the website content herself.

5 Tyne Co-op said (that) the team were making improvements to their video until the last minute.

6 FruitStore told us (that) they hadn't had a website before. It was really making a difference to their business.'

7 Bill Rylands asked how long it took to make a typical video.

8 Alpha asked if/whether they'd provided the quality we'd expected.

VOCABULARY

6

• Explain that students should use the other words in the sentences to decide whether the incomplete words are nouns or adjectives. They then complete the word stems.

Answers

1 imaginative   2 artistic   3 unrealistic   4 precision
5 analytical   6 emotion   7 dynamism

7

• Ask students to complete the text with verbs that make collocations connected with customer service.

Answers

1 make   2 behaved   3 offer   4 pay   5 pay   6 give

DISCUSSION

8

• Put students into pairs to discuss the questions.

• **Question 2.** Remind students to use conditional sentences in response to this question.

Answers

1 Students' own answers, though they may say that they could be influenced by one of the factors only if this had impressed them very much.

2 Students' own answers, though they may mention *friendly interactions with customers*, *personal attention* and *professionalism* (from the list in question 1).

SPEAKING

9

• Ask students to use the word prompts to write complete sentences and questions. They could check their sentences and questions in the Useful language boxes in Unit 9.4

• You could check answers by asking a stronger pair to read out the conversation to the rest of the class.

Answers

1 What do you think about

2 How about you

3 I just wanted to say

4 What are your thoughts

5 Let me just say

6 I'd like to know what you think

7 would you like to say anything?

8 If I could say something here.

WRITING

10

• Look at comment 1 and the first sentence as an example with the class. Elicit that *warned* is a reporting verb and that *us that restaurants are very hard to get right* goes in the gap.

• Ask students to read the other comments and then to insert them into the text after the reporting verbs using the correct reported speech patterns.

Answers

1 warned us that restaurants are very hard to get right

2 replied that we had a lot of confidence

3 advised us to research the market well

4 agreed to give us a loan

5 suggested trying out / that we try out our recipes

6 told us not to change anything. It was just great as it was!

11

• Put students into pairs to check their answers and to compare the reporting patterns they used.

• Check answers with the class. Ask individual students to read out one sentence each.

11 Resources

LEAD IN

• Books open. To gauge students' prior knowledge of the unit vocabulary, draw their attention to the photo on pages 118–119 and its caption, and ask them to identify the resources that they can see. Possible answers could be: *agricultural resources, e.g. grass and cereals, energy, e.g. solar power and wind power, construction materials, e.g. bricks, wood, plastic that have been used to build the houses, and human resources, i.e. the people who live in the houses in the photo.* Write key words for resources on the board as students mention them.

• Bring in students' own experiences. Put students into pairs or small groups to discuss these questions: *How often do you take some time to just stop and look at the view from your window or to go outside and take in the view? What do you think the benefits of doing this are? Are there any drawbacks?* Conduct whole-class feedback, and focus on the advantages and disadvantages of taking time out to stop and look at the world around us. Write the advantages and disadvantages on the board as students mention them, and establish a consensus as to whether there are more advantages or disadvantages.

TED TALKS
BACKGROUND

1

• Ask students to read the text about Gavin Pretor-Pinney and his talk.

• Put students into pairs to discuss the questions.

• **Question 1.** Tell students that although the adjective *idle* is a negative personality adjective, the verb *to idle* usually has a neutral meaning. It's fine to spend some time idling in order to unwind and relax.

• **Question 2.** Encourage students to go into a little more detail than 'they like clouds' and be more specific about what they think this society actually does.

• **Question 3.** Let students know that *busy* is a relative term: one person's idea of *busy* may not be the same as someone else's. Students should use their own definition of *busy* here.

• Conduct whole-class feedback. Confirm what the Cloud Appreciation Society actually is and what its members do. Ask: *Is this a society that you would consider joining?*

Background information

The Cloud Appreciation Society

The Cloud Appreciation Society is an organization which was founded to promote the value of cloudspotting. The organization's manifesto says that they are fighting the 'banality' of 'blue-sky thinking', a management jargon cliché meaning that looking up to the skies will help you to find inspiration because there's nothing there, only blue skies. In contrast, the Cloud Appreciation Society believes that there definitely is something there, and it's something of great interest and beauty. See: https://cloudappreciationsociety.org/ for more information.

KEY WORDS

2

• Ask students to try to guess the meaning of the words in bold and then to match them with their definitions.

Answers

1 b   2 d   3 a   4 f   5 c   6 e

• Put students into pairs to ask and answer the questions. Monitor students while they're speaking, offering help where necessary. Then conduct whole-class feedback.

AUTHENTIC LISTENING SKILLS Vowels: sounds and spelling /aʊ/ and /əʊ/

3a

- Ask students to read the information about vowels: sounds and spelling /aʊ/ and /əʊ/ in the Authentic listening skills box.

- Elicit some more examples of words which contain an /aʊ/ sound, e.g. a<u>llow</u>, a<u>mount</u>, back<u>ground</u>, brown, down, f<u>low</u>er, found, house, loud, <u>mount</u>ain, now, our, owl, proud, <u>show</u>er, sur<u>round</u>, <u>thous</u>and, wow, and words with an /əʊ/ sound, e.g. a<u>lone</u>, be<u>low</u>, boat, bone, both, don't, go, gold, no, owe, own, phone, road, so, win<u>dow</u>. Check that students notice the difference in spellings between the words which share these two sounds.

- Give students time to read the sentence. If necessary, clarify the meaning in this context of:

    moan – make a complaint which is usually seen as trivial and not taken seriously (line 1)

- 🔊 58 Play the recording so that students can underline the words with an /aʊ/ sound and circle the words with an /əʊ/ sound.

Transcript

Clouds. Have you ever noticed how much people moan about them?

- Check answers with the class. Write the sentence on the board. Ask individual students to underline and circle words. If necessary, play the recording again.

Answers
/aʊ/: clouds, how, about
/əʊ/: moan

3b

- Ask students to read the words in the box and to decide which ones have an /aʊ/ sound and which have an /əʊ/ sound.

- 🔊 59 Play the recording so that students can check their answers. If necessary, play the recording again.

Transcript

They get a bad rap. If you think about it, the English language has written into it negative associations towards the clouds. Someone who's down or depressed, they're under a cloud. And when there's bad news in store, there's a cloud on the horizon. I saw an article the other day. It was about problems with computer processing over the Internet. 'A cloud over the cloud,' was the headline.

- Check answers and ask students to practise saying all the words in the box in pairs so that they can hear the difference in the sounds they contain.

Answers
/aʊ/: down
/əʊ/: associations, processing, over

11.1 Cloudy with a chance of joy

TEDTALKS

1

- Books open. Draw students' attention to the title of the talk: *Cloudy with a chance of joy*. Elicit or explain that this title is linked to *Cloudy with a chance of rain* which is used in weather forecasting.

> #### Background information
>
> ##### Cloudy with a chance of …
>
> The phrase *Cloudy with a chance of show*ers was originally a popular phrase used in weather forecasts. However, in recent years it's been appropriated in other contexts. For example in 2013, a film was made with the title *Cloudy with a Chance of Meatballs*. The film is based around a freak weather incident in which meatballs fall from the sky. Gavin Pretor-Pinney has also appropriated the stem of the phrase and added *joy* to the end of it to show his belief that clouds can bring joy. Appropriating and modifying well-known phrases or slogans is a commonly used communication strategy amongst native speakers of English and its intention is often to get the audience's attention and generate humour.

- Ask students to look at the sentence parts. If necessary, clarify the meaning in this context of:

    the exotic – things or people which are very different, strange or unusual to us (part c)

- Elicit that the opposite of *the exotic* would be *the ordinary*.

- Ask students to match the two parts of the sentences.

- ▶ 11.1 Play the whole talk once so that students can check their answers. Students can then check their answers in pairs.

Transcript

0.14   *Clouds. Have you ever noticed how much people moan about them? They get a bad rap. If you think about it, the English language has written into it negative associations towards the clouds. Someone who's down or depressed, they're under a cloud. And when there's bad news in store, there's a cloud on the horizon. I saw an article the other day. It was about problems with computer processing over the Internet. 'A cloud over the cloud,' was the headline.*

0.47   *It seems like they're everyone's default doom-and-gloom metaphor. But I think they're beautiful, don't you? It's just that their beauty is missed because they're so omnipresent, so, I don't know, commonplace, that people don't notice them. They don't notice the beauty, but they don't even notice the clouds unless they get in the way of the sun. And so people think of clouds* *as things that get in the way. They think of them as the annoying, frustrating obstructions, and then they rush off and do some blue-sky thinking.*

1.22 (Laughter)

1.24 *But most people, when you stop to ask them, will admit to harbouring a strange sort of fondness for clouds. It's like a nostalgic fondness, and they make them think of their youth. Who here can't remember thinking, well, looking and finding shapes in the clouds when they were kids? You know, when you were masters of daydreaming?*

1.51 *Aristophanes, the ancient Greek playwright, he described the clouds as the patron goddesses of idle fellows two and a half thousand years ago, and you can see what he means. It's just that these days, us adults seem reluctant to allow ourselves the indulgence of just allowing our imaginations to drift along in the breeze, and I think that's a pity. I think we should perhaps do a bit more of it. I think we should be a bit more willing, perhaps, to look at the beautiful sight of the sunlight bursting out from behind the clouds and go, 'Wait a minute, that's two cats dancing the salsa!'*

2.31 (Laughter) (Applause)

2.33 *Or seeing the big, white, puffy one up there over the shopping centre looks like the Abominable Snowman going to rob a bank.*

2.44 (Laughter)

2.47 *Perhaps you're having a moment of existential angst. You know, you're thinking about your own mortality. And there, on the horizon, it's the Grim Reaper.*

3.01 *But one thing I do know is this: The bad press that clouds get is totally unfair. I think we should stand up for them, which is why, a few years ago, I started the Cloud Appreciation Society. Tens of thousands of members now in almost 100 countries around the world. And all these photographs that I'm showing, they were sent in by members. And the society exists to remind people of this: Clouds are not something to moan about. Far from it. They are, in fact, the most diverse, evocative, poetic aspect of nature. I think, if you live with your head in the clouds every now and then, it helps you keep your feet on the ground. And I want to show you why, with the help of some of my favourite types of clouds.*

3.49 *Let's start with this one. It's the cirrus cloud, named after the Latin for a lock of hair. It's composed entirely of ice crystals cascading from the upper reaches of the troposphere, and as these ice crystals fall, they pass through different layers with different winds and they speed up and slow down, giving the cloud these brush-stroked appearances, these brush-stroke forms known as fall streaks. And these winds up there can be very, very fierce. They can be 200 miles an hour, 300 miles an hour. These clouds are bombing along, but from all the way down here, they appear to be moving gracefully, slowly, like most clouds. And so to tune into the clouds is to slow down, to calm down. It's like a bit of everyday meditation.*

4.31 *Those are common clouds. What about rarer ones, like the lenticularis, the UFO-shaped lenticularis cloud? These clouds form in the region of mountains. When the wind passes, rises to pass over the mountain, it can take on a wave-like path in the lee of the peak, with these clouds hovering at the crest of these invisible standing waves of air, these flying saucer-like forms, and some of the early black-and-white UFO photos are in fact lenticularis clouds. It's true.*

5.00 *A little rarer are the fallstreak holes. All right? This is when a layer is made up of very, very cold water droplets, and in one region they start to freeze, and this freezing sets off a chain reaction which spreads outwards with the ice crystals cascading and falling down below, giving the appearance of jellyfish tendrils down below.*

5.19 *Rarer still, the Kelvin–Helmholtz cloud. Not a very snappy name. Needs a rebrand. This looks like a series of breaking waves, and it's caused by shearing winds – the wind above the cloud layer and below the cloud layer differ significantly, and in the middle, in between, you get this undulating of the air, and if the difference in those speeds is just right, the tops of the undulations curl over in these beautiful breaking wave-like vortices.*

5.48 *All right. Those are rarer clouds than the cirrus, but they're not that rare. If you look up, and you pay attention to the sky, you'll see them sooner or later, maybe not quite as dramatic as these, but you'll see them. And you'll see them around where you live. Clouds are the most egalitarian of nature's displays, because we all have a good, fantastic view of the sky. And these clouds, these rarer clouds, remind us that the exotic can be found in the everyday. Nothing is more nourishing, more stimulating to an active, inquiring mind than being surprised, being amazed. It's why we're all here at TED, right? But you don't need to rush off away from the familiar, across the world to be surprised. You just need to step outside, pay attention to what's so commonplace, so everyday, so mundane that everybody else misses it.*

6.42 *One cloud that people rarely miss is this one: the cumulonimbus storm cloud. It's what produces thunder and lightning and hail. These clouds spread out at the top in this enormous anvil fashion, stretching ten miles up into the atmosphere. They are an expression of the majestic architecture of our atmosphere. But from down below, they are the embodiment of the powerful, elemental force and power that drives our atmosphere. To be there is to be connected in the driving rain and the hail, to feel connected to our atmosphere. It's to be reminded that we are creatures that inhabit this ocean of air. We don't live beneath the sky. We live within it. And that connection, that visceral connection to our atmosphere feels to me like an antidote. It's an antidote to the growing tendency we have to feel that we can really ever experience life by watching it on a computer screen, you know, when we're in a wi-fi zone.*

7.43 *But the one cloud that best expresses why cloudspotting is more valuable today than ever is this one, the cumulus cloud. Right? It forms on a sunny day. If you close your eyes and think of a cloud, it's probably one of these that comes to mind. All those cloud shapes at the beginning, those were cumulus clouds. The sharp, crisp outlines of this formation make it the best one for finding shapes in. And it reminds us of the aimless nature of cloudspotting, what an aimless activity it is. You're not going to change the world by lying on your back and gazing up at the sky, are you? It's pointless. It's a pointless activity, which is precisely why it's so important.*

8.31 *The digital world conspires to make us feel eternally busy, perpetually busy. You know, when you're not dealing with the traditional pressures of earning a living and putting food on the table, raising a family, writing thank you letters, you have to now contend with answering a mountain of unanswered emails, updating a Facebook page, feeding your Twitter feed. And cloudspotting legitimizes doing nothing.*

9.01 *(Laughter)*

9.03 *And sometimes we need –*

9.05 *(Applause)*

9.12 *Sometimes we need excuses to do nothing. We need to be reminded by these patron goddesses of idle fellows that slowing down and being in the present, not thinking about what you've got to do and what you should have done, but just being here, letting your imagination lift from the everyday concerns down here and just being in the present, it's good for you, and it's good for the way you feel. It's good for your ideas. It's good for your creativity. It's good for your soul.*

9.48 *So keep looking up, marvel at the ephemeral beauty, and always remember to live life with your head in the clouds.*

9.58 *Thank you very much.*

9.59 *(Applause)*

Answers

1 d 2 b 3 c 4 a

• Note the differences in North American English and British English shown at the foot of the spread. In this unit, these focus on pronunciation, spelling and vocabulary differences.

2

• Give students time to read the sentences. If necessary, clarify the meaning of:

   the Grim Reaper – a mythical figure who is believed to come for the dead and take them away (sentence 2a)

   the Abominable Snowman – a mythical creature that is believed to live in the mountains in the Himalayas. It's also known as *the Yeti* (sentence 2b)

• ▶**11.1** Play the first part (0.00–3.49) of the talk so that students can choose the correct option.

Answers

1 don't notice   2 a third, 2 b second, 2 c first
3 a hundred

3

• Look at the types of clouds with the class and say their names for students to hear, e.g. cirrus /'sɪrəs/ and cumulonimbus /'kjuːmjʊlə 'nɪmbəs/. If necessary, clarify the meaning of:

   flying saucers – mythical disc-shaped spaceships that are believed to be flown by aliens (type b)

   tendrils – thin, thread-like parts of a plant or sea creature which often grow in a spiral form (type c)

• If possible, you could also find photos or pictures of the different types of clouds online to show students or ask students to use their mobile devices to find photos or pictures.

• ▶**11.1** Play the second part (3.49–7.43) of the talk and ask students to listen for the names of the different types of clouds and to tick the types that they have seen themselves.

• Conduct whole-class feedback and try to find out which type of cloud is the one that the largest number of students have seen.

4

• Look at the instructions and the sentences with the class. If necessary, clarify the meaning of:

   paraphrase – a summary of information in different words (line 2)

• If necessary, clarify that *cloudspotting* is the activity of looking at clouds. Elicit other hobbies which end with the suffix *-spotting*, e.g. *trainspotting, planespotting, birdspotting*.

• ▶**11.1** Play the third part (7.43 to the end) of the talk so that students can check whether the statements are accurate paraphrases of what Gavin Pretor-Pinney says.

Answers

1 yes   2 no   3 yes   4 yes

5

• Look at the instructions and the sentences with the class. Elicit or explain that an *idiom* is *a group of words used together with a meaning that is different from the meanings of the individual words*. You could ask students to translate an idiom from their first language directly into English and tell the rest of the class what it means.

• Put students into pairs to complete the idioms. Remind students that there's one extra word which they won't need.

• Students could check their answers by finding the idioms in the transcript of the TED Talk on page 181.

• Ask students to discuss the meaning of the idioms in sentences 3 and 4.

Answers

1 under   2 horizon   3 sky   4 head, feet

Background information

Meanings of idioms in sentences 3 and 4

Blue horizon thinking, also known as *blue sky thinking*, is original or creative thinking which isn't limited by conventional norms. It is often used in management jargon and is thought to have its origins in the fact that blue skies are clear and don't contain anything. This fits in with the idea of abandoning convention and starting afresh. When *you have your head in the clouds*, you're out of touch with the real world around you and more interested in an unreal, day-dream-like view of the world.

When *you keep your feet on the ground*, you stay grounded in the realities of day-to-day life. The idea is that although these two states seem contradictory, you can combine them by daydreaming, while also remaining grounded in reality.

Extra activity

Using idioms

Give students sentences which include idioms and ask them to work out their meaning from the context. For example: *You're barking up the wrong tree if you think Bernardo's got a promotion – he isn't going anywhere!*, *Those two couldn't be more different – they're like chalk and cheese*. Then give students other idioms which they have to include in sentences. For example: *put the cart before the horse*, *get the wrong end of the stick*, *straight from the horse's mouth*, *you can't swing a cat in here*, *like a bull in a china shop*. If you have internet access, students could go online and clarify the meanings of these idioms. Students then work in pairs and read out their sentences to their partner, who has to guess the meaning of the idiom.

VOCABULARY IN CONTEXT

6

• ▶ 11.2 Play the clips from the TED Talk. When each multiple-choice questions appears, pause the clip so that students can choose the correct definition.

Transcript and subtitles

1 *It seems like they're everyone's default **doom-and-gloom** metaphor.*
   a *relaxation*
   b *optimism*
   c *pessimism*

2 *The **bad press** that clouds get is totally unfair.*
   a *appreciation*
   b *lack of understanding*
   c *negative comments*

3 *I think we should **stand up for** them.*
   a *attack*
   b *defend*
   c *get on our feet*

4 *Clouds are not something to moan about. **Far from it.***
   a *The opposite is true.*
   b *They are too far away.*
   c *We don't understand them.*

5 *If you close your eyes and think of a cloud, it's probably one of these that **comes to mind.***
   a *you care about*
   b *crosses the sky*
   c *you think of*

Answers

1 c 2 c 3 b 4 a 5 c

7

• Put students into pairs to discuss the questions.

Suggested answers

1 Things that come to mind when you think of your English classes could be: learning language, having fun, finding out more about other cultures, preparing yourself for the world of work.

2 People who get a bad press are usually in the public eye, such as a politician, a businessperson or a celebrity.

3 Others might need to stand up for: the young, the disabled, women, people from ethnic minorities, people living under oppressive regimes.

CRITICAL THINKING Identifying the 'take away' message

8

• Elicit or explain that the important message people take away from a talk can also be called the talk's *'take away' message*.

• Ask students to think about the message Gavin Pretor-Pinney wanted people to 'take away' from his talk and what the 'take away' message was for them, if that was different.

• Conduct whole-class feedback. You could collect students' ideas about what Gavin Pretor-Pinney wanted people to 'take away' and distil these into a single-sentence summary, which you could write on the board.

9

• Ask students to read the comments about the TED Talk and to match each comment with the main idea the viewer has taken away from the talk.

Answers

1 Taddeu   2 G. Murphy   3 Roshan

PRESENTATION SKILLS Being enthusiastic

10

• Ask students to read about being enthusiastic in the Presentation skills box. Ask: *How important do you think enthusiasm is to the success of a presentation? How important is presenting with enthusiasm in your culture?*

- ▶ 11.3 Play the clips so that students can identify which techniques Gavin Pretor-Pinney uses.

Transcript

1   *It seems like they're everyone's default doom-and-gloom metaphor. But I think they're beautiful, don't you? It's just that their beauty is missed because they're so omnipresent, so, I don't know, commonplace, that people don't notice them. They don't notice the beauty, but they don't even notice the clouds unless they get in the way of the sun. And so people think of clouds as things that get in the way. They think of them as the annoying, frustrating obstructions, and then they rush off and do some blue-sky thinking. (Laughter) But most people, when you stop to ask them, will admit to harbouring a strange sort of fondness for clouds. It's like a nostalgic fondness, and they make them think of their youth. Who here can't remember thinking, well, looking and finding shapes in the clouds when they were kids? You know, when you were masters of daydreaming?*

2   *I think we should be a bit more willing, perhaps, to look at the beautiful sight of the sunlight bursting out from behind the clouds and go, 'Wait a minute, that's two cats dancing the salsa!'*

- Students could discuss their answers in pairs before you check with the whole class. You could pause after the first clip and discuss the techniques Gavin Pretor-Pinney uses, and then play the second clip.

Answers
He uses all four techniques.

11

- Look at the photo with the class. Elicit or explain that this man is making a wooden toy and that it's his hobby.

- Ask students to choose something they know a lot about and enjoy doing. Students may say that there isn't anything they know a lot about, but everyone will have something that they enjoy doing. You could give an example of something you enjoy doing to get students started and also say the three things you would want to communicate about it.

- Ask students to choose three things that they want to communicate about their topic and to make brief notes. Remind them not to write whole sentences.

- If students have photos on their phones or can find photos of the things they want to talk about by doing internet searches, they can also use these in their presentations.

- Students think about how they can use the techniques in their presentation and practise giving it. Tell students to aim to speak for around two minutes.

12

- Put students into groups of three. They take turns to give their presentation and to give each other feedback on how well they used the techniques.

▶ Set Workbook pages 104–105 for homework.

11.2 Sharing our resources

VOCABULARY Resources

1

- Books open. Look at the lists of resources and examples with the class. If necessary, clarify the meaning of:

  wheat – a cereal grain which is used to make flour (bottom right)

- Ask students to match the resources with the examples.

Answers
agricultural – wheat, financial – money, human – employees, information – the Internet, mineral – copper, natural – water, non-renewable – oil

- **Optional step.** Put students into pairs to brainstorm further examples of each resource type. Further examples of agricultural resources could include: *oats, barley, corn, vegetables, fruit, cotton.*

GRAMMAR Articles

2

- Look at the infographic with the class. If necessary, clarify the meaning of:

  commodities – raw materials or agricultural produce which can be bought and sold (title)

- Ask students to find the things in the infographic.

Answers
1 Russia, USA, Canada, Norway, Denmark (including Greenland), Finland, Sweden, Iceland

2 gold, copper   3 oil, natural gas

4 Gold is found in every mobile phone and computer. All plastic comes from oil.

3

- Look at the Grammar box with the class. Ask students to underline nouns with *a/an, the* and with no (zero) article in the sentences and then to answer the question.

- Students can check their answers and overall understanding of articles by turning to the Grammar summary on page 160.

Answers
a/an: countable singular (a member, an organization, an [oil-based] product)

the: countable singular (the [Arctic] region), countable plural ([unexplored] deposits), uncountable (natural gas)

no (zero) article: countable plural ([significant] amounts, [natural] resources, [synthetic] fibres), uncountable (oil, gold)

- You could ask students to identify articles in the infographic and to say why these articles have been used in this context. For example, use of *the*: **The** *whole region is . . .* , *Ten per cent of* **the** *world's fresh water is in Greenland,* **the** *Arctic Ocean . . .* ; use of no (zero) article: **Gold** *is found in . . .* ; use of *a*: **A** *typical home contains . . .* .

- If you feel that students need more controlled practice before continuing, they could do one or both of Exercises 1 and 2 in the Grammar summary. Otherwise, you could continue on to Exercise 4 in the unit and set the Grammar summary exercises for homework.

Answers to Grammar summary exercises

1

1 an   2 the   3 the   4 a   5 the   6 the   7 an   8 a

2

1 –   2 –   3 –   4 The   5 the   6 the   7 the   8 –
9 –   10 –

4

- Look at an example with the class. Ask students to read the news items until they find a noun whose article has been removed. Elicit that *the* has been removed before *resources* in line 1.

- Students add the other eight missing articles to the news item. Encourage them to look at the example sentences in the Grammar box.

- If necessary, clarify any uncertainties about how articles should be used in the news item. Students may add unnecessary articles, especially *the*. Where appropriate, remind students to avoid adding unnecessary articles and point out that they can only use up to a maximum of nine words.

Answers

1 the resources   2 the Arctic   3 a thick layer   4 the ice
5 the area   6 The Arctic Council   7 a small organization
8 an important focus of attention   9 the future

GRAMMAR Quantifiers

5

- Ask students to read the sentences in the Grammar box and to find the words in bold in the infographic. They then answer the question.

- If necessary, clarify what countable and uncountable nouns are. Note that in students' previous English learning experience, they may have used alternative names, e.g. *count* and *uncount nouns* instead.

- Students decide what type of noun the quantifiers are used with. They can do this in pairs.

- Students can check their answers and overall understanding of articles by turning to the Grammar summary on page 160.

Answers

every: countable singular; *few*: countable plural;
a large amount of: uncountable; *all*: uncountable

- If you feel that students need more controlled practice before continuing, they could do some or all of Exercises 3–6 in the Grammar summary. Otherwise, you could continue on to Exercise 6 in the unit and set the Grammar summary exercises for homework.

Answers to Grammar summary exercises

3

1 the whole   2 much   3 several   4 much   5 a small amount of   6 many   7 all   8 much

4

1 a few   2 little   3 a little   4 few   5 little   6 few
7 a few   8 few

5

1 neither   2 all   3 any   4 a lot of   5 no   6 either

6

1 I download a lot of music from **the Internet**.

2 I love my new job – I'm **an analyst** for a big oil company.

3 A big challenge for us all is ~~the~~ **climate change**.

4 I really have ~~few~~ **little time** to finish all my work.

5 I can't choose between the city and the country – I like ~~the~~ **both**.

6 I listen to English online **all day** ~~days~~ (or **every day**).

- **Optional step.** Elicit or explain that *fewer* is a comparative adjective used with countable nouns and *less* is a comparative adjective used with uncountable nouns. However, it's also worth pointing out that *less* is now also commonly used to refer to countable nouns by native English speakers.

6

- Ask students to choose the correct options to complete the comments. Students can do this in pairs.

Answers

1 every   2 Both   3 any   4 amount   5 several
6 no   7 few   8 little

7

- Look at the instructions with the class. If necessary, clarify the meaning of

  internet sensation – a person or thing that becomes famous very quickly through the Internet (lines 1–2)

- **Optional step.** Elicit examples of internet sensations, either people, animals or things, which students are familiar with.

- Students complete the paragraph with quantifiers and articles.

- Check answers. Explain that using no article for gap 7 would also be grammatically correct.

Answers

1 a 2 every 3 few 4 a lot of 5 –, 6 a huge number of 7 any 8 Both 9 a few 10 no 11 the

SPEAKING How much is too much?

8 **21st CENTURY OUTCOMES**

- Explain that students will have the chance to fulfil the 21st CENTURY OUTCOME by taking part in a quiz.

- Draw students' attention to the title of the quiz: *How much is too much?* Elicit that different people may interpret quantities differently. For example, in the case of sugar, what is too much for one person could be not enough for another.

- Ask students to complete the quiz with the nouns. Then check answers.

- Ask students to choose and underline the option which is true for them.

Answers

1 paper 2 electricity 3 food 4 information
5 money 6 things

TEACHING TIP

Students' levels of experience

Depending on your students' age and background, they may not always have a lot of experience of certain topics, especially those related to international and environmental issues. If this is true for your students, encourage them to draw on the experience they do have and not to feel that their lack of experience of these topics makes them unable to discuss them.

9

- Put students into groups of three to compare their answers.

- Ask students to give more information about three of their answers. They can give more information by being more specific about what that amount, e.g. *a lot*, means to them in that context. For example, if a student thinks he/she prints a lot of things out, he/she can say how many pages a week he/she prints out on average. The other students can then say whether they agree that this constitutes a small or large amount.

▶ Photocopiable communicative activity 11.1: Go to page 233 for further practice of articles and quantifiers. The teaching notes are on page 247.

▶ Set Workbook pages 106–107 for homework.

11.3 International movements

READING Life in the slow lane

1

- Books open. Draw students' attention to the section heading: *Life in the slow lane*. Explain that this is a play on words of *life in the fast lane*, which refers to a life filled with excitement.

- You could put students into groups to discuss what fast food they eat and what they think the term 'slow food' means.

- Conduct whole-class feedback, but don't confirm answers at this stage.

2

- Ask students to read the article to confirm what the term 'slow food' means.

Answers

The 'slow' movement is a reaction against the idea that faster is always better. The slow food movement started in Italy, and aimed to promote and protect local and traditional foods. Events and activities focus on building links between people, with food at the heart of everything.

3

- Ask students to read the headings. They then match the headings with the paragraphs.

Answers

1 C 2 B 3 A

4

- Look at sentence 1 as an example with the class. Elicit that the slow movement began in 1986, so the sentence can be changed to *The slow movement started in the 20th century.*

- Put students into pairs to compare each sentence with what the text says. They should identify the inaccuracies and change one or more words, or rewrite the sentences so that they agree with the information in the article.

Suggested answers

1 The slow movement started in the 20th century.

2 The movement believes everything should go at its own speed: the one which gives the best quality results.

3 Slow food promotes local and traditional foods

4 Terra Madre Day is a world-wide event.

5 Slow travel encourages you to connect with local people.

6 You can embrace slow travel on a package holiday – you can buy a ticket and get on a local bus or train, rather than join an organized coach tour, for example.

7 Slow goods tend to be of high quality.

8 There are lots of types of slow movement.

5

• Look at item 1 as an example with the class. Elicit that the verb in line 2 of the article is *has grown* and the preposition that follows is *into*.

• Ask students to find forms of the verbs in the article and to write the preposition that follows each verb.

> **Answers**
> _____
> 1 grown into   2 focus on   3 connecting with
> 4 searching for   5 appeal to   6 spreading around

• You could also point out that other prepositions can also follow the verbs *grow*, *search* and *spread*. For example, other verb + preposition combinations with *grow* include: *grow up*, *grow into*, *grow from*, *grow to.* You could draw students' attention to the difference in meaning between some of the verb + preposition combinations, e.g. *grow up* refers to the process of becoming an adult, whereas *grow into* refers to becoming accustomed to or confident in a specific role or position.

6

• Ask students to complete the sentences. Remind them that they may have to change the forms of the verbs.

> **Answers**
> _____
> 1 focuses on   2 appealed to   3 grown into
> 4 connect with   5 spread about   6 searching for

• Ask students to decide whether any of the sentences are true for them and, where necessary, to change the underlined words to make them true.

• **Optional step.** You could put students into pairs to compare sentences and to ask each other questions to find out more information about the sentences they've written.

7

• Check that students can remember the meaning of *drawback*. It featured in the email in Unit 8.4 on page 93.

• Elicit the three movements described in the article: *slow food*, *slow travel*, *slow goods*. Put students into pairs to list one benefit and one drawback of each of the three movements. This is not a memory test, so encourage students to refer to the article while they're doing this.

• Put pairs together to compare their ideas. Students discuss what they think about the 'slow' philosophy. Ask: *Do you think the 'slow' philosophy has more benefits than drawbacks or more drawbacks than benefits?* Then conduct whole-class feedback.

VOCABULARY Quantities

8

• Students should be able to deduce the meaning of any unknown vocabulary items either by looking at the pictures or based on the other word they're combined with.

• **Optional step.** Elicit or give other examples of quantities, e.g. *a bunch of bananas*, *a loaf of bread*.

> **Answers**
> _____
> 1 m   2 g   3 k   4 e   5 b   6 i   7 c   8 n   9 f
> 10 j   11 a   12 l   13 h   14 d

9

• Look at clue 1 as an example with the class. Elicit that you need *slices of bread* to make *sandwiches*.

• Ask students to read the clues and to write the words from Exercise 8 which they refer to. Remind them that they might need to use plural forms of the units, e.g. *barrel, bowl*.

> **Answers**
> _____
> 1 slices of bread   2 a pad of paper   3 a piece of cake   4 a barrel of oil   5 a tube of toothpaste   6 a tank of petrol   7 tins of paint   8 containers of goods

• **Optional step.** Ask students to write similar clues for the other six items in Exercise 8 or any other word combinations for quantities. They could then work in pairs and give each other their clues to complete with the correct words.

SPEAKING Making a difference

10   `21st` **CENTURY OUTCOMES**

• Tell students that in this exercise and in Exercise 11 they're going to read and think about environmental issues and discuss solutions for them in order to fulfil the 21st CENTURY OUTCOME.

• Put students into groups of four to share and compare what they know about the four organizations.

> **Background information**
>
> **Red Cross** and **Red Crescent**
>
> The name *Red Cross* is used in Christian countries and the name *Red Crescent* is used in Islamic countries.

11

• Ask students to decide who is Student A, Student B, Student C and Student D. Students then read their information on page 164. Monitor students while they're reading and clarify any unfamiliar vocabulary items.

• Ask students to give the other students in their group a summary of what they read about the organization, without reading out the information if possible. When students have all summarized their information, they should discuss the questions.

• Conduct whole-class feedback in order to gauge students' opinions on which organization(s) has/have had the most impact and which movement(s) they would join. Ask any students who thought of movements that they would like to start, to tell the class about these movements. Ask: *What would your rationale and aims be? Who would your supporters be?*

- **Optional step.** Students who have thought of a movement they would like to start could prepare and do a presentation of that movement for the rest of the class. The other students could watch the presentations and then vote for the movement they would most like to join.

Extra activity

The $1 million donation

Students work in the same groups of four. Tell students that they have $1 million (or the equivalent in their local currency) to donate to one of the four organizations they've just talked about and they have to agree on which one they should give it to. Students discuss which organization they think is the most worthy beneficiary, and why. They then tell the other groups what they've decided to do with the money, giving reasons for their choice.

▶ Set Workbook pages 108–109 for homework.

11.4 Come and join us

LISTENING Making enquiries

- Books open. You could ask students to discuss the questions in pairs.

- Even if students say that they don't belong to any clubs or societies or go to any classes or courses (apart from their English course), they're likely to have some hobby or interest that they pursue in their free time on their own or with their families, e.g. cooking, reading books, gardening.

2

- 🎧 60 Play the recording so that students can answer the questions.

Transcript

A = Assistant, B = Enquirer

1

A: *Good morning.*

B: *Hi there. Is this the right place to find out about the job club?*

A: *Yeah, sure. You mean help with job applications and interviews, that sort of thing?*

B: *Yes, a friend told me they run sessions here.*

A: *We do, yes. Have a seat, please and I'll get you the information. Just a second.*

B: *OK, thanks.*

…

A: *Right, here are all the details. The next sessions are after the holidays. Can I help you with anything else?*

B: *No thanks. I'll have a read through this first. Thanks for your help.*

2

A: *Can I help you?*

B: *Yeah, hi. I was wondering if there are any places left on the jewellery-making course? It's this one here, JF2.2 …*

A: *Let me check. OK, yes, it was full, but we've had a few cancellations at the last minute.*

B: *Oh, good!*

A: *So that's the advanced course, for people with some experience of working with gold and silver.*

B: *Yeah, that's the one.*

A: *OK, we'll need proof of payment of fifty per cent of the course fee before confirming your place.*

B: *Can you write the details down for me?*

A: *It's OK, it's all here in this leaflet.*

3

A: *Hello, Matfield Leisure Centre.*

B: *Hi, I'm ringing to ask about the judo classes on Thursday evenings. Could you tell me how much they cost?*

A: *The judo classes for adults?*

B: *Yes, that's right. On Thursdays.*

A: *If you could hold on just one moment, please. … There are different rates depending on whether you're already a member of the Centre, what payment plan you'd follow or if you want to pay by the hour. Would you like the address of our website? That's probably the best way to find what you need.*

B: *Oh, I see. No, it's OK. I can probably find it myself, thank you.*

Answers

conversation 1: 1 the job club, 2 yes

conversation 2: 1 a jewellery-making course, 2 yes

conversation 3: 1 the judo classes on Thursday evenings, 2 no

3

- Look at the Useful language box with the class. Go through the first expression as an example with the class: this expression is used in conversation 1. Elicit that you would say *Is this the right place to find out about … ?* in a face-to-face conversation.

- Elicit that conversations 1 and 2 are face-to-face conversations and conversation 3 is on the phone. Tell students to write the numbers 1, 2 and 3 next to the expressions as they hear them.

- 🎧 60 Play the recording again so that students can identify the expressions used in each conversation.

- Check answers with the class. Invite individual students to read out an expression from the conversations each, and to say which conversation and whether it was face-to-face or on the phone. Then ask students to decide if the expressions could be used in both situations. They can do this in pairs.

4

• You could put students into pairs to discuss whether the other expressions in the Useful language box could be used in both situations or in only one.

Pronunciation   Linking with /r/

5a

• Elicit or explain that sometimes the /r/ sound at the end of a word is pronounced and sometimes it isn't.

• 🔊61 Play the recording and ask students to focus on whether the /r/ sound at the end of the word is pronounced.

Transcript

| 1 after | 3 your | 5 hour |
| 2 for | 4 member | 6 our |

• Check that students noticed that the /r/ sound isn't pronounced. Play the recording again if necessary.

5b

• Explain that students are now going to listen to the same words in connected speech.

• 🔊62 Play the recording and ask students to focus on whether the /r/ sound at the end of the word is pronounced.

• Check that students noticed that the /r/ sound at the end of the word is pronounced before a vowel and explain that this is 'linking with /r/'. Remind students that they practised linking with /w/ in Unit 7.4 on page 82. Play the recording again if necessary. Draw students' attention to the way the /r/ sound in 'for each' in phrase 5a is pronounced.

SPEAKING   Finding out about a club

6

• Put students into small groups to talk about the clubs and classes they mentioned in Exercise 1.

WRITING   Short emails

7

• Ask students to read the four emails and to match the emails that are part of the same exchange.

• Ask students to complete the subject line. Remind students that effective subjects are short, and clearly communicate the main point of the email.

• Ask students which exchange is less formal, and why.

Writing skill Fixed expressions

8a

- Look at the instructions with the class. If necessary, clarify the meaning of:

    a fixed expression – a combination of words which is always used together in a specific context

- **Optional step.** Tell students that a lot of fixed expressions are used in English emails, and using them can make email writing easier and make emails sound more natural. Elicit an example of a fixed expression which is commonly used in emails, e.g. *Look forward to hearing from you.*

- Ask students to underline eleven fixed expressions in the emails. They then look at the forms which follow the expressions and add the expressions to the three groups.

- Check the answers with the class. Elicit or explain that: *I'm sorry for, We look forward to, Thanks for, Looking forward to* (all in *-ing* group) can all be used with nouns as well. In group 2, *We look forward to …* is the most formal version of this phrase and other more informal variations are also possible. For example: *We're / I'm looking forward to … , Looking forward to … , Look forward to … .* Also elicit or explain that in group 3, alternatives to *Don't hesitate to get in touch with me* could be *Don't hesitate to phone/call/contact me.*

Answers

1 … + noun

Thank you for your, I am writing with reference to,

Please accept my apologies for, Please find attached

2 … + -ing

We look forward to, Thanks for, Looking forward to

3 … + verb clause

I'm pleased to say that, I'm afraid that,

don't hesitate to (get in touch), I would be grateful if

8b

- Look at sentence 1 as an example with the class. Then ask students to complete the other sentences with an appropriate expression from Exercise 8a.

Answers

1 I regret that / I'm afraid that
2 Thanks for
3 I'm sorry for (Please accept my apologies for *is also possible*)
4 We look forward to
5 Please find attached
6 Don't hesitate
7 I would be grateful if
8 Looking forward to

---

9 *21st* CENTURY OUTCOMES

- Elicit or explain that students can fulfil the 21st CENTURY OUTCOME by using fixed expressions in their emails.

- Look at the instructions and the topics with the class. If necessary, clarify the meaning of:

    courier charges – a payment you make to a company, or to an employee of a company, that transports commercial packages and documents – this company is a courier (last item)

- Ask students to choose one of the topics and to write a short email to enquire about it. Alternatively, you may prefer to tell students which email to write. Fast finishers could write an email about more than one topic.

- **Optional step.** Students could use their mobile devices to type their email and then send it to the person they're going to exchange emails with in Exercise 10.

10

- Put students into pairs to exchange emails. They write a response to the email they receive.

▶ Photocopiable communicative activity 11.2: Go to page 234 for further practice of making and responding to enquiries. The teaching notes are on page 247.

▶ Set Workbook pages 110–111 for homework.

▶ Set Workbook Presentation 6 on pages 112–113 for homework.

12 Change

LEAD IN

• Books open. Draw students' attention to the unit title, and to the photo and its caption on page 128. Ask: *Does what you can see in the photo surprise you? If so, what exactly surprises you about it?* Possible answers could be: *The fact that Buddhist monks eat at Burger King! The contrast between the tradition that you connect with the Buddhist monk and the modernity of fast food.* Bring in students' own experiences. Ask: *Can you remember a time when you've seen a surprising combination of people and things similar to the one you can see in the photo?* Students could discuss the questions in pairs.

• Remind students that fast food outlets like Burger King have only existed for the last fifty or sixty years and that fast food shows us how food has changed in recent years. Bring in students' own experiences. Ask: *What other examples of change have you experienced during the course of your life? How have you dealt with these changes? What impact have they had on your life?* Put students into small groups to discuss these questions. Conduct whole-class feedback, and compare and contrast students' experiences of change.

TEDTALKS
BACKGROUND

1

• Ask students to read the text about Margaret Heffernan and her talk. If necessary, clarify the meaning of:

  conventional wisdom – what is generally agreed to be true (last line)

• **Question 1.** A *reputation for saying unexpected things* could include anything and everything from being inappropriate, mistaken, controversial to challenging the status quo depending on the context you're teaching in. If students can't think of any famous people who have (or had) a reputation for saying unexpected things, they could think about someone they know who has this reputation.

• **Question 2.** Students may use the third conditional when answering this question, e.g. *If I'd known … , I wouldn't have done … .* If they use the third conditional incorrectly, correct their sentences while you're monitoring their conversations or during whole-class feedback and tell students that they will look at using conditionals in more detail later in this unit.

• **Question 3.** Even if students don't find it difficult to disagree themselves, encourage them to think about possible reasons why other people could feel this way.

• Conduct whole-class feedback.

> **Answers**
>
> 1 Students' own answers
>
> 2 Students' own answers
>
> 3 Students' own answers, though they may suggest that people don't tell other people they disagree with them because they want to avoid conflict.

KEY WORDS

2

• Ask students to try to guess the meaning of the words in bold and then to match them with their definitions.

> **Answers**
>
> 1 b 2 e 3 a 4 c 5 f 6 d

AUTHENTIC LISTENING SKILLS
Grammatical chunks

3a

• Ask students to read the information about grammatical chunks in the Authentic listening skills box. If necessary, clarify that *grammatical chunks* are groups of words that are often found together. Ask students to look at the underlined chunks in sentences 1 and 2 for some examples of grammatical chunks.

- Ask students to read the sentences and to decide whether they think the underlined chunks are stressed or unstressed. Advise students to read out the sentences as they do this.

- 🔊 63 Play the recording and ask students to notice whether the underlined chunks are stressed or unstressed. Then ask whether the message would still be clear without the chunks.

Transcript

1   In Oxford in the 1950s, there was a fantastic doctor, who was very unusual, named Alice Stewart.

2   And Alice was unusual partly because, of course, she was a woman, which was pretty rare in the 1950s.

Answers

The underlined chunks are unstressed. The message would be clear without these chunks.

3b

- Ask students to read the third and fourth sentences, and to identify and underline the chunks they think will be unstressed.

- 🔊 64 Play the recording so that students can check their answers.

Transcript and answers

(underlining = unstressed words)

3   And she was brilliant, she was one of the, at the time, the youngest Fellow to be elected to the Royal College of Physicians.

4   She was unusual too because she continued to work after she got married, after she had kids, and even after she got divorced and was a single parent, she continued her medical work.

- **Optional step.** Students could work in pairs and take turns to practise reading out the two sentences from the transcript. They should focus on how they say the chunks. While one student is reading, the other can listen and then give feedback on their partner's use of stress.

12.1 Dare to disagree

TEDTALKS

1

- Books open. Give students time to read the list of areas.

- ▶12.1 Play the whole talk once so that students can identify the areas Margaret Heffernan mentions.

Transcript

0.13   In Oxford in the 1950s, there was a fantastic doctor, who was very unusual, named Alice Stewart. And Alice was unusual partly because, of course, she was a woman, which was pretty rare in the 1950s. And she was brilliant, she was one of the, at the time, the youngest Fellow to be elected to the Royal College of Physicians. She was unusual too because she continued to work after she got married, after she had kids, and even after she got divorced and was a single parent, she continued her medical work.

0.46   And she was unusual because she was really interested in a new science, the emerging field of epidemiology, the study of patterns in disease. But like every scientist, she appreciated that to make her mark, what she needed to do was find a hard problem and solve it. The hard problem that Alice chose was the rising incidence of childhood cancers. Most disease is correlated with poverty, but in the case of childhood cancers, the children who were dying seemed mostly to come from affluent families. So, what, she wanted to know, could explain this anomaly?

1.25   Now, Alice had trouble getting funding for her research. In the end, she got just 1,000 pounds from the Lady Tata Memorial prize. And that meant she knew she only had one shot at collecting her data. Now, she had no idea what to look for. This really was a needle in a haystack sort of search, so she asked everything she could think of. Had the children eaten boiled sweets? Had they consumed coloured drinks? Did they eat fish and chips? Did they have indoor or outdoor plumbing? What time of life had they started school?

1.56   And when her carbon-copied questionnaire started to come back, one thing and one thing only jumped out with the statistical clarity of a kind that most scientists can only dream of. By a rate of two to one, the children who had died had had mothers who had been X-rayed when pregnant. Now that finding flew in the face of conventional wisdom. Conventional wisdom held that everything was safe up to a point, a threshold. It flew in the face of conventional wisdom, which was huge enthusiasm for the cool new technology of that age, which was the X-ray machine. And it flew in the face of doctors' idea of themselves, which was as people who helped patients, they didn't harm them.

2.49   Nevertheless, Alice Stewart rushed to publish her preliminary findings in The Lancet in 1956. People got very excited, there was talk of the Nobel Prize, and Alice really was in a big hurry to try to study all the cases of childhood cancer she could find before they disappeared. In fact, she need not have hurried. It was fully 25 years before the British and medical – British and American medical establishments abandoned the practice of X-raying pregnant women. The data was out there, it was open, it was freely available, but *nobody wanted to know. A child a week was dying, but nothing changed. Openness alone can't drive change.*

3.46 *So for 25 years Alice Stewart had a very big fight on her hands. So, how did she know that she was right? Well, she had a fantastic model for thinking. She worked with a statistician named George Kneale, and George was pretty much everything that Alice wasn't. So, Alice was very outgoing and sociable, and George was a recluse. Alice was very warm, very empathetic with her patients. George frankly preferred numbers to people. But he said this fantastic thing about their working relationship. He said, 'My job is to prove Dr Stewart wrong.' He actively sought disconfirmation: different ways of looking at her models, at her statistics, different ways of crunching the data in order to disprove her. He saw his job as creating conflict around her theories. Because it was only by not being able to prove that she was wrong, that George could give Alice the confidence she needed to know that she was right.*

4.57 *It's a fantastic model of collaboration – thinking partners who aren't echo chambers. I wonder how many of us have, or dare to have, such collaborators. Alice and George were very good at conflict. They saw it as thinking.*

5.23 *So what does that kind of constructive conflict require? Well, first of all, it requires that we find people who are very different from ourselves. That means we have to resist the neurobiological drive, which means that we really prefer people mostly like ourselves, and it means we have to seek out people with different backgrounds, different disciplines, different ways of thinking and different experience, and find ways to engage with them. That requires a lot of patience and a lot of energy.*

5.59 *And the more I've thought about this, the more I think, really, that that's a kind of love. Because you simply won't commit that kind of energy and time if you don't really care. And it also means that we have to be prepared to change our minds. Alice's daughter told me that every time Alice went head-to-head with a fellow scientist, they made her think and think and think again. 'My mother,' she said, 'My mother didn't enjoy a fight, but she was really good at them.'*

6.38 *So how do we develop the skills that we need? Because it does take skill and practice too. If we aren't going to be afraid of conflict, we have to see it as thinking, and then we have to get really good at it. So, recently, I worked with an executive named Joe, and Joe worked for a medical device company. And Joe was very worried about the device that he was working on. He thought that it was too complicated and he thought that its complexity created margins of error that could really hurt people. He was afraid of doing damage to the patients he was trying to help. But when he looked around his organization, nobody else seemed to be at all worried. So, he didn't really want to*

say anything. After all, maybe they knew something he didn't. Maybe he'd look stupid. But he kept worrying about it, and he worried about it so much that he got to the point where he thought the only thing he could do was leave a job he loved.

7.45 *In the end, Joe and I found a way for him to raise his concerns. And what happened then is what almost always happens in this situation. It turned out everybody had exactly the same questions and doubts. So now Joe had allies. They could think together. And yes, there was a lot of conflict and debate and argument, but that allowed everyone around the table to be creative, to solve the problem, and to change the device.*

8.20 *Joe was what a lot of people might think of as a whistle-blower, except that like almost all whistle-blowers, he wasn't a crank at all, he was passionately devoted to the organization and the higher purposes that that organization served. But he had been so afraid of conflict, until finally he became more afraid of the silence. And when he dared to speak, he discovered much more inside himself and much more give in the system than he had ever imagined. And his colleagues don't think of him as a crank. They think of him as a leader.*

9.05 *So, how do we have these conversations more easily and more often? Well, the University of Delft requires that its PhD students have to submit five statements that they're prepared to defend. It doesn't really matter what the statements are about, what matters is that the candidates are willing and able to stand up to authority. I think it's a fantastic system, but I think leaving it to PhD candidates is far too few people, and way too late in life. I think we need to be teaching these skills to kids and adults at every stage of their development, if we want to have thinking organizations and a thinking society.*

9.52 *The fact is that most of the biggest catastrophes that we've witnessed rarely come from information that is secret or hidden. It comes from information that is freely available and out there, but that we are willfully blind to, because we can't handle, don't want to handle, the conflict that it provokes. But when we dare to break that silence, or when we dare to see, and we create conflict, we enable ourselves and the people around us to do our very best thinking.*

10.34 *Open information is fantastic, open networks are essential. But the truth won't set us free until we develop the skills and the habit and the talent and the moral courage to use it. Openness isn't the end. It's the beginning.*

10.56 (Applause)

Answers

She mentions areas a, b, c and d.

- Note the differences in North American English and British English shown at the foot of the spread. In this unit, the differences focus on vocabulary and spelling differences. See page 6 of the Introduction for ideas on how to present and practise these differences.

2

- ▶12.1 Play the first part (0.00–3.46) of the talk so that students can check their answers.

Answers

1 T

2 F (When she analysed the results of her study, they were very clear.)

3 T

4 F (It took twenty-five years for Alice Stewart's findings to have an effect on medical practices.)

3

- ▶12.1 Play the second part (3.46–6.38) of the talk so that students can check their answers.

Answers

1 different   2 mistaken   3 challenge   4 didn't enjoy

- **Optional step.** Draw students' attention to the contrasting pairs of adjectives and verbs that they've just looked at, i.e. *correct / mistaken*, *similar / different*, *agree with / challenge* and ask students to brainstorm other examples of contrasting word pairs that they know.

4

- Look at the questions with the class. If necessary, clarify the meaning of:

  stand up to (something or someone) – to challenge the authority of people or organizations so as to not allow yourself to be treated unfairly by them (sentence 4)

- Elicit or explain that this meaning is different from the meaning of *stand up* ('defend') in 11.1 Vocabulary in context.

- Put students into pairs. You could ask them to predict the answers based on what they can remember from the first time they watched this part of the talk.

- ▶12.1 Play the third part (6.38 to the end) of the talk so that students can answer the questions.

Answers

1 They didn't seem to be worried.

2 He did discuss his fears.

3 Everyone worked together to change the device.

4 She thinks that getting students to stand up to authority is a fantastic idea.

5 She thinks that this fear stops us from enabling ourselves to do our best thinking.

5

- Put students into small groups to complete the sentences about Margaret Heffernan's message with four of the six words.

- Check answers and then ask students to discuss the extent to which they agree with Margaret Heffernan's ideas.

- **Optional step.** Review expressions for generalizing and qualifying, e.g. *on the whole*, *typically*, *generally / in general*, *to some extent*, *to some degree*, *in some respects*, and encourage students to use these during their discussions.

- Conduct whole-class feedback. Ask a representative of each group to tell the rest of the class how far they agree with Margaret Heffernan's ideas, and why.

Answers

1 change   2 together   3 agree   4 leaders

VOCABULARY IN CONTEXT

6

- ▶12.2 Play the clips from the TED Talk. When each multiple-choice question appears, pause the clip so that students can choose the correct definition.

Transcript and subtitles

1 And that meant she knew she only had one **shot** at collecting her data.
   a attempt
   b technique
   c time frame

2 This really was a **needle in a haystack** sort of search.
   a excessively complicated to carry out
   b extremely difficult to find the answer
   c particularly expensive to do

3 Now that finding **flew in the face** of conventional wisdom.
   a proved the relevance of
   b was the opposite of
   c was in line with

4 different ways of **crunching the data** in order to disprove her.
   a analysing statistics
   b applying research techniques
   c collecting information

5 Alice's daughter told me that every time Alice **went head-to-head** with a fellow scientist, they made her think and think and think again. 'My mother,' she said, 'My mother didn't enjoy a fight, but she was really good at them.'
   a asked for help from
   b directly confronted
   c had a discussion with

6 It comes from information that is freely available and out there, but that we are **wilfully blind** to
   a can't understand
   b don't agree with
   c refuse to see

Answers

1 a 2 b 3 b 4 a 5 b 6 c

7

• Students complete the sentences in their own words, then compare them in pairs.

• Conduct whole-class feedback. You could ask several students to read out their sentence and then elicit responses from the rest of the class. For example, ask: *Does anyone else feel the same about those quiz shows? Does anyone have a different opinion about them?*

CRITICAL THINKING Relevant background information

8

• Put students into pairs to discuss why they think these pieces of background information were relevant to Margaret Heffernan's main message. Encourage students to use the words in the brackets to help them. This is a critical thinking rather than a memory activity, so also encourage students to look at the transcript of the talk on page 182 to help find reasons for the relevance of the sentences to Margaret Heffernan's main message. Then conduct whole-class feedback.

Answers

1 It shows she wasn't afraid to be unconventional compared to what women were expected to do in the 1950s.

2 It establishes that she was exceptional in her field.

3 It shows how important having confidence in your ideas is when you are going to challenge conventional wisdom.

4 He was afraid to say what he knew was true and to be the only one to speak.

5 He was courageous and gave others the courage to say what they also thought.

9

• Put students into pairs to read the comments and to discuss how they think the background information about Alice and Joe added to the viewers' understanding of the talk. Explain that students can use the transcript of the talk and the points from Exercise 8 to help them. Then conduct whole-class feedback.

PRESENTATION SKILLS Using pauses

10

• Ask students to read about using pauses in the Presentation skills box. Ask: *What effect can pauses have in a presentation? To what extent do they contribute to the success of a presentation?*

• ▶12.3 Play the clips so that students can identify and use lines to mark where Margaret Heffernan pauses.

Transcript and answers

1 　*By a rate of two to one, | the children who had died | had had mothers who had been X-rayed | when pregnant.*

2 　*In fact, | she need not have hurried. | It was fully 25 years before the British and medical – | British and American medical establishments – | abandoned the practice | of X-raying pregnant women.*

11

• Put students into pairs to think of a surprising news items they've read or heard about recently. This could be from the local, national or international news.

• Students make brief notes on the background to the story and the facts which make it a surprising story. If possible, students could go online to look up the news story and to check the facts or to find out some more information.

• Ask students to practise telling the story several times in pairs, using pausing in different places in order to assess what is the most effective way of using pauses. Once they've established the most effective way of using pauses, students can mark these in on their notes about the news item.

TEACHING TIP

Using a hook in storytelling

A 'hook' is an opening statement, question or quote that gets your audience's attention at the start of a story or presentation and makes them want to listen to the rest of it. Here are some tips you could give your students for creating effective hooks for their stories:

1 State the opposite of a widely accepted point of view.

2 Ask a rhetorical question or a series of them.

3 Use a catchy phrase, slogan or soundbite.

4 Use the word *imagine*, e.g. *Imagine a world where … .*

5 Make a confession.

6 Use a quote from a celebrity or a well-known film or television programme.

12

• Put students into new pairs. Take turns to tell each other their stories.

• Encourage students to respond to each other's story, showing interest in what the other person said. They should also say to what extent they were surprised by the story and what specifically they were surprised by. Students could also give each other feedback on how effectively they used pauses.

▶ Set Workbook pages 114–115 for homework.

12.2 Moments of change

GRAMMAR Third conditional

1

• Books open. Put students into pairs to discuss the questions. Make sure that students think about the answers to the questions themselves first before they look at the information about 'big data'. Even if students don't know the answers to the questions, they can speculate.

• **Optional step.** Conduct whole-class feedback, but don't confirm answers at this stage.

• Ask students to read the information about 'big data' in the infographic and to check their answers. Then check answers with the class. You could encourage students to work out how many million or billion emails are sent/received every day.

Answers

1 Big data is data that is more complex than data collected using traditional tools.

2 We get big data from: people interacting online; people sending information to machines; machines collecting information.

3 29 million emails every second (x 60 x 60 x 24 = 2,505,600 million emails or 2,505.6 billion emails); 400 million tweets every day

---

Background information

Uses of big data

There are several uses of 'big data' and the number of applications is likely to increase in the future. Here are some examples: personalized recommendations on websites, such as video-streaming sites; identifying the best places to advertise products and services; weather forecasting; personalized learning applications; and finding out how diseases, e.g. malaria, are spread.

2

• Give students time to read the sentences. If necessary, clarify the meaning of:

blackspot – a place where a problem is particularly bad or where it very frequently arises (sentence 4)

• 🔊 65 Play the recording so that students can answer the questions.

Transcript

P = Presenter, J = Journalist

P: *If you spend any time at all online, whether you are actually shopping or just looking for information about a new camera, listening to music or streaming videos, then you will almost certainly have noticed that,*

increasingly, the Internet makes suggestions to you about books you might like to read next, films you might like to watch or products you might want to buy. How does this happen? Well, it's just one example of how businesses are using something called 'big data' to market themselves more efficiently. So what is this thing called big data? How's it different from simple 'data'? That's what we're going to be looking at in today's programme with the help of business journalist Samira Jones. Samira?

J: *Hi, well, essentially big data is data that we can now access because of our digital world – it's a huge volume of information that can be extremely complex to analyse using traditional methods. To give a simple example, whereas traditionally a company had to design a market research survey and actually ask customers for responses, these days digital technology keeps track of all kinds of customer behaviour, and in real time. And this information shows trends and changes in behaviour that a company might not have thought about including in their market research. Basically, if traditional data gave enough information, big data wouldn't have become such an important marketing tool.*

P: *So, let's take the case of a particular toothpaste company that launched a new food line, which was a complete disaster. If they'd had access to big data, would they have marketed the product better? Is that the idea?*

J: *Yes, in theory, that's one way big data could work. Or perhaps if they'd known more about the market, they wouldn't have made that particular product line. But it's not only in business that big data is useful. It has all kinds of implications. Take the area of health and disease, and one of the big health epidemics of recent times, bird flu. It would have affected many more people if the health authorities hadn't spotted certain trends in the way it was spreading. Even an illness as common as flu can show up quickly because people do online searches for flu medicines. According to one report, a flu epidemic in the USA was predicted ten days before it reached its peak. If the online searches hadn't been tracked, this prediction wouldn't have been possible.*

P: *And what about for us as individuals? How can big data help us to make decisions in our daily lives?*

J: *Well, there's an interesting example in Australia. Cycling is becoming more and more popular there and a lot of cyclists use an app to track all of their journeys. This data provides a useful map of accident blackspots – places where the most accidents happen – so you can change your route if you want to and avoid those spots. It works because so many cyclists downloaded the app. If they hadn't, they wouldn't be able to use the information.*

- Draw students' attention to the jounalist's American accent and her pronunciation of route /raʊt/. The British pronunciation is /ruːt/.

3

- **Optional step.** Elicit examples of the second conditional and that this is formed with *if + would, + past simple*.
- Look at the Grammar box with the class. Ask students to read the sentences – which are from the recording – and to choose the correct option to complete the rules for using the third conditional. They can do this in pairs.
- Students can check their answers and overall understanding of the third conditional by turning to the Grammar summary on page 162.

- If you feel that students need more controlled practice before continuing, they could do one or both of Exercises 1–2 in the Grammar summary. Otherwise, you could continue on to Exercise 4 in the unit and set the Grammar summary exercises for homework.

4

- Before students read the story, ask if they've heard of Richard Doll and if they know what he's famous for discovering. Don't confirm the answer at this stage.
- Ask students to read the story and to use the information to complete the conditional sentences.

- Check answers with the class and clarify any issues regarding the use of the third conditional.

5

- **Optional step.** Ask students to raise their hands if they use Facebook and notice how many students raise their hands. Then ask students to raise their hands if they use Yahoo! and notice how many students raise their hands this time. You would expect significantly more students to use Facebook than Yahoo! Elicit possible reasons for this difference. For example: *The Facebook brand is stronger than the Yahoo! brand, More people you want to connect with use Facebook than Yahoo! Facebook has moved with the times, whereas Yahoo! hasn't to the same extent.*
- Ask students to read the story and then to summarize its content by writing sentences using the third conditional.
- Check answers with the class. Slight variations from the sentences in the answer key are possible, so check with individual students if they have written something that's different and which they believe to be correct.

GRAMMAR Mixed conditional sentences

6

- Explain that we can also mix clauses from two different types of conditionals – second and third – in one grammatically correct sentence.
- Look at the Grammar box with the class. Elicit or explain that *pattern* refers to *mixed third + second conditional* and *mixed second + third conditional*. Also explain that the word after *mixed* (*second* or *third*) in the patterns refers to the verb form that follows *if*.

- Ask students to read the sentences and to answer the questions.

- Students can check their answers and overall understanding of mixed conditionals by turning to the Grammar summary on page 162.

- If you feel that students need more controlled practice before continuing, they could do Exercises 3–4 in the Grammar summary. Otherwise, you could continue on to Exercise 7 in the unit and set the Grammar summary exercises for homework.

- Note that there is also an Extension section and exercise in the Grammar summary on *wish*.

7

- Look at item 1 as an example with the class. Elicit that a possible sentence for this situation is: *If social networks weren't so popular* (second), *I wouldn't have tracked down my old school friends* (third).

- Put students into pairs to write the other mixed conditional sentences based on the information in the situations.

- Check the answers with the class. Slight variations from the sentences in the answer key are possible.

- Ask students to discuss with their partner whether any of the sentences are true for them.

- Conduct whole-class feedback. Encourage students to use conditionals in their responses.

- **Optional step.** Ask students to make sentences of their own using mixed conditionals. You could give an example from your own life to get them started.

SPEAKING What if … ?

8   *21st* **CENTURY OUTCOMES**

- Before starting this exercise, refer students to the 21st CENTURY OUTCOMES at the foot of the page. Elicit or explain that when we evaluate information critically, we consider both its good and bad points and take both into account when drawing our conclusions.

- Look at the example with the class. Encourage students to make other statements about this event. For example: *If Tim Berners-Lee hadn't invented the Web, he wouldn't be so famous today.*

- Put students into groups of three. If this isn't possible, put students into pairs and ask one student to read both Student B's and Student C's information or into groups of four and ask two students to read Student C's information.

- Ask students to decide who is Student A, Student B and Student C. Give them time to read their information on page 164.

- Students take turns to read out the information about an event from the past. The other students then imagine and discuss the situation if this thing hadn't happened. Remind students to refer to the example on page 133.

- **Optional step.** Students may not be familiar with all the scenarios described and their implications. If you have internet access, students could go online to do some research about the historical events they have to make sentences about.

- Conduct whole-class feedback and invite students to discuss each situation in turn.

1980: If CNN hadn't been founded in 1980, we wouldn't have had 24-hour news coverage until later in the decade.

Student B

1962: If the Decca record company had signed the Beatles, they would have made a fortune.

2003: If the human genome hadn't been decoded, it would be much harder to treat some diseases.

Student C

1977: If the first Star Wars film hadn't been released, a lot of people would have a different favourite film.

2014: If a contestant on a TV quiz show in the USA had been able to pronounce 'Achilles' correctly, he would have won a million dollars.

9

• Ask students to identify a key event (or key events) in each of the areas and to discuss how the world might be different now if it hadn't happened. Encourage students to use a variety of structures in their sentences, i.e. not to have a third conditional starting with *if* in every sentence.

• Conduct whole-class feedback. You could ask students to think about whether the fact that this happened is a positive or a negative thing.

Suggested answers

Music: If Kurt Cobain hadn't committed suicide, he wouldn't have become a music idol.

Technology: Ron Wayne would be a billionaire if he hadn't left Apple in 1976.

Sport: Germany wouldn't have won the World Cup in 2014 if they'd had a different manager.

Economics: There wouldn't have been such high unemployment levels over the last few years if the financial crisis hadn't happened.

Science: If Marie Curie had decided to stop working after getting married, we wouldn't have had X-rays as early as we did.

Entertainment: If the original *Star Wars* film hadn't been such a big success, they wouldn't have made so many sequels.

Extra activity

Presentation and Q&A

Ask students to do team or individual presentations on the differences we would see in the world if the key events they discussed hadn't happened. In their presentations, students could focus on several events which happened in one of the areas or events which happened in a range of different areas. These presentations could be followed by a Q&A session in which the other students can ask questions and have their say on whether they agree with the presenters.

▶ Photocopiable communicative activity 12.1: Go to page 235 for practice of third and mixed conditional sentences. The teaching notes are on page 248.

▶ Set Workbook pages 116–117 for homework.

12.3 The benefit of hindsight

READING A letter to my younger self

1

• Books open. Draw students' attention to the spread title: *The benefit of hindsight.* If necessary, clarify the meaning of:

hindsight – understanding of a situation or event after it has happened

• Ask students if they've ever used the *benefit of hindsight* or if they know anyone who tends to use it.

• Look at the instructions and the word list with the class. Draw students' attention to the Glossary at the end of the article to clarify the meaning of *primatologist*.

• Put students into pairs to brainstorm the personal qualities they think would help people to succeed in these five professions.

• Conduct whole-class feedback and elicit a list of personal qualities for each profession. Write the qualities on the board as students mention them.

Suggested answers

actor: bold, brave, dramatic, outgoing, self-confident, sociable

athlete: brave, independent, self-confident, sensible human rights campaigner: assertive, brave, courageous, passionate, self-confident

primatologist: adventurous, brave, curious

writer: anxious, modest, shy

2

• Ask students to look at the extracts from the letters and to identify the profession of each person. Ask students to read the extracts and to focus on identifying the personal qualities each person seems to have. Students compare the personality adjectives they thought of for each profession in Exercise 1 with what the people say about themselves. Ask: *Do these people seem to have the personal qualities you expected them to have? How are they the same as or different to what you expected?* Students can discuss the questions in pairs. Then conduct whole-class feedback.

Background information

Roger Bannister

Roger Bannister was the first person to *break* the four-minute mile, meaning he was the first person to run a mile (or 1.6 kilometres) in under four minutes. He did that in Oxford on 6 May 1954. When Roger Bannister says that he was focused on 'getting to Oxford', he's referring to the famous university located in that city.

3

• Give students time to read the sentences. If necessary, model and drill the pronunciation of anxious: /ˈæŋkʃəs/ (sentence 2).

• Look at an example with the class. Ask students to read the extract about Jane Goodall and to find the sentence that refers to her (sentence 5).

• Ask students to read the extracts again and to find the sentences that refers to the other four people.

Answers

1 Roger Bannister   2 Peter Capaldi   3 Meera Syal
4 Shami Chakrabarti   5 Jane Goodall

4

• Tell students to look at what comes before and after each expression to identify the context in which it is used.

• Students match the expressions (1–8) with the expressions (a–h) which have similar meanings. They can do this in pairs.

Answers

1 c   2 b   3 g   4 f   5 e   6 h   7 d   8 a

5

• Ask students to think about what they were like when they were 16. If students are, in fact, 16 or 17 years old, ask them to think about what they were like at a younger age, e.g. 14 years old. You could give an example from your own life.

• Put students into pairs to discuss the questions.

Extra activity

A letter to my younger self

Ask students to write a letter to their 16-year-old self in which they: a) show empathy for how their younger self is feeling right now; b) reassure their younger self that everything is going to be OK; c) give their younger self some advice for the future.

VOCABULARY Personality adjectives (2)

6

• **Optional step.** Students have previously looked at personality adjectives in Unit 9 and you could ask them to look at page 102 to review these first.

• Ask students to look at the groups of adjectives and to choose the odd one out in each group. Most of these adjectives are likely to already be familiar to students, but monitor students while they're doing this activity and either offer clarification on unknown adjectives or ask them to consult a dictionary. Alternatively, they can do the activity in pairs.

• Check answers with the class. Also check that students are able to pronounce the adjectives correctly as they may need them in Exercises 8 and 9. In particular, students are likely to find the pronunciation of the following adjectives challenging: argumentative /ˌɑːgjʊˈmentətɪv/, courageous /kəˈreɪdʒəs/, sociable /ˈsəʊʃəbl/, assertive /əˈsɜːtɪv/ and irresponsible /ˌɪrɪsˈpɒnsəbl/. Model and drill the pronunciation, as necessary. Draw students' attention to the syllable stress patterns in these adjectives.

Answers

1 argumentative   2 arrogant   3 terrified   4 cold
5 anxious   6 sensible

7

• Look at sentence 1 as an example with the class. Elicit that the correct option is *brave*.

• Ask students to choose the correct option to complete the other sentences. They can do this in pairs.

Answers

1 brave   2 outgoing   3 argumentative   4 arrogant
5 wild   6 anxious

• **Optional step.** Students write similar sentences with the adjectives that weren't the correct options, e.g. *sensible* in sentence 1. These could be sentences which are true for students. Check students' sentences, focusing on whether they've used the personality adjectives correctly.

SPEAKING Never again!

8 21st CENTURY OUTCOMES

- Tell students that in this exercise they're going to reflect critically on someone else's past experiences and then in Exercise 9 they will have the chance to reflect critically on their own past experiences in order to fulfil the 21st CENTURY OUTCOME.
- Give students time to read the story.
- Put students into pairs to say how they would describe the person's friend. Encourage them to use some of the personality adjectives that they've just looked at. Monitor students while they're speaking, noting whether they're using the personality adjectives from Exercise 6 and doing so correctly.
- Conduct whole-class feedback and ask students to tell you the adjectives they would use to describe the person's friend.

9

- Ask students to think about experiences they've had with two people they know or used to know.
- Put students into groups to describe these two people, using appropriate personality adjectives. Tell students that they should conclude their stories by saying whether they think the people were a positive or negative influence on them, giving reasons for or evidence to support their choice.

▶ Set Workbook pages 118–119 for homework.

12.4 Could I have a quick word?

LISTENING Managing change

1

- Books open. Draw students' attention to the spread title: *Could I have a quick word?* Elicit or explain that this question would be used by native speakers when they want to ask someone to do something or to change something, or when they want to give them feedback or criticism in private.
- 66 Play the recording so that students can match the options under each heading with the conversations.

Transcript

1

A: *So, basically we've had a good month and you have met your targets, well done. The last thing I want to talk about is opening times. If you remember, we carried out extensive market research last month. It's clear that our customers want us to be open later in the evenings and that will affect you.*

B: *I understand that we have to respond to what customers want, of course. At the moment, this could create some difficulty for me as I have a lot of commitments in the evenings. I wonder if you could look at whether some of my colleagues have more flexibility?*

2

C: *Dan, could I have a quick word? I notice that I haven't had any work from you for a while. You know that this term you're expected to do one assignment a week.*

D: *Ah, yes. I'm doing my best to keep up with the course. I have a lot on right now. I should explain that I'm in the middle of moving house. It's only a temporary problem, really. I intend to get back on track in the next couple of weeks. I was hoping you could give me some extra time?*

3

E: *Look, we have to do something about the state of this flat. Now that we're all out at work all day, nobody does any housework at all!*

F: *OK, you're right, we need to talk about it. The thing is, I really haven't got time.*

E: *I appreciate that, but I'm in the same position. And you don't work in the mornings, so …*

F: *That's true, but I'm still busy. Perhaps we could get a cleaner for a few hours a week? It would really make a difference. And it wouldn't cost much if we shared the cost between us.*

Answers

1 at work, work later, evening commitments
2 at college, do more work, moving house
3 at home, take on some extra tasks, busy all day

TEACHING TIP

Listening to English outside the classroom

If students are now coming to the end of their English course, you may want to draw their attention to the fact that continued exposure to listening material in English outside the classroom will help them to continue developing their listening skills and to build their learner autonomy. Students are also free to choose what they listen to outside the classroom, which should help to make this experience a motivating one. If students travel a lot or commute, they can also do some listening on their smartphones, MP3 or CD players while they're on the move. Encourage students to use what they've learned about listening techniques up to now to help them when they're listening on their own, e.g. how to understand fast speech and connected speech or how to listen for gist.

You can help to motivate students to do some listening in their own time by suggesting sources of podcasts and videos – www.ted.com is a good place to start!

2

- 🎧 66 Play the recording again so that students can answer the questions.

- **Question 2.** Tell students that they should take the situations in which the suggestions are made into account when decide how reasonable they are.

- Check answers to question 1. Then refer students to the transcript of the conversations on page 173 to read the suggestions themselves.

- Conduct whole-class feedback on students answers to questions 2 and 3. Ask students to give their response to each suggestion.

Answers

1 conversation 1: I wonder if you could look at whether some of my colleagues have more flexibility?

conversation 2: I was hoping you could give me some extra time?

conversation 3: Perhaps we could get a cleaner for a few hours a week?

2 Students' own answers

3 Students' own answers

Focus on register

At this level, students should be aware of and be able to use different registers. Draw students' attention to differences in register where appropriate, for example in the conversations students listen to in Exercises 1 and 2, where conversation 1 is in a formal register and conversations 2 and 3 are in an informal register. Encourage students to not only identify the register of a text or transcript, but also the features which indicate what the register is, e.g. formal/informal vocabulary or more/less indirect language. If you have two conversations or texts where the same message is being communicated in a formal register in one and an informal register in the other, you could also ask students to compare and contrast how this difference manifests itself in the language used. In the transcript for Exercises 1 and 2, for example, you can compare *I have a lot of commitments* in conversation 1 with *I have a lot on right now* in conversation 2.

Pronunciation Tone and meaning

3a

- Look at the instructions with the class. If necessary, review the meaning of *stress* and *intonation*. Tell students that the stress and intonation we use when speaking helps to give our speech a certain tone.

- If necessary, clarify the difference between being *assertive* (speaking in a strong and confident way) and being *aggressive* (speaking forcefully, often in an angry way). Elicit or explain that being assertive is acceptable in all situations whereas being aggressive isn't usually acceptable. Also, if necessary, clarify the meaning of:

> *ineffective* – unlikely to achieve the results that are wanted (line 5)

- Explain that students are going to listen to sentences that use some of the expressions in the Useful language box and decide what tone the speaker uses. Tell students that some of the sentences they will hear have been designed to show you how not to sound and some are good examples of use of tone.

- 🎧 67 Look at sentence 1 as an example with the class. Play the recording and pause. Elicit that the tone the speaker uses is assertive.

- Play the rest of the recording and ask students to write either *AS* (assertive), *AG* (aggressive) or *I* (ineffective) for the tone of each sentence. Students could check their answers in pairs before you check with the whole class.

Transcript

1   *I want to talk about how we spend our money.*

2   *I appreciate that you find this difficult.*

3   *I intend to make some changes around here.*

4   *I'm doing my best to keep everyone happy.*

5   *I was hoping you could do some extra work.*

6   *Perhaps we could discuss this some time next week?*

Answers

1 assertive   2 assertive   3 aggressive   4 ineffective
5 assertive   6 assertive

3b

- 🎧 67 Play the recording again and pause after each sentence so that students can listen and repeat the assertive sentences (1, 2, 5 and 6).

SPEAKING Tricky situations

4   21st CENTURY OUTCOMES

- Before starting this exercise, refer students to the 21st CENTURY OUTCOMES at the foot of the page. You could get students thinking about how they deal with setbacks and criticism by asking them to work in pairs and to tell each other about times when they've suffered setbacks or criticism, and how they responded to them.

- Put students into small groups to discuss what they would say in these situations in order to get the change they want. Encourage students to consider the relationships between the two people involved, e.g. two friends, boss–employee, teacher–students, and how power is distributed in these relationships, i.e. the boss has more power than the employee. Students should also consider the appropriate register for each situation.

• You could also encourage students to use *wish* when discussing what they would say. (See Grammar summary, page 162.)

• **Optional step.** Ask students to think about and discuss the role that culture plays in these interactions. Ask, for example: *Would people from different cultures, such as a native speaker from the USA and a non-native speaker from Germany, communicate differently in these situations, and why?* Students could compare how people from their culture would be likely to communicate differently to people from other countries. If you have a multicultural group and you put students from a mixture of cultures in each group, they could compare ideas in their groups.

• Conduct whole-class feedback on what students would say in each situation. You could write example sentences for each situation on the board, one after the other, so that students can easily compare the length and register of the sentences for each situation.

WRITING Letter of complaint

5

• Explain that students are going to read an email in which someone makes a complaint. You could ask students whether, based on this information, they expect the register of the text to be formal or informal, giving reasons for their answers.

• Look at the email with the class. Elicit or explain that we do not know if H P Jones is a man or a woman.

• Give students time to read the email and to answer the questions.

• Check answers with the class. Elicit or explain that *re* means 'about' or 'on the subject of' and is used mainly in formal writing, especially business letters.

Answers
1 a The credit card used to pre-pay the car hire was not acceptable and he/she had to provide a different card. b The staff member was particularly unhelpful and unable to explain the reasons why he could not accept his first card. c There were no cars available in the category he/she requested and he/she was offered a smaller car. d It is now ten days since he/she returned the car and he/she still has not received the refund which is due for the lower category car. 2 a The company should have informed him about the changes to the website. b The staff member should have been more helpful and explained the reasons why he could not accept his first card. c H P Jones should have been given a larger car as there was one available. d He/She should have received the refund immediately.

3 He/She would appreciate the company's co-operation in processing his/her refund on receipt of the letter and looks forward to a clarification of their policy re credit cards and car categories.

6

• Ask students to read the list of features of formal communication.

• Students identify and underline the parts of the email that show the features of formal communication. They can do this in pairs.

• Check answers with the class. Elicit or explain that *Yours faithfully* rather than *Yours sincerely* is used when the name of the recipient is unknown. You could draw students' attention to the final words of the third paragraph: *did he offer* is an example of inversion and this sentence means 'he didn't offer an apology at any time'. Again, inversion is used in formal writing.

Answers
From: HP_Jones@Jones.co.uk To: Customer Service@OnTheRoadCars.com (a) <u>Subject: Complaint: Car Hire Gatwick Airport ref 4159763</u> (b) <u>Dear Sir / Madam</u> (d) <u>I am writing to draw your attention to the poor service at the Gatwick Airport office of your company.</u> In February of this year, I booked a car online for the dates 11–15 April, booking reference 4159763. (e) <u>On arriving to pick up the vehicle, I was informed that the credit card used to pre-pay the car hire was not acceptable and I had to provide a different card.</u> This could have left me without a car, but fortunately, I had another card. (e) <u>The staff member I dealt with, 'Paul', was particularly unhelpful and unable to explain the reasons why he could not accept that card.</u> It then transpired that there were no cars available in the category I requested and I was offered a smaller car. This was not adequate for my needs. Your employee could have provided me with a larger car as there was one available, yet he said this was not company policy. (e) <u>It is now ten days since I returned the car and I still have not received the refund which is due for the lower category car.</u> I now notice that the terms and conditions on your website changed in March. (e) <u>I believe you should have informed customers with existing bookings about these changes.</u> (e) <u>I also feel the refund should have been made into my account immediately.</u> (e) <u>Equally, your employee could have handled the matter in</u> a <u>more professional manner: at no time did he offer an apology.</u> (f) <u>I would appreciate your co-operation in processing my refund on receipt of this letter and look forward to a clarification of your policy re credit cards and car categories.</u> (c) <u>Yours faithfully</u> H P Jones

Writing skill Past modals (2)

7a

- Ask students to underline the verbs in the sentences and to decide which sentences are criticisms and which refer to possible actions. They can do this in pairs. Explain that looking at the sentences in context in the email and/or reading out the sentences as they would naturally say them should help students to identify their functions.

- Students can check their answers and overall understanding of past modals by turning to the Grammar summary on page 162.

> **Answers**
>
> 1 This <u>could have left</u> me without a car … (possible action)
>
> 2 Your employee <u>could have provided</u> me with a larger car … (possible action)
>
> 3 I believe you <u>should have informed</u> customers with existing bookings about these changes. (criticism)
>
> 4 I also feel the refund <u>should have been made</u> into my account immediately. (criticism)
>
> 5 Equally, your employee <u>could have handled</u> the matter in a more professional manner. (possible action)

- If you feel that students need more controlled practice before continuing, they could do Exercises 6–7 in the Grammar summary. Otherwise, you could continue on to Exercise 7b in the unit and set the Grammar summary exercises for homework.

> **Answers to Grammar summary exercises**
>
> **6**
>
> 1 should have   2 must have   3 could have
> 4 shouldn't have   5 couldn't have   6 might have
>
> **7**
>
> 1 If you ~~would have~~ **had** worked harder, you'd have passed your exam.
>
> 2 Tom wouldn't be ill if he ~~would have~~ **had** taken his tablets.
>
> 3 I wouldn't have been ~~successful, if~~ **successful if** you hadn't supported me.
>
> 4 If the epidemic had spread, more people would **have** died.
>
> 5 If we ~~didn't have bought~~ **hadn't bought** the tablet, we would have bought a laptop.
>
> 6 What ~~you would~~ **would you** have done if you had failed the exam again?
>
> 7 I'm sorry I'm late – I ~~must~~ **should** have phoned you to let you know.
>
> 8 I often think I ~~would~~ **should** have chosen a different career.

7b

- Look at the instructions, the sentences and the functions with the class. If necessary, clarify the meaning of:

  deduction – the process of using logic or reason to reach a conclusion about something (function b)

- Ask students to complete the customer's comments with the modal verbs.

- Check answers with the class. Then ask students to match the comments with the functions. They can do this in pairs.

> **Answers**
>
> 1 should: d a regret
>
> 2 shouldn't: a a criticism
>
> 3 must: b a deduction
>
> 4 could: a possibility

8

- Ask students to read the situation and to work on their own to write an email using the structure of the email in Exercise 5 as a model. Remind them to use at least one past modal form.

9

- Put students into pairs. They read each other's email, and focus on whether their complaint and the action expected is clear. Students then give each other feedback on these points. They could also give each other feedback on other aspects of their letter, e.g. register, structure, style, use of vocabulary, use of grammar, spelling and punctuation.

- Encourage students not only to praise each other's email, but also to feel free to offer criticism where appropriate. Tell students that when their partner criticizes their email, they should respond assertively, e.g. by defending and giving reasons for their use of a particular expression.

- Monitor students while they're giving each other feedback on their emails, encouraging them to criticize each other and react to criticism assertively, where appropriate.

▶ Photocopiable communicative activity 12.2: Go to page 236 for practice of personality adjectives and expressions for 'being assertive'. The teaching notes are on page 248.

▶ Set Workbook pages 120–121 for homework.

▶ Set Workbook Writing 6 on pages 122–123 for homework.

REVIEW 6 | UNITS 11 AND 12

READING GiveMeTap

1

• Ask students to read the article quickly and to match one of the headings with each paragraph.

Answers

1 E   2 B   3 D   4 A   5 C

2

• Ask students to read the article again and to find words from the article to complete the sentences.

Answers

1 water   2 brand   3 dirty water   4 earn money
5 experience

GRAMMAR

3

• Ask students to complete the sentences with the correct articles and quantifiers.

Answers

1 an   2 little   3 Each   4 The   5 a few   6 no
7 the   8 –   9 All

4

• Ask students to complete the conditional sentences with the appropriate forms of the verbs in brackets.

Answers

1 wouldn't have known … hadn't talked

2 would have died … hadn't installed

3 hadn't built … would have to

4 wasn't … would (we) have created

VOCABULARY

5

• Ask students to complete the sentences with appropriate expressions for quantities that are used with the items.

Answers

1 slices   2 barrel   3 carton   4 containers   5 piece
6 tank   7 pad   8 tin

1 two   2 depends when you are using the book
3 students' own answer   4 there are about 15 million containers so a large number will be moving at any one time   5 students' own answer   6 depends when you are using the book   7 students' own answer   8 a DIY store or a hardware shop

6

• Ask students to choose the correct options to complete the text. Encourage them to read through the whole sentence and deduce the correct option from the context.

Answers

1 self-confident   2 assertive   3 mad   4 outgoing
5 shy   6 co-operative

DISCUSSION

7

• Put students into pairs to discuss the questions.

SPEAKING

8

• Ask students to use the word prompts to write complete sentences or questions. They could check their sentences and questions in the Useful language box in Unit 11.4.

Answers

1 I'm ringing to ask

2 Would you like the address of our website?

3 I'd like to talk to the person who handles

4 Let me check

5 Just a second.

6 Have I got the right number

7 If you could hold on one moment,

8 Is this the right place to find out

9 Here are all the details.

WRITING

9

• Ask students to imagine they are Ms Brooks and to write a reply to Rosa. Remind them to use the same register as in the original email in their reply.

Suggested answer

Dear Ms Greer

Thank you for your email about the hotel's conference facilities. I'm afraid the facilities aren't available the weekend of 13th–14th July. They are, however, available on 6th–7th and also the previous weekend. We would be able to accommodate 25–30 people for two overnight stays in either individual or double rooms. Could you confirm how many of each type you would like and whether you require half or full board? Please find attached our list of rates.

Yours sincerely

Leila Brooks

10

• Put students into pairs to exchange emails and compare the information they included.

VOCABULARY

1 Complete the sentences with the words or expressions in the box. There are three extra words or expressions you do not need. The first one is done for you.

assist	committed to	co-ordinate	create	deal with	earn	focus on
give	head up	interested in	involved in	offer	passionate about	responsible for

0 It's clear that he's _____committed to_____ working for this company. He's been here for thirty-five years now and he tells everyone that he never wants to leave.

1 I'm a secretary in the Quality Control department, so I _____ the head of department and the other managers by answering the phone and doing the paper work.

2 I've come to this event because I'm _____ meeting other professionals with similar interests.

3 I regularly _____ customers in China, so I need to improve my English.

4 As a design engineer working for a construction company, I'm always _____ the design of different types of buildings.

5 I _____ a team of twenty people and recently I've been working on my leadership skills so that I can do that as well as I can.

6 As a fashion house, we want to _____ amazing designs that will make the people who wear them feel wonderful.

7 She gave some of her responsibilities to other people so that she could just _____ technical services.

8 As the project manager, it's my job to _____ the different stages of the project and to make sure we get everything done on time.

9 Severine is _____ the timetable. She decides who does what and when.

10 They're _____ helping other people – they would do it even if they didn't get paid for it.

Marks (out of 10): _____

2 Read the text and choose the expression (A–D) which best fits each gap. The first one is done for you.

I left school at the age of sixteen without any academic **(0)** _C_ . Instead of staying at school, I decided to look for a job and I found a starting **(11)** _____ as an office junior at an insurance company. All I wanted to do was earn a **(12)** _____ so that I could start buying the things that I wanted. When I was seventeen, I got my driving **(13)** _____ and bought myself a car. I also realized how useful it was to get some workplace **(14)** _____ because you're going to be at work for a long time and you need to know how to get up early, get to work and work together in a team.

My boss was happy with my performance at work and she suggested I work towards getting some professional **(15)** _____ by taking courses in the evening. I think I was the only person on the course who didn't have a high school **(16)** _____ , so I found it quite difficult. Fortunately, the teachers helped me to develop some of the academic **(17)** _____ I hadn't learned at school, like how to scan-read a book and take notes.

Going back to school has made me realize that gaining professional **(18)** _____ is important, but studying can also give you more employment **(19)** _____ . In my case, my boss suggested I apply for a more senior position in the company. I was successful and now I have a managerial position with a higher salary and a lot more job **(20)** _____ .

0 A opportunities	**B** position	**C** qualifications	**D** experience
11 A security	**B** experience	**C** salary	**D** position
12 A diploma	**B** licence	**C** salary	**D** position
13 A licence	**B** security	**C** experience	**D** qualification
14 A opportunities	**B** security	**C** skills	**D** experience
15 A qualifications	**B** experience	**C** diplomas	**D** skills
16 A position	**B** qualification	**C** diploma	**D** licence
17 A qualifications	**B** experience	**C** opportunities	**D** skills
18 A salaries	**B** experience	**C** opportunities	**D** security
19 A opportunities	**B** qualifications	**C** skills	**D** experience
20 A experience	**B** qualifications	**C** opportunities	**D** security

Marks (out of 10): _____

GRAMMAR

3 Complete the second sentence so that it has a similar meaning to the first sentence, using the word given. Do not change the word given. You must use between two and four words, including the word given. The first one is done for you.

0 Seminars on personal branding are provided once a month by the team from Brandit! **seminars**
The team from Brandit! _____*provide seminars*_____ on personal branding once a month.

21 The email addresses of visitors to our website are collected and saved by an add-on that we've installed. **and**
An add-on that we've installed _____ the email addresses of visitors to our website.

22 A local TV station is streaming this event so that music-lovers in over 100 countries can join in. **streamed**
This event _____ so that music-lovers in over 100 countries can join in.

23 At the end of June, I will complete my studies. **have**
By the end of June, I _____ my studies.

24 The support team deals with hundreds of enquiries from our users every hour. **with**
Hundreds of enquiries from our users _____ by our support team every hour.

25 Today is a day that it's impossible to forget. **never**
I _____ today.

26 A number of possibilities for improving our brand image are being investigated by the marketing department. **is**
The marketing department _____ a number of possibilities for improving our brand image.

27 More people are running their own businesses now than ever before and this trend will continue over the next ten years. **be**
I think more people _____ their own businesses in ten years' time than ever before.

28 The ability to promote yourself is viewed very positively by our recruitment manager. **ability**
Our recruitment manager _____ to promote yourself very positively.

29 He earns a lot of money, so he plans to retire before he's forty. **earned**
He _____ enough money to retire before he's forty.

30 I've decided to spend the whole summer working with disabled children. **will**
I _____ the whole summer working with disabled children.

Marks (out of 10): _____

4 Read the text. Use the correct form of the word given in CAPITAL LETTERS at the end of some of the lines to fill the gap in the same line. Do not write more than three words in each gap. The first one is done for you.

The five biggest trends of the next ten years

1 The number of internet users is increasing rapidly and it's predicted that it
(0) _____*will reach*_____ five billion in the next few years. Around half of these **REACH**
(31) _____ tablets to access the Internet. By 2020, connected devices **USE**
(32) _____ so integrated into our daily lives that we **BECOME**
(33) _____ them as 'digital assistants' that help us with everything we do. **SEE**

2 Today, thousands of items **(34)** _____ online every minute and it is expected **SELL**
that every retail company **(35)** _____ an online presence in ten years' time with **HAVE**
nineteen per cent of retail sales being made online.

3 It's likely that in ten years' time we **(36)** _____ even more than we do now and **TRAVEL**
we **(37)** _____ smart technology to make our journeys easier and faster. **USE**

4 Today's cities **(38)** _____ to be mega-cities in the twenty-first century. It **GROW**
(39) _____ that by 2025 the population of the area between Boston and **ESTIMATE**
Washington DC in the USA will be nearly 60 million people.

5 When it comes to social trends, we **(40)** _____ in a world where the number of **LIVE**
older people is constantly increasing right now. This trend will continue over the next
ten years and there'll also be more ethnic and cultural diversity in our societies.

Marks (out of 10): _____

READING

5 You are going to read an article about people who start their own business. Choose the answer (A–D) which best fits according to the text. The first one is done for you.

Are solopreneurs the next generation of entrepreneurs?

Have you just lost your job? Maybe you've just graduated from university? Some would say there's no such thing as job security nowadays, so instead of looking for another corporate job, why not go it alone and work for yourself? But how exactly do you build up your own business when you're starting from nothing? It's essential that you're 100 per cent committed to your business and passionate about what you're doing. You also have to be prepared to put in the hours to make it a success.

Here are some top tips that will help solopreneurs to get started:

1 Brand yourself

Solopreneurs have to create their own brand. Instead of using your own name to promote your business, think of a brand name and use that in your website URL, Twitter username and Facebook page. Also ensure that when people see that name, they think of your company. This will help you to get work.

2 Get on Twitter

We sometimes see Twitter as being a site where people post about what they had for breakfast, but when used effectively for the purposes of marketing it can be a very powerful tool. Start following people who share your interests and especially those who are in your industry or area. This should help you to build relationships with people who may be interested in buying your products or services and these relationships can translate into sales.

3 Make full use of professional networking sites

A lot of people set up a profile on a professional networking site and then forget all about it. Don't be one of those people. If you take the time to really make your profile stand out and update it regularly, you will see the benefits. People are more likely to contact you with work opportunities. Don't overlook the groups that exist on a lot of these sites either. Join groups that fit your interests and start networking.

4 Start a blog

If you've never blogged before, now's as good a time as any to start. Setting up a blog is easier than you'd think and it's an excellent way of establishing your brand online. Fill your blog with interesting, well-written posts and your readers will think that you're an expert in your area, which will, in turn, help them to trust and listen to you. The best thing about a blog, however, is probably the fact that it allows you to sell yourself in a non-commercial way.

5 Don't forget your email signature

Although it's great to use websites, blogs and social media to brand yourself, email is still likely to be the means of written communication that you'll be using the most, so brand that as well. Make sure that anyone who receives an email from you knows exactly what you do and how they can find out more about you. Do you teach yoga? Let people know about that and also make sure they can find a link to a webpage with information about where and when your classes are in case they want to come along.

6 Go to local and international events

As great as online professional networking can be, there's nothing quite like meeting potential customers and partners face-to-face at an event. People are more likely to remember you and get in touch if they've met you in person. If possible, do some research into who will be at the event before you go and identify people who you think could help you with your business. Make a point of talking to these people before you leave and give them a business card or exchange numbers.

7 Don't be afraid to do something you've never done before

You may not be the kind of person who enjoys putting yourself out there, using social media and chatting to people you don't know at conferences, but if you want to be a successful solopreneur, you shouldn't be afraid to try something new and do some of those things that you don't naturally enjoy doing. Nothing that's worth having comes easily and that includes your own business.

0 A solopreneur is

   A someone who starts and runs a business on their own. ✓

   B someone who sells goods online. ☐

   C someone who provides venture capital to start-ups. ☐

   D someone who doesn't want to work with other people. ☐

41 If you want to be a solopreneur, you need to

   A have enough capital to fund your business. ☐

   B have enough time to spend working on your business. ☐

   C have enough knowledge of the product or service you want to sell. ☐

   D have other people who can support you when you get started. ☐

42 Instead of using your own name, you should

   A set up an anonymous Facebook page and Twitter account. ☐

   B use your Twitter username. ☐

   C think of a different name. ☐

   D find a brand name for your business. ☐

43 It's important to use a name that

   A doesn't make people think of existing companies. ☐

   B includes the name of your product or service. ☐

   C is connected to the type of business you want to run. ☐

   D is easy for people to remember. ☐

44 People sometimes don't realize

   A what a useful networking tool Twitter can be. ☐

   B that you can use Twitter to sell things. ☐

   C that Twitter is great for telling people about your everyday life. ☐

   D that you can advertise on Twitter. ☐

45 In order to make the most of professional networking sites, you should

   A set up a profile and then forget all about it. ☐

   B concentrate on joining as many groups as you can. ☐

   C keep your profile regularly updated. ☐

   D make people think that you're better than you really are. ☐

46 Setting up a blog is

   A something that people may think is easy. ☐

   B a must if you want to establish your brand online. ☐

   C something you should already have done. ☐

   D something that people may think is difficult. ☐

47 Blogs are useful because

   A they allow you to sell yourself. ☐

   B they can demonstrate your expertise. ☐

   C they're non-commercial. ☐

   D they're free to set up. ☐

48 It's important to brand your email signature too,

   A despite the fact that you'll communicate more through social media than by email. ☐

   B because most of your written communication will be by email. ☐

   C because people pay more attention to email signatures than blogs or websites. ☐

   D because then people will be able to contact you more easily. ☐

49 The writer advises that before going to an event, you should

   A do some networking with the people who will be there online. ☐

   B order some business cards so that you can give them out. ☐

   C use social media to tell other people that you'll be there. ☐

   D find out who will be there and who can help you with your business. ☐

50 The writer thinks that

   A success comes easily to those who do the things they naturally enjoy doing. ☐

   B successful solopreneurs need to be prepared to do things they find difficult. ☐

   C the most important thing is for solopreneurs to have a strong social media presence. ☐

   D the most successful solopreneurs spend all their time on their business. ☐

Marks (out of 10): _____

LISTENING

6 🎧 **68** Listen to a job interview. Complete the interviewer's notes with a word or short phrase. The first one is done for you.

Name: Daniela **(0)** _____*Fisher*_____ .

After school, she worked in **(51)** _____ .

She studied business studies at **(52)** _____ and specialized in **(53)** _____ .

She then worked at BMI for **(54)** _____ years.

She is looking for a new job so that she can spend more time **(55)** _____ .

In ten years' time, she'd like to have a global **(56)** _____ and **(57)** _____ customers from all over the world.

Her biggest **(58)** _____ is that she's a perfectionist.

She sees herself as a natural **(59)** _____ .

In her free time, she likes to go **(60)** _____ .

Marks (out of 10): _____

SPEAKING

7 Make an arrangement with your teacher to discuss and get some feedback on the CV you've written in English. You should include the following in your discussion:

- Begin by stating the purpose of the meeting.
- Ask about your teacher's availability.
- Suggest a date/time.
- Your teacher is not available at that time and will suggest a different time.
- Agree and make an arrangement.
- Say what you will do to prepare for the meeting.

You can receive ten marks for including all the points above, using a range of language for making arrangements and using appropriate future forms.

Marks (out of 10): _____

WRITING

8 You're applying for your dream job. Write a formal letter that you could send with your curriculum vitae to the employer you're applying to. Tell the employer why you would be the right person for the job and what your career goals are. Write 140–190 words.

You can receive ten marks for following the conventions for letter writing, writing in an appropriate style and using appropriate language for academic qualifications, professional experience and career goals.

Marks (out of 10): _____

TEST 2 | Units 3 and 4

VOCABULARY

1 Complete the words with the correct endings. The first one is done for you.

0 We could con*sider*_____ other ways of letting people know about this issue.

1 In recent years, we've seen dramatic grow_____ in Chinese cities.

2 We want to ensure that women in India feel saf_____ when they go out to get water.

3 Emerging economies have the potential to become very economically succ_____ .

4 A culture of aspiration can motiv_____ children to try to get out of poverty.

5 We can use indices such as GDP to measure quantit_____ economic differences.

6 We're optim_____ that we can reduce poverty in Bangladesh.

7 Our aim is to sec_____ a ninety per cent child survival rate by 2025.

8 There may be no such thing as perf_____ statistics, but they do give us a good idea of what is going on.

9 We have made improvements to the qualit_____ of the education children receive.

10 Countries like China and India are becoming increasingly influen_____ .

Marks (out of 10): _____

2 Read the text and choose the word (A–D) which best fits each gap. The first one is done for you.

The life coach

I have the best job in the world – I'm a life coach. I say I have the best job in the world because I get to spend my days helping people to **(0)** _C_ their potential. A lot of the time, people come to me because they're depressed and feel like they're a **(11)** _____ because they haven't achieved something they'd always imagined they would. Maybe they've experienced some kind of personal **(12)** _____ which has made them lose confidence and they just don't know what to do next.

The **(13)** _____ is though, that a lot of these people have just been pushing themselves too hard and have burnt out. When you find out what these people have done in their careers, you think wow he or she has really **(14)** _____ . I mean I've had CEOs, top journalists and even politicians come through my door. People who have so much **(15)** _____ in their respective fields and who are admired and respected for the expertise they have in the areas they've worked in, but they just couldn't care **(16)** _____ about all of that anymore. They've climbed to the top of the career ladder, but they've come to the conclusion that all you really need is to find some peace of mind. And I couldn't agree **(17)** _____ with them. If we don't have peace of mind, what do we have?

I tell them it's not their **(18)** _____ that they feel this way – a lot of very successful people do. I also help them to focus on what's really important in life and give them the tools and the **(19)** _____ that they need to find contentment. In the same way that you can't have a successful career without doing some forward **(20)** _____ , you also need to consider your route to peace of mind. You could say I'm the guide who helps my clients to plan that route.

0 A build	**B** notice	**C** achieve	**D** create
11 A failure	**B** catastrophe	**C** mistake	**D** fault
12 A disaster	**B** truth	**C** experience	**D** blame
13 A experience	**B** knowledge	**C** fault	**D** truth
14 A done it	**B** made it	**C** pushed it	**D** earned it
15 A success	**B** experience	**C** knowledge	**D** truth
16 A less	**B** more	**C** enough	**D** any
17 A at all	**B** enough	**C** less	**D** more
18 A mistake	**B** error	**C** blame	**D** fault
19 A knowledge	**B** truth	**C** experience	**D** success
20 A success	**B** planning	**C** knowledge	**D** expertise

Marks (out of 10): _____

GRAMMAR

3 Complete the second sentence so that it has a similar meaning to the first sentence, using the word given. Do not change the word given. You must use between two and four words, including the word given. The first one is done for you.

0 Up until the 1970s, environmental issues were unimportant for most people, but now there's a lot
more awareness of them. **unimportant**
Environmental issues _____ *used to be unimportant* _____ for most people, but that's all changed now.

21 In the 1970s, people started to be more and more interested in what was happening to the environment. **become**
Since the 1970s, people _____ more and more interested in
what is happening to the environment.

22 The Habitat Conservation Consultancy was founded to support sustainable environmental projects
in 1998 in Sweden and it continues to do that today. **supporting**
The Habitat Conservation Consultancy _____ sustainable
environmental projects since 1998.

23 The Habitat Conservation Consultancy's founder Nathan Rasmussen is a biologist who began
his professional life as a field researcher eighteen years ago. **been**
The Habitat Conservation Consultancy's founder Nathan Rasmussen _____
a biologist for eighteen years.

24 Nathan Rasmussen decided at the very beginning that The Habitat Conservation Consultancy would
only accept donations from organizations or governments with ethical policies. **has**
Since it was established, The Habitat Conservation Consultancy _____
donations from ethical organizations or governments.

25 Nathan Rasmussen is now the director of The Habitat Conservation Consultancy, but when he was younger
he spent three years researching the feeding habits of birds on the island of Madagascar. **research**
Nathan Rasmussen _____ the feeding habits of birds on the island
of Madagascar.

26 The Habitat Conservation Consultancy started to grow sixteen years ago when Nathan Rasmussen took
on two employees to work with him, and this growth continues today. **growing**
The Habitat Conservation Consultancy _____ for the last sixteen years.

27 After ten years of hard work, The Habitat Conservation Consultancy received the first of
several awards for its work. **working**
The Habitat Conservation Consultancy _____ hard for ten years before
it received the first of several awards for its work.

28 In the beginning, Nathan Rasmussen was unsure whether the organization would be a success, but
he stopped feeling that way when he saw what it was achieving. **been**
Nathan Rasmussen _____ unsure whether the organization would
be a success until he saw what it was achieving.

29 The Habitat Conservation Consultancy was based in Gothenburg for twelve years. Then it moved
to Stockholm six years ago. **been**
The Habitat Conservation Consultancy _____ in Gothenburg for
twelve years before it moved to Stockholm.

30 The Habitat Conservation Consultancy started regularly using social media to let people know about
its work six months ago. **been**
The Habitat Conservation Consultancy _____ social media to let
people know about its work for the last six months.

Marks (out of 10): _____

4 Read the text and choose the word (A–D) which best fits each gap. The first one is done for you.

The Cambridge Five

The Cambridge Five **(0)** ___A___ British spies employed by the Russian (or Soviet) government who got their name from the fact that they had all studied at the University of Cambridge in the 1930s. We **(31)** _____ the names of four of the five for some time now. Some claim that all five men **(32)** _____ as Russian spies before they left Cambridge.

Donald Maclean: Maclean **(33)** _____ as a student Communist Party campaigner in Cambridge for some time when he was recruited by the Soviets. After completing his studies in 1934, he started work at the Foreign Office in London where he **(34)** _____ messages on to Moscow on a regular basis.

Guy Burgess: Burgess also went into the diplomatic service after being recruited by the Soviets. However, he **(35)** _____ an increasingly wild and irresponsible life, and the Russians started to see him as a problem As a result, Burgess **(36)** _____ Britain for Russia with Maclean in 1951.

Kim Philby: Philby had also spent a lot of time taking part in Communist Party activities when he was a student at Cambridge. Later, he **(37)** _____ an underground Communist Party organization in Vienna and was then recruited by the Soviets during World War II. Philby **(38)** _____ to hold high-profile positions in the British diplomatic service.

Anthony Blunt: Blunt was recruited into the NKVD, which would later become the KGB. He was recruited into MI5 (the British secret intelligence agency) where he passed decrypted Enigma messages to the Soviet Union during World War II. Blunt **(39)** _____ his activities as a spy for forty years when they were finally revealed in 1979 and he was stripped of the knighthood he **(40)** _____ in 1956.

0	**A** were	**B** had been	**C** have been	**D** were being
31	**A** knew	**B** had known	**C** have known	**D** know
32	**A** worked	**B** had worked	**C** have worked	**D** had been working
33	**A** was working	**B** used to work	**C** would work	**D** had been working
34	**A** has passed	**B** has been passing	**C** would pass	**D** had been passing
35	**A** was living	**B** had lived	**C** would live	**D** had been living
36	**A** was leaving	**B** used to left	**C** left	**D** had been leaving
37	**A** joined	**B** had joined	**C** was joining	**D** had been joining
38	**A** was going on	**B** had gone on	**C** went on	**D** had been going on
39	**A** was concealing	**B** used to conceal	**C** concealed	**D** had been concealing
40	**A** was receiving	**B** had received	**C** received	**D** had been receiving

Marks (out of 10): _____

READING

5 You're going to read an article about problems that companies have had with their brands. For the items below, choose from the sections from the article (A–E). The first one is done for you.

Brand blunders

A

Companies' success or failure often depends on the success of their brands. But even companies who we see as having very strong brands, such as Coca Cola, sometimes get it terribly wrong and experience what we could call brand blunders. These disasters usually result from the process of rebranding, where a company decides to change an aspect of its brand such as the name, the packaging or the product's ingredients. The aim of this process is, of course, to make the brand more popular and commercially successful. Indeed, if done correctly, rebranding can lead to tremendous success for a company, as it has done for brands like *Old Spice* and *Target*. However, as many companies have discovered to their cost, when rebranding goes wrong it can really go wrong and companies are often forced to reverse the changes they've made. Let's take a look at four examples where exactly this happened and try to figure out what the reasons for these brand blunders were.

B

The Ford motor company has built up a reputation as one of the most successful car manufacturers in the world, but even Ford has had its share of brand blunders over the years. In 1958, for example, Ford started selling a car called the Edsel, which has come to be seen as an example of how not to market a product amongst people who work in marketing. There were several reason for its lack of success. Firstly, the car was more expensive than the better-value cars bought by working people, but cheaper than the more exclusive models that the wealthy preferred. Then there was the fact that the Edsel was enormous at a time when smaller cars were becoming fashionable. Many people also thought that the car's design was very unattractive. It's believed that the car's disastrous sales performance cost Ford around $400 million.

C

Up until 1997, the British national carrier British Airways had always used the Union flag on the tail fins of its entire fleet of aeroplanes. However, in that year, the company decided to refresh its brand image and the Union flag was replaced by a range of colourful designs created by artists from around the world. According to British Airways' CEO, the aim was to give the company a more modern image and reflect changes in British life and culture. Many customers complained about the new designs. They actually liked the fact that the company represented Britishness and British values and that's what they wanted it to continue to represent. In 2001, British Airways reverted to the original Union flags on their aircraft and they've been there ever since.

D

Sometimes it's the rebranded product's name rather than its brand identity or image which causes problems as the manufacturers of 'Vegemite', the vegetable-based sandwich spread popular in Australia, found out when they decided to rename 'Vegemite' as 'iSnack 2.0' in 2009. Apparently, the letter 'i' was chosen because of the popularity of Apple devices, such as the iPod and iPhone and the company thought that the new name would help to give its products a 'cooler' image and make them more appealing to young people. The problem was that there was no connection between the world of personal technology and the food industry. Unlike the name 'Vegemite', which gives you a clear idea of what to expect from the product, 'iSnack 2.0' resulted in more confusion than connections amongst consumers and, unsurprisingly the name was changed back to just 'Vegemite' within five days.

E

Logos are an important component of brand identity and play an important role in determining its success. Effective logos are eye-catching, attractive and memorable. The credit card company MasterCard, therefore, ran into difficulties when it changed its logo to a new one that some consumers thought was downright ugly. The dark orange and yellow circles that we associate with MasterCard remained but another circle was super-imposed on top of them which was brown in colour, and it was this brown colour that people didn't like. Eventually, MasterCard admitted that the new logo wasn't working and went back to the original one.

Which paragraph

0	explains what a brand blunder is?	*A*
41	states that logos are an important part of brand identity?	_____
42	shows that even companies with very strong brands sometimes suffer brand blunders?	_____
43	gives an example of a company who wanted to adopt a cooler image?	_____
44	shows how important it is to give a product the right price?	_____
45	suggests that some companies rebrand in order to show that they're moving with the times and staying up-to-date?	_____
46	gives examples of companies for whom the rebranding process has been a success?	_____
47	mentions the connection people make between brands and national identities?	_____
48	mentions the importance of making a connection between the brand name and the product?	_____
49	suggests that consumers respond negatively to the use of some colours in brands?	_____
50	shows how consumer trends can affect a brand's success?	_____

Marks (out of 10): _____

LISTENING

6 🎧 **69** Listen to five short voicemails from people who want to contact Anna. Choose the option (A–H) from the list which best summarizes each voicemail. Use each letter only once. There are three extra letters which you do not need to use.

A someone who's helping Anna to buy a new home?
B someone who's helping Anna to organize her finances?
C someone Anna has to interview for a job?
D someone who's sold Anna something?
E someone Anna wants to sell her home to?
F a potential employer?
G someone who has bought something from Anna?
H a friend of Anna's?

51 Extract 1: _____
52 Extract 2: _____
53 Extract 3: _____
54 Extract 4: _____
55 Extract 5: _____

Marks (out of 10 – 2 points per correct answer): _____

SPEAKING

7 Prepare a two-minute presentation for your teacher about how your home country has changed over the last fifty years. You have five minutes to think of three ways in which your home country has changed. When you are ready, begin your presentation. Include the following in your presentation:
- the three ways in which your country has changed: these could be economic, social, political or cultural changes
- possible reasons for these changes
- what you think the future trends in these areas of change will be

After five minutes, give your presentation to your teacher. Make sure you include all three of the points above. Your teacher will ask you a question at the end.

You can receive ten marks for including all the points above, using the appropriate language for talking about the process and results of change, using the appropriate vocabulary for the changes you talk about and answering the teacher's question effectively.

Marks (out of 10): _____

WRITING

8 A city held a street food festival last weekend and it wants to hold another one in three months' time. Read the list of things that didn't go well at the event:
- there were complaints about the fact that visitors weren't allowed to bring their own drinks into the festival site
- there were long queues at almost all of the food trucks and some people had to wait up to 30 minutes
- there weren't enough parking spaces for everyone who wanted to park near the site
- there weren't enough rubbish bins and the visitors left a lot of rubbish on the festival site
- some people said that there could have been more signposts to help people to find the way to the festival site

Write a report on the event in which you make suggestions for how things could be done better next time. Write 140–190 words.

You can receive ten marks for making suggestions in response to the five points above, following the conventions for report writing, writing in an appropriate style and using appropriate language for making suggestions.

Marks (out of 10): _____

Name of student: _____

Total score out of 80 = _____ marks

VOCABULARY

1 Complete the text with the words in the box. There are three extra words you do not need. The first one is done for you.

budget	broke down	charge	~~control~~	cut back	deal	fees
partnership	into	invest	make	on	out	the

Financial matters

Ellen: I work in a bank and help our customers to **(0)** _____control_____ their finances. You might be surprised to hear that when I was a student, I got **(1)** _____ a lot of debt. Then I started working in a call centre, **(2)** _____ on the amount of money I was spending on clothes, and paid all of it back. After a few years, I decided to go travelling. While I was preparing for the trip, I had to work **(3)** _____ a budget and I realized I liked working with numbers. That was when I applied for a job at the bank.

Pietr: Last year, I set up a start-up. I got a lot of funding through *Kickstarter* and this enabled us to **(4)** _____ an offer for an old bakery. At first, I wanted to go it alone. But when I met Mina, I saw the benefits of forming a **(5)** _____ with another like-minded person and we've been working together ever since. Our company makes cupcakes and recently we made a **(6)** _____ with a local café to sell our cupcakes there.

Jurgen: When I first joined my current company, the finances were in a terrible state and I had to balance **(7)** _____ books. For example, our bank wanted to **(8)** _____ us a lot for our transactions, and I had to deal with that. We're with a new bank now and we don't have to pay such high **(9)** _____ for services like overseas bank transfers and they also give us good advice on how to **(10)** _____ our profits so that we get good returns.

Marks (out of 10): _____

2 Read the text and choose the word or expression (A–D) which best fits each gap. The first one is done for you.

Smartphone mania

Jenny: One day I was **(0)** __D__ the budget for an event which a client had agreed to **(11)** _____. Then we got talking and he **(12)** _____ his smartphone and started showing me some photos of his wife and children. I'm amazed by the fact that some people are so **(13)** _____ their phones that they'd rather interact with their electronic devices than old friends.

Rattan: I tried to cut back on the amount of time I spent using my smartphone, but I found that wasn't **(14)** _____ . A friend of mine told me that it was **(15)** _____ difficult for her to stop using hers and she'd decided to get rid of it. But what if I **(16)** _____ on the motorway and I need to call for help? One day, I went out to get some Chinese food to **(17)** _____ and on the way back, I decided to check the latest news on my phone. A police officer saw me, reported it and I was given a fine.

Sascha: One day I was making an international call while my phone was charging and the phone just **(18)** _____ , leaving me with hundreds of pieces of glass and plastic to clean up and **(19)** _____ . I had some notes for a presentation saved on the phone, but fortunately I was able to remember them and the presentation **(20)** _____ well anyway.

0	**A** cutting back	**B** getting into	**C** turning out	**D** working out
11	**A** charge	**B** invest	**C** sponsor	**D** balance
12	**A** picked out	**B** whipped out	**C** worked out	**D** turned out
13	**A** tied to	**B** slowed down by	**C** inspired by	**D** defended by
14	**A** doable	**B** workable	**C** getable	**D** makeable
15	**A** absolutely	**B** incredibly	**C** ultimately	**D** brilliantly
16	**A** break down	**B** break away	**C** break up	**D** break in
17	**A** mingle with	**B** take a shot at	**C** turn out	**D** take away
18	**A** blew up	**B** blew out	**C** blew away	**D** blew in
19	**A** throw off	**B** throw into	**C** throw from	**D** throw away
20	**A** turned out	**B** turned off	**C** turned on	**D** turned away

Marks (out of 10): _____

GRAMMAR

3 Complete the second sentence so that it has a similar meaning to the first sentence, using the word given. Do not change the word given. You must use between two and four words, including the word given. The first one is done for you.

0 I called you three times this morning, but I wasn't able to get through to you.   **couldn't**

I called you three times this morning, but I _____*couldn't get through*_____ to you.

21 Jasmine was able to convince her family to become vegetarian.   **managed**

Jasmine _____ convince her family to become vegetarian.

22 The IT training course that Ricardo went to last week was optional.   **have**

Ricardo _____ go to the IT training course last week.

23 I always ask my sister for advice when I need to make decisions.   **have**

If I _____ a decision, I always ask my sister for advice.

24 I've been on a lot of camping trips where the weather hasn't been good, but this year the weather was much worse than it usually is.   **particularly**

When I went camping this year, the weather was _____ .

25 It was impossible for us to get tickets for the festival.   **able**

We _____ get tickets for the festival.

26 Going running always helps me to relax after a difficult day at work.   **go**

If I've had a difficult day at work, I _____ .

27 Can you show me what to do?   **wonder**

I _____ show me what to do.

28 Richard made the visitors feel welcome when they came to the Stockholm office.   **succeeded**

Richard _____ the visitors feel welcome when they came to the Stockholm office.

29 I'm not worried about getting into debt next year because I have a lot of money in my savings account.   **have**

If I get into debt next year, I _____ enough money in my savings account to support myself for a while.

30 The connection speed of my new router is absolutely astonishing.   **really**

I'm _____ by the connection speed of my new router.

Marks (out of 10): _____

4 Read the text. Use the correct form of the word given in CAPITAL LETTERS at the end of some of the lines to fill the gap in the same line. Do not write more than three words in each gap. The first one is done for you.

Médecins Sans Frontières (MSF), or Doctors Without Borders to give it its English name, is an international organization that goes into conflict and disaster zones to provide medical assistance to people in need. When assistance **(0)** _____*is needed*_____ in a specific area, MSF doctors and support staff go into it and help the   **NEED**
people who live there, regardless of their race, religion or politics. If MSF **(31)** _____ there   **BE**
on the ground to help people in need, thousands more lives would be lost in these extreme situations. MSF was
founded in 1968 by a group of young French doctors who thought that the world **(32)** _____   **BE**
a better place if people went out and provided emergency help to anyone who needed it. If you're not genuinely
interested in helping people in need, you probably **(33)** _____ work with MSF. However, if   **COULD**
you're the type of person who wants to really make a difference, you **(34)** _____ the   **FIND**
experience incredibly rewarding. In addition, you **(35)** _____ be a doctor or a nurse to work   **HAVE TO**
with MSF. If you're an office worker who wants to get involved, you **(36)** _____ to find   **BE ABLE**
opportunities suitable for you too – just go to the MSF website. MSF wouldn't be able to do the work it does if it
(37) _____ donations from the public and funds from governments and other organizations.   **RECEIVE**
So if you **(38)** _____ to make a donation to MSF, you will also be contributing to its work. And   **BE ABLE**
you can also be sure that your money **(39)** _____ to an independent organization whose   **GO**
top priority is the health of the often neglected people who get caught up in wars and natural disasters, and which
(40) _____ in staying neutral during conflicts.   **SUCCEED**

Marks (out of 10): _____

READING

5 You're going to read a newspaper article in which a campaigner for standing at work discusses the effects that sitting or standing at work can have on people. Six sentences have been removed from the article. Choose from the sentences A–G the one which fits each gap. There is one extra sentence which you don't need to use. The first one is done for you.

Sitting – A twenty-first century disease?

In today's knowledge economy, we work with our heads rather than our hands. **(0)** ___D___ However, I would like to challenge that assumption and promote a new working culture where we don't sit, but stand.

You may have heard some scare-stories in the media about how bad sitting can be for your health. Some news outlets have been running stories where they've said sitting is more dangerous than smoking. **(41)** _____ The American Medical Association (AMA) says research studies have shown that sitting for long periods of time can, indeed, be bad for your health. Amongst the conditions which can be caused or worsened by extended periods of sitting, they list: diabetes, bowel cancer, high blood pressure, obesity and depression. Even if you don't develop diabetes or high blood pressure, you may still find yourself feeling a certain mental fogginess or malaise where you feel like you can't think clearly or concentrate on anything. The obvious solution would seem to be to tell people to go out, get some fresh air and get moving when they're not at work. **(42)** _____ Some experts have also suggested that the damage caused by ten hours of sitting cannot simply be undone by one hour of exercise.

So what can those of us who have to work in an office but also want to take care of our health do? Well, for me the obvious solution is to stand at work. Standing can have the same health benefits that walking does: it burns calories, boosts your energy levels, tones your muscles, improves your circulation and improves your posture. People who've managed to stand at work for longer periods of time, such as 3–6 months, have noticed the difference. **(43)** _____ Why pay for an expensive gym membership when you can get fit while you work? People love standing at work too! After trying standing at work for a while, the vast majority just don't want to go back to sitting.

We have to be realistic here though – standing at work all day may not be practical. It's natural that people would want to stop and sit down at times to take a break or to help them concentrate on something they have to work on closely and intensively. **(44)** _____ We recommend that people use an adjustable desk which can be used for either sitting or standing so that they can easily change between the two ways of working.

If you want to try standing at work, it's important that you stand properly. Stand with your toes facing forwards and pull your stomach in slightly. Make sure your back is straight too. You don't need to flex or tense up your body, but be aware of what is happening in your body. Once you've got the right posture, try doing regular shoulder rolls. It's also a good idea to go for regular walks around the office about once every hour and shake out your arms and legs.

If you notice any pain or discomfort at any time while either sitting or standing, make a change in your position or posture. If the problem continues for a longer period of time, you'll need to visit your doctor and get it checked out. It's also worth remembering that you don't have to work standing up every day, just making that change for two or three days out of five would be beneficial. **(45)** _____ Always remember to stay active and stay healthy too.

A Yet, our increasingly busy lives make it difficult for a lot of office workers to find the time – and just as importantly the energy – to do that.

B We have no problem whatsoever with people doing that.

C However you decide to work, it's important that you do it in a way that you feel comfortable with.

D Up until now we've thought that the best way to transfer our knowledge through our computers is by sitting down for anywhere from eight to fourteen hours a day.

E They've succeeded in losing weight they had been trying to get rid of for years, they have more energy and they feel more mentally alert.

F We would strongly advise against that.

G Well, let's look at the facts – what effects can sitting have on our bodies?

Marks (out of 10 – 2 points per correct answer): _____

LISTENING

6 ⒶⓉⒹ **70** Listen to a woman called Raquel talking about a company called 'Tea and Scones' which she runs. Complete the sentences with a word or short phrase. The first one is done for you.

0 Raquel started 'Tea and Scones' _____ *five* _____ years ago.

46 Raquel says that at the beginning she used her _____ to buy the equipment she needed.

47 Raquel started off selling tea and scones at _____ events.

48 Raquel decided to get a loan so that she could buy a _____ .

49 Raquel explains that using social media to promote her business helped her to get into contact with other _____ .

50 Raquel says she then started using _____ to get funding for her business.

51 Raquel was _____ by how much money people gave to her business through the site.

52 Raquel says she gave people the option of giving money in _____ funding units on the site.

53 Raquel says she then started using other funding sites where she had to write a _____ .

54 Raquel says that she also had to keep _____ updated on her business activities.

55 Raquel is now going to open a _____ in Highgate in London.

Marks (out of 10): _____

SPEAKING

7 Work in pairs, Student A and Student B.

Step 1

Student A: Talk about what personal technology is popular today, and say why you think it is.

Student B: Talk about what we can do to be ethical consumers, and why ethical consumerism is important.

Make sure you both:
- describe and explain trends in either personal technology use or ethical consumerism
- give reasons for these trends and explain the significance of them
- talk about the effects these trends have had

You have two minutes to think about what you are going to say. Student A, you go first.

Step 2

You are going to ask your partner about either personal technology or ethical consumerism.

Make sure you ask about:
- what effects it has had on their everyday life
- how it influences their purchasing decisions
- what trends they expect to see in the future

Student A: You ask Student B questions first.

Student B: Now you ask Student A.

You can receive ten marks for including all the points above and using a range of language.

Marks (out of 10): _____

WRITING

8 A website wants to write an article about consumers' experiences with different mobile phones and is looking for contributions. Write a review of your mobile phone. Include some basic facts about the phone, its features and what you like and don't like about it. Write 140–190 words.

You can receive ten marks for writing a review of your mobile phone and using intensifier + adjective combinations correctly.

Marks (out of 10): _____

Name of student: _____

Total score out of 80 = _____ marks

VOCABULARY

1 Complete the text with the words in the box. There are three extra words you do not need. The first one is done for you.

allowed	developed	enabled	encouraged	exploited	figured out	got round
inspired	introduced	messed around	put	recharged	replaced	switched off

The development of email

In 1971, ARPANET (Advanced Research Projects Agency Network) was just a large network which **(0)** _____*allowed*_____
computers at the US Defence Department to connect with each other. Nobody was sure how this new technology should best
be **(1)** _____ in order to benefit the public. Richard W. Watson, for example, **(2)** _____
that messages and files could be delivered to printers, but the 'Mail Box' protocol he created was never
(3) _____ into practice. That same year, ARPANET programmer Ray Tomlinson had
(4) _____ a local inter-user mail programme called SNDMSG which had been around from the early 1960s
and this new version of SNDMSG **(5)** _____ users to write, address and send messages to other users for
the first time. Up until then, electronic messages could only be sent by adding information to an existing file, but Tomlinson
(6) _____ the concept of sending messages directly by using an experimental file transfer programme
called CPYNET. This **(7)** _____ the problem of not being able to edit, delete or add to the original message
and eventually **(8)** _____ SNDMSG. After Tomlinson had **(9)** _____ with a few test
messages containing made-up words, he was ready to show the system to his colleagues. The breakthroughs that Tomlinson
had made **(10)** _____ other software engineers to continue developing email programmes and, as they say,
the rest is history.

Marks (out of 10): _____

2 Read the text and choose the word or expression (A–D) which best fits each gap. The first one is done for you.

Need a better work–life balance?

The number of people reporting symptoms of extreme physical, mental and emotional stress, also known as burnout, is
increasing year on year. Why are so many of us finding it difficult to **(0)** ___*D*___ and what can we do about it?

The fast-paced and constantly-connected nature of modern life can make it difficult for us to switch **(11)** _____ and relax and,
unfortunately, some people just can't. If you never take any time to **(12)** _____ your head and **(13)** _____ your batteries, you
can get sucked into a dangerous cycle of exhaustion and anxiety. No matter how often people tell you to **(14)** _____ it easy,
the thought of stopping and take a day **(15)** _____ feels scarier than carrying on. Work becomes such a dominant part of
your life that you just can't imagine what you would do if you had to take some of your annual **(16)** _____ , so you don't.

The first step to take when you want to break the cycle and regain a more normal work–life balance is to recognize that you
have a problem and to talk to people you can trust about it. Secondly, try to undo the damage by managing your stress levels,
for example by setting aside a few days when you can just **(17)** _____ from it all, **(18)** _____ your feet up and relax. Then you
just need to sustain those positive habits over a longer period of time. You could do this by setting aside a certain amount of
time every day, perhaps an hour at first and then longer, in which you spend **(19)** _____ doing things that make you feel good.
Once you've been doing that for a while, you may want to take a holiday. It doesn't really matter where you go, the
(20) _____ will do you a lot of good.

0	**A** put their feet up	**B** take a day off	**C** go out	**D** unwind
11	**A** off	**B** out	**C** on	**D** up
12	**A** unwind	**B** chill	**C** clear	**D** refresh
13	**A** recharge	**B** refresh	**C** take	**D** catch up with
14	**A** take	**B** make	**C** do	**D** feel
15	**A** on	**B** off	**C** in	**D** out
16	**A** scene	**B** quality time	**C** days off	**D** leave
17	**A** get away	**B** go away	**C** get lost	**D** forget
18	**A** take	**B** recharge	**C** refresh	**D** put
19	**A** feet up	**B** a day off	**C** leave	**D** quality time
20	**A** change of scene	**B** feeling refreshed	**C** chilling out	**D** day off

Marks (out of 10): _____

GRAMMAR

3 Complete the second sentence so that it has a similar meaning to the first sentence, using the word given. Do not change the word given. You must use between two and four words, including the word given. The first one is done for you.

0 The finished products are transported to this area where the machines then package them.
The finished products that _____*have been transported*_____ to this area are then packaged by machines. **been**

21 It will still be possible for changes to be made later.
Changes _____ later. **could**

22 When he came back to work, he saw that someone else had taken his desk.
When he came back to work, he saw that his desk _____ by someone else. **been**

23 We will give a prize of $10,000 to the inventor of the most innovative new product.
A $10,000 prize _____ to the inventor of the most innovative new product. **will**

24 The new boss said that the employees must have a break every 3–4 hours.
The new boss said that the employees must _____ a break every 3–4 hours. **remember**

25 The technicians in our lab have been investigating new ways of exploiting gene cell technology for the last six months.
The technicians in our lab _____ new ways of exploiting gene cell technology six months ago. **started**

26 In order to finish this project on time, I'll need to spend another twenty hours on it by the end of the week.
If I don't spend another twenty hours on this project by the end of the week, it _____ on time. **will**

27 My suggestion is that we take thirty minutes at the end of the day to unwind.
I _____ thirty minutes at the end of the day to unwind. **suggest**

28 We should publish this research before someone gets there before us.
This research _____ before someone gets there before us. **be**

29 I'm sorry I phoned my accountant so late at night.
I _____ my accountant so late at night. **regret**

30 It would be a good idea to examine this problem from a lot of different angles.
This problem _____ from a lot of different angles. **should**

Marks (out of 10): _____

4 Complete the text with the correct forms of the verbs in the box. The first one is done for you.

buy	chat	~~get~~	go	go out	meet
put	see	spend	think	use	

Jeremy

I'm a keen runner and like **(0)** _____to get_____ outside and run as often as I can. Recently, I found a website where runners can connect with each other and there's this community area with forums where you can chat to other runners. I sometimes post questions, but I usually forget **(31)** _____ back and check if there are any replies to the things I've posted! But this time I did and I remember **(32)** _____ a message from Graham there. I'd asked a question about whether I should use the same running shoes all the time and Graham suggested **(33)** _____ another pair of running shoes so that I'd have two pairs instead of just one. He said that then I would avoid **(34)** _____ too much pressure on one pair, but that I wouldn't notice any differences between the two pairs either. Graham and I carried on **(35)** _____ in the forums and then I found out that he lives near me! So we decided **(36)** _____ up for a run the following week. Now we go running together every week.

Liz

Well, I started **(37)** _____ the Matchmaking site about a year ago. You register, set up an online profile, and other people can view your profile and send you a direct message. One day, I checked my inbox and saw that I had a direct message from a guy called Patrick. I remember **(38)** _____ 'Wow, he seems like a really nice guy.' So we arranged **(39)** _____ for coffee. Funny thing was, when I walked into the café, I couldn't see Patrick anywhere. Then, I noticed someone waving at me. It was Patrick, but he looked completely different to his profile picture. He had clearly used a photo of someone else on Matchmaking! I felt deceived and hurt. Well, since then I've stopped **(40)** _____ time on online dating websites. I'd rather meet someone face-to-face.

Marks (out of 10): _____

READING

5 You're going to read a newspaper article about how we can use technology to improve people's lives. For the items below, choose from the sections from the article (A–E). The first one is done for you.

Tech for good

A

Nowadays when we think of the latest technology and what is currently state-of-the-art or cutting edge, we tend to think first of technology that we can use to communicate, like smartphones, or technology that's there to entertain us, like games consoles. What we usually don't realize is that technology can also make life easier for people with disabilities or illnesses by helping them with everyday tasks or helping them to manage their conditions. The Nominet Trust is an organization which identifies and promotes examples of what it calls 'tech for good', or, in other words, technology which can help to make people's lives better. They hope that by drawing public attention to these inventions they will be able to attract investment in them. Many of the innovations that the Nominet Trust promotes are designed to deal with social issues that arise in developing countries, but some can also help people anywhere in the world.

B

One of the most impressive innovations that the Nominet Trust has drawn attention to recently is a piece of wearable technology which allows blind people to see more than they could before. We've all heard about how wearable technology can help us to stay connected and to find the information we need even more easily, but few of us are probably aware of the fact that wearable technology can use 3D cameras to greatly improve the light perception of visually impaired people. As a result, they can manage to see outlines of close-up objects when before they would only have been able to see dark, blurred shapes. People who've tested the innovative glasses so far at Oxford University have described the effects as miraculous.

C

Then there's Jerry the bear, an interactive teddy bear that teaches children how to manage diabetes. It sounds improbable that a stuffed animal would be able to do such a thing, but this is a teddy bear with a difference. Jerry helps children to figure out how much insulin they will need to inject and enables them to practise injecting insulin in his legs and arms. Children can check Jerry's blood sugar levels by looking at sensors on his paws and a computer screen on his stomach that displays how much insulin needs to be injected into him. Jerry makes what can be a scary experience for children into something that's easier for them to deal with and provides them with a friend who'll always be there for them as they come to terms with having diabetes.

D

We're all familiar with navigation apps which can show us how to get from A to B, but if you're a wheelchair user, these apps won't necessarily be that helpful for you. Wheelchair users don't only need to know how to get from A to B, they also need to know which route they will be able to access in their wheelchairs. Now a website called Euan's Guide has been set up which shows routes and local businesses and facilities which can be accessed by the disabled in over 350 towns in the UK. The site even uses voice recognition technology so that it can also be accessed by the blind. Euan's Guide was awarded funding by British Telecom after winning an award for innovation in 2014 and it plans to use this award to extend its activities further so that it can help even more disabled people.

E

More and more people living in developed countries are feeling disconnected from the communities they live in and this problem is particularly widespread among the over-50s. This was the impetus for the setting up of an online service known as The Casserole Club which connects people by bringing them together to eat. It works in a similar way to an online dating website by allowing neighbours to get in touch with each other online and then arrange to meet up in one of their homes and eat together. For the elderly or disabled who don't get to eat a hot or home-cooked meal as often as they'd like to, these meals have a very positive impact on their lives. It's not only the food that they enjoy, but also having someone to talk to.

Which paragraph

0	gives an example of an innovation that is specifically designed to help children?	*C*
41	tells us about a company that is supporting an innovation?	_____
42	suggests that technology can help children to deal with the challenges they face?	_____
43	says that some people feel alone despite being surrounded by people?	_____
44	describes an organization that promotes innovations which can improve people's lives?	_____
45	gives an example of an innovation whose effects have been extremely surprising?	_____
46	gives an example of an innovation which enables people to meet each other?	_____
47	suggests that we usually think of technology for communication or entertainment when we think of technological innovations?	_____
48	mentions plans to increase the scope of a digital innovation?	_____
49	gives an example of a piece of technology which can act as a companion?	_____
50	mentions the number of places where a technological innovation can be used?	_____

Marks (out of 10): _____

LISTENING

6 🔊 **71** Listen to five short extracts in which people are talking about their work–life balance. Choose the option (A–H) from the list which best summarizes what each person says. Use each letter only once. There are three extra letters which you do not need to use.

    A feels the negative effects of not taking enough time to relax

    B uses yoga and meditation to help them unwind

    C thinks that it isn't possible to have it all

    D is told by friends and family that they need to slow down

    E thinks that you have to be a workaholic in order to succeed at work

    F has started spending more quality time with their family

    G is planning to limit the amount of time they spend looking at a screen

    H thinks we would be more relaxed if we stopping checking our phones all the time

    51 Speaker 1: _____

    52 Speaker 2: _____

    53 Speaker 3: _____

    54 Speaker 4: _____

    55 Speaker 5: _____

Marks (out of 10 – 2 points per correct answer): _____

SPEAKING

7 Work in pairs, Student A and Student B.

    Step 1: Imagine that a town by the sea wants more tourists to visit it. Take two minutes on your own to think of some ways in which the town could attract more visitors.

    Step 2: You now have two minutes to tell each other what you think the town could do and to explain why you think your ideas would work.

    Step 3: You now have two minutes to discuss the options you've both thought of together and decide on three things you would recommend to the town.

You can receive ten marks for using the appropriate language for discussing options.

Marks (out of 10): _____

WRITING

8 Write a short essay about an invention that you think is important. Include the following in your essay:
- What the invention is and how it works
- What its purpose is and what problem it solves
- Why you think it's an important invention

Write 140–190 words.

You can receive ten marks for including the above information in your essay, following the conventions for essay writing and using appropriate language for describing technological developments.

Marks (out of 10): _____

TEST 5 | Units 9 and 10

Name of student: _____

Total score out of 80 = _____ marks

VOCABULARY

1 Complete the sentences with the correct form of the word in CAPITAL LETTERS. The first one is done for you.

0 He's so _____*unrealistic*_____ – he'll never be able to save that much money on his salary. **REAL**

1 We stopped under trees by a lake – a perfect _____ for a picnic. **SET**

2 I know I'm being _____ , but I'm scared of snakes getting into my house. **RATIONAL**

3 I always get very _____ when I go to a wedding. **EMOTION**

4 They act very _____ towards people who are different to them. **OFFEND**

5 She's so _____ ! When I asked her how many users we have, she said 1,654,327. **PRECISION**

6 These ideas from the agency are very _____ – we've seen them a hundred times before. **IMAGINE**

7 The sales assistant didn't behave very _____ – she told me that the dress looked awful on me! **PROFESSION**

8 For me, it's _____ to take that route, when we could go another way and get there much faster. **LOGIC**

9 She's always been very _____ , so it's not surprising that she's working in strategic operations now. **ANALYZE**

10 These days I spend _____ ten hours a day staring at a screen. **ROUGH**

Marks (out of 10): _____

2 Read the text and choose the word or expression (A–D) which best fits each gap. The first one is done for you.

Customer service around the world

I'm a sales representative for a multinational company and, as a result, I have to travel a lot. I think I must have been to about twelve different countries in the last six months alone. When you travel as much as I do, you start to notice how people in different countries do customer service differently.

Let's start with the US. I go there quite a lot and every time I do, I notice that the serving staff in the restaurants where I eat are really friendly – that's definitely **(0)** __*C*__ with a smile for you. They always behave so **(11)** _____ , asking you how you are, calling you 'Sir' and wishing you a nice day. I'm not sure if they really mean it though. They're just waiting for you to ask for the **(12)** _____ and then **(13)** _____ them a big tip. I think 15–20 per cent is the norm over there.

Then there are the Germans. They tend to have quite a different attitude to customer service. You usually don't have to pay for **(14)** _____ like bread and water which they would **(15)** _____ you for in a country like Italy, but they don't always behave **(16)** _____ towards the customers, not greeting them or looking them in the eye, and speaking to them very abruptly. It can also take a long time to get the bill at the end of your meal. I have sometimes **(17)** _____ about bad service when I've been staying there.

Finally, you have the Brits. I once ate out in London and there was a mix-up with my order – they brought me something that I hadn't asked for. I got an **(18)** _____ for the mistake from the waiter which lasted for at least five minutes! I told him that it was OK and I was happy to eat the spaghetti carbonara he'd brought me, but they insisted on giving me a **(19)** _____ for the drinks I'd already paid for at the bar and **(20)** _____ me a free meal at the restaurant the next time I come to London.

0 **A** waitresses	**B** servers	**C** service	**D** restaurants
11 **A** politely	**B** inappropriately	**C** easily	**D** kindly
12 **A** invoice	**B** service charge	**C** complaint	**D** bill
13 **A** provide	**B** leave	**C** offer	**D** make
14 **A** side orders	**B** services	**C** extras	**D** additional items
15 **A** pay	**B** purchase	**C** charge	**D** order
16 **A** impolitely	**B** appropriately	**C** clearly	**D** badly
17 **A** made an apology	**B** complained	**C** charged	**D** rejected
18 **A** awareness	**B** order	**C** offer	**D** apology
19 **A** discount	**B** refund	**C** tip	**D** service charge
20 **A** provided	**B** offered	**C** paid	**D** made

Marks (out of 10): _____

GRAMMAR

3 Complete the text. Use only one word in each gap. In some cases, more than one word is possible. The first one is done for you.

The Campaign to End Loneliness is a non-profit organization **(0)** ___*that/which*___ was launched in 2011 in order
to help older people **(21)** _____ feel alone. They want to reach people **(22)** _____ friends or family
don't live nearby. Director Laura Ferguson **(23)** _____ us that some people they work with only get the chance to
spend time with others at the get-together events **(24)** _____ the campaign organizes.

Research into the effect of loneliness on people's mental and physical health, **(25)** _____ was done by the
University of Nottingham in 2014, showed that spending long periods of time alone can shorten people's life expectancy
by up to five years and this is just the scenario **(26)** _____ the campaign wants to prevent. The area
(27) _____ the organization has made the most progress is that of community action. Ferguson explained
that they **(28)** _____ made tremendous progress in building up a network of over 2,000 volunteers
(29) _____ organize community events. She added that their next target **(30)** _____ to increase that
number to 3,000 community volunteers over the next five years.

Marks (out of 10): _____

4 Complete the second sentence so that it has a similar meaning to the first sentence, using the word given. Do not change
the word given. You must use between two and four words, including the word given. The first one is done for you.

0 'This tower was built in 1443,' the tour guide said.   **built**
The tour guide told us that the tower ____*had been built*____ in 1443.

31 'Hackers have attacked the accounts of 2.4 million customers,' the CEO said.   **attacked**
The CEO said that hackers _____ the accounts of 2.4 million customers.

32 Hay-on-Wye is a small Welsh town known for its bookshops and it's formed a partnership with Timbuktu in Mali.   **formed**
Hay-on-Wye, _____ a partnership with Timbuktu in Mali, is a small Welsh
town known for its bookshops.

33 'We will be introducing an innovative new way of dealing with customer complaints,' the company
announced.   **would**
The company announced that they _____ an innovative new way of
dealing with customer complaints.

34 'How many of you were told to stop doodling at school?' asked the presenter.   **got into**
The presenter asked how many people in the audience _____ trouble
for doodling at school.

35 A colleague of mine never listens to people properly and nobody in the office likes her.   **listens**
A colleague of mine _____ to people properly is very unpopular
in the office.

36 'I have already spoken to two customer service advisors today!' the customer told me.   **spoken**
The customer told me that she _____ to two customer service
advisors that day.

37 'I will continue learning English next year because I really enjoyed it this year,' the student said.   **learning**
The student said that she _____ English next year because
she had really enjoyed it this year.

38 My cousin's home is in Helsinki. It is a very cosmopolitan city.   **lives**
Helsinki, _____ , is a very cosmopolitan city.

39 'Our travel agent won't give us a refund for our holiday,' the woman complained.   **refused**
The woman complained that the travel agent _____ give her a refund.

40 'I'm going to work on improving my listening skills,' said the teenager.   **going**
The teenager said she _____ work on improving her listening skills.

Marks (out of 10): _____

READING

5 You're going to read an article about a campaign to support women who have Asperger Syndrome. Choose the answer (A–D) which best fits according to the text. The first one is done for you.

My name is Mairi Sinclair and two years ago, I started a blog called *Happy with Asperger's* to reflect on my experiences as a woman who has Asperger Syndrome. After being diagnosed with Asperger Syndrome a few years ago, I trawled the Internet for information about what living with this psychological and emotional disorder is like. All I found was webpages about how uncomfortable sufferers feel and how unfriendly other people perceive them to be. I wanted to bring some more positivity to the conversation about what living with Asperger Syndrome is like. In fact, I believe that we can even see having the disorder as a gift because sufferers tend to be highly intelligent. They can also be individuals who think in a very logical way with strong analytical skills or who are very imaginative and have tremendous creativity. Since I began, I've received so many comments and emails from other sufferers who've told me how invaluable they've found my blog. They tell me it's given them a lot of hope and courage as they move forward in their lives because it paints such a realistic picture of everyday life with Asperger Syndrome without dwelling on the things that sufferers can't do.

Asperger Syndrome has received quite a lot of media attention recently as awareness of its existence has grown. We've heard about how everyone from the composer Wolfgang Amadeus Mozart to the inventor of the computer Alan Turing probably had Asperger Syndrome and there's even a television programme going out in the UK at the moment called *The Autistic Gardener* which features an Asperger Syndrome sufferer who uses his analytical thinking skills to design beautiful gardens! One thing that Mozart, Turing and the Autistic Gardener have in common though is their gender – they're all male – and Asperger Syndrome has typically been thought of as a disorder which affects men and boys. Indeed, experts have claimed that male Asperger Syndrome sufferers outnumber female sufferers by a ratio of 4:1. However, it has also been suggested that there are far more female Asperger Syndrome sufferers out there than we'd previously thought – because so many women and girls are unaware of the fact that they have the condition. Experts also think that females are better at hiding the symptoms of Asperger Syndrome than men because they naturally tend to be more sensitive than their male counterparts. Females with Asperger Syndrome are more likely to be shy and hide away from social contact whereas male sufferers tend to be louder and need more attention. The result is that a lot of women remain undiagnosed without knowing why they don't quite fit in with the people around them.

One of the first posts which I wrote on my blog was about how non-verbal signals can be unclear for Asperger Syndrome sufferers when they're interacting with other people. For example, someone could be giving me non-verbal signals which people would normally be able to interpret as meaning that the other person is irritated or annoyed by what I'm saying, but I would be unable to pick up on those signals and realize that I should either shut up or talk about something else instead. This kind of thing can make social interaction quite intimidating for us and make other people think we're very impolite. Lots of other people with Asperger Syndrome – female and male – commented on the blog post to say that they knew exactly what I meant and they'd had similar experiences. It's the kind of thing we usually can't talk to people about because only other Asperger Syndrome sufferers would be able to imagine what it feels like, but sharing these experiences is so valuable.

After building up a community of blog subscribers, some people told me that I should take it further. As a result, I decided to hold a live online discussion forum on the topic of understanding non-verbal signals. Instead of saying people with Asperger Syndrome react to non-verbal signals inappropriately, I wanted to look at what we can actually do to help us to tackle this issue. Since the first online discussion forum, we've held four more. What started as a blog has become a campaign to promote a dialogue between sufferers which focuses on how they can just live normal lives while minimizing the negative effects that the disorder can have on them.

0 Two years ago Mairi Sinclair started a blog about

   A what's it's like to be a blogger with Asperger Syndrome. ☐

   B how to blog about your experiences if you're a woman with Asperger Syndrome. ☐

   C how to reflect on your experiences if you have Asperger Syndrome. ☐

   D what's it's like for women to live with Asperger Syndrome. ✓

41 When she started looking for information about Asperger Syndrome online, Mairi found a lot of information about

   A the positive conversation that's going on about Asperger Syndrome. ☐

   B how many famous people have had Asperger Syndrome. ☐

   C the advantages that having Asperger Syndrome can bring. ☐

   D how difficult life with Asperger Syndrome can be. ☐

42 According to the article, other people often think that Asperger Syndrome sufferers are

   A insensitive. ☐

   B unfriendly. ☐

   C highly intelligent. ☐

   D impolite. ☐

43 One of the positive characteristics of Asperger Syndrome sufferers is how

   A realistic they can be. ☐

   B analytical they can be. ☐

   C positive they can be. ☐

   D friendly they can be. ☐

44 In recent years, public awareness of Asperger Syndrome

   A has declined. ☐

   B has remained more or less the same. ☐

   C has risen. ☐

   D has reached a peak. ☐

45 Statistics about the ratio of male to female Asperger Syndrome sufferers suggest that

   A there are four times more female sufferers. ☐

   B there are four times more male sufferers. ☐

   C male sufferers are four times more likely to be diagnosed. ☐

   D female sufferers are four times more likely to be diagnosed. ☐

46 Compared to male sufferers, female sufferers are more likely to

   A be highly intelligent. ☐

   B need a lot of attention. ☐

   C be insensitive. ☐

   D be quiet and reserved. ☐

47 Asperger's sufferers usually find it difficult to understand

   A unclear language. ☐

   B verbal signs. ☐

   C non-verbal signals. ☐

   D written language. ☐

48 People with Asperger Syndrome find being able to share experiences with other sufferers

   A inappropriate. ☐

   B impressive. ☐

   C invaluable. ☐

   D illogical. ☐

49 Mairi has now organized a number of

   A blog posts. ☐

   B live online forums. ☐

   C campaign meetings. ☐

   D events where sufferers can meet face-to-face. ☐

50 The focus of Mairi's campaign is on helping people with Asperger's to

   A live their lives as normally as possible. ☐

   B understand how other people feel. ☐

   C communicate with other sufferers online. ☐

   D let other people know how difficult their lives are. ☐

Marks (out of 10): _____

LISTENING

6 🔊 **72** Listen to a discussion between three colleagues. Complete the sentences with a word or short phrase. The first one is done for you.

   0 Marise welcomed Richard and Bonnie to the discussion about the _____*product launch*_____ .

51 The new product will be launched in the first week of _____ .

52 Marise asked her colleagues what they thought about giving customers a _____ discount.

53 Richard thought the best approach would be to give away some _____ .

54 Bonnie made the point that people often take free samples and then _____ and buy the product when it's on sale at its full price.

55 Marise then asked Richard how he felt about giving customers a _____ .

56 Marise wanted to hear Richard's and Bonnie's views on ways of launching the product _____ .

57 Richard suggested using sites such as Facebook and Twitter to _____ .

58 Marise suggested using a range of _____ on social media so that the posts aren't too repetitive.

59 Bonnie also said there could be an _____ .

60 Marise brought the meeting to a close and they agreed to meet again _____ at ten o'clock.

Marks (out of 10): _____

SPEAKING

7 Work in pairs, Student A and Student B.

Step 1

Student A: Talk about what you think it's like to work in a call centre where you're dealing with customer's complaints.
Student B: Talk about what you think it's like to work in a restaurant in the USA.

Make sure you both:
- describe the personal characteristics you need in order to do this job
- say what challenges and benefits this job brings the people who do it
- say whether you would like to do this job, giving reasons for your answer

You have two minutes to think about what you are going to say and two minutes to speak. Student A, you go first.

Step 2

You are going to ask your partner about the job they have, or have done or would like to do. You have two minutes to ask questions.

Make sure you ask about:
- the personal characteristics you need in order to do this job
- the challenges and benefits for the people who do this job
- whether they like this job, and why they like or don't like it

Student A: You ask Student B questions first.
Student B: Now you ask Student A.

You can receive ten marks for including all the points above and using a range of language.

Marks (out of 10): _____

WRITING

8 Write an article about either a good or bad customer service experience. Include the following in your article:
- The context in which you had this experience, i.e. where? when? what happened?
- What made it good or bad for you
- How you reacted to it
- How it will affect your future purchasing decisions

You can receive ten marks for including the above information in your article, following the conventions for article writing and using appropriate language for customer service.

Write 140–190 words.

Marks (out of 10): _____

TEST 6 | Units 11 and 12

Name of student: _____

Total score out of 80 = _____ marks

VOCABULARY

1 Complete the text with the words in the box. There are three extra words you do not need. The first one is done for you.

appreciate	barrel	carton	~~face~~	intend	mind	packet
piece	press	shot at	slice	stand up	tin	tube

Foodbanks in the UK

The unemployed are often seen as lazy money-grabbers, but the evidence which I've collected over the last ten years flies in the **(0)** _____*face*_____ of that stereotype. In fact, it's the last thing that comes to **(1)** _____ when I think of them. Many of the people who live below the poverty line have had a difficult start in life: some are mentally or physically disabled and they need someone to **(2)** _____ for them. Food banks want to give people in need a **(3)** _____ eating normally and hopefully also healthily. We've seen people who have so little food that they were sometimes only able to eat one **(4)** _____ of bread a day.

People come in and donate things to us. Even if you can only spare a **(5)** _____ of soup or a **(6)** _____ of toothpaste, we would be very grateful and will then distribute those items amongst the people who come into our food bank. I remember a child who came in the other day. I gave her a **(7)** _____ of biscuits and her eyes just lit up, she was so excited. Then there was this elderly lady who came and she was very happy to receive a **(8)** _____ of eggs. She said that she loved omelettes, but she couldn't usually afford to buy eggs. Another day, someone brought us a cake and the people who came into the food bank that day and got a **(9)** _____ of it were so pleased. I **(10)** _____ that some people think that these people should be helping themselves instead of getting help from us, but, personally, I couldn't turn them away.

Marks (out of 10): _____

2 Read the text and choose the correct word or expression (A–D) for each gap. The first one is done for you.

Why do young people get such a bad press?

We hear a lot in the media about how many problems young people cause, but is the **(0)** _*B*_ that they get really justified? I've heard so many negative things said about young people – one old lady even told me that finding a good sixteen-year-old was about as difficult as **(11)** _____ ! This old lady went on to tell me that the young people who hang around at the park near her home make her feel uncomfortable and even **(12)** _____ . I had to turn around and tell her that she was wrong. If I hadn't spent my life working with young people, I wouldn't have felt **(13)** _____ enough to do that.

I'm a youth worker and I run programmes to help troubled young people in Baltimore. The word 'troubled' probably makes you think of **(14)** _____ , out-of-control teenagers, but, in fact, the kids who come to us are very **(15)** _____ and lovely to be around ninety-five per cent of the time. There's just that other five per cent of the time when they lose control and sometimes become very **(16)** _____ , shouting at us and not being willing to accept the ground rules that we've laid down for them. As I mentioned, though, this is very much the exception rather than rule.

Sometimes I feel like the media is just **(17)** _____ what young people are really like. They should come down to visit some of my programmes and find out what the truth is. Far from being **(18)** _____ and thinking that they know it all, a lot of the young people we work with are actually quite **(19)** _____ and aren't aware of how much potential they have. These young people are, however, having to **(20)** _____ with other young people who've had a much more stable early life when it comes to getting places at a university or jobs, and that's not always easy for them.

0	**A** shot	**B** bad press	**C** needle in a haystack	**D** anxiety
11	**A** going head-to-head	**B** robbing a bank	**C** finding a needle in a haystack	**D** flying in the face of other people
12	**A** argumentative	**B** irresponsible	**C** outgoing	**D** anxious
13	**A** self-confident	**B** sensible	**C** wild	**D** arrogant
14	**A** wild	**B** independent	**C** terrified	**D** courageous
15	**A** irresponsible	**B** assertive	**C** courageous	**D** pleasant
16	**A** insecure	**B** sociable	**C** argumentative	**D** irresponsible
17	**A** flying in the face of	**B** wilfully blind to	**C** giving a bad press to	**D** daring to disagree with
18	**A** mad	**B** terrified	**C** insecure	**D** arrogant
19	**A** insecure	**B** self-confident	**C** independent	**D** arrogant
20	**A** feel anxious	**B** go head-to-head	**C** find a needle in a haystack	**D** be brave

Marks (out of 10): _____

GRAMMAR

3 Complete the second sentence so that it has a similar meaning to the first sentence, using the word given. Do not change the word given. You must use between two and four words, including the word given. The first one is done for you.

0 There's no mobile phone reception in this part of the building.   **isn't**
There _____ *isn't any* _____ mobile phone reception in this part
of the building.

21 The tourists didn't buy the city discount card because they didn't know about it, but now they wish
that they had.   **bought**
If the tourists had known about the city discount card, they _____ it.

22 She thought that big data was difficult to work with, so she said no to the job.   **realized**
If she _____ that big data wasn't actually difficult to work with,
she wouldn't still be looking for a job now.

23 GDL Electronics has sold over three million of these devices so far.   **huge**
A _____ of these devices have been sold so far by GDL Electronics.

24 I wish I could use the 3G on my phone to download more data – then I wouldn't need to use Wi-Fi at all. **able**
If I _____ use the 3G on my phone to download more data,
I wouldn't need to use Wi-Fi at all.

25 A motorbike rider came around the corner at a great speed and nearly knocked me down. If that had
happened, it's possible that I would have been paralyzed.   **left**
The motorbike rider _____ me without the use of my legs if he'd
knocked me down.

26 I had two careers advisors at school and both of them told me that law wasn't a career for girls. **neither**
_____ careers advisors I had at school thought that law was a
career for girls.

27 She became a model because someone from a modelling agency spotted her in a shopping centre
and offered her a contract.   **been**
If she _____ in the shopping centre on that day, she wouldn't have
been spotted by someone from a modelling agency and become a model.

28 Some delegates mistakenly didn't download the app which included the most up-to-date version
of the conference programme.   **downloaded**
If the delegates _____ the app, they wouldn't know the most
up-to-date version of the conference programme.

29 I only like a small number of films – it's difficult to please me!   **films**
There are only _____ that I like – it's difficult to please me!

30 I bought a more expensive tablet with extra memory capacity because I mistakenly thought I would
use it all.   **paid**
I _____ more money for the extra memory capacity if I'd have
known that I wouldn't use it all.

Marks (out of 10): _____

TEST 6 | Units 11 and 12

4 Complete the text. Use only one word in each gap or write a dash (–) if the gap should be left blank. The first one is done for you.

Chimamanda Ngozi Adichie

Chimamanda Ngozi Adichie is **(0)** _____*a*_____ well-known Nigerian novelist, short-story writer and activist. She was born in **(31)** _____ university town of Nsukka in Nigeria, where her father was a professor. After leaving school, Chimamanda originally studied **(32)** _____ medicine and pharmacy at the University of Nigeria before moving to Philadelphia in the USA. She went on to study creative writing and African studies at Johns Hopkins University and Yale, **(33)** _____ of which are top American universities. If Chimamanda had stayed in Nigeria, her work **(34)** _____ show the great awareness of the experience of immigration which it does.

Chimamanda Ngozi Adichie's first novel *Purple Hibiscus* was published in 2003 and won the Orange Prize for fiction **(35)** _____ following year. If Chimamanda had stopped writing there, we wouldn't have **(36)** _____ able to read her next two novels and the volume of short stories she published subsequently. A **(37)** _____ of people have watched her 2009 TED Talk 'The danger of a single story' and since then she has gone on to give **(38)** _____ other high-profile lectures and talks, which have also been well received, and another talk at TEDx in 2012. Chimamanda has famously said that if people wanted to call her a feminist, she **(39)** _____ be happy with that label. She says that if there are **(40)** _____ young girls out there who want to write, they should have the courage to go ahead and tell their stories.

Marks (out of 10): _____

READING

5 You're going to read a magazine article about change management. Six sentences have been removed from the article. Choose from the sentences A–G the one which fits each gap. There is one extra sentence which you don't need to use. The first one is done for you.

Managing the dynamics of change management

If you go into any workplace, you're likely to find people who have more influence than others. These tend to be quite self-confident and bold individuals that others go to when they have fears or concerns, people whose opinions are trusted, and any comments that they make tend to be passed around the workplace. **(0)** __*D*__ An important thing you need to know about these people though, is that they can be divided into two types – the champions and the antagonists – and the two need to be handled differently. **(41)** _____

The champions are co-operative influencers who will happily support their leader at times of change and actively encourage other employees to get on board. **(42)** _____ You cannot and should not be the only one who's out there in the workplace actively encouraging people to support the change you want to introduce. To give you an example: one manager I know who heads up an eighty-person team wanted to introduce a more systematic and standardized way of meeting training and development needs so that the more insecure employees would benefit from the company's training programmes as much as the more self-confident ones. **(43)** _____ They said they'd encourage their colleagues to jump on board with it. He thought this was great and then it occurred to him that if he'd known he had employees with that kind of attitude in his team to start with, he'd have thought of a strategy for using their support and this would have made the implementation of the changes he wanted to make go a little more smoothly.

However, you can't expect your champions to just magically appear. You have to be proactive, get out there and make them like you. The typical office champion would be a secretary or personal assistant as they tend to be very pleasant, sociable people that others feel they can rely on and trust. You may also find that people doing other jobs are more suitable champions though, so don't restrict your search for champions to them. Actually make the time to listen to what your employees say to each other and pay attention to how they interact.

Unfortunately though, some managers are not only failing to identify their champions, they're actually going directly to the people who are going to give them the least support. **(44)** _____ An antagonist is someone who is hostile to and opposes the change that their managers want to implement. A huge number of managers are attracted to these people because they're working under the misapprehension that if you get the people who are likely to oppose you on your side, everyone else will agree with you too. **(45)** _____ If you go to your antagonists first and they don't accept your pitch for change, you've effectively just built up a group of angry, unco-operative people who are likely to spread negativity around their workplace and make it harder for your champions to generate support. My advice would be to forget about the antagonists to begin with and start by working with your champions. This should ensure that a positive message, is spread around the office and give you the strong platform you need. In short, all you need to know is that successful change management can only be achieved by managers who are able to harness the influence of their champions.

A We all know that this is how successful managers strike the right balance.
B Let me tell you a little bit more about each of these types.
C Unfortunately though, this isn't always how it works.
D So if you're planning to bring about change at work, you would want to get these influencers on your side.
E After he'd introduced the initiative, some employees came up to him and told him what a good idea it was.
F These are the people that I call the antagonists.
G Furthermore, these people are particularly important during large-scale changes, such as when you want your team to start using a new piece of technology or follow a new procedure for completing routine tasks.

Marks (out of 10 – 2 points per correct answer): _____

LISTENING

6 🎧 **73** Listen to Carlo Zizzo talking about his work and his philosophy. Listen and choose the best answer (A–C).

0 Carlo Zizzo lives in
  A Naples. ☐
  B Salerno. ✓
  C Sicily. ☐

46 Carlo Zizzo is a
  A food critic. ☐
  B chef. ☐
  C philosopher. ☐

47 Carlo Zizzo learned to cook from his
  A uncle. ☐
  B grandmother. ☐
  C school friends. ☐

48 When Carlo was young, he
  A did the washing up for his grandmother. ☐
  B prepared food for a restaurant. ☐
  C worked in his uncle's hotel. ☐

49 At Zizzo's, Carlo tries to serve foods that
  A people have stopped eating. ☐
  B people ate during the middle ages. ☐
  C people don't usually want to eat. ☐

50 One of the things that Carlo likes to serve is
  A fish tails. ☐
  B fresh fish. ☐
  C fish collars. ☐

51 Carlo found out about the slow food movement after
  A deciding he didn't want to throw any food away. ☐
  B deciding he wanted to do something to protect his food heritage. ☐
  C becoming interested in forgotten foods. ☐

52 Carlo says that it's important to him to respect
  A his food heritage. ☐
  B his customers. ☐
  C fresh flavours. ☐

53 The result of Carlo's slow food cooking is that the customers in his restaurant get more
  A consistency. ☐
  B unusual foods. ☐
  C variety. ☐

54 As a result of the way he cooks, Carlo is able to support
  A local fishmongers. ☐
  B small local food producers. ☐
  C his customers. ☐

55 Carlo can't understand why anyone would
  A want to eat mass-produced, processed food. ☐
  B want to eat food at anyone else's restaurant. ☐
  C want to eat dishes that don't contain forgotten foods. ☐

Marks (out of 10): _____

SPEAKING

7 Work in pairs, Student A and Student B.

Step 1

Student A: Talk about the movements or causes that you support, and say why you support them.

Student B: Talk about someone you admire, and say why you admire this person.

Make sure you both:
- describe the movement/cause or person
- give reasons for your choices
- talk about what effect the movement/cause or person has had on your life

You have two minutes to think about what you are going to say and two minutes to speak. Student A, you go first.

Step 2

You are going to ask your partner about changes they would like to happen. You have two minutes to ask questions.

Make sure you ask about:
- what changes they would make in their lives if they were able to go back in time
- what changes they would like to make in their own lives
- what changes they would like to make to the world if they could

Student A: You ask Student B questions first.

Student B: Now you ask Student A.

You can receive ten marks for including all the points above and using a range of language.

Marks (out of 10): _____

WRITING

8 You have received this email from Francesca Melcher who wants to stay at the Bed & Breakfast you run. Read the email and then write your reply. You don't have any rooms free on the dates when Francesca wants to stay at your Bed & Breakfast, so you suggest an alternative. Write 140–190 words.

> Dear Sir or Madam
>
> We will be visiting Porto in August and came across an advertisement for your Bed & Breakfast. I would like to book one double room for the nights of 12–16 August. Could you please confirm the booking for us?
>
> Many thanks in advance.
>
> Kind regards
>
> Francesca Melcher

You can receive ten marks for responding to the email above, writing your email in an appropriate style, and using appropriate language for apologizing and suggesting alternatives.

Marks (out of 10): _____

Answer key

To score each test as a percentage, take the total mark (e.g. 60), divide by 80 (e.g. 0.75) and multiply by 100 = 75%.

Test 1 (Units 1 and 2)

VOCABULARY

1

1 assist   2 interested in   3 deal with   4 involved in
5 head up   6 create   7 focus on   8 co-ordinate
9 responsible for   10 passionate about

2

11 D   12 C   13 A   14 D   15 A   16 C   17 D   18 B
19 A   20 D

GRAMMAR

3

21 collects and saves   22 is being streamed
23 will have completed   24 are dealt with   25 'll/will never forget   26 is investigating   27 will be running   28 views the ability   29 'll/will have earned   30 will be spending

4

31 will be using   32 will have become   33 'll/will see
34 are being sold   35 will have   36 'll/will be travelling
37 'll/will be using   38 'll/will grow   39 is estimated
40 're/are living

READING

5

41 B   42 D   43 A   44 A   45 C   46 D   47 A   48 B
49 D   50 B

LISTENING

6

51 an office   52 university   53 marketing   54 five
55 at home   56 role   57 deal with   58 weakness
59 leader   60 climbing

Transcript 68

S = Stefan, D = Daniela

S: Hello. You must be Daniela Fisher. Nice to meet you. My name's Stefan.

D: Nice to meet you, Stefan.

S: Please take a seat. … So, we're looking for someone to join our sales team as a key account manager. Maybe you could start by telling me something about your academic qualifications.

D: Yes, of course. First I trained as an office clerk and then I went to university and did a degree in business studies, specializing in marketing.

S: OK, great. And what did you do after you completed your studies?

D: I was at BMI for five years and I gained a lot of insights into selling software to large companies.

S: OK, but now you want to make a move into more of an office-based job?

D: Yes. I enjoyed my previous job and I learned a lot from it, but I've just bought a place of my own and I'd like to spend more time at home.

S: OK, so what do you think you will be doing in five years' time?

D: I certainly hope that I'll be working here as a key account manager.

S: OK, great. And what about in ten years' time?

D: I'd like to have a global role in your company where I can deal with customers from all over the world.

S: OK, and what would you say your greatest weakness is?

D: Well, I'm definitely the type of person who is always looking to develop professionally. But if I had to think of a weakness I have, it would probably be that I'm a perfectionist. I always want to do things to the best of my ability and I get frustrated if that's not possible.

S: OK, why would that not be possible?

D: Well, it could be that the other people I'm working with aren't doing their jobs to the best of their ability.

S: OK, so then tell me: what kind of team player are you?

D: I love working in teams, but I think I'm a natural leader. I'm good at leading and inspiring other people, but I also know how to delegate.

S: So what do you like to do in your free time?

D: Well, my main interest is climbing. I like to get outdoors in the mountains at the weekend.

S: Wow, that sounds dangerous!

D: It's all perfectly safe. You've got your helmet and other equipment. And all the climbers look out for each other while we're out there.

S: OK, but rather you than me! Right, well it's been great talking to you, Daniela. We should be able to give you a definite answer either way by the end of the week.

D: Thanks very much. Bye.

S: Bye.

SPEAKING

7

Use these criteria to award a maximum of ten marks. Give two marks if the student meets each criterion well, one mark if their performance is satisfactory, and no marks if they do not meet the criterion at all.

Did the student …

- complete the task, i.e. talk about everything they were asked to?
- speak fluently, i.e. without too much hesitation?

- speak accurately, with correct grammar and vocabulary, and a clear pronunciation?
- interact with you appropriately?
- use language for making arrangements presented in Unit 2?

WRITING

8

Use these criteria to award a maximum of ten marks. Give two marks if the student's writing meets each criterion well, one mark if their writing is satisfactory, and no marks if they do not meet the criterion at all.

Did the letter …

- have an appropriate greeting and ending?
- use appropriate language to explain why the student is the best person for the job?
- use appropriate language to explain what the student's career goals are?
- use accurate grammar and vocabulary, and good punctuation and paragraphing?
- have an appropriate formal style?

Test 2 (Units 3 and 4)

VOCABULARY

1

1 growth   2 safe   3 successful   4 motivate
5 quantitative   6 optimistic   7 secure   8 perfect
9 quality   10 influential

2

11 A   12 A   13 D   14 B   15 B   16 A   17 D   18 D
19 A   20 B

GRAMMAR

3

21 have become   22 has been supporting   23 has been
24 has only accepted   25 used to research
26 has been growing   27 had been working   28 had been
29 had been based   30 has been using

4

31 C   32 D   33 D   34 C   35 A   36 C   37 A   38 C
39 D   40 B

READING

5

41 E   42 A   43 D   44 B   45 C   46 A   47 C   48 D
49 E   50 B

LISTENING

6

51 F   52 A   53 H   54 B   55 D

Transcript 69

1

Hello, Anna. You'll be pleased to hear that we've decided to shortlist you for an interview at Johnson & Johnson. We'd like to see you at 1 pm on 10th April and the interview will take place in the showroom in building 66. Come to reception and our receptionist will tell you how to get there. Bye.

2

Hello, Anna. John Webster from David Carr Estate Agents here. You may remember that you asked me to contact the owners of that house you were interested in and set up a time for you to view it. Well, I've been in touch with them and they said you could call round on Friday afternoon from four o'clock onwards. Could you let me know if that's a good time for you? Then I can get back to the owners and confirm it with them. Many thanks. Bye.

3

Hi Anna, this is Tara. I thought we were meeting at the bistro at 12, but it's 12.15 now and I can't see you anywhere. I've looked inside and outside. I'm just standing in front of the entrance, so if you're coming up from the high street you should be able to see me. If you could give me a call back to let me know where you are, that would be great. See you later, bye.

4

Hello, Anna. My name's Clark Simpson from Sanderson & Sanderson. You asked me to give you a call when I had finished calculating how much tax you would have to pay for the last financial year, but I see you're not available at the moment. Would it be possible for you to come into the office on either the 21st or 22nd to discuss a couple of things with us? We're open from nine until five. Look forward to hearing from you.

5

Hi, Anna. This is Frederick Sandy. Because you bought a car from us two years ago, you're now eligible for a discount on a new vehicle if you let us take your old one off your hands. This means that you could get up to twenty per cent off one of our brand new models. I'll be in the office until 6 pm if you want to call me back today. Otherwise, I'll be back in the office tomorrow from 9. Talk to you later.

SPEAKING

7

Use these criteria to award a maximum of ten marks: see Test 1.

Did the student …

- complete the task, i.e. talk about everything they were asked to?
- speak fluently, i.e. without too much hesitation?
- speak accurately, with correct grammar and vocabulary, and a clear pronunciation?
- respond to your question appropriately?
- use language for talking about the process and results of change presented in Unit 3?

WRITING

8

Use these criteria to award a maximum of ten marks: see Test 1.

Did the report …

- introduce and outline the context?
- respond to the list of things that didn't go well
- use language for making suggestions presented in Unit 4?
- use accurate grammar and vocabulary, and good punctuation and paragraphing?
- use the appropriate register for a report?

Test 3 (Units 5 and 6)

VOCABULARY

1

1 into   2 cut back   3 out   4 make   5 partnership
6 deal   7 the   8 charge   9 fees   10 invest

2

11 C   12 B   13 A   14 A   15 B   16 A   17 D   18 A
19 D   20 A

GRAMMAR

3

21 managed to   22 didn't have to   23 have to make
24 particularly bad   25 weren't able to   26 go running
27 wonder if you can   28 succeeded in making
29 'll/will have   30 really astonished

4

31 wasn't   32 would be   33 couldn't   34 'll/will find
35 don't have to   36 'll/will be able   37 didn't receive
38 're/are able   39 will go   40 succeeds

READING

5

41 G   42 A   43 E   44 B   45 C

LISTENING

6

46 (personal) savings   47 small local / small / local
48 van   49 entrepreneurs   50 *Kickstarter*   51 surprised
52 £15 / 15 pound   53 business plan   54 investors
55 shop

Transcript 70

I started 'Tea and Scones' five years ago after I'd graduated from university. I used my personal savings to buy some basic equipment for making tea and scones, and I started off at some small local events near to where I live in North London. I got really positive feedback from customers and some people suggested I should buy a van so that I could travel around to different events more easily. But I couldn't afford that then, so

I decided to go to the bank and get a £5,000 loan. That was quite a big step and I was worried about getting into debt.

That was also when I started using the Internet to let people know about what I was doing. I set up a Facebook page, a Twitter account and a company website. Social media also helped me to make contact with other entrepreneurs with similar businesses and they told me about Kickstarter. It's a site where you can ask for funding for your business. If other people see your business on the site and they want to invest in it, they can. I set my funding units at £15, so you could give me £15 or 30, 45, 60, and so on. Within about an hour of joining and posting on the site, eight people had already contacted me, and within a week two hundred had agreed to fund me. I was really surprised – I had never expected that at all!

I started to expand the business and go to more events and festivals. I also took on my first employee. But after a while I realized that if I was really going to make a living from this, I would need to find a funding model that would be more appropriate for the type of larger-scale company that I wanted to build. That was when I found another site where you can get investment in return for shares in your business and some of the investors on there were interested in me! It was just a bit scary because I had to write a proper business plan and send it to them. I also had to keep them updated on my income and outgoings on a weekly basis. And I had to update them as soon as anything changed, like when I took on another person to work with me.

I'd love to own a shop in London, and now I'm going to open one in Highgate, so that's a massive step for me. I'll wait and see how that goes before I decide whether I've made it!

SPEAKING

7

Use these criteria to award a maximum of ten marks: see Test 1.

Did the student …

- complete the task, i.e. talk about everything they were asked to?
- speak fluently, i.e. without too much hesitation?
- speak accurately, with correct grammar and vocabulary, and a clear pronunciation?
- ask natural questions and interact with their partner appropriately?
- use appropriate language for talking about technology and ethical consumerism?

WRITING

8

Use these criteria to award a maximum of ten marks: see Test 1.

Did the review …

- include everything the student was asked to include?
- explain what the student likes and dislikes about their mobile phone?
- use intensifier + adjective combinations?

- use accurate grammar and vocabulary, and good punctuation and paragraphing?
- follow the conventions for review writing?

Test 4 (Units 7 and 8)

VOCABULARY

1

1 exploited   2 figured out   3 put   4 developed
5 enabled   6 introduced   7 got round   8 replaced
9 messed around   10 encouraged

2

11 A   12 C   13 A   14 A   15 B   16 D   17 A   18 D
19 D   20 A

GRAMMAR

3

21 could (still) be made   22 had been taken   23 will be
given   24 remember to have   25 started investigating /
to investigate   26 won't / will not be finished   27 suggest
taking   28 should be published   29 regret phoning
30 should be examined

4

31 to go   32 seeing   33 buying   34 putting   35 chatting
36 to meet   37 using   38 thinking   39 to go out
40 spending

READING

5

41 D   42 C   43 E   44 A   45 B   46 E   47 A   48 D
49 C   50 D

LISTENING

6

51 D   52 E   53 B   54 F   55 C

Transcript 71

1

I'm a teacher and I usually work about 70 hours a week. I know that some of the people close to me are a bit worried because they see how exhausted I am all the time. One of them suggested I try yoga or meditation, but that's not really my thing to be honest. They think that I should be working less, basically, and taking it easy. I'm not sure how I'm going to manage that and get everything done for school though.

2

I've always worked a lot. Even when I was at school, I preferred reading and studying to playing football or going out with friends! It seems strange to most people I suppose, but looking back, my work ethic has helped me to get where I am today. I'm a Chief Market Analyst at an international bank and I've had to work very

long hours to make my way up the career leader. You really have to let your work take over your life if you want to get on.

3

I work in customer service, so I sit at my computer all day. My eyes can get really sore. Recently though, I've started going to a yoga class once a week and it does me such a lot of good. Afterwards, I feel completely refreshed and I've forgotten all about the customers who've called me to complain that day. Sometimes, I do a little bit of meditation too. I found it hard to clear my mind and think of nothing at first, but now that I've been doing it for a few months, it comes much easier to me.

4

A few months ago, I saw this TED Talk about work–life balance. This guy told a story about how he had spent an afternoon messing around with his son, and his son told him it had been the best day of his life. That really made me stop and think. I couldn't remember the last time I did something like that with my children. After that, I decided to make an effort to spend time with my kids at the weekend. We've had some really good times together, and now I make sure that I never work on Saturday or Sunday and I just enjoy spending the whole day with my children.

5

I had always been a career woman. Then my husband and I decided to start a family. I thought I could take a few months off to be with the baby and then carry on working as I'd done before. Things didn't work out quite as I'd planned though. When I was at work, I was constantly worrying about my daughter. Then when I was with her, I was completely worn out and constantly checking my phone. That was when I decided to choose my family over my career, rather than trying to have both at the same time. I feel much happier as a result.

SPEAKING

7

Use these criteria to award a maximum of ten marks: see Test 1.

Did the student …

- complete the task, i.e. talk about everything they were asked to?
- speak fluently, i.e. without too much hesitation?
- speak accurately, with correct grammar and vocabulary, and a clear pronunciation?
- use appropriate language for making suggestions?
- use language for discussing options presented in Unit 8?

WRITING

8

Use these criteria to award a maximum of ten marks: see Test 1.

Did the essay …

- include everything the student was asked to include?
- have an introduction, a main body and a conclusion?
- use language for describing technological developments?

- use accurate grammar and vocabulary, and good punctuation and paragraphing?
- follow the conventions for essay writing?

Test 5 (Units 9 and 10)

VOCABULARY

1

1 setting 2 irrational 3 emotional 4 offensively
5 precise 6 unimaginative 7 professionally
8 illogical 9 analytical 10 roughly

2

11 A 12 D 13 B 14 C 15 C 16 B 17 B 18 D
19 B 20 B

GRAMMAR

3

21 that/who 22 whose 23 told 24 that/which
25 which 26 that/which 27 where 28 had
29 who 30 was

4

31 had attacked 32 which has formed 33 would be
introducing 34 had got into 35 who never listens
36 had (already) spoken 37 would continue learning
38 where my cousin lives 39 refused to 40 was going to

READING

5

41 D 42 B 43 B 44 C 45 B 46 D 47 C
48 C 49 B 50 A

LISTENING

6

51 May 52 ten per cent / 10% 53 free samples
54 don't come back 55 discount 56 online 57 promote
the launch 58 images and messages / messages and
images 59 online competition 60 next Monday

Transcript 72

M = Marise, R = Richard, B = Bonnie

M: So, hello Richard, hello Bonnie. Thanks for coming, guys. Great to have you here. As you know, today we're here to discuss the launch of our new product – Soda Life. We'll be launching Soda Life at the start of May. We need to decide the best way to launch the product. I was thinking that we could offer a ten per cent discount on the product's recommended retail price. What are your thoughts on that?

R: Well, Marise, I'm not so sure about the discount idea, to be honest. As far as I'm concerned, the best way is to give away free samples instead. People always love free samples.

M: OK, thanks for that, Richard. How about you, Bonnie? Do you agree?

B: Erm, well, I just wanted to say that people do love free samples, but then most of them don't come back so they never buy the product when it's on sale at its full price afterwards. I'm more in favour of giving a discount.

M: OK, so it looks like two out of three of us are in favour of giving a discount. How do you feel about that, Richard?

R: I think I can live with that, Marise.

M: Great, thank you, Richard. Now, I'd be interested in your opinions on how to launch the product online. Do either of you have any thoughts on that?

R: Well, my suggestion is that we should, of course, promote the launch on our Facebook page as much as we can and do the same on Twitter.

M: Sure, that sounds good to me. How about having some different images and messages that we can use in the posts so that they don't get too repetitive?

R: Great idea.

B: Yes, we can do that. And one more thing, we could have a competition that people can enter online and win Soda prizes.

M: I like that … yeah … Richard, I know you've done this kind of thing before, what do you think is the best way to organize the competition?

R: Just give me a bit of time to think about that and I'll get back to you with some ideas right away.

M: Great. So, just to sum up, we've agreed to offer a ten per cent discount when we launch and run a full social media marketing campaign with a competition. And I'll look forward to hearing from you later about how to organize the competition, Richard. Bonnie, maybe you can work on the images and messages for the social media posts.

B: Sure.

R: Yeah, will do.

M: Great. Let's meet next Monday at ten o'clock then …

SPEAKING

7

Use these criteria to award a maximum of ten marks: see Test 1.

Did the student …

- complete the task, i.e. talk about everything they were asked to?
- speak fluently, i.e. without too much hesitation?
- speak accurately, with correct grammar and vocabulary, and a clear pronunciation?
- ask natural questions and interact with their partner appropriately?
- use personality adjectives and language for customer service presented in Units 9 and 10?

WRITING

8

Use these criteria to award a maximum of ten marks: see Test 1.

Did the article …

- include everything the student was asked to include?
- use language for customer service presented in Unit 10?
- accurately use reported speech where appropriate?
- use accurate grammar and vocabulary, and good punctuation and paragraphing?
- follow the conventions for article writing?

Test 6 (Units 11 and 12)

VOCABULARY

1

1 mind   2 stand up   3 shot at   4 slice   5 tin
6 tube   7 packet   8 carton   9 piece   10 appreciate

2

11 C   12 D   13 A   14 A   15 D   16 C   17 B   18 D
19 A   20 B

GRAMMAR

3

21 would have bought   22 'd/had realized   23 huge number
24 was/were able to   25 could have left   26 Neither of the
27 hadn't been   28 hadn't downloaded   29 a few films
30 wouldn't have paid

4

31 the   32 –   33 both   34 wouldn't   35 the   36 been
37 lot   38 –   39 would   40 any

READING

5

41 B   42 G   43 E   44 F   45 C

LISTENING

6

46 B   47 B   48 C   49 A   50 C   51 C   52 A   53 C
54 B   55 A

Transcript 73

My name is Carlo Zizzo. I live in the town of Salerno, which is just to the south of Naples in Italy. I'm a chef and my cooking style is typical southern Italian. My grandmother is the one who taught me how to cook and then my uncle, who had a hotel in Salerno, asked me if I wanted to come and work in the kitchen in his hotel in my summer holidays when I was at secondary school. I loved every minute of those summer holidays. I started off just doing the washing up and taking the trash out, and then later on they allowed me to help out with the food preparation, which I thought was absolutely fascinating. If you'd told me

back then that I would go on to become a real chef one day, I would have been absolutely overjoyed, I can tell you.

Anyway, now I have my own restaurant, it's called Zizzo's, and what I tried to do there is to find forgotten Italian food that nobody really eats anymore and put it on people's plates again. These are just simple things like varieties of cheese or tomatoes that people don't really eat any longer. I love fresh fish and I cook with fish collars, the meaty bit on fish's backs that people often just throw away – they're the best part of the fish! You can use just about every part of a fish. When I started to get interested in forgotten foods, I found out about the slow food movement because protecting those types of foods is one of the things they want to do too. The aim is to protect our food heritage going back hundreds of years and this is something that is really important to me personally. It's also all about keeping centuries-old culinary expertise alive today and when we do that, not only do we keep our cultural traditions alive, we also help to ensure that people will have more choice and flavour when they go out to eat. Otherwise, there is a bit of a tendency to move towards a kind of monotone food culture, where everyone is basically eating different combinations of the same ingredients, cooked in the same way. And who wants that?

The plates of food I serve up are fresh, they're full of flavour and, by eating them, my customers help to champion the small-scale producers I work with and make sure that their own food traditions are preserved. What more could you want? I know that's how I want to eat!

SPEAKING

7

Use these criteria to award a maximum of ten marks: see Test 1.

Did the student …

- complete the task, i.e. talk about everything they were asked to?
- speak fluently, i.e. without too much hesitation?
- speak accurately, with correct grammar and vocabulary, and a clear pronunciation?
- ask natural questions and interact with their partner appropriately?
- use language for movements and looking back on life with the benefit of hindsight presented in Units 11 and 12?

WRITING

8

Use these criteria to award a maximum of ten marks: see Test 1.

Did the email …

- start with a greeting and a reference to the previous email?
- inform the reader about the situation?
- include an apology and an alternative suggestion?
- use accurate grammar and vocabulary, and good punctuation and paragraphing?
- include a friendly ending?

Communicative activities

1.1 This page is unavailable

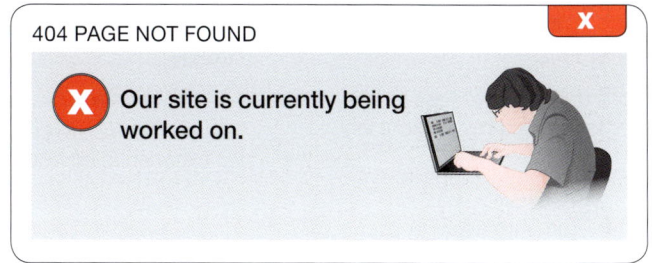

This page is unavailable.   **X**

X We are currently working on our site.

404 PAGE NOT FOUND   **X**

X Our site is currently being worked on.

1 Work in pairs and discuss the questions.

  1 Do you have your own website?
  2 Does your company have a website?
  3 Are you a member of an association, club or group that has its own website?

2 Choose one website and tell your partner what features or types of information visitors to this website can see.
For example, are there any pictures, colours, logos or any other features that visitors can see more than once on the website?
Write short sentences about your partner's website. For example:
There are pictures of people playing tennis.
It has lots of different blues.

_____

_____

_____

_____

_____

3 Think up an appropriate message that visitors to a language school's website will see when the site is down or the page they want is still being developed. Write the message on the empty webpage below. Make notes about the type of image, photo or video you would use to accompany the message.

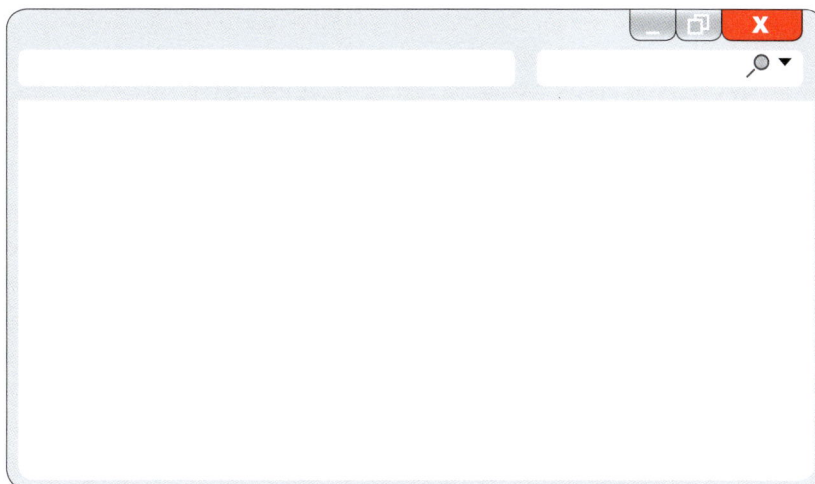

4 Create a message that visitors will see when a website from one of these types of business is unavailable.

building company	café / restaurant	car hire	comic shop
dental practice	flower delivery service	gardener	hairdresser
rubbish collection	sports studio	tourist information	

5 Present your ideas to the class. Also, tell other students how their messages and images make you (the visitor to the website) feel.

1.2 What do we have in common?

1 Complete the sentences with information about yourself.

    1 I live _____ (where).

    2 I speak _____ (languages).

    3 I started my present job _____ (when).

    4 I have _____ (months/years) experience of working in / studying _____ (field of business or topic).

    5 I am interested in _____ (free-time activities).

2 Choose the option to make the sentences true for you.

    1 *I write / I don't write* a blog.

    2 *I've tried / I've never tried* to start up my own business.

    3 *I'm involved / I'm not involved* in a charity.

    4 *I've done / I haven't done* voluntary work.

    5 *I'm taking/ I'm not taking* another course at the moment.

    6 *I post / I don't post* updates and photos on social media.

3 Mingle and have small-talk conversations. Use opening sentences to start the conversations and then ask follow-up questions to try to find something in common with every person you talk to. Make notes.

Opening sentences

> Hello, I don't think we've met. I'm …

> Do you mind if I join you?

> I believe you live/work … ?

Follow-up questions

> Do we both … ?

> So, how do you like … ?

> Are you currently … ?

Things I have in common with:

_____ _____

_____ _____

_____ _____

_____ _____

_____ _____

_____ _____

_____ _____

2.1 Hopes and plans

1 Complete the table with verbs and adjectives that naturally and frequently appear before the word *goal*.

Verbs	Adjectives	
		GOAL

2 Find two more words that mean the same as *goal* and write them in the third column of the table.

3 Use the words in the **Questions** column of the table to write questions for your survey.

Questions	Interviewee 1	Interviewee 2	Interviewee 3
holiday / next year *Where are you going to go on holiday next year?*			
plans / retirement			
aims / short-term			
targets / work			
live / ten years' time			
goals / twelve months			

4 Use your survey to interview other students. Ask follow-up questions where appropriate. Make notes in the table. Continue on a second page if required.

5 Compare and discuss the answers the interviewees gave you. How effective were your questions? How could you improve them?

WEB DESIGNER	JOURNALIST	BANK CLERK
COMPUTER PROGRAMMER	TRANSLATOR	PSYCHOLOGIST
CHEF/COOK	PARCEL DELIVERY PERSON	TRAIN DRIVER
SUPERMARKET CASHIER	(ENGLISH) LANGUAGE TEACHER	TRAVEL AGENT
TAX ADVISOR / ACCOUNTANT	CHILDMINDER	HOUSE PAINTER
INSURANCE SALESPERSON	NURSE / CARE ASSISTANT	SECRETARY / PA (PERSONAL ASSISTANT)

3.1 Have you made a donation?

Text A

The UK Giving Study was started in _____ by the Charities Aid Foundation (CAF). Every year since then, it [1] *has collected and analysed / has been collecting and analysing* information about the donations that people in the UK make to charities each year.

Since 2005, the CAF [2] *have interviewed / have been interviewing* more than 25,000 people. Some of their more recent findings [3] *have shown / have been showing* that:

- Just over half (52%) of the UK population give to charity each year. The average amount that people donate [4] *has remained / has been remaining* at around _____ for a few years.

- Women have always been more likely to donate than men.

- 66% of women aged 45–64 donate to charity and usually donate the largest amounts.

- _____ are the least likely to give to charity (52%), but it was found that when they did donate they usually gave more – £42 on average.

Throughout the study, _____ has always been the most common donation method. Unsurprisingly, more and more donations are now being made online, although donating via direct debit [5] *has increased / has been increasing* too.

Medical research has consistently been the cause that most people supported, followed by hospitals and hospices, and _____. In general, more women [6] *have given / have been giving* money to these causes than men. The only causes that men have donated more to than women have been sports-related charities.

The study also discovered that the types of charities people donated to often depended on the age of the person giving. Those aged over 65 years often support ▩▩▩▩▩▩▩▩▩ while younger people are more likely to support ▩▩▩▩▩▩▩▩▩ .

✂ -

Text B

The UK Giving Study was started in 2005 by the Charities Aid Foundation (CAF). Every year since then, it [1] *has collected and analysed / has been collecting and analysing* information about the donations that people in the UK make to charities each year.

Since 2005, the CAF [2] *have interviewed / have been interviewing* more than _____ people. Some of their more recent findings [3] *have shown / have been showing* that:

- Just over half (52%) of the UK population give to charity each year. The average amount that people donate [4] *has remained / has been remaining* at around £30 for a few years.

- Women have always been more likely to donate than men.

- _____ of women aged 45–64 donate to charity and usually donate the largest amounts.

- Londoners are the least likely to give to charity (52%), but it was found that when they did donate they usually gave more – _____ on average.

Throughout the study, cash has always been the most common donation method. Unsurprisingly, more and more donations are now being made online, although donating via _____ _____ [5] *has increased / has been increasing* too.

Medical research has consistently been the cause that most people supported, followed by hospitals and hospices, and children and young people. In general, more women [6] *have given / have been giving* money to these causes than men. The only causes that men have donated more to than women have been _____ charities.

The study also discovered that the types of charities people donated to often depended on the age of the person giving. Those aged over 65 years often support ▩▩▩▩▩▩▩▩▩ while younger people are more likely to support ▩▩▩▩▩▩▩▩▩ .

3.2 Sleep survey

1 Put the words in order to make survey questions.

2 Work with four other students. Write their names here. Ask your questions.

A _____ B _____ C _____ D _____

3 Discuss and report your findings.

Questions	A	B	C	D
1 _____? go / what / to / do / sleep / you / time / usually				
before 10 pm				
between 10 pm and midnight				
after midnight				
2 _____? time / wake / do / what / usually / you / up				
before 6 am				
between 6 am and 7 am				
after 7 am				
3 _____? many / how / average / you / hours' / sleep / do / get / on				
less than 6				
6–8				
more than 8				
4 _____? the / many / during / times / wake / do / you / up / how / night				
zero				
1–3				
more than 3				
5 _____? room / how / is / your / sleep / when / dark / you				
completely dark				
mostly dark				
not dark at all				
6 _____? enough / do / how / you / sleep / you / often / get / think				
always				
mostly				
sometimes				
never				
7 _____? you / important / to / how / is / night's / good / a / sleep				
very important				
neither unimportant nor very important				
not important				

4.1 Listen, sketch and retell

Text A

Gloria has been living in Paris for almost fifteen years now. Before moving to France, she lived with her mother and father in Togo. She didn't have any brothers or sisters, so she was expected to help her parents on the small family farm.

Gloria was a quiet child who had a real talent for drawing. She often used to get into trouble with her parents and her school teacher as she would be so focused on her drawing that she would forget to milk the goat, get the water or do her homework. All she ever used to think about was where to get pencils and paper for her drawings.

When she was fifteen, an art teacher from Paris visited Gloria's school on an exchange programme. This teacher recognized Gloria's talent and decided that she would do everything she could to help her. It took two years and a lot of paperwork, but when Gloria was seventeen the teacher managed to get her a free place at an art college in Paris.

Since then, Gloria has had three exhibitions in Paris, and has written and illustrated a best-selling book for children about growing up in Togo. Due to the success of her first book, Gloria was able to send money back to her parents in Togo. Her parents have built themselves a new house in which there is a special room where the local children have art lessons with Gloria when she visits. Gloria is currently working on her second book, which is expected to be a great success.

✂ -

Text B

Until recently, Raul lived in a small, sleepy town in the south of Spain. At the weekends and in the school holidays, he used to work in his family's restaurant in the town square. It was boring work as there really weren't many customers in those days. Raul was always a small boy with a huge passion for dance. In the opinion of Raul's father, dancing, unless it was Spanish flamenco dancing, was not something that boys or men did.

Raul's uncle arranged for Raul to take bull-fighting classes in the next town – Raul attended once and never went back again! Instead, he secretly took dancing lessons with a retired ballerina.

Very soon, Raul was inventing his own dance routines with the hope that one day he would be able to attend the ballet academy in Madrid.

One of Raul's friends filmed Raul dancing and posted the video on the Internet. To Raul's amazement, the video went viral. At first, Raul's father was angry, but it didn't take him long to realize that his son's dancing talent could bring in a lot of business.

Within a few weeks, tourists were going to his family's restaurant hoping to see him dance. For the past two years, when he is not at the ballet academy in Madrid, Raul has been dancing for customers in the restaurant. Raul's father has bought the empty building next door and plans to expand the restaurant, as these days, if you want to eat there, you have to book a table at least a month in advance.

4.2 Improving the partnership

1 Work in groups. Decide whether you want to talk about your school or your town. Then complete the text by choosing between the alternatives and writing the missing information.

> **Situation**
>
> Your school/town has a relatively new partnership with a school/town in _____ (where).
>
> _____ (number) visitors from your partner school/town have just left. They visited you for _____ (number) days. It was their first visit, and it was a disaster for many reasons!
>
> Next _____ (when), you are going to visit them in their school/town. They are probably not looking forward to your visit.
>
> How are you going to make things better between you? This is an important partnership and you want to have a good and friendly relationship when you visit them. Additionally, you want to learn from the things that went wrong so that next year's visit (you hope it will still take place) will be much more of a success.

2 Make a list of all the things that went wrong during your partners' visit.

> **What went wrong**
>
> _____
> _____
> _____
> _____
> _____
> _____
> _____
> _____
> _____
> _____
> _____
> _____
> _____

3 Hold a meeting. Discuss the points on your list. Make and respond to suggestions about how to address these problems and improve the relationship between you and your partners. Make notes.

4 Write the minutes from your meeting.

5 Present your suggestions and plan of action to the rest of the class.

5.1 A short collaborative story

1 Use your imagination to complete some basic biographical details about the person in your story.

Name: _____

Age: _____

Nationality: _____

Occupation: _____

Lives in _____

with _____

2 Write the first sentence of a short story about the person in your story: line a. Include the modal verb and any other words or information given.

3 Pass the story on to other students so that they write a sentence each: b–f. Continue in this way until the story is complete.

a _____ couldn't _____

_____

b Therefore, he/she wasn't able to _____

_____

c It was because (*make an excuse*) _____

_____

d But he/she had to have _____

_____

e _____ managed to _____

_____

f _____ succeeded in _____

_____

4 Get your story back from the student who wrote sentence f. Read your story. Is it similar to or different from what you expected?

5.2 Financing a new business idea

1 Work in pairs. What is your new business or idea?

_____

_____

_____

2 What are the three best ways to finance your new business or idea?

| angel investors | banks | crowd funding | personal savings | private loan | shareholders |

1st choice: _____

Positive and negative aspects of this type of financing

_____

_____

Questions you have about this type of financing

_____

_____

_____

2nd choice: _____

Positive and negative aspects of this type of financing

_____

_____

Questions you have about this type of financing

_____

_____

_____

3rd choice: _____

Positive and negative aspects of this type of financing

_____

_____

Questions you have about this type of financing

_____

_____

_____

3 Tell the class about your new business or idea and talk about how you could fund it. Ask for other students' feedback and suggestions, and answer any questions they might have.

6.1 If ....

If it **snows** today,	If you've lost your **keys**,
If the **bees** all died,	If someone shouts '**shark!**',
If you go to the **Grand Canyon**,	If your new **phone** breaks,
If you are looking at the **Pyramids**,	If my friends were more **passionate about** _____ ,

✂

6.2 Can I just check that?

Call 1: Hotel requirements for Student A

You want to book a hotel for you and your partner for a relaxing weekend break. You like walking and sightseeing, and eating out in the evening (your partner is a vegetarian). You plan to travel there by car – arriving around 4pm Friday afternoon – and would appreciate something to eat after your long drive.

✂ ---

Call 1: Hotel information for Student B (the receptionist at each hotel)

Castle Hotel: 20 rooms with shower or bath, toilet, TV and cosy seating area. Large buffet breakfast. Traditional grill restaurant open 6 pm – 10 pm. Reception open 8 am – 6 pm. Parking €5 per day (booking required). Free Wi-Fi in reception area. Located in beautiful hilly countryside. Nearest town 7 km. Lake 2 km.

Park hotel: Located next to the river in the old town centre park. 10 double, 4 single rooms, all with shower and toilet. Free parking and bicycle hire. Wi-Fi in all rooms. Free newspapers in the breakfast room. Breakfast only. Check in 2 pm. Check out 11 am. Special weekend rates available (includes theatre tickets). Distance to town centre: 500 metres. Lake 10 km.

Green sports hotel: A modern low-energy hotel located close to the romantic lake with various facilities for cycling, jogging and walking. The restaurant is open from 7 am – 11 pm and offers local dishes as well as food for special diets. 60 spacious rooms. Free parking and Wi-Fi. Swimming pool, sauna, fitness room and spa treatment area. Sports bar with large TV. Path to the lake. Town centre 5 km (free bus service).

✂ ---

Call 2: Conference venue requirements for Student B

Student B: Your medium-sized company needs a venue for a five-day sales and marketing conference. You need at least four rooms for workshops and talks. You expect about 200 participants from all over the world; some of them will be visiting your country for the first time.

✂ ---

Call 2: Conference venue information for Student A (the manager at each venue)

1 New multi-purpose centre in city centre, next to train station. Airport 30 minutes by train. 8 meeting rooms, plus large theatre-style room (holds 300). Drinks and finger food can be provided at extra cost. Technical equipment can be hired by the day. From £700 per day.

2 Large popular conference centre at the airport. £40 per person per day. Includes two tea and coffee breaks, and buffet lunch. City centre 30 minutes by train. Parking £20 per day. Walkway to airport hotels. 45 rooms of different sizes, some with projectors and speakers.

3 Former factory, now conference and event centre. 8 large adaptable spaces. Café/bar with alcohol licence. Modern lighting and sound system. Large car park. Near motorway. 70 miles from international airport. Town centre 3 miles. From £1,000 per day.

e-bike

airport body scanner

satellite navigation systems for cars

barcode

bionic arm

Wi-Fi

Electric bikes are often described as new and revolutionary, but they are probably older than you think. An electric bicycle was invented and patented in 1897 by Hosea W Libbey of Boston. That bike was driven by a double electric motor.

Today e-bikes are popular in Europe – for example, they are ridden by German postal workers – but they are banned in some US cities such as New York!

Full-body scanners were first introduced as a part of airport security in 2007 and by 2010 they had been installed at all US airports. However, they were replaced by new scanners, called millimetre-wave scanners, after passengers complained that security staff were able to see the outline of their bodies.

It has been reported that since this change, four out of five Americans now support the use of Advanced Imaging Technology at US airports.

Satellite-based global positioning technology was first developed for the US military in the 1960s, but satellite navigation systems for cars did not become widely available until 2000. Even then, only a few cars were equipped with sat nav systems.

These days most new cars are sold with sat navs (or GPS) already installed – as we would be lost without them!

The first patent for a barcode was issued to inventors Joseph Woodland and Bernard Silver in 1952. It took many years before the barcode was used commercially as there were no industry standards until the 1970s.

George J Laurer is considered to be the inventor of UPC, or Uniform Product Code, which was invented in 1973 and is still used today.

The first product to have a barcode included was a packet of chewing gum.

The bionic arm is a prosthetic that is fitted to people who have lost their arm in an accident. The first bionic arm prototype was developed and tested between 2007 and 2011.

In 2013, a soldier who was wounded in Afghanistan was fitted with a prosthetic arm that can be controlled by thoughts. He was the first British person to receive a bionic arm and is now called 'The Six Million Dollar Man' by his friends after a character in an old US TV show.

Wireless local area networks (Wi-Fi) was made available to everyone in the US in 1985. Shortly after that, the IEEE (Institute of Electrical and Electronics Engineers) and the Wi-Fi Alliance were formed to help develop and regulate wireless technology worldwide.

The term Wi-Fi began to be used commercially in 1999. The name is often written as WiFi or Wifi.

7.2 Create, adapt, enable

Situation

You have been asked to put forward an idea for a special garden for people who are unable to see.

The garden is behind the school for the visually-impaired and the blind. It is approximately 500 square metres in size and is surrounded on three sides by a two-metre high wall. There are currently two old trees in the garden: a cherry tree and an apple tree. There is also a small pond in one corner and a broken path, and the garden has grown wild as it has not been used since the school moved into the building five years ago.

The school has 55 day-pupils who are 6–18 years old. The head teacher has asked for interesting technological elements to be included in the garden.

There is a budget of £20,000 for the whole project.

1   Work in groups. Think about things that would make the garden interesting for visually-impaired pupils. Brainstorm things that you would like to put in the garden. Write them on the mind map.

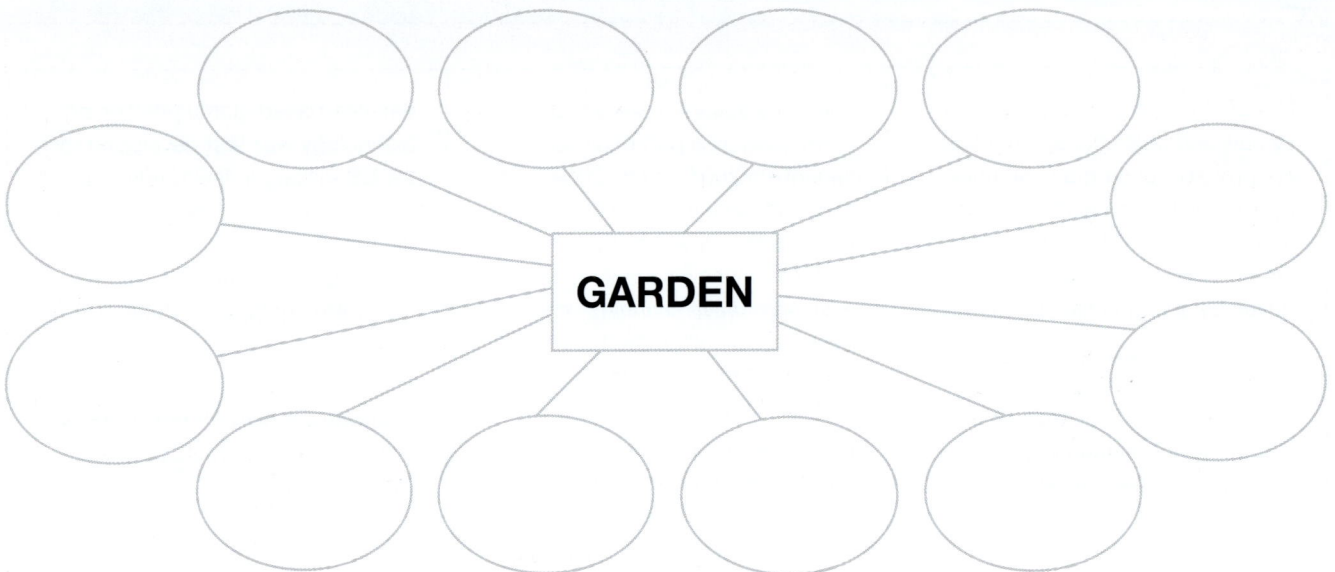

GARDEN

2   Discuss the contents of your mind map in greater detail. Do you really want to include everything in the garden? Do you need to improve or adapt some of the things to suit the school and the pupils' needs? What benefits will they bring? Choose 6–8 things that you will include in your garden idea and make notes.

_____

_____

_____

_____

_____

3   Think about layout and design, the costs, the weather, the pupils' special needs, the educational and emotional benefits your garden would bring to the pupils, problems you might come across and ways to deal with these. Prepare a presentation.

4   Present your ideas to the class.

8.1 About us and our lives

Statements	1 false	2 almost false	3 neither true nor false	4 almost true	5 true
1 I spend at least an hour each day relaxing.	1	2	3	4	5
2 I never check my work emails before going to bed.	1	2	3	4	5
3 I don't mind being without internet access for a day.	1	2	3	4	5
4 I plan to take at least two weeks' holiday this year.	1	2	3	4	5
5 I enjoy socializing with my colleagues.	1	2	3	4	5
6 I try to do sports at least twice a week.	1	2	3	4	5
7 I make time each month to help other people.	1	2	3	4	5
8 I try not to stay at work late or do overtime more than once a week.	1	2	3	4	5
9 I regularly make time to go for a walk.	1	2	3	4	5
10 I enjoy cooking for (or eating with) my friends and family.	1	2	3	4	5

Statements	1 false	2 almost false	3 neither true nor false	4 almost true	5 true
1	1	2	3	4	5
2	1	2	3	4	5
3	1	2	3	4	5
4	1	2	3	4	5
5	1	2	3	4	5
6	1	2	3	4	5

Communicative activities

8.2 The best option

Option A

Name: Castle House

What: An old large country house.

Rooms: 12 rooms, each with 4 beds and its own bathroom. 2 large seminar rooms. Indoor and outdoor eating area.

Cost: €150 per person for 5 nights.

Food: Additional €10 for breakfast only, or €30 for breakfast and dinner (non-alcoholic drinks included). No private use of kitchen.

Getting there: 1.5 hours by coach, 2 hours by train.

Additional information: Near to castle ruins. Large park/garden. May have to share the accommodation with another group.

Option B

Name: Lakeside Lodge

What: Basic accommodation building belonging to a mountain climbers' association.

Rooms: Upstairs: 4 dormitories, each with 8 beds, plus 4 basic bathrooms. Downstairs: large communal room and kitchen.

Cost: €1,000 for the week.

Food: No food provided, but you can use the kitchen.

Getting there: 3–4 hours by coach.

Additional information: Need to bring sleeping bags and food. Barbecue place with seating next to lake. 10-minute drive or 30-minute walk to nearest village with shops.

Option C

Name: Sea View Hotel

What: Small hotel available out of season for private group hire.

Rooms: 10 double and 6 single rooms, all with bathroom.

Cost: €2,500 for 5 nights.

Food: Breakfast included. Dinner available upon request (extra charge).

Getting there: 5 hours by train plus 30 minutes by boat.

Additional information: On quiet island with large natural beach. Free bicycle hire available.

9.1 Where, who, which, whose

Disneyland	Eiffel Tower, Paris	Hollywood
Wall Street, New York	Buckingham Palace, London	Las Vegas
Porsche	Coca Cola	The Red Cross
Nike	Apple	Chanel
Hillary Clinton	Nelson Mandela	Elvis Presley
The Beatles	Cristiano Ronaldo	Neil Armstrong

Communicative activities

9.2 A great event

Agenda for the kick-off meeting	Information	Notes
1 Where to hold the event?	The small local park is available. Alternatively, the police will allow you to close one quiet street for the event.	
2 Day of the week, and time?		
3 What entertainment / music / games should be provided?	All age groups are expected to attend – from families with small children to pensioners.	
4 What food and drink should be provided?	Consider the weather and time of year.	
5 How much should a ticket cost?	There is no budget or funding. Do you want to raise money beforehand or cover all the costs through ticket sales?	
6 What sort of decorations should there be?		
7 What other practical or organizational aspects should you talk about?	Consider safety, electricity, rubbish collection, noise, etc.	

Basic details

The event: _____ (what) will take place on _____ (when)
from _____ o'clock until _____. It will be held _____ (where).

Tickets will cost _____ (how much).

We plan to provide _____ (what).

Sub-committee members:

Finance: _____

Entertainment: _____

Decoration: _____

Catering: _____

10.1 The visitors' book

Student A

Comments	Name	Email
Lovely exhibition, although I would have put the green vase in the same room as the blue lion as these obviously belonged together. Well done to all the volunteers!	Joseph Brown	J.Brown@brownbros.com
We loved the tree painting and tried to buy it, but unfortunately it wasn't for sale. What a shame!	Sophie Davis	sophie@davisfamily.com
The flyer said: Doors open at 10. My wife and I arrived on time (as always) and waited five minutes outside in the rain, under our golf umbrellas, until someone unlocked the main door.	Reginald Davenport (Mr)	R.Davenport@telecom.net
Thank you for the delightful exhibition. Our only complaint is that the toilets were on the second floor and the lift was broken. I had to push my wife to the library two streets away so that she could use the disabled toilet there.	Frank and Dorothy Sayer	thesayers@talktalk.com
The exhibition was OK, but the queue for the tea and coffee was too long, and the cake was not fresh.	Christine Simon	info@ChrisSi_systems.net

✂ -

Student B

Comments	Name	Email
A fantastic exhibition and a great idea to allow the scouts to sell tea and cake. My son helped out on the tea stand today. They made nearly £200 which they will put towards buying a new tent for their scout camp.	Anna Ivanov	a.ivanov@ivanov.org
What a great exhibition! Well done! I would happily have paid an entrance fee. How can I make a donation to your charity?	Doris O'Brien	DOB@dmail.edu
We visited the exhibition today with our children. My husband enjoyed it, but the children were bored. Sorry about the broken mirror.	The Andrews family	andrews@family.com
We enjoyed the exhibition very much. May I suggest that next time you have a cloakroom where people can leave their umbrellas? Someone's large umbrella must have dripped all the way through Room 1. My 89-year-old father slipped and banged his head. Luckily, he wasn't seriously injured.	Maria Rossi	info@rossi.co.uk
My partner wanted to see the exhibition, but it wasn't my kind of thing at all. I'd wanted to stay at home and watch the football. She enjoyed it though and told me I should write something nice So, ... cheers!	Dave Hunter	theman@davethebuilder.com

10.2 Cultural tips

Write up a list of helpful cultural tips for someone who is coming from another country and plans to work at your company / attend your school or university.

_____ is considered inappropriate because _____

_____

To avoid misunderstandings, _____

_____

People here might think that _____ is impolite because _____

_____

At first, you might feel that the people here are _____

_____

You might be unaware that _____

_____

In a restaurant you _____,
but in a works canteen or school cafeteria _____

If something is unclear, it is normal behaviour to _____

_____

If you make a mistake, _____

_____

In order to ensure that people think you are behaving professionally, you should _____

_____

Be careful, _____ might be considered offensive behaviour.

It is important to remain polite and formal when _____

_____

If you feel uncomfortable, _____

_____

One last piece of invaluable information is _____

_____

11.1 Energy

1 Write these energy sources under the two headings: **Renewable** and **Non-renewable**. Write any other energy sources you can think of in the table.

coal   gas   hydro   nuclear   oil   solar   wind

Renewable	Non-renewable

2 Use some or all of these words to write eight questions about energy.

availability	collection	companies	cost
future	homes	industry	pollution
providers	source	storage	transport

Questions	Answers given / Information found

Communicative activities

11.2 Can you help me?

The phone-call scenarios

1	You want to join a new yoga course. Find out whether it is possible to attend a free trial lesson as well as any other useful information.	**4**	You want to change to a renewable energy provider. You'd like someone to come and talk to you about the option.
2	You want to book a room in a small hotel that was recommended by a friend. You can't find any booking information on their website.	**5**	You have books, clothes and CDs to give to charity. Can someone collect them from you or do you have to take them somewhere?
3	You don't have time to look after a dog, but you have heard that the dog home sometimes needs people to walk their rescue dogs.	**6**	You'd like to volunteer to read to children. A friend told you that the library runs a reading club, but you don't know any further details.

The phone-call sequence

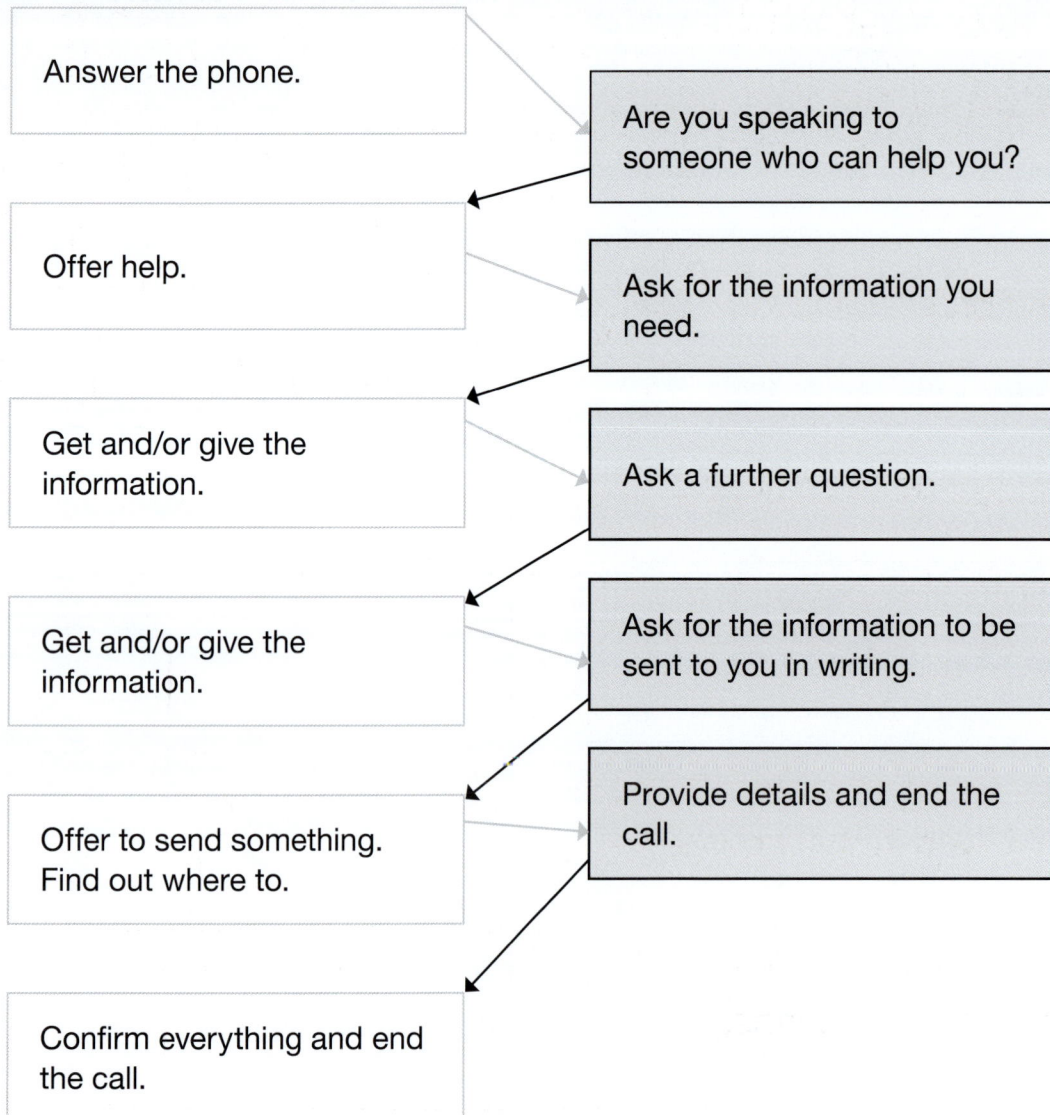

Answer the phone.	Are you speaking to someone who can help you?
Offer help.	Ask for the information you need.
Get and/or give the information.	Ask a further question.
Get and/or give the information.	Ask for the information to be sent to you in writing.
Offer to send something. Find out where to.	Provide details and end the call.
Confirm everything and end the call.	

12.1 A different life

✂

If I'd started to learn English in primary school,	
If I could go back and learn a different profession,	
If I hadn't gone on that holiday,	
If I'd gone to a different school,	
If I'd been born 50 years earlier,	
If I hadn't grown up in my country,	
If my family had been richer,	
If I hadn't asked for help,	
If I hadn't lived in that house,	
If I'd had different friends,	

12.2 Personality challenge

anxious	argumentative	arrogant	co-operative
easygoing	insecure	irresponsible	outgoing
self-confident	sensible	shy	terrified

✂ -

Discuss which restaurant or café to go to for your end-of-course dinner. Decide on the time and who will book it.	Talk about what clothing it's appropriate to wear to the office in temperatures of 30 degrees and over.
You plan to go to the cinema together to watch a film in English. Decide which film you will go and see, as well as where and when you'll see it.	You're going to paint your classroom or meeting room. Talk about what colour to paint it, as well as who will do the painting and when.
Your teacher is getting married and you want to buy a present from the group. Talk about what to buy, who will buy it, and how much to spend.	Two members of your group always arrive fifteen minutes after the lesson has started. When they arrive, they always ask what you've done up to that point. This can be disturbing and annoying.
You've been asked to look after your boss's fifteen-year-old son while he's doing four weeks' work experience at your company. You're so busy with the new project that you don't know how you'll find the time.	Your teacher used to set homework after every lesson. But as only half the class did it, the teacher stopped setting homework. Talk about whether you'd like to have homework again.

Communicative activities | Teacher's notes

1.1 This page is unavailable

A pairwork activity in which students discuss websites, and write error or maintenance messages before presenting the websites in class.

Language

Present tenses: active and passive

Computer- and website-related vocabulary

Preparation

Make a copy of the worksheet for each student.

In class

1 Hand out a copy of the worksheet to each student. Students read the two messages at the top of the worksheet and decide which tense and which form is used in each (present continuous, active and passive).

2 Ask students to tell you which websites they use regularly and whether they have a website of their own.

3 **Exercise 1.** Students discuss the questions in pairs.

4 **Exercise 2.** Each student chooses one of the websites they use regularly and tells their partner about its features. They then write short sentences about their partner's website.

5 Conduct whole-class feedback. Invite individual students to read out some of the sentences they have written. Then ask them whether there has ever been a time when the websites they talked about were unavailable. If any of them answer that there was, ask them for more information. Ask: *Was the whole site unavailable, or just a particular page? Do you know why this was? Did visitors to the site receive a message saying that it was unavailable? If yes, what did the message say, and were there any graphics with it?*

6 **Exercise 3.** Students read the instructions and think up an appropriate message that visitors to a language school's website will see when the site is down or the page is being worked on, updated, etc. Once they have agreed on a message, they should write this into the empty webpage. Next to this, they should make notes about the type of image, photo or video they would use to accompany the message. Remind them to try to make a connection between the image and text and the brand and type of business – you can watch the TED Talk again to see the examples given there. Emphasize that the task is not about students' artistic talents but about their imaginative and appropriate use of language and images.

7 **Exercise 4.** Students continue to work in pairs and do the task again but this time for a well-known everyday type of business. If possible, get students to write and to illustrate their ideas either on flipchart paper or on something that can be projected so that everyone can see and share ideas.

8 **Exercise 5.** Pairs present their work to the class who guess what kind of website each notice is for and say how the message makes them (as visitors to that website) feel. For example: Is the message clear? Is it funny? Do they feel like the company cares about their customers?

1.2 What do we have in common?

A mingling group activity in which students try to find things that they have in common with others in the class.

Language

Small talk / Networking language: making an impression

Vocabulary for talking about yourself

Open-ended questions and reflecting comments

Preparation

Make a copy of the worksheet for each student.

In class

1 Hand out a copy of the worksheet to each student.

2 **Exercises 1 and 2.** Give students five minutes to complete the sentences with information about themselves and by choosing the option to make the sentences true.

3 Ask students to offer suggestions as to how they could ask other people – people they don't know very well or even at all – about the things in Exercises 1 and 2. Encourage them to look again at the Useful language box: *Making an impression* in Unit 1.4 and to formulate open-ended questions that they could use during the following mingling activity.

4 Set the scene by asking students where and in which situations they might mingle and make small talk with more than one person, e.g. at a conference, during a break at a training seminar, before or after a lesson.

5 **Exercise 3.** Explain that the task is now to talk to other people and to (tactfully and indirectly) try to find things that they have in common with the people they talk to. For example, instead of asking simply *Where do you live?*, students could say something like *I really like living close to the centre of the city. Are you a city person too?* Draw students' attention to the speech bubbles as well as to the Useful language box and suggest that they use these prompts to help the conversations get started and to flow smoothly. The sentences in Exercises 1 and 2 will provide them with plenty of discussion topics. Remind students to make notes of what they have in common with the people they speak to.

6 Monitor while students are mingling and talking, noting any good language they use – in particular open-ended questions and reflecting comments. Let the task run for about twenty minutes or until you see that students do not have anyone new to talk to.

7 Conduct whole-class feedback. Invite individual students to tell the rest of the class about things they have in common with other students. Praise students' good language use.

2.1 Hopes and plans

A pairwork activity in which students ask each other about their future hopes and plans.

Language

Future forms

Vocabulary for plans and goals

Preparation

Make a copy of the worksheet for each student.

In class

1 Hand out a copy of the worksheet to each student.
2 **Exercise 1.** Put students into pairs to complete the table. If students are struggling to do this, tell them to type *collocations with goal* into an internet search field or use a collocation dictionary. If necessary, elicit or explain that *collocations* are words that very often appear together. Draw the table on the board. Elicit students' suggestions and complete the table (see **Suggested answers** below).
3 **Exercise 2.** In the same way, other words for *goal* can be found by searching for *goal* synonyms. Elicit students' suggestions and add the words to the table on the board.
4 **Exercise 3.** Look at the example with the class. Still in their pairs, students write survey questions using the words. The last section at the bottom of the first column is for any further question they want to add. Check students' questions and make any necessary corrections. Model some of the answers that they might give to the example question. Make sure you use future forms in your answers and remind students to do the same. For example: *Where are you going to go on holiday next year? I think we'll probably go to Spain, but we don't know where exactly.*
5 **Exercise 4.** Tell students that they should use their survey and talk to at least three other people, making notes of the information they are given. Set a time limit on this task of fifteen minutes, but let it run longer if students are talking a lot and communicating well. Listen in and make notes about good language you heard as well as mistakes. Encourage students to use future forms in their answers.
6 Conduct whole-class feedback. Use your notes to help with and praise students' language use.
7 **Exercise 5.** Ask students to reflect on how effective their questions were and to discuss improvements they would make to a second version of their survey. Encourage them to talk about interesting or surprising answers they received (with permission from the person who provided them). They can do this in pairs or as a whole class.

Suggested answers

verbs: *achieve, evaluate, fix, have, reach, refine, rethink, set, work towards*

adjectives: *business / personal, clear / specific, common, easy / impossible, life, long-term / short-term, major / minor, (un)achievable, (un)important, (un)obtainable, (un)realistic*

GOAL: *aim, target*

2.2 A job a minute

A group game in which students try to talk about specific jobs for up to one minute.

Language

Career collocations

Revision of future forms

Preparation

Make a copy of the worksheet for each group of four students. Cut out the cards.

In class

1 Put students into groups of four. Hand out a set of job cards to each group. Allow groups 2–3 minutes to read through the jobs and to discuss what they are or ask you if they do not know what this person does. Get students to mix up the cards and place them face down on the table in front of them so that the cards can't be read.
2 Explain that each card shows the name of an everyday job. If students can talk about a job for one minute, they will get 3 points. If they can talk for only for half a minute, they will get 1 point. Make sure that each group is able to time how long each person talks – either by using the stopwatch function on their smartphone or looking at the second hand on a watch or wall clock.
3 Before students start the game, elicit points that they could talk about (many of which will have been discussed to a certain degree in Unit 2.3) and write them on the board underlining the key words. For example: *Is it a <u>traditional</u> or <u>new</u> type of job? Will the job become <u>more common</u>? Is it likely to <u>disappear</u>? Does it have a <u>future</u> at all? How might it <u>change</u>? What <u>professional or academic qualifications</u> are needed? What <u>skills or experience</u> should someone have to do it? What kind of <u>salary</u> could someone expect to <u>earn</u>? Could you <u>do</u> this job? Would you <u>want to</u>?*
4 Explain that in addition to the points students will get for speaking, they can get an extra bonus point for using career collocations from Unit 2.3. The other students in their group will decide whether to award these bonus points.
5 Start the game. The first student starts by taking one card, reading the job out loud and then talking about it for 60 seconds (or less). The other students time the speaker, listen carefully to what is said and award points accordingly.
6 Let the game run for about twenty minutes. If students are in groups of three, the game should run until all the cards have been used; if they are in groups of four, each student should have four turns so that each student speaks an equal number of times. At the end of the game, students add up the points to find out who is the winner in their group.
7 Conduct whole-class feedback. Invite individual students to tell everyone which jobs were the easiest to talk about and which were the most difficult. Discuss why they think this is. Also ask which of these jobs students would most or least like to do, and why.

3.1 Have you made a donation?

A pairwork information-gap activity in which students choose the correct grammar forms and fill in the missing information in their texts by asking their partner questions.

Language

Present perfect simple and present perfect continuous

Vocabulary for facts, studies and surveys

Preparation

Make a copy of the worksheet for each pair of students. Cut the worksheet along the dotted lines to separate the texts. You could also make a copy for yourself, and copy the answers given in one of the texts into the other.

In class

1 Put students into pairs so that there is a Student A and a Student B in each pair. Hand out a copy of text A to each Student A and a copy of text B to each Student B. Tell students that their texts are each missing five pieces of information and that their partner has the information they need to fill the gaps. All they have to do is ask for the information! Explain that after they have formulated and asked questions, and received the information they need, the last sentence in both texts will still be incomplete. In their pairs, they should decide what information is missing and how they would write this information in the sentence.

2 Before they do this, students first read their versions of the text quietly and decide whether the options 1–6 in *italics* should be in the present perfect simple or present perfect continuous forms. Before they ask each other for the missing information, check answers with the class.

3 Students take turns to ask each other questions to obtain the missing information, *In which year ... ?* To ensure that this remains a communicative task and not a reading one, remind them not to show their text to their partner!

4 After they have filled all the gaps in their texts, conduct whole-class feedback to find out how they decided to complete the final sentence. The actual answers are shown in brackets.

5 Check answers with the class and, depending on your class, by conducting a whole-class discussion about donating to charity.

Answers

*1 has been collecting and analysing   2 have interviewed
3 have shown   4 has remained   5 has increased
6 have given*
Grey tinted gaps: *religious causes, children's causes*
Missing information, Student A: *2005, £30, Londoners, cash, children and young people*
Missing information, Student B: *25,000, 66%, £42, direct debit, sports-related*

3.2 Sleep survey

A pairwork and group activity in which students survey each other about their sleep habits – sleep being our most important need according to Maslow.

Language

Survey language

Sleep-related vocabulary

Preparation

Make a copy of the worksheet for each student.

In class

1 Hand out a copy of the worksheet to each student.

2 **Exercise 1.** Put students into pairs to put the words in order (1–7) to make seven questions. Check students' questions (see **Answers** below).

3 **Exercise 2.** Give students twenty minutes to ask four other students about their sleep habits by asking them the questions. Tell them to write the name of each person they speak to next to one of the letters, e.g. *A Angela, B Thomas.* Point out that the letters in the top line of the survey correspond to the names of the students.

4 **Exercise 3.** After students have surveyed four people, get them to sit together in groups of 3–5 and ask them to discuss their findings. For example: *Only one of the people I surveyed went to bed before 10 pm, but they all said they sleep in rooms that are mostly dark.* Also encourage students to ask and answer other questions. *For example: How do you feel when you haven't had enough sleep? How could you improve the quality of your sleep?*

5 Conduct whole-class feedback about the importance of sleep during which students can talk about the answers they were given to the questions.

6 **Extension.** Get students to discuss, agree on and write up their top tips for a good night's sleep on flipchart paper. They could either write seven tips based on the seven questions in the survey, or they could add more tips of their own and write ten tips.

Answers

1 What time do you usually go to sleep?
2 What time do you usually wake up?
3 How many hours' sleep do you get on average?
4 How many times do you wake up during the night?
5 How dark is your room when you sleep?
6 How often do you think you get enough sleep?
7 How important to you is a good night's sleep?

4.1 Listen, sketch and retell

A pairwork speaking and listening activity in which students read, listen to, sketch and retell stories. This can be extended into a writing activity.

Language

Narrative tenses (past simple, past continuous, past perfect simple, past perfect continuous)

Used to and *would*

Preparation

Make a copy of the worksheet for each pair of students. Cut the worksheet along the dotted line to separate the texts.

In class

1 Put students into pairs so that there is a Student A and a Student B in each pair. Hand out a copy of half of the worksheet to each student so that they have a text each.

2 Tell students that this activity tests their listening skills and their ability to retell a story. Explain that while their partner is reading the story out loud, they should remain quiet and make sketches relating to what they hear. Tell them that they may also make a note of names and numbers but nothing else – all their other notes must be in sketch form. For example, if the text is about a boy and a dog they should draw a simple quick sketch of a boy and a dog. Reassure them that they do not need to be talented artists as nobody apart from themselves is going to look at their drawings! Explain that these sketches will be their 'notes' which they will use as prompts and reminders when they come to retell the story to a different partner.

3 Students take turns to read their text slowly and clearly to their partner. Tell them to read the text twice. During the first reading, partners should just listen. During the second reading, they should draw their sketches on a blank piece of paper or on the back of the worksheet.

4 When both students in each pair have read their text and drawn their sketches, put students into new pairs so that each Student A now works with a different Student B. Using their sketches, students take turns to retell the story that they listened to. New partners should give feedback as to how well the story was retold, i.e. Was anything missed out?, Was anything in the wrong order? If yes, what were these things?

5 **Extension.** This activity can be extended in two ways:

   1 In new pairs, students tell each other similar narrative stories of their own (one they know to be true or one they have made up).

   2 Students write up their original partner's story using only their sketches as memory aids. Check students' use of the narrative tenses as well as *used to* and *would*.

4.2 Improving the partnership

A group activity in which students hold a meeting to discuss what went wrong in a recent visit and how to improve the situation in the future. The activity leads to a short writing task and a group presentation.

Language

Making and responding to suggestions

Writing a plan of action after a meeting

Preparation

Make a copy of the worksheet for each student.

In class

1 Hand out a copy of the worksheet to each student.

2 **Exercise 1.** Put students into groups of four (five or six will also work). Tell students to read the situation and to decide how to fill in the missing information. The situation may differ between groups, but all the members in each separate group must have the same completed text.

3 **Exercise 2.** Each group brainstorms what went wrong during the recent visit to their school or town and they all complete their list of problems. Tell them that their list must be identical with those of the other students in their group. Allow about ten minutes for this task. If students need help with ideas, tell them to refer to Unit 4.4.

4 **Exercise 3.** Once each group has decided on the situation and agreed on their list, they should use this as the basis for a meeting in which they will discuss what went wrong, what they can do so that this will never happen again, how to repair the damaged relationship with their partners, and what they might do before or during their forthcoming visit to their partners in order to make amends for everything that went wrong. Remind them that the partnership is important and they do not want to lose it. Students can be assigned particular roles, e.g. chairperson, manager, communications officer, marketing assistant and secretary / personal assistant. Get students to look at the Useful language box: *Making and responding to suggestions* in Unit 4.4 before they start the meeting. Monitor and make a note of good language used and some errors which you can deal with later in whole-class feedback.

5 Stop the meetings when they have come to their natural conclusion or after twenty minutes. Conduct whole-class feedback.

6 **Exercise 4.** Give the groups a further ten minutes to reflect on what they decided in their meeting and to write up a plan of action, i.e. what they will do now and in which order.

7 **Exercise 5.** Each group presents their situation and their plan of action to the rest of the class. The listeners should ask any questions they have and students from the group that is presenting should answer these.

5.1 A short collaborative story

A collaborative group activity in which students write parts of a story and then turn it into a storyboard and/or act it out.

Language

Modals and related verbs: past forms

Making excuses

Preparation

Make a copy of the worksheet for each student.

In class

1 Hand out a copy of the worksheet to each student.
2 **Exercise 1.** Ask students to use their imagination to fill in the basic biographical information in the box. Explain that the information they write here will create the character which the following short story will be about. They can write anything they like, but they should try to make sure it sounds real and believable.
3 **Exercise 2.** Tell students that the collaborative short story which follows will be about the person in the box and that they should now write the first line of their story. This must include the modal verb that is already written on line a.
4 **Exercise 3.** After the first line of the story has been written, students pass their worksheet to the student on their right. When all students have a new worksheet, they should read the biographical information about the character and the first line before writing the second line of the story, line b, using the information provided. Explain that what they write should logically follow what has been written already.
5 When students have written sentence b, they all pass the worksheets on again to the student on their right. Again, they should read the biographical information, and lines a and b, before writing line c. Continue in this way until all the story lines have been written (each line a–f is for a different student).
6 **Exercise 4.** After line f has been written, students pass the worksheet back to the person who wrote the biographical information. Students now read through the stories they started and the others finished.
7 Conduct whole-class feedback. Ask students whether their story and characters developed in a way that they had expected. Or had they imagined that the story would be completely different? Are they pleased with the way the story turned out?
8 **Extension.** Students work in pairs and add dialogue to the stories. They could do this by drawing a basic storyboard (as in a comic strip) and adding the dialogue in speech bubbles. Make sure that the excuse in sentence c is part of the dialogue! When students have added the speech bubbles, get them to act out the story using the dialogue they have written and with the help of other students if their dialogue requires more than two speakers.

5.2 Financing a new business idea

A pairwork activity in which students present a new business or a new idea, and get suggestions and feedback about funding from other students.

Language

Finance vocabulary

Funding and entrepreneurial vocabulary

Negative, indirect and tag questions

Preparation

Make a copy of the worksheet for each student.

In class

1 Put students into pairs. Hand out a copy of the worksheet to each student so that they can all make their own notes throughout the activity.
2 **Exercise 1.** Explain that students are going to think of ways to fund or finance a new business or idea. As the whole activity stems from students deciding which business or idea they want to work with, it would be good to provide them with extra input at this stage and also to limit the time you want them to spend on this research. In order to 'force' them into making a decision, limit the time to 15–20 minutes. Tell students that they do not need to come up with a completely new idea – they may adapt one that already exists. This can either be one that they know of, e.g. an event in their town, or a new business idea that they have heard of. Or they can simply 'steal' an idea from one of the many start-up or crowd-funding websites that are easily found on the Internet.
3 **Exercise 2.** Once students have chosen their idea, they should decide on the three best ways to finance it. They should make a note of these in the three boxes. They should also include the positive and negative aspects of each way of funding, and any questions they would like to ask the other students regarding these ways of financing the business or idea. Set a time limit of a further 5–10 minutes.
4 **Exercise 3.** In their pairs, students stand up at the front, and tell the rest of the class about their idea and their top three choices of how to fund it. With help from the other students (who should try to use negative, indirect and tag questions to get further information), they should decide on the one best way to fund their new business or idea. If you have a very large class, students could do this in groups of 6–8.
5 After each pair has presented their idea and chosen their method of funding with help from the others, conduct whole-class feedback in which everyone discusses which idea they like best and which they would most likely invest their own personal savings in.

6.1 If …

A pairwork activity in which students think of humorous ways to finish conditional sentences – leading to a memory game which can be played by groups of four.

Language

Zero, first and second conditionals

Preparation

Make a copy of the worksheet for each pair of students. Either cut out the cards in advance or make sure you take scissors to the class.

In class

1 Put students into pairs. Hand out a copy of the worksheet or a set of sixteen cards to each pair.

2 Give students ten minutes to think of three different ways to finish each of the eight sentence starters on the word cards. If possible, the sentence endings should be humorous. Note that students need to provide some missing information in one of the sentence starters.

3 Ask students to choose their favourite ending for each sentence and to write it on a blank card. Check that students' sentence endings are grammatically correct before they write on the blank card!

4 Students cut out the cards if this has not already been done. Each pair should then exchange their sixteen cards with another pair. Students mix up their 'new' set of cards. They place them face down on the table in front of them and play a memory game – turning over two cards at a time to try to find matching sentence halves. If the sentence halves match, that student keeps the two cards and has another turn. If the halves do not match, the cards are turned over again and the other student in the pair has a turn. The game should continue until all the sentence halves have been matched. This game can be extended by two pairs of students getting together and mixing their cards to make a larger set of 32 cards.

5 **Extension.** Point out that in each of the eight sentence beginnings, there are some words in bold. Students create new cards and write new sentence beginnings by changing the words in bold to other words. For example: *If it* **rains** *today, … .* They then give these sentence starters to another pair of students who think up and write humorous endings to each of the new sentences.

6.2 Can I just check that?

A two-part pairwork activity in which students request information and clarification during two phone calls in order to decide on the best hotel or conference venue to suit their needs.

Language

Requesting and giving clarification

Preparation

Make a copy of the worksheet for each pair of students. Cut the worksheet along the dotted line to separate the four sections.

In class

1 Put students into pairs so that there is a Student A and a Student B in each pair. Explain that this is a two-part task and involves students in making two phone calls. In call 1, Student A wants to book a hotel and Student B has hotel information. Student B will play the role of the receptionist at each of the three hotels that Student A calls. In call 2, Student B wants to book a conference venue and Student A is the manager at each of the three venues. If possible, get partners to sit back to back during the task so that they can't see each other (as in a phone call) and, because of this, they will need to use the expressions from the Useful language box: *Requesting and giving clarification* in Unit 6.4. Allow students to keep their books open at this page during the activity.

2 **Call 1.** Hand out a copy of the hotel requirements text to each Student A and a copy of the information about the three hotels to each Student B. Explain that Student A should call all three hotels, ask for information and make notes during the phone calls. Student A can ask for any further information that would be helpful, and Student B can use their imagination and experience to invent any information that is missing. Give them a few minutes to read through their information before they start their first phone call.

3 Monitor students while they're speaking, noting any good language use you hear as well as mistakes that need correcting. Deal with these later in whole-class feedback. After Student A has made the three calls, he/she should note which hotel he/she wants to book. Conduct whole-class feedback and ask each Student A about which hotel he/she would like to book, and why. Did they all decide on the same hotel? If not, why not? Find out whether they could use many of the Useful language expressions and how these helped them.

4 **Call 2.** Students change roles, and in the same way and with the new conference information that you will hand out to them, they should prepare for and hold the second set of three phone calls about a conference venue.

5 Conduct whole-class feedback again and find out which venues students booked, and why. Find out whether they were able to use more of the Useful language expressions during the second set of calls.

6 **Variation.** Instead of working in pairs, get students to work in groups of three. Student C is an observer who listens to each phone call and makes notes, and ticks the expressions from the Useful language box as they are used. Student C should also give feedback to Student A and Student B on how effective the phone calls were, how well students seemed to understand each other, and anything else he/she noted.

7.1 Latest inventions

A pairwork activity which deals with inventions.

Language

Passives

Preparation

Make a copy of the worksheet for each pair of students. Cut out the picture cards and the text cards, and keep them in two separate batches.

In class

1 Put students into pairs. Hand out a set of six picture cards (these six cards only at the moment) to each pair. Ask students to decide quietly (so that the other pairs don't hear) which of the things on the cards was invented first. Without getting any answers from them at this stage, tell students to place this card on the table to make the beginning of a timeline. After this, they should decide in which order the remaining things were invented and place them in chronological order (from left to right across the table) with the one they think was invented most recently at the end of the line.

2 Students should now all get up and look at the other pairs' timelines. Are they all the same? If not, they should ask each other why they think X was invented before Y and not the other way around. For example: *We think that the barcode was invented before the satellite navigation system. Why do you think that it wasn't?*

3 Tell students to rearrange their cards if, after having talked to other students, they would like to change the order.

4 Give each pair a set of six text cards. Ask students to read the texts out to each other one card at a time. When each text card has been read out, it should be placed in a new timeline below the picture cards. At this stage, students may not change the order of their picture cards.

5 After all the texts have been read out and each pair or group has a new complete timeline, students should compare the order that they placed the picture cards in with the order in which they now know the things were invented. Conduct whole-class feedback to find out whether students placed the picture cards in the right order at the beginning and whether they changed the order of their cards after talking to other students (see **Answers** below). After reading the texts, which cards did they still need to move to get the chronological order right? Did they find any of the information in the texts surprising? Which of the inventions would they like to find out more about? Set this task as homework!

Answers

e-bikes 1897
barcode 1952/1973
Wi-Fi 1985
car satellite navigation system 2000
airport body scanners 2007
bionic arm 2007–2011 / 2013

7.2 Create, adapt, enable

A group activity in which students discuss, create, design and present their idea for a school garden for pupils with special needs.

Language

Innovation: verbs

Revision of passives

Preparation

Make a copy of the worksheet for each student.

In class

1 Put students into groups (3–5 students). Hand out a copy of the worksheet to each student.

2 Ask students to read the situation. Elicit that a *blind* person is someone who is unable to see, though the term visually impaired is often used instead and also for people who may be able to see to a certain degree. (Alison Patrick, the triathlete in Unit 5.2, is visually impaired.) If any students know someone who is visually impaired, ask them to talk about what that person is able to do despite not being able to see properly.

3 **Exercise 1.** Deal with any questions about the situation on the worksheet – invent any further necessary details, then give groups five minutes to brainstorm a minimum of twelve things that they would like to have in the garden and to write them on the mind map. Tell them to be creative in their ideas, and not to be afraid to 'think outside the box' as not everything they write now needs to be in their final garden design. Provide language help as required.

4 Explain that students should now go through the points on their mind map one by one and discuss whether to include them in the garden. For example: *Do we really want to have more trees? Are roses a good idea?* Tell them to choose 6–8 things from their mind map that they will definitely include in their garden idea. To force students into making a decision, set a fairly short time limit of ten minutes.

5 **Exercise 2.** Groups should further expand and discuss the merits of each point using the 'innovation' verbs from Unit 7.3 where possible and passive forms where appropriate. For example: *A garden house will enable the pupils to … , A new wider path could be built … , The old path could be replaced by … .* Tell students to make notes on the lines provided. As these notes will form the basis of their presentation, they should be as detailed as possible. Allow a further 10–15 minutes for this stage.

6 **Exercise 3.** Each group should now prepare a five-minute presentation of their idea. They could draw a sketch of their garden idea on flipchart paper and use this to illustrate their presentation.

7 **Exercise 4.** Groups should now present their ideas to the rest of the class. After all the ideas have been presented, everyone should vote for the one they like best.

8.1 About us and our lives

A pairwork and whole-class activity in which students decide to what extent statements are true or false for them and then compare their answers.

Language

Verb patterns with -ing and infinitive

Preparation

Make a copy of the worksheet for each student.

In class

1 Hand out a copy of the worksheet to each student. Tell students that they should read the statements and decide to what extent each statement is true or false for them, marking this by circling one of the numbers on the line. Using sentence 1 as an example: if they mostly (but not always) spend at least an hour each day relaxing, they might circle the number 4. But, if they hardly ever spend an hour a day relaxing, then they might want to circle number 2 on the line. Ask them to circle a number for all ten statements.

2 When students have done this, tell them to connect their circles with lines so that they end up with something that looks like a graph that is on its side.
For example:

1	1	②	3	4	5
2	1	2	3	④	5
3	1	2	3	4	⑤
4	1	2	3	4	⑤
5	1	②	3	4	5

3 Put students into pairs to compare their 'graph' lines and their answers. How similar or different do their graph lines look?

4 Ask students to discuss their answers with their partner by asking questions or just providing further information. For example:

Student A: *I see that you circled 2 for statement 5. Why is that?*
Student B: *Well, I'm happy to work with my colleagues, but I don't want to see them in my free time too. What about you?*
Student A: *I circled 5 as we often go out socializing after work, and I enjoy it.*

Allow 10–15 minutes for this stage.

5 Either pin the worksheets on a wall next to each other or lay them out on a table. Get students to look at them all and to make comments. How similar or different are the lines? Are there any statements where nearly everyone has answered in the same way? Why do they think this is?

6 **Extension.** Put students into pairs to write six more statements about their daily lives. They can then exchange their statements with another pair. Again, partners can compare their 'graph' lines.

8.2 The best option

A group activity in which students discuss three accommodation options for a team-building week and write an email explaining their decision.

Language

Discussing options

Linking expressions

Preparation

Make a copy of the worksheet for each student.

In class

1 Write *Someone became very ill* and *The barbecue set on fire* on the board. Ask students to suggest what other things might go wrong on a week away with twenty male and female 18–20-year-olds.

2 Put students into groups (3–5 students). Explain that they all work for the same (imaginary) company and are responsible for the trainees there. Elicit the type of company they work for, e.g. a bank, an energy company, a car company. Groups can choose to work for different companies if they like. Tell them that they are going to discuss three venues / accommodation options for a team-building week with the new trainees. Explain that further information about the situation and the trainees is given at the top of the worksheet, and the three options that they need to discuss are below it. Note that there is no further information about the 'near disaster'. Students may decide for themselves what happened last year.

3 Explain that students have twenty minutes to discuss the options and to make a decision. Now hand out a copy of the worksheet to each student and tell them to read the information thoroughly. Deal with any vocabulary questions that arise before they start discussing. Refer them to the Useful language box: *Discussing options* in Unit 8.4.

4 While students are discussing, monitor and make notes of good language used and some errors which you can deal with later in whole-class feedback.

5 When the twenty minutes is up, conduct whole-class feedback in which each group says which of the three options they chose, and why.

6 Explain that students need to put their decision into an email to the company's managing director. Refer them to the email and *Linking expressions* in Unit 8.4, and ask them to decide in their groups what they will write before they actually start writing.

7 When each group has written an email, they should 'send' this to another group of students who should read and discuss it, and give the writers feedback before it is sent on to the managing director. Do they understand why the decision was made? Do they still have any questions?

8 Students get their email back with comments and rewrite the email if necessary so that they have the 'perfect' email to send to their managing director.

9.1 Where, who, which, whose

A group activity in which students give clues using relative clauses and the others guess who, what or where they are talking about.

Language

Relative clauses

Preparation

Make a copy of the worksheet for each group of four students. Cut out the cards and keep them in two separate batches. Shuffle the eighteen word cards.

In class

1   Put students into groups of four. Hand out a set of eighteen word cards to each group. Tell students to place the cards face down on the table in front of them so that they can't see what is written on them. Keep the nine blank cards to one side until later.

2   Explain that each card contains the name of a famous person, place, or company or organization. Taking turns, students take the top card, read what is on it and give clues to the others in their group – the clues should contain relative clauses. Provide help by writing on the board:

> This is the place where XXX
> This is the person who/whose XXX
> This is the company/organization which/whose XXX

For example:

> Disneyland: *This is the place where children can meet Mickey Mouse.*
> Apple: *This is the company which is famous for its designs.*
> Neil Armstrong: *This is the person who did something very famous in 1969.*

The others in the group try to guess what is written on the card. The speaker should keep on giving more clues until someone guesses correctly. The student who guesses correctly keeps the card. Then the next student takes a card and the game continues in the same way until all the cards have been used. The student with the most cards at the end of the game is the winner.

3   This game can be extended by getting each group to write three more places, people, companies/organizations on the blank cards. While they are deciding what to write, they should discuss their choices using relative clauses. This will allow them to judge whether other students will be able to work with the new cards – by giving clues and guessing what is written on the extra cards in the same way as they did with the eighteen printed cards.

4   When the new cards have been prepared, they should be exchanged with another group, then shuffled and placed face down in a pile on the table. The game now continues as before with each group using the cards another group has prepared for them.

5   Conduct whole-class feedback and ask students to say who or what is easiest or hardest to talk about using relative clauses.

9.2 A great event

A meeting activity in which students brainstorm ideas for a neighbourhood celebration and decide who should do what.

Language

Turn-taking expressions

Personality adjectives

Preparation

Make a copy of the worksheet for each student.

In class

1   This activity can be carried out with the whole class working together or in groups of up to six. Hand out a copy of the worksheet to each student.

2   Elicit reasons for big public or national celebrations and write them on the board. For example: *to celebrate a national day or a country's independence, to celebrate the wedding or anniversary of a very important public figure.*

3   Explain that there is going to be a big national celebration in four months' time. Tell students that they all live in the same few streets, and that they are attending a kick-off meeting to discuss the party or street party they want to hold in their neighbourhood. Ask them to agree on the reason for the celebration from the list on the board.

4   In each group, appoint a chairperson who is responsible for the smooth running of the meeting. Explain that this is an informal open meeting in which they can all say what they want, but that they should use the Useful language expressions in Unit 9.4 to ensure that the meeting does not get out of hand. The chairperson should also make sure that all the points in the agenda column are discussed.

5   In each group, appoint a meeting secretary who will keep notes of any decisions that are made and help the chairperson by keeping an eye on the time, and reminding him/her to move onto the next point.

6   Give students 5–10 minutes to read through the points on the agenda and the information given for some of the points. They then make notes with their ideas and suggestions next to each one. Suggest a time limit of twenty minutes plus or minus five minutes depending on group size.

7   The chairperson should officially open the meeting by greeting everyone and reminding them why they are there.

8   After the meeting, the secretaries should recap the decisions that were made so that everyone in the group can complete the missing information in the basic details section.

9   Students decide which members of the group would be best suited to join which sub-committee in order to plan the event. Students should use the personality adjectives in Unit 9.3 to suggest others or themselves for these roles.

10.1 The visitors' book

A pairwork activity in which students read comments in a visitors' book, report what was written to their partner, and decide which comments they should reply to.

Language

Reported speech

Preparation

Make a copy of the worksheet for each pair of students. Cut the worksheet along the dotted line to separate the texts.

In class

1 Put students into pairs so that there is a Student A and a Student B in each pair. Hand out a copy of half of the worksheet to each student so that they have five comments each.

2 Tell students that they recently helped out at a local exhibition. Now that the exhibition has finished, they have been asked to go through the comments in the visitors' book and to decide which, if any, they should respond to. Explain that they have five comments each which they should first read and then report to their partner. Point out that all the comments have email addresses with them, so students are able to contact the writers if they want to.

3 Give students about five minutes to read their five comments and to think how they will explain them to their partner. They should not show their partner the worksheet or read out the comment – instead, they should use reported speech to explain what is written.

4 Partners take turns to explain the comments on their worksheet. If necessary, remind them to use reported speech to explain what is written. For example: *In my first comment, the writer has said that … .* After each individual comment has been explained, students should quickly decide together whether this is a serious comment and one that they should respond to.

5 After students have each reported their five comments, they should decide again which comments they feel they should respond to. Now that they know about more comments, their opinion on this may have changed.

6 Working together, partners write emails responding to at least two of the comments they have read. Write on the board: *In our visitors' book, you wrote that XXXXX,* and tell students that they must include this sentence beginning somewhere in each email.

7 Pairs of students can now work together, exchange their emails and read what the other students have written.

8 Conduct whole-class feedback. Find out if everyone has decided to respond to the same comments, what students thought of the emails they read, and how they thought the comment writers would feel when they received the emails.

10.2 Cultural tips

A pairwork activity in which students brainstorm ideas, and write up a list of helpful cultural tips for someone who is coming from another country and plans to work at their company or attend their school or university.

Language

Customer service vocabulary

Cross-cultural awareness vocabulary

Revision of reported speech

Preparation

Make a copy of the worksheet for each student.

In class

1 Put students into pairs. Explain that a new colleague is joining the company or that a new student is going to attend their school or university. (You can choose whether you would like the activity to be more business-oriented or general.) Tell students that this person is coming from a different culture. Elicit where this person might be coming from, although it's not important for students to know anything about the culture of the other country. If you are teaching a multinational class, everyone should write about the country in which they are studying.

2 Tell students that they have been asked to inform this person about life in their country and the culture at their school or company in order to make their stay there as easy as possible. Explain that they are going to write a list of useful cultural points and tips which will be sent to this person before they arrive.

3 Elicit some tips and write them on the board. For example: *Always be on time. Don't wear shorts in the office.* Encourage students to include whatever they consider to be helpful when writing their list.

4 Hand out the worksheet to each student. Draw students' attention to the gaps and explain that the format is already prepared and that they just need to fill in the useful information. Tell them that there are many ways of doing this and that later on they will have the chance to compare the cultural tips. Before they start writing, they should read through the gapped text, and discuss how they would like to complete it and what tips they would like to include.

5 Allow about fifteen minutes for the writing stage – extend the time if necessary. Monitor and provide help where required. Ensure that the tips students write fit grammatically into the gapped sentences.

6 Get pairs to exchange their text for one written by another pair. In their pairs, they should read and comment on what the other students wrote. How does it compare to their own text?

7 Conduct whole-class feedback in which students say which tips they think are the best. Combine these and get students to write them up so that they have one definitive list of tips which could really be used.

11.1 Energy

A pairwork and whole-class information gathering task in which students find out about energy use amongst other students and people in their area or country.

Language

Articles

Quantifiers

Preparation

Make a copy of the worksheet for each student.

In class

1 Hand out a copy of the worksheet to each student.
2 **Exercise 1.** Put students into pairs to complete the table. You can then check answers with the class (see **Answers** below).
3 **Exercise 2.** Still in pairs, students use the words to write eight questions they would like to ask about energy use and consumption. These questions can be used when talking to other students, or used as the basis of internet research. For example: *How much pollution is caused by oil? How many energy providers are there in your area? How many homes in your neighbourhood have solar panels?*
4 There are two ways that this activity can be carried out. Which one you choose will depend on your own preference and whether there is internet access in your classroom.

   Version 1. If you have internet access in class, get students to research answers to their questions and write them under 'Information found'.

   Version 2. If you have no internet access in class, students should talk to each other to find out about what kind of energy they each use as well as getting other students' answers to the questions they wrote. Remind students to record everyone's answers under 'Answers given'.
5 Regardless of which version you choose, students should assess the information they have found or gathered, write this up in report form using quantifiers and paying attention to the use of articles. For example: *We found that a large number of people get their energy from a green provider. Only a few homes have solar panels in our town. There are no nuclear power companies in this area at all.*
6 Students should present their findings to the class, giving as much information and as many examples as possible.
7 Conduct whole-class feedback to find out how 'green' students are, or how 'green' energy use and consumption is in their country.

Answers

Renewable	*Non-renewable*
hydro, solar, wind	*coal, gas, nuclear, oil*
also: *biofuel, biomass, geothermal energy, tidal power, wave power*	also: *groundwater, petroleum, uranium*

11.2 Can you help me?

A pairwork activity in which students make and answer phone enquiries.

Language

Making and responding to enquiries

Preparation

Make a copy of the worksheet for each student.

In class

1 Put students into pairs. Hand out a copy of the worksheet to each student. Ask students to read the six phone-call scenarios and to look at the phone-call sequence. Elicit or explain that in the first scenario, one of the partners works at a yoga studio or at a sports centre and is the person who answers the phone.
2 Refer students to the Useful language box: *Making and responding to enquiries* in Unit 11.4 and remind them to use these expressions in their phone calls.
3 Tell students to carry out phone calls 1 and 2 with their partner. During the calls, they should follow the steps in the sequence as closely as possible and invent any information they need. The student making the call should keep a note of the information he/she receives. For the second phone call, they should change roles so that the student who made the first phone call now receives the second call. Allow about ten minutes for these two calls.
4 Get students to work with a new partner and to carry out phone calls 3 and 4 in the same way as before.
5 Get students to work with another new partner and to carry out phone calls 5 and 6.
6 Conduct whole-class feedback and get students to talk about the information they received, how helpful the person providing the information was, and whether making and receiving the calls became easier as they practised more.

12.1 A different life

A pairwork and group activity in which students write the second halves of sentences about themselves, then exchange them with another pair who match the halves and decide who wrote what.

Language

Third and mixed conditional sentences

Preparation

Make a copy of the worksheet for each pair of students. Make sure you take scissors to the class so that students can cut up their sentences.

In class

1 Put students into pairs. Hand out a copy of the worksheet to each pair of students. Tell them that they should take turns to finish the sentences (so that they finish five different ones each) with information about their lives and what they might have been like if certain aspects were different or hadn't happened. Before students write on the worksheets, get them to talk to each other and decide exactly what they want to write. You could suggest that they write their sentence endings on another piece of paper so that you can check for logical or grammatical mistakes before one of them writes the sentence endings on the worksheet. It's important that only one student in each pair writes all the sentences endings so that the handwriting is the same on all ten!

2 When all the sentences have endings, students cut out the sentence halves so that each pair has twenty sentence halves.

3 Each pair of students exchanges their sentence halves for those of another pair.

4 Pair A should lay Pair B's sentence halves out on the table and try to match them. When they think they have done this correctly, they should decide who they think completed which sentence, and why. They then divide them up into two sets of five complete sentences – one set for each student who they think wrote the endings.

5 Pairs now work together. Pair B should read out Pair A's sentence halves and say who they think wrote the sentence ending. For example: *'If I hadn't grown up in my country,'* plus *'I wouldn't know how to dance the tango.' We think Maria wrote this sentence because she comes from South America.* Pair A should tell Pair B if they have matched the sentence halves and identified the writer correctly.

6 Pairs then change roles and repeat the step above.

7 Give a further ten minutes for each group of four students (Pairs A and B) to talk further about any of the sentences and information they find interesting and want to know more about.

8 Conduct whole-class feedback if there is enough time and students don't mind having these aspects of their 'different lives' discussed openly.

12.2 Personality challenge

A group activity in which students discuss given topics in the personality and style that is written on their card.

Language

Personality adjectives
Expressions for 'Being assertive'

Preparation

Make a copy of the worksheet for each group of 4–6 students. Cut out and shuffle the twelve personality cards and the eight topic cards in two separate batches.

In class

1 Write the twelve adjectives from the personality cards on the board and, if necessary, clarify any meanings. Tell students that you are now going to ask them to do something in the style of one of the personalities you've written on the board and they should guess which personality you are using. Ask them to do something related to the lesson. For example: *Please turn to page 136 in your Student's Book.* Ask them in an insecure way. Now ask them to guess which adjective best describes the personality you just took on. Model a couple more personality adjectives with other sentences or questions and get students to guess which ones you are modelling.

2 Put students into groups of 4–6, and hand out a set of personality cards and a set of topic cards to each group. Place these two sets face down in separate piles on the table so that students can't look at them yet. Tell them that the personality cards contain only the adjectives that you have written on the board.

3 Explain that students are going to pick up a personality card from the pile and then discuss the topics written on the topic cards in the style of the personality adjective written on their card. Refer students to the Useful language box: *Being assertive* in Unit 12.4 and ask them to use these sentence beginnings when appropriate in their discussion.

4 Before they start, all but one of the students in the group should take a personality card. It is important that they do not tell the others what is written on the card! Explain that they should discuss one topic for about five minutes and that it is important that each person says something. The task of the student who did not take a personality card (the observer) is to read out the topic card for the others, and to listen to the discussion and decide what is written on the other students' personality cards.

5 The observer may stop the discussion when he/she thinks he/she knows which personalities the other students have on their cards. The observer should then tell the others and find out how many he/she got right.

6 Students place their personality cards back in the pile and shuffle them. They repeat the activity with a new topic, new personalities and a new observer.

7 Conduct whole-class feedback to find out which of the personalities students found easiest to take on in English, and why.